Simple Steps for Fifth Grade

Thinking Kids™
An imprint of Carson-Dellosa Publishing LLC
P.O. Box 35665
Greensboro, NC 27425 USA

Thinking Kids™
Carson-Dellosa Publishing LLC
P.O. Box 35665
Greensboro, NC 27425 USA

ISBN 978-1-4838-2675-2

01-335157784

Table of Contents

Table of Contents

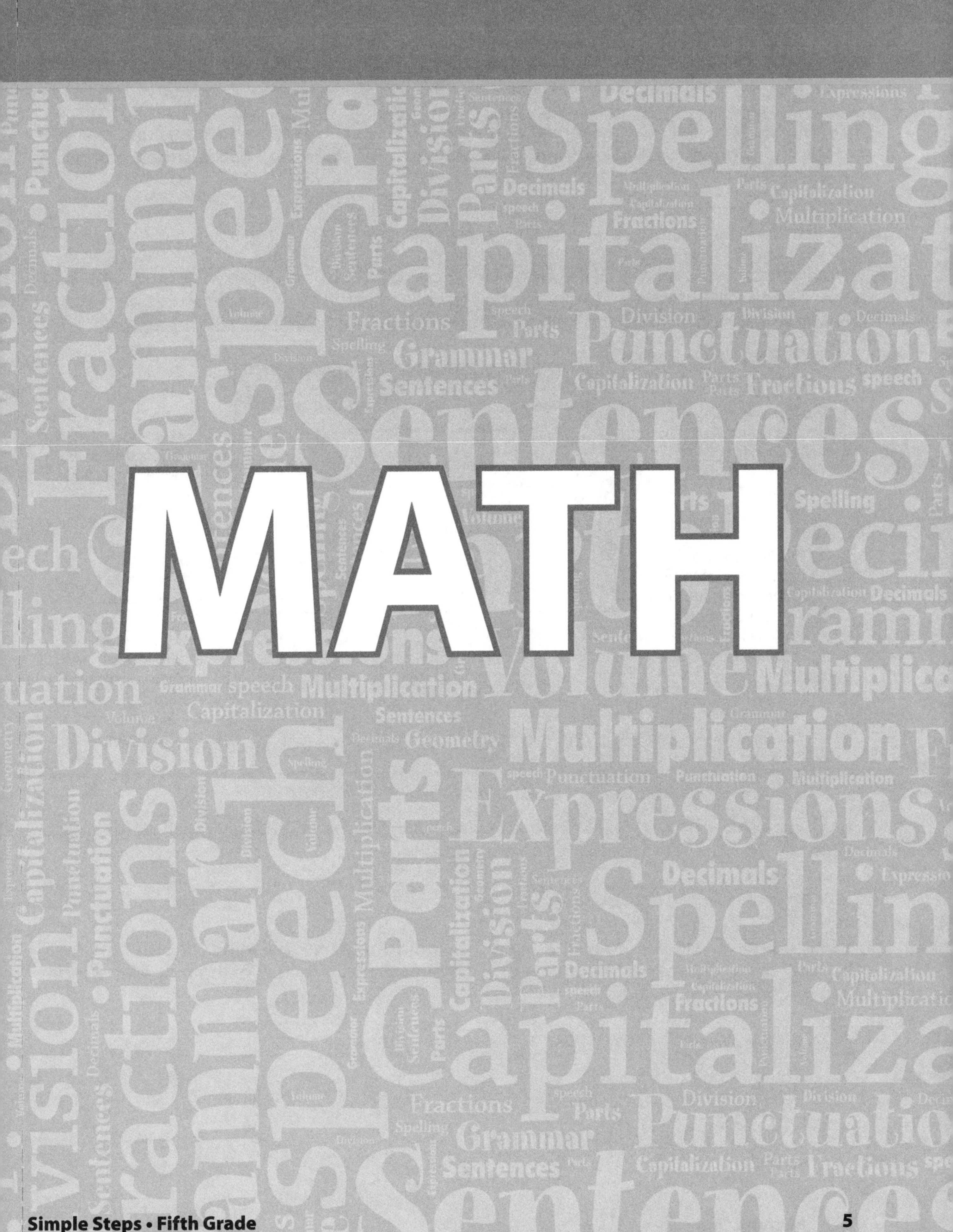

MATH

Introduction

Simple Steps for Fifth Grade uses a combination of step-by-step examples and color coding designed to build students' math skills and deepen their understanding of math concepts.

Instructions

The instructional sections of this book are organized around step-by-step examples. In these sections, key math concepts and terms are assigned colors. This can help students visualize a connection between the skill they are learning and the way that it is applied.

1. **The left side explains each step of the math skill being taught.**

2. **The right side shows how to apply the skill to each step of a specific problem.**

The Order of Operations

The order of operations is used to find the value of an expression with more than one operation.

Solve: $3 \times (4 + 5) + 6 \div 3$

First, do all operations within parentheses or other grouping symbols.	$3 \times (4 + 5) + 6 \div 3$ $3 \times 9 + 6 \div 3$
Second, multiply and divide in order, from left to right.	$3 \times 9 + 6 \div 3$ $27 + 6 \div 3$ $27 + 6 \div 3$ $27 + 2$
Finally, add and subtract in order, from left to right.	$27 + 2 = 29$

3. **On the left, the word parentheses is colored blue. The words multiply and divide are colored green. The words add and subtract are colored purple.**

4. **On the right, parentheses ( ) are colored blue in the corresponding example step. Multiplication and division operations are colored green. The addition operation is colored purple.**

Practice

Practice problems follow the concepts after they are explained, giving students an opportunity to work with what they have just learned.

Review

Review sections are included throughout each chapter, along with a chapter review section at the end of each chapter and an overall math review at the end of the math section.

Multi-Digit Multiplication

Multiplication is the way to find sums of equal groups of numbers. Follow these steps to multiply numbers with more than one digit. Be careful to regroup as needed. Use zeros as placeholders to help you line up partial products correctly.

Solve: 54 × 37

First, write the problem vertically. Place the factor with the most digits on top.

```
   2
  54
× 37
 378
```

Next, use **place value** to break the smaller factor up. 37 can be broken up into 30 and 7.

```
  54      54
× 30    ×  7
```

Then, **multiply** 54 by 30 and by 7. Work right to left.

```
  54      54
× 30    ×  7
1620     378
```

Finally, **add** the results to find the **final product**.

```
 1620      54
+ 378    × 37
 1998   1,998
```

Practice

1. 73 × 21

2. 45 × 44

3. 76 × 32

4. 93 × 39

Multi-Digit Multiplication

Follow these steps to multiply by larger numbers.

When you multiply by a three-digit number, you also add a row with two zeros to align your third product starting in the **hundreds** column.

$$\begin{array}{r} 872 \\ \times\ 494 \\ \hline 3488 \\ 78480 \\ +\ 348800 \\ \hline 430{,}768 \end{array}$$

When you multiply by a four-digit number, you will also insert another row with three zeros to align your answer starting in the thousands column.

$$\begin{array}{r} 2312 \\ \times\ 1341 \\ \hline 2312 \\ 92480 \\ 693600 \\ +\ 2312000 \\ \hline 3{,}100{,}392 \end{array}$$

Practice

Solve the following problems. Show your work.

1. 143×142
2. 1503×741
3. 4610×1239
4. 1225×242
5. 774×455
6. 1811×1021
7. 3789×532
8. 5925×1112
9. 596×589

Dividing by 2-Digit Numbers

To divide by two-digit numbers, set up the division problem using a long division symbol. Be careful to keep columns aligned correctly, and remember to write the remainder at the top when you finish.

Solve: $14\overline{)718}$

First, estimate to find the first digit in the quotient. Think: How many times does the divisor go into the hundreds and tens place of the dividend?

$$\begin{array}{r} 5 \\ 14\overline{)718} \end{array}$$

14 goes into 71 at least 5 times. The tens digit of the quotient is 5.

Then, multiply the tens digit of the quotient by the divisor. Subtract the result from the hundreds and tens place of the dividend. Bring down the ones place from the dividend to get the total number of ones left in the dividend.

$$\begin{array}{r} 5 \\ 14\overline{)718} \\ -70\downarrow \\ \hline 18 \end{array}$$

14 x 5 = 71.

71 – 70 = 1

There are 18 ones left in the dividend.

Finally, repeat the process for the ones digit. Estimate how many times the divisor goes into the ones. Multiply the ones digit of the quotient by the divisor. Subtract the result from the total number of ones to get the remainder. Record the remainder with the rest of the quotient.

Hint: The remainder must always be less than the divisor.

$$\begin{array}{r} 51 \text{ r}4 \\ 14\overline{)718} \\ -70\downarrow \\ \hline 18 \\ -14 \\ \hline 4 \end{array}$$

14 goes into 18 at least 1 time. The ones digit of the quotient is 1.

14 x 1 = 14

18 – 14 = 4

14 cannot divide 4, so the remainder is 4.

Practice

1. $17\overline{)770}$

2. $29\overline{)850}$

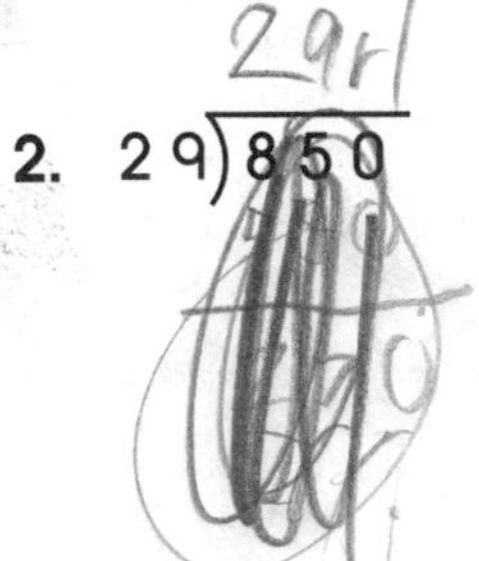

3. $52\overline{)989}$

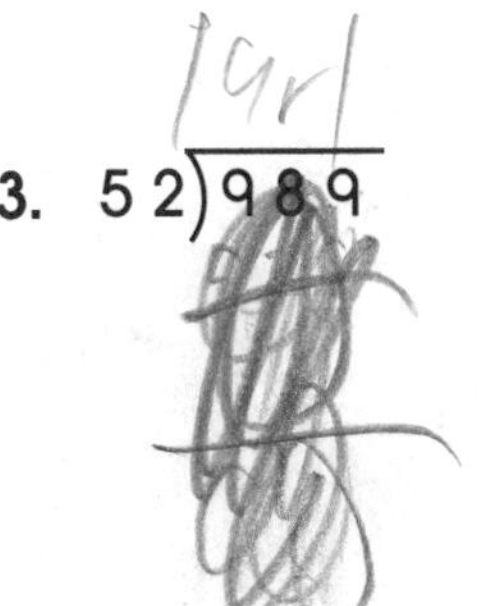

Dividing by 2-Digit Numbers

For longer dividends, continue repeating the steps of division until there are no digits left in the dividend to divide.

Solve: $32\overline{)7980}$

First, estimate how many times the **divisor** goes into the thousands and hundreds place of the **dividend**.

Multiply the **hundreds digit** of the quotient by the **divisor**. Subtract the result from the thousands and hundreds place of the **dividend**. Bring down the tens place to get the total number of tens left in the dividend.

```
      2
32)7980
  -64↓
   158
```

32 goes into 79 at least 2 times. The hundreds digit of the **quotient** is 2.

32 x 2 = 64

79 – 64 = 15

There are 158 tens left in the dividend.

Then, continue to estimate, multiply, subtract, and bring down until there are no digits left in the dividend to divide. Finally, write the remainder at the top.

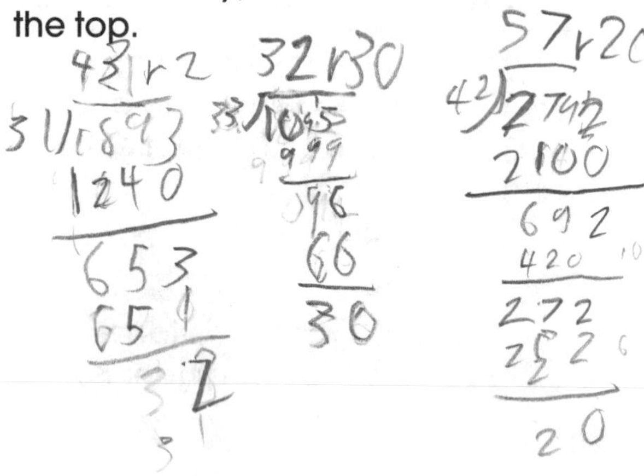

```
     249r12
32)7980
  -64↓
   158
  -128↓
    300
   -288
     12
```

32 goes into 158 at least 4 times.

32 x 4 = 128

158 – 128 = 30.

There are 300 ones left in the dividend.

32 goes into 300 at least 9 times.

32 x 9 = 288

300 – 288 = 12

The remainder is 12.

Practice

Solve the following problems.

1. $31\overline{)1893}$

2. $33\overline{)1095}$

3. $42\overline{)2792}$

Dividing by 2-Digit Numbers

Math

Practice

Solve the following problems.

1. $23\overline{)264}$

2. $46\overline{)857}$

3. $58\overline{)2439}$

4. $32\overline{)571}$

5. $28\overline{)635}$

6. $21\overline{)4,670}$

7. $21\overline{)491}$

8. $19\overline{)412}$

9. $17\overline{)4,990}$

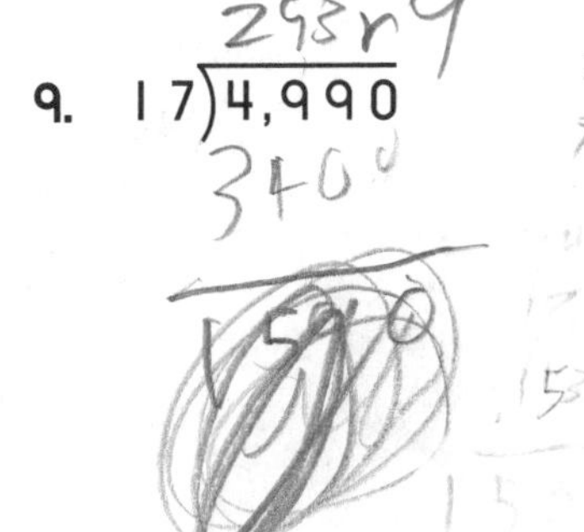

10. $38\overline{)1460}$

11. $33\overline{)1812}$

12. $42\overline{)2792}$

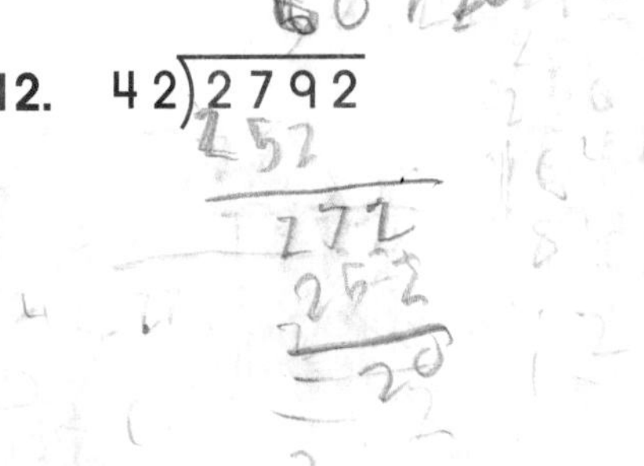

Problem Solving

You can use the multiplication strategies you have learned so far to solve more difficult problems.

First, underline the important information that you will need to solve the problem.

Students in Thornton's schools are collecting cans and bottles for a charity drive. They are having a contest to see which students and which schools collect the most cans and bottles. The contest lasts 15 weeks. One student, Raul, collects 33 cans per week. How many cans does Raul collect during the contest?

Next, determine which operation is best for solving the problem.

Raul collects the same number of cans each week. So, we can multiply the number of cans collected per week, 33, by the number of weeks, 15.

$$\begin{array}{r} 33 \\ \times\ 15 \\ \hline \end{array}$$

Then, write the problem, with the digits aligned.

Multiply by 5 ones and regroup 1 ten.

$$\begin{array}{r} {\scriptstyle 1} \\ 33 \\ \times\ 15 \\ \hline 165 \end{array}$$

Multiply by 1 ten. Use a zero as a placeholder.

$$\begin{array}{r} 33 \\ \times\ 15 \\ \hline 165 \\ +\ 330 \\ \hline 495 \end{array}$$

Finally, solve the problem.

Raul collected 495 cans.

Practice

Solve the problem. Show your work in the space provided.

1. Elmhurst has 328 students. Each student collects 28 cans during the charity drive contest. How many cans do the students collect?

1.

Math

Problem Solving

You can use the division strategies you have learned so far to solve more difficult problems.

First, underline the important information that you will need to solve the problem.

Several students at Milton Middle School talk about the trips they took last summer. They compare the distances and times they spent traveling. Alice's family drove a total of 495 miles in 11 hours. What was their average speed for the trip?

Next, determine which operation is best for solving the problem.

Speed compares the total distance traveled to the total time. To find the average speed in miles per hour, we will divide the distance, 495 miles, by the time, 11 hours.

$$11\overline{)495}$$

Then, write the problem.

$$\begin{array}{r} 45 \\ 11\overline{)495} \\ -44\downarrow \\ \hline 55 \\ -55 \\ \hline 0 \end{array}$$

Compare: 49 > 11.
Multiply: 4 × 11
Subtract: 49 – 44. Bring down 5.
Compare: 55 > 11. Multiply: 5 × 11.
Subtract: 55
No remainder

Finally, solve the problem.

The average speed for the trip was 45 miles per hour.

Practice

Solve the problems. Show your work in the space provided.

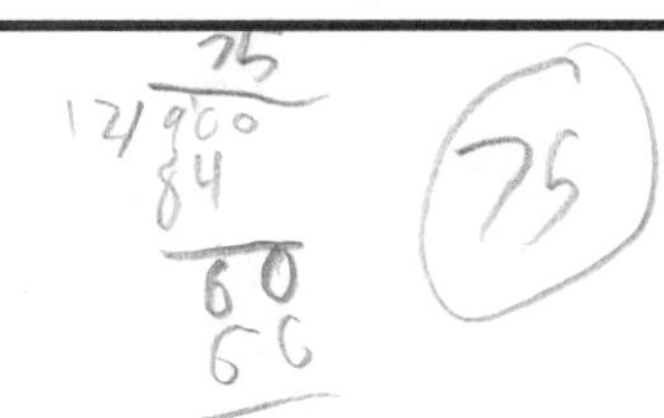

1. Ming's family drove 900 miles in 12 days. What was the average distance they drove each day?

1.

2. The Mendoza family drove 336 miles through national parks. It took them 14 hours to drive this distance. What was their average driving speed?

2.

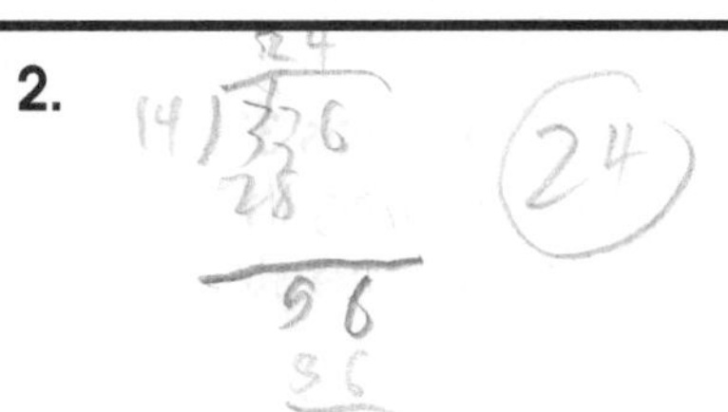

Math

Chapter Review

Solve the multiplication and division problems.

1. 243 × 8 = ________
2. 221 × 628 = ________
3. 5,432 ÷ 55 = ________
4. 9 × 6,418 = ________
5. 2,720 ÷ 6 = ________
6. 989 × 62 = ________
7. 289 ÷ 72 = ________
8. 487 × 12 = ________
9. 4,277 ÷ 18 = ________
10. 53 × 28 = ________
11. 420 × 24 = ________
12. 5,859 ÷ 55 = ________
13. 2,566 ÷ 42 = ________

The soldier and the teacher are answering the question, "How's business?" To decode their answers, solve the problems above. Find the answers in the codes below. Write the letter of each problem above the answer.

Soldier

14. "Mine is

___	___	___	___	
138,788	453 r2	1,944	98 r42	
5,844	106 r29	61,318	57,762,	
98 r42	61 r4	61,318	1,484	1,944."

Teacher

15. "Mine is

___	___	___	___	___	___ ."
237 r11	10,080	61 r4	1,944	1,944	4 r1

Solve the word problems. Show your work in the space provided.

Athletes spend different amounts of times practicing. The number of hours that teams or individual athletes practice depends on the sport. Students at one school compared practice times for different sports.

16. A swim team has 31 swimmers. The total practice time for the team is 22,320 hours each season. How many hours per season does each swimmer practice?

1.

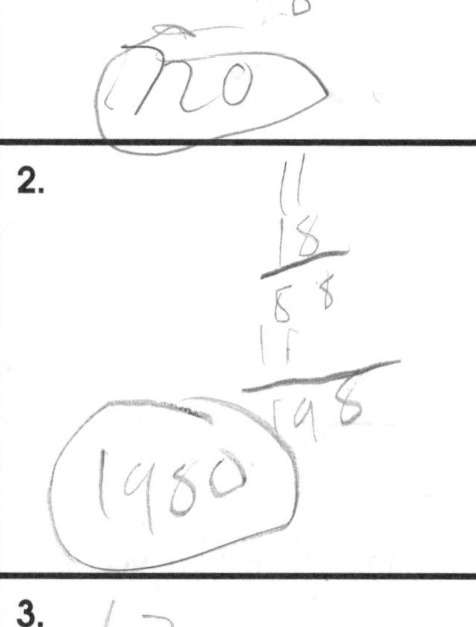

17. There are 18 players on the soccer team. Each player spends 110 hours at practices and games during the season. How many hours in total are spent at practices and games?

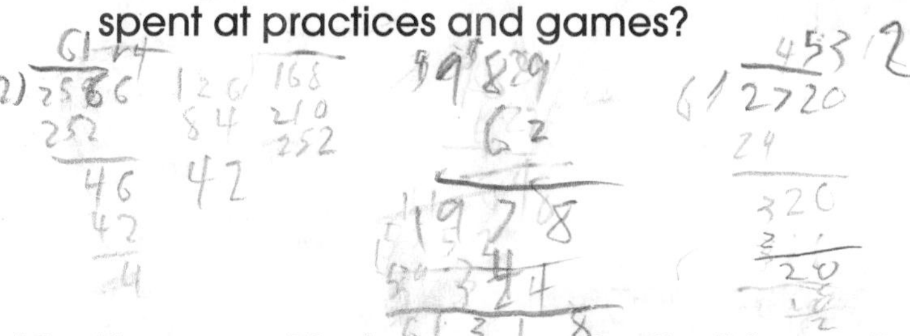

2.

18. There are 73 players on a football team. Each player practices 60 hours per season. What is the total practice time for the football team?

3.

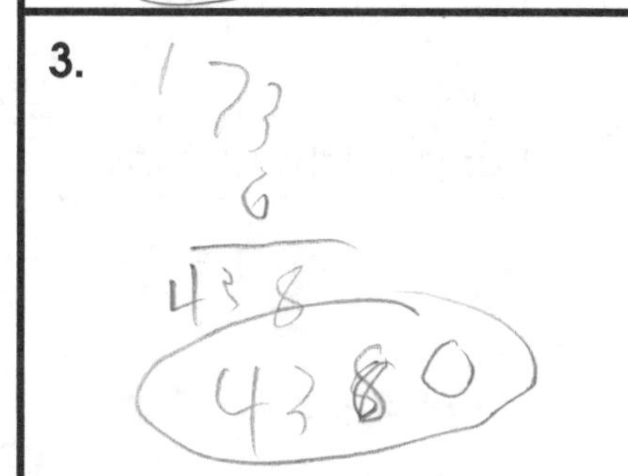

19. A baseball team spends 3,267 hours in practice each season. There are 27 players on the team. How many hours does each player practice per season?

4.

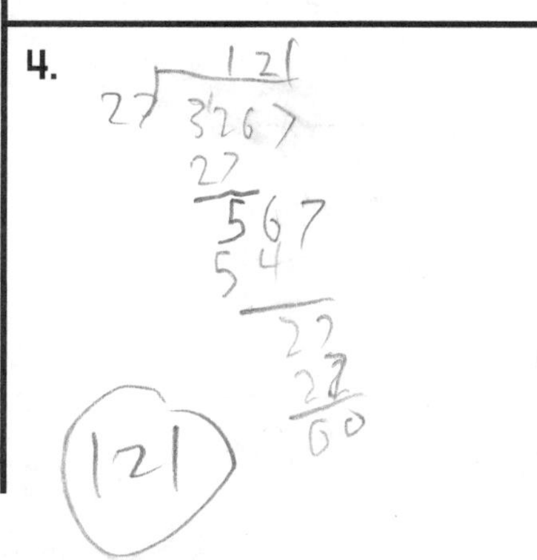

Math

Place Value

When you write a number, the position of a digit indicates the digit's value. The value of each place is 10 times the value of the place to the right.

Solve: Write the value of the underlined digit: 2,325,976

Visualize a place-value chart to see that 2 is in the **ten thousands** place.

So, 2 has a value of **2 ten thousands**, or **20,000**.

Millions	Hundred Thousands	Ten Thousands	Thousands	Hundreds	Tens	Ones
2	3	2	5	9	7	6

Math

Practice

Write the numerical value of the digit in the place named.

1. 5,363,246
   hundred thousands
   ____

2. 952,418
   thousands
   ____

3. 4,510,367
   millions
   ____

4. 8,123,405
   hundreds
   ____

5. 9,867,823
   ten thousands
   ____

6. 567,345
   ones
   ____

7. 1,328,976
   tens
   ____

8. 5,004,002
   millions
   ____

9. 2,982,023
   ten thousands
   ____

You can also use place value to determine the value of decimals.

Solve: In 1,324.973, what is value of the 9?

Visualize a place-value chart to see that 9 is in the tenths place.

So, 9 has a value of $\frac{9}{10}$, or 0.9.

thousands	hundreds	tens	ones	tenths	hundredths	thousandths
1	3	2	4 .	9	7	3

Practice

Write the place of the given digit.

1. 3 in $10.03

   ____

2. 7 in 7,000.2

   ____

3. 9 in 691

   ____

4. 4 in 1.43

   ____

Write the digit that is in the given place.

5. 731.045
   ones

   ____

6. 30.146
   hundredths

   ____

7. 2,910.42
   ones

   ____

8. 8.773
   thousandths

   ____

9. 16.51
   hundredths

   ____

10. 481.265
    hundreds

    ____

Powers of Ten

An exponent is a number that shows how many times a base number is to be used in multiplication. A power of 10 is a number with an exponent and the base number 10.

$10^1 = 10 = 10$
$10^2 = 10 \times 10 = 100$
$10^3 = 10 \times 10 \times 10 = 1,000$
$10^4 = 10 \times 10 \times 10 \times 10 = 10,000$

Solve: Convert 10^5 to a standard number.

First, look at the exponent to determine how many times the base number 10 is used in the number. Note how the exponent is equal to the number of zeros.	$10^5 = 10 \times 10 \times 10 \times 10 \times 10$
Next, multiply to determine the standard number.	$10 \times 10 \times 10 \times 10 \times 10 = 100,000$

Practice

Convert the powers of ten to standard numbers.

1. $10^3 =$ 1000
2. $10^6 =$ 1,000,000
3. $10^7 =$ 10,000,000
4. $10^{12} =$ __________

Convert each value below to a power of ten.

5. 100 = 10^2
6. 100,000,000 = 10^8
7. 1,000,000,000 = 10^9
8. 10,000,000,000 = 10^{10}

Patterns of Zeros and Decimals

To multiply a number by a power of 10, count the number of zeros in the power of 10. Move the decimal point in the product that many places to the right. Insert zeros as needed.

To multiply by 10, move the decimal point one place to the right.	0.4 → 4. 10 × 0.4 = 4
To multiply by 100, move the decimal point two places to the right.	0.40 → 40. 100 × 0.4 = 40
To multiply by 1,000, move the decimal point three places to the right.	0.400 → 400. 1,000 × 0.4 = 400

Practice

0.0245 × 100 = 2.45

Multiply by the power of ten to find the product.

1. 21.48 × 10 = 214.8
2. 6.07 × 1,000 = 6070.
3. 7.58 × 100 = 758
4. 7.434 × 100,000 = 743,000
5. 4.43 × 10,000 = 44,300
6. 0.571 × 10 = 05.71

0.571 × 100 = 57.1

5.07 × 1000 = 5070

Patterns of Zeros and Decimals

To divide a number by a power of 10, count the number of zeros in the power of 10. Move the decimal point in the quotient that many places to the left. Insert zeros as needed.

To divide by 10, move the decimal point one place to the left.

265800. → 26580.0

265,800 ÷ 10 = 26,580

To divide by 100, move the decimal point two places to the left.

265800. → 2658.00

265,800 ÷ 100 = 2,658

To divide by 1,000, move the decimal point three places to the left.

265800. → 265.800

265,800 ÷ 1,000 = 265.8

Math

Practice

Divide by the power of ten to find the quotient.

1. 13.4 ÷ 10 = ____________
2. 27.65 ÷ 100 = ____________
3. 3.457 ÷ 100 = ____________
4. 726.9 ÷ 1,000 = ____________
5. 1,533,211 ÷ 10,000 = ____________
6. 27.75 ÷ 10 = ____________

Numbers in Expanded Form

Expanded form is a way to write a number that shows the sum of the values of each digit of a number.

Solve: Write 39,572 in expanded form.

First, visualize a place-value chart.

Ten Thousands	Thousands	Hundreds	Tens	Ones
3	9	5	7	2

Next, write the values of the digits as a sum.

The expanded form of 39,572 is
30,000 + 9,000 + 500 + 70 + 2.

Solve: Write 72,998 in expanded form.

First, visualize a place-value chart.

Ten Thousands	Thousands	Hundreds	Tens	Ones
7	2	9	9	8

Next, write the values of the digits as a sum.

The expanded form of 72,998 is
70,000 + 2,000 + 900 + 90 + 8.

Practice

Write each number in expanded form.

1. 21,343 = ____________________

2. 983 = ____________________

3. 430 = ____________________

4. 721 = ____________________

5. 9,465 = ____________________

6. 73,628 = ____________________

Math

Numbers In Expanded Form

Decimals can also be written in expanded form.

Solve: Write 96.524 in expanded form.

First, visualize a place-value chart.

Tens	Ones	.	Tenths	Hundredths	Thousandths
9	6	.	5	2	4

Next, write the values of the digits as a sum.

The expanded form of 96.524 is
90 + 6 + 0.5 + 0.02 + 0.004.

Solve: Write 106.74 in expanded form.

First, visualize a place-value chart.

Hundreds	Tens	Ones	.	Tenths	Hundredths
1	0	6	.	7	4

Next, write the values of the digits as a sum.

The expanded form of 106.74 is
100 + 6 + 0.7 + 0.04.

Practice

Write each number in expanded form.

1. 519.5 = ______________________
2. 14.514 = ______________________
3. 332.115 = ______________________
4. 38,966.3 = ______________________
5. 2.568 = ______________________
6. 987.654 = ______________________
7. 987.654 = ______________________

Math

Review

Use everything you have learned so far about place value to answer the questions.

What is the place value of the underlined digit?

1. 83,7<u>6</u>4 ____________________

2. 328.36<u>7</u> ____________________

Write the digit that is in the given place.

3. 32.476—thousandths __________

4. 3,798.142—hundreds __________

5. 109,433—tens __________

6. 47.335—hundredths __________

Answer the following questions.

7. How many hundredths are in 0.4? __________

8. How many tens are in 215? __________

Convert each power of ten to a standard number.

9. 10^9 = ____________________

10. 10^5 = ____________________

11. 10^4 = ____________________

12. 10^2 = ____________________

Multiply or divide by the given power of ten.

13. 532.4 × 100 = __________________

14. 12.22 ÷ 10 = __________________

15. 7.217 x 1,000 = __________________

16. 3356.7 ÷ 100 = __________________

Write each number in expanded form.

17. 3,465 = ____

18. 83.926 = ____

Math

Comparing and Ordering Decimals

Comparing decimals is similar to comparing whole numbers.

The symbol < means that the number on the left is less than the number on the right. The symbol > means that the number on the left is greater than the number on the right.

Solve: Compare 0.08 and 0.8 using <, >, or =.

0.08 ◯ 0.8

First, line up the digits by place value.	0.08 0.8
Next, compare the digits with the greatest place value.	0.08 0.8 Both numbers have 0 ones.
Finally, compare the digits in the next place value.	0.08 0.8 0 tenths < 8 tenths, so: 0.08 (<) 0.8

Practice

Compare using <, >, or =.

1. 0.94 ◯ 0.84
2. 21.3 ◯ 21.4
3. 1.03 ◯ 1.06
4. 2.234 ◯ 2.244
5. 19.75 ◯ 19.750
6. 107.702 ◯ 107.072
7. 14.64 ◯ 14.7
8. 3.227 ◯ 3.226

Comparing and Ordering Decimals

Practice

Compare using <, >, or =.

1. 0.007 ◯ 0.07
2. 0.9 ◯ 0.90
3. 2.159 ◯ 2.259
4. 101.05 ◯ 101.005
5. 10.05 ◯ 10.005
6. 9.50 ◯ 7.05
7. 201.102 ◯ 202.102
8. 1.230 ◯ 1.23

Compare the numbers, and place them in order from least to greatest.

9. 0.7, 1.7, 0.07, 0.06 ____________________
10. 2.2, 2.3, 0.23, 0.3 ____________________
11. 3.032, 3.031, 4.032, 3.3 ____________________
12. 0.92, 0.902, 2.902, 0.95 ____________________
13. 5.7, 5.6, 5.06, 15.07 ____________________
14. 102.1, 101.2, 102.2, 101.1 ____________________
15. 7.89, 7.98, 8.99, 7.098 ____________________

Rounding Whole Numbers and Decimals

Rounding a number means choosing a simpler number that is close to the original number's value.

Solve: Round 10.84 to the nearest whole number.

First, visualize 10.84 on a number line. It is between 10 and 11.	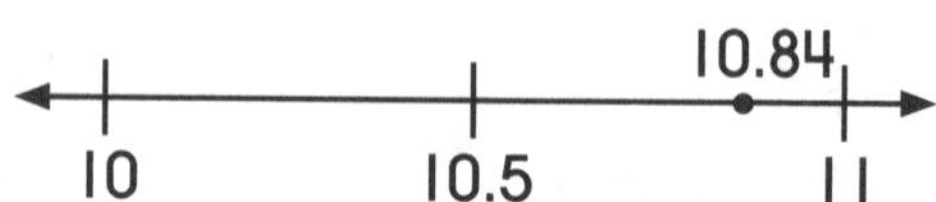
Next, round to the closer whole number.	10.84 is closer to 11. It rounds up to 11.

You can also round by looking at the digits in a number. Round 17.361 to the nearest whole number.

First, find the digit in the ones place. This is the place you are rounding to. Then, find the digit to the right of that place.	17.361 3 is to the right of the 7.
If that digit is 4 or less, round down. If it is 5 or more, round up.	3 is less than 4, so 17.361 rounds down to 17.

Practice

Round to the nearest whole number.

1. 8.4 = ____________________
2. 0.6 = ____________________
3. 2.24 = ____________________
4. 19.9 = ____________________
5. 4.449 = ____________________
6. 7.52 = ____________________
7. 91.121 = ____________________
8. 3.98 = ____________________
9. 22.7 = ____________________
10. 36.099 = ____________________

Math

Rounding Whole Numbers and Decimals

A decimal can also be rounded to the nearest place. You can use a number line or use the digits in the number to round.

Solve: Round 0.461 to the nearest tenth.

First, find the digit in the tenths place. Then, find the digit to the right of that place.	0.461 6 is to the right of the 5.
If that digit is 4 or less, round down. If it is 5 or more, round up.	6 is greater than 5, so 0.461 rounds up to 0.5.

Solve: Round 1.872 to the nearest hundredth.

First, find the digit in the hundredths place. Then, find the digit to the right of that place.	1.872 2 is to the right of the 7.
If that digit is 4 or less, round down. If it is 5 or more, round up.	2 is less than 5, so 1.872 rounds down to 1.87.

Practice

Round to the nearest tenth and the nearest hundredth.

	nearest tenth	nearest hundredth
1. 8.434	__________	__________
2. 5.851	__________	__________
3. 19.235	__________	__________
4. 27.088	__________	__________

Math

Problem Solving

You can use the strategies you have learned about rounding to estimate measurements in real life.

First, underline the important information that you will need to solve the problem.

In Zion's science class, students are recording the masses of rocks they found during a nature walk. Ms. Essa wants each measurement rounded to the tenth of a unit. Zion's rock had a mass of 0.137 kilogram, according to the digital scale. What number should he record?

Next, determine which strategy is best for solving the problem.

To find a mass to the nearest tenth of a unit, round to the nearest tenth.

Then, represent the problem using a number line.

0.137 is between two tenths: 0.1 and 0.2. Plot those tenths on a number line. Then plot 0.137 on the same line.

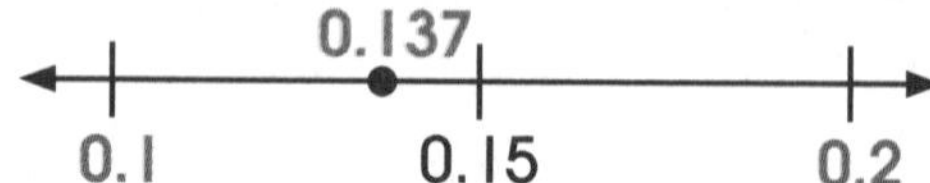

Finally, the problem.

0.137 is closer to 0.1 than to 0.2. So, round down. Zion should record the mass as 0.1 kilogram.

Practice

Solve the problems. Show your work in the space provided.

1. Arturo will buy a sweater that costs $37.68. Arturo wants to know about how much money to bring. What is the cost of the sweater to the nearest dollar?

   1.

2. The sign at a gas station says that regular gasoline costs $3.259 per gallon. What is the cost per gallon to the nearest hundredth of a dollar?

   2.

Math

Review

Use everything you have learned so far about comparing and rounding numbers to solve the problems.

Compare using <, >, or =.

1. 0.99  0.009
2. 214.01 ◯ 214.001
3. 30.249 ◯ 30.429
4. 9.008 ◯ 9.08
5. 8.2 ◯ 8.20
6. 23.4 ◯ 2.34

Compare the numbers, and place them in order from least to greatest.

7. 0.7, 1.7, 0.07, 0.06 ______________________________
8. 9.81, 9.081, 9.091, 9.082 ______________________________

Round to the nearest whole number.

9. 95.945 __________
10. 8.67 __________
11. 99.198 __________
12. 33.333 __________

Round to the nearest tenth and the nearest hundredth.

	nearest tenth	nearest hundredth
13. 0.638	__________	__________
14. 1.454	__________	__________
15. 3.770	__________	__________
16. 6.923	__________	__________

Math

Chapter Review

What is the place value of the underlined digit?

1. 1,5$\underline{3}$9.86 ____________________
2. 8$\underline{9}$6,742 ____________________
3. 3$\underline{5}$,263.8 ____________________
4. $\underline{3}$,524,291.4 ____________________
5. 105.8$\underline{5}$6 ____________________
6. 9,557.40$\underline{4}$ ____________________
7. 8,702,$\underline{3}$38 ____________________
8. 2$\underline{2}$.234 ____________________
9. 3,543.$\underline{5}$4 ____________________
10. 7$\underline{7}$7.73 ____________________

Write the digit that is in the given place.

11. 30.146—hundredths __________
12. 1,325.12—thousands __________
13. 1.325—tenths __________
14. 2,852.643—thousandths __________
15. 31,257,908—millions __________
16. 39.029—tens __________
17. 288,356—ten thousands __________
18. 4,900.007—thousandths __________

Answer the following questions.

19. How many ones are in 153? __________
20. How many hundreds are in 1,234? __________
21. How many tenths are in 15.03? __________
22. How many hundredths are in 0.3? __________
23. How many tens are in 227? __________

Convert each power of ten to a standard number.

24. 10^2 ____________________ 25. 10^8 ____________________

26. 10^3 ____________________ 27. 10^6 ____________________

Multiply by the given power of ten.

28. 8.75 × 1,000 = __________ 29. 4.567 × 100 = __________

30. 91.95 x 10 = __________ 31. 0.0377 x 10,000 = __________

Divide by the given power of ten.

32. 7,643 ÷ 100 = __________ 33. 34,981 ÷ 1,000 = __________

34. 1,154,040 ÷ 10,000 = __________ 35. 88.93 ÷ 10 = __________

Write each number in expanded form.

36. 592,682 = ____

37. 78.364 = ____

38. 97,933.4 = ____

39. 11.579 = ____

40. 1,523,899 = ____

41. 248.31 = ____

42. 2,202.477 = ____

43. 88,356.6 = ____

Chapter Review

Compare using <, >, or =.

44. 0.004 ◯ 4.00

45. 614.05 ◯ 614.05

46. 6.041 ◯ 6.401

47. 8.26 ◯ 8.026

48. 5.8 ◯ 50.8

49. 2.9 ◯ 2.009

Round to the nearest whole number.

50. 45.288 ____________

51. 97.5 ____________

52. 12.003 ____________

53. 72.71 ____________

54. 61.51 ____________

55. 34.598 ____________

Round to the nearest tenth and hundredth.

	nearest tenth	nearest hundredth
56. 7.953	____________	____________
57. 4.438	____________	____________
58. 5.299	____________	____________
59. 8.171	____________	____________
60. 0.562	____________	____________
61. 3.424	____________	____________

Adding Decimals to Hundredths

You can add decimals in the same way you add whole numbers. When writing the problem, be sure to keep the decimal points aligned and include the decimal point in the correct place in the sum.

Solve: 46.83 + 21.59

First, write the addition problem vertically, with decimal points aligned. Write the decimal point in the sum.	46.83 + 21.59 ——— .
Next, add the hundredths: 3 + 9 = 12. Write the 2 under the hundredths. Regroup 10 hundredths as 1 tenth.	1 46.83 + 21.59 ——— .2
Then, continue adding from right to left. Add the **tenths**, then the ones, and finally the tens. Regroup as needed.	1 1 46.83 + 21.59 ——— 68.42

Practice

Solve the following problems.

1. 54.45 + 19.26 = ______
2. 732.84 + 21.25 = ______
3. 102.90 + 0.26 = ______
4. 103.36 + 34.21 = ______
5. 91.44 + 81.64 = ______
6. 217.77 + 109.47 = ______
7. 37.21 + 13.98 = ______
8. 455.16 + 80.28 = ______
9. 79.56 + 47.31 = ______

Math

Adding Decimals to Hundredths

When solving word problems that require adding decimals, align the decimals when you write the equation. Add like you would with whole numbers. Make sure to include the decimal point in the correct place in the answer.

Solve: Ginny took the money she earned babysitting and went to the movies. She spent $8.50 for her ticket. Then, she spent half of the remaining money on popcorn. On the way home, she bought an ice cream cone for $1.49. When she got home, she had $0.81 left of her earnings. How much did she earn babysitting?

First, work backward. Add the amount left at the end, $0.81, to the cost of the ice cream cone. Regroup as needed. This sum shows half of the amount she had left after she bought the ticket.

```
   1 1
   0.81
 + 1.49
 ------
 $ 2.30
```

The other half, also $2.30, is what she spent on popcorn. So, next, add $2.30 + $2.30 to find the total amount she had left after buying the ticket.

```
   2.30
 + 2.30
 ------
 $ 4.60
```

Finally, add the $8.50 she spent on the ticket to find out how much she earned babysitting.

```
   1
   4.60
 + 8.50
 ------
 $13.10
```

She spent $13.10 babysitting.

Practice

Solve the problem. Show your work in the space provided.

1. Kento mowed three lawns. He deposited $9.50 of his earnings in his savings account at the bank. Then, he bought his friend a birthday present for $6.84. When he arrived at the party, he had $4.66 left. How much money did Kento earn mowing lawns?

1.

Math

Adding Decimals to Hundredths

Practice

Solve the problems. Show your work in the space provided.

1. A pair of running shoes costs $22.29 for a store to buy from the manufacturer. The store owner wants to make a profit of $18.50. What should be the selling price of the shoes?

1.

2. Malcolm spent $48.74 on new speakers and $25.39 on computer games. After his purchases, he only had $0.58 left. How much money did Malcolm have before he went shopping?

2.

3. Opal is buying groceries for dinner. Salad costs $4.25, pasta costs $3.15, and bread costs $3.50. How much do Opal's groceries cost?

3.

4. Sheila bought three books for $12.63, $9.05, and $14.97. How much did she spend?

4.

Math

Subtracting Decimals to Hundredths

You can subtract decimals in the same way you subtract whole numbers. Be sure to align the decimal points and to include the decimal point in the correct place in the difference. Regroup as needed.

Solve: 79.62 − 38.89

First, write the subtraction problem vertically, with decimal points aligned. Write the decimal point in the sum.	79.62 − 38.89 ——— .
Start with the hundredths. Since 2 < 9, regroup 1 tenth in 6 tenths as 10 hundredths. Add 10 hundredths to the 2 hundredths to get 12 hundredths. Subtract hundredths.	5 12 79.~~6~~~~2~~ − 38.89 ——— . 3
Continue subtracting from right to left. Subtract the tenths, the ones, and the tens. Regroup as needed.	8 15 12 7~~9~~.~~6~~~~2~~ − 38.89 ——— 40.73

Practice

Solve the following problems.

1. 8.86 − 5.29
2. 9.40 − 3.62
3. 75.13 − 23.21
4. 19.49 − 8.56
5. 83.94 − 22.47
6. 7.39 − 2.82
7. 41.72 − 31.34
8. 17.67 − 9.81
9. 95.09 − 27.21

Math

Subtracting Decimals to Hundredths

When solving word problems that require subtracting decimals, align the decimals when you write the equation. Subtract like you would with whole numbers. Make sure to include the decimal point in the correct place in your answer.

Solve: An owner of a clothing store bought a dress for \$36.25 and sold it for \$53.99. What was her profit?

First, write the problem vertically. Line up the decimal points and put the decimal point in the answer.

$$\begin{array}{r} 53.99 \\ -\ 36.25 \\ \hline . \end{array}$$

Next, subtract the hundredths

$$\begin{array}{r} 53.99 \\ -\ 36.25 \\ \hline .\ 4 \end{array}$$

Continue subtracting from right to left. Subtract the tenths, the ones, and the tens. Regroup as needed.

$$\begin{array}{r} {\scriptstyle 4\ 13} \\ \not{5}\not{3}.99 \\ -\ 36.25 \\ \hline 17.74 \end{array}$$

The store owner made \$17.74 in profit.

Practice

Solve the problems. Show your work in the space provided.

1. A scale shows the mass of a box of books to be 12.79 kilograms. After removing a book, the mass is 10.98 kilograms. What is the mass of the removed book?

2. The height of the water in a barrel is 49.27 centimeters. After one month, due to evaporation, the height of water in the barrel is 29.52 centimeters. What is the decrease in water height during the month?

1.

2.

Math

Subtracting Decimals to Hundredths

Math

Practice

Solve the problems. Show your work in the space provided.

Pedro researches the amount of snowfall in a mountain town that is popular for skiing. The amount of snow measured last November was 21.23 inches. In December, the snowfall was 25.67 inches, and in January it was 24.78 inches. In February, the snowfall measured 22.17 inches.

1. Pedro compares the snowfall amounts in December and January. What is the difference between the two amounts?

1.

2. How much more snow fell in December than in February?

2.

3. What is the difference between the amount of snow measured in January and in February?

3.

Inserting Zeros to Add and Subtract

When adding and subtracting decimals, you may need to insert zeros after the decimal point to help you keep the digits aligned. The value of a decimal does not change if you add zeros after the last nonzero digit. For example, 0.6 = 0.60 = 0.600 = 0.6000.

Solve: 0.6 + 0.39 + 1.23

First, write the problem vertically. Insert a zero as a placeholder in 0.6 to align the digits. Bring down the decimal point.

$$\begin{array}{r} 0.60 \\ 0.39 \\ +\ 1.23 \\ \hline . \end{array}$$

Then, add from right to left. Add hundredths, tenths, and ones. Regroup as needed.

$$\begin{array}{r} 1\ 1 \\ 0.60 \\ 0.39 \\ +\ 1.23 \\ \hline 2.22 \end{array}$$

Solve: 4.8 – 2.13

First, write the problem vertically. Insert a zero as a placeholder in 4.8. Bring down the decimal point.

$$\begin{array}{r} 4.80 \\ -\ 2.13 \\ \hline . \end{array}$$

Then, subtract from right to left. Subtract hundredths, tenths, and ones. Regroup as needed.

$$\begin{array}{r} 7\ 10 \\ 4.\cancel{8}\cancel{0} \\ -\ 2.13 \\ \hline 2.67 \end{array}$$

Practice

Add or subtract, inserting placeholder zeros as needed.

1. $\begin{array}{r} 2.1 \\ +\ 0.25 \\ \hline \end{array}$

2. $\begin{array}{r} 0.87 \\ -\ 0.4 \\ \hline \end{array}$

3. $\begin{array}{r} 14.37 \\ +\ 3.1 \\ \hline \end{array}$

Inserting Zeros to Add and Subtract

Practice

Solve the problems. Show your work in the space provided.

1. Nancy watched a video for 0.2 hours in the morning. At night, she continued watching the video for 0.87 hours. How much longer did she watch the video at night?

1.

2. Kento spends 8.45 hours per week watching TV and 6.5 hours per week practicing the piano. Each week, how much more time does he spend watching TV?

2.

3. Mr. Wilson just received his bill for $1,867.85 for the wedding dinner party for his daughter. His budget for the dinner was $2,000. How much less did the dinner cost than he expected?

3.

Math

Review

Use everything you have learned so far about adding and subtracting decimals to solve the problems.

Add or subtract, inserting placeholder zeros as needed.

1. $\begin{array}{r} 46.38 \\ +\ 21.25 \\ \hline \end{array}$

2. $\begin{array}{r} 64.81 \\ +\ 7.3 \\ \hline \end{array}$

3. $\begin{array}{r} 3.08 \\ -\ 0.72 \\ \hline \end{array}$

4. $\begin{array}{r} 78.6 \\ -\ 38.89 \\ \hline \end{array}$

5. $\begin{array}{r} 12.7 \\ +\ 3.26 \\ \hline \end{array}$

6. $\begin{array}{r} 8.81 \\ +\ 0.13 \\ \hline \end{array}$

Solve the word problems. Show your work in the space provided.

7. Chung's hat measures 6.37 units. His friend's hat measures 6.75 units. What is the difference in the hat sizes?

8. In Benson Park, workers clear 1.64 acres of trash in an hour. At Alto Park, workers clear 1.77 acres in an hour. What total area is cleared in one hour?

9. Last month, Chou watched a movie that was 2.5 hours long. Yesterday, he watched a movie that was 1.38 hours long. How much longer was the movie he watched last month?

10. The Maxwells volunteered and pulled weeds at a playground. They worked 2.35 hours on Saturday and 1.8 hours on Sunday. How many hours altogether did they work?

7.
8.
9.
10.

Multiplying Decimals to Hundredths

To multiply decimals, first multiply as you would with whole numbers. Then, count the total number of decimal places in each factor. That is the number of decimal places to use in the product.

Solve: 8.7 × 0.3

First, multiply the numbers without their decimal points. Line up the numbers by place value.

$$\begin{array}{r} 8.7 \\ \times\ 0.3 \\ \hline \end{array}$$

Think: 87 × 3 = 261.

Next, count the decimal places in each factor.

$$\begin{array}{rl} 8.7 & \rightarrow \text{1 decimal place} \\ \times\ 0.3 & \rightarrow \text{1 decimal place} \\ \hline 261 & \end{array}$$

Then, add the number of decimal places to find out how many decimal places the product will have. This is how many numbers will be to the right of the decimal point in your answer.

$$\begin{array}{r} \text{1 decimal place} \\ +\ \text{1 decimal place} \\ \hline \text{2 decimal places} \end{array}$$

Finally, write the decimal point in your product.

$$\begin{array}{rl} 8.7 & \\ \times\ 0.3 & \\ \hline 2.61 & \rightarrow \text{2 decimal places} \end{array}$$

Practice

Underline the decimal places in each factor, then multiply.

1. $\begin{array}{r} 0.5 \\ \times\ 0.1 \\ \hline \end{array}$

2. $\begin{array}{r} 0.9 \\ \times\ 0.3 \\ \hline \end{array}$

3. $\begin{array}{r} 1.2 \\ \times\ 4.8 \\ \hline \end{array}$

4. $\begin{array}{r} 2.6 \\ \times\ 7.7 \\ \hline \end{array}$

5. $\begin{array}{r} 1.8 \\ \times\ 0.8 \\ \hline \end{array}$

6. $\begin{array}{r} 3.4 \\ \times\ 3.6 \\ \hline \end{array}$

7. $\begin{array}{r} 0.7 \\ \times\ 0.7 \\ \hline \end{array}$

8. $\begin{array}{r} 9.6 \\ \times\ 0.9 \\ \hline \end{array}$

Multiplying Decimals to Hundredths

Practice

Underline the decimal places in each factor, then multiply.

1. $\begin{array}{r} 199.6 \\ \times \quad 8 \\ \hline \end{array}$

2. $\begin{array}{r} 19.96 \\ \times \quad 8 \\ \hline \end{array}$

3. $\begin{array}{r} 199.6 \\ \times \quad 0.8 \\ \hline \end{array}$

4. $\begin{array}{r} 300.4 \\ \times \quad 6 \\ \hline \end{array}$

5. $\begin{array}{r} 30.04 \\ \times \quad 6 \\ \hline \end{array}$

6. $\begin{array}{r} 300.4 \\ \times \quad 0.6 \\ \hline \end{array}$

7. $\begin{array}{r} 250.2 \\ \times \quad 5 \\ \hline \end{array}$

8. $\begin{array}{r} 25.02 \\ \times \quad 5 \\ \hline \end{array}$

9. $\begin{array}{r} 250.2 \\ \times \quad 0.5 \\ \hline \end{array}$

10. $\begin{array}{r} 15.84 \\ \times \quad 0.5 \\ \hline \end{array}$

11. $\begin{array}{r} 42.6 \\ \times \quad 0.6 \\ \hline \end{array}$

12. $\begin{array}{r} 21.9 \\ \times \quad 0.4 \\ \hline \end{array}$

13. $\begin{array}{r} 21.7 \\ \times \quad 4.2 \\ \hline \end{array}$

14. $\begin{array}{r} 63.1 \\ \times \quad 2.2 \\ \hline \end{array}$

15. $\begin{array}{r} 3.41 \\ \times \quad 6.2 \\ \hline \end{array}$

Multiplying Decimals to Hundredths

Practice

Multiply. Underline the decimal places in the products.

1. 5.44×901.02

2. 25.9×47.6

3. 291.23×4.34

4. 3.08×608.8

5. 908.01×4.11

6. 92.5×50.7

7. 901.3×8.2

8. 11.4×22.4

9. 109.21×32.2

10. 47.1×12.9

11. 81.75×2.7

12. 211.7×4.5

13. 18.08×18.7

14. 28.6×26.8

15. 727.3×7.0

Math

Dividing Decimals to Hundredths

To divide a decimal by a whole number, determine the correct placement of the decimal point in your answer, then divide as usual.

Solve: 2.5 ÷ 4

First, write the decimal point in the quotient. Then, divide as you would divide whole numbers.

```
   0.6
4)2.5
 -2 4
 ----
     1
```

4 goes into 25 at least 6 times.

4 x 6 = 24

25 - 24 = 1

Next, instead of writing 1 as the remainder, write a **zero** in the hundredths place and bring it down. Continue dividing.

```
   0.6 2
4)2.5 0  <-- Write a zero here.
 -2 4 ↓
 ------
     1 0
   -   8
   -----
       2
```

Write a zero here.

4 goes into 10 at least 2 times.

4 x 2 = 8

10 - 8 = 2

Finally, instead of writing 2 as the remainder, write a **zero** in the thousandths place and bring it down. Estimate, multiply, and subtract to get the final answer.

```
   0.6 2 5
4)2.5 0 0  <-- Write a zero here.
 -2 4 ↓ |
 ------ |
     1 0 |
   -   8 ↓
   -------
       2 0
     - 2 0
     -----
         0
```

Write a zero here.

4 goes into 20 at least 5 times.

4 x 5 = 20

20 - 20 = 0

Practice

Divide.

1. 5)2.7

2. 5)4.19

3. 4)0.31

Dividing Decimals to Hundredths

When dividing by a decimal, change the divisor into a whole number by moving the decimal point to the right. Then, move the decimal point in the dividend the same number of places to the right to write an equivalent division problem.

Solve: 24.15 ÷ 1.05

First, make the divisor a whole number. To do this, move the decimal point in 1.05 two places to the right. Then, move the decimal point in the dividend the same number of places.

$1.05\overline{)24.15} = 105\overline{)2415}$

You can also think of this as multiplying by the same power of ten:

$1.05 \times 10^2 = 105$

$24.15 \times 10^2 = 2415$

$2415 \div 105 = 23$

$24.15 \div 1.05 = 23$

Finally, divide the whole numbers as usual.

$$\begin{array}{r} 23 \\ 105\overline{)2415} \\ -210 \\ \hline 315 \\ -315 \\ \hline 0 \end{array}$$

Practice

Rewrite each problem with a whole number divisor. Then, divide.

1. $1.2\overline{)6.0}$
2. $0.24\overline{)7.92}$
3. $0.8\overline{)8.24}$
4. $2.4\overline{)14.4}$
5. $3.3\overline{)23.1}$
6. $0.7\overline{)28.98}$

Math

Dividing Decimals to Hundredths

Practice

Divide to solve the problems.

1. $0.03\overline{)45.6}$
2. $1.7\overline{)20.4}$
3. $3.8\overline{)16.72}$
4. $7.4\overline{)28.86}$
5. $1.07\overline{)67.41}$
6. $0.22\overline{)8.03}$
7. $0.08\overline{)2.52}$
8. $0.02\overline{)6.56}$
9. $1.5\overline{)8.4}$
10. $0.65\overline{)0.91}$
11. $0.08\overline{)0.17}$
12. $0.17\overline{)3.06}$
13. $2.92\overline{)23.36}$
14. $0.17\overline{)42.67}$
15. $6.3\overline{)2526.3}$

Math

Problem Solving

You can use the decimal division strategies you have learned so far to solve more difficult problems.

First, underline and identify the important information that you will need to solve the problem. Be sure to look in the table as well as in the problem.

Sound energy can be measured in watts. This table shows the energy output of some musical instruments.

Instrument	Energy Output
Piano	0.44 watts
Trombone	6.4 watts
Snare Drum	12.3 watts
Human Voice	0.000024 watts

How many snare drums would it take to produce 73.8 watts of energy?

Next, determine which operation is best for solving the problem.

One snare drum has an energy output of 12.3 watts. So, we can divide the total number of watts, 73.8, by 12.3, to find the number of snare drums needed to produce that energy output.

Then, write the problem.

$12.3\overline{)73.8}$

Finally, solve the problem. Move the decimal point in 12.3 one place to the right. Move the decimal point in the dividend one place to the right also. Then, divide.

$12.3\overline{)73.8} = 123\overline{)738}$

$$\begin{array}{r} 6 \\ 123\overline{)738} \\ -738 \\ \hline 0 \end{array}$$

6 snare drums are needed.

Math

Practice

Use the table above to solve the problem. Show your work in the space provided.

1. How many trombones would it take to produce 1,280 watts of energy?

1.

Use everything you have learned so far about decimal operations to solve the problems.

Multiply or divide.

1. 6.2×0.4

2. 3.05×2.83

3. 5.73×2.83

4. 4.03×1.1

5. $0.25\overline{)65}$

6. $0.04\overline{)19}$

7. $0.7\overline{)13.23}$

8. $1.3\overline{)2.86}$

Solve the problems. Show your work in the space provided.

9. Roberto bought a 12-pack of bottled water. Each bottle held 0.75 liters. How many liters of water did he buy?

9.

10. A hike is 26.4 miles. Alicia wants to divide it equally over 3 days. How far does she need to hike each day?

10.

11. There are 6.75 buckets of sand in a sandbox. If each full bucket holds 4.32 pounds of sand, how many pounds of sand are there in the sandbox?

11.

Chapter Review

Math

Add or subtract.

1.
$$\begin{array}{r} 0.23 \\ +\ 0.91 \\ \hline \end{array}$$

2.
$$\begin{array}{r} 78.07 \\ +\ 1.34 \\ \hline \end{array}$$

3.
$$\begin{array}{r} 9.06 \\ +\ 2.78 \\ \hline \end{array}$$

4.
$$\begin{array}{r} 48.78 \\ +\ 9.03 \\ \hline \end{array}$$

5.
$$\begin{array}{r} 29.08 \\ -\ 2.10 \\ \hline \end{array}$$

6.
$$\begin{array}{r} 13.73 \\ -\ 8.64 \\ \hline \end{array}$$

7.
$$\begin{array}{r} 3.89 \\ -\ 1.47 \\ \hline \end{array}$$

8.
$$\begin{array}{r} 33.04 \\ -\ 6.75 \\ \hline \end{array}$$

9.
$$\begin{array}{r} 0.98 \\ +\ 0.87 \\ \hline \end{array}$$

10.
$$\begin{array}{r} 26.32 \\ +\ 1.14 \\ \hline \end{array}$$

11.
$$\begin{array}{r} 42.55 \\ -\ 3.75 \\ \hline \end{array}$$

12.
$$\begin{array}{r} 81.12 \\ +\ 56.29 \\ \hline \end{array}$$

13. Add 12.7 and 3.26.

14. Subtract 2.21 from 8.3.

15. Add 5.63 and 2.1.

16. Add 26.3 and 5.25.

Multiply or divide.

17. 586×3.7

18. 2.1×0.8

19. 3.50×2.6

20. 38.2×7.58

21. 98×0.4

22. 370×6.4

23. 7.02×9

24. 42.36×13

25. $2.5\overline{)10}$

26. $0.03\overline{)36}$

27. $9\overline{)7.2}$

28. $8\overline{)5.6}$

29. $4.8\overline{)24.96}$

30. $0.37\overline{)2.96}$

31. $9.06\overline{)63.42}$

32. $1.21\overline{)4.84}$

Chapter Review

Math

Solve the problems. Show your work in the space provided.

33. Jeff wants to buy a vase for $32.75. He only has $25.15. How much does Jeff need to borrow from his brother to buy the vase?	**33.**
34. Booker needs to pay his rent. He has $1,252.45 in the bank. His rent is $672.30. How much money will Booker have left in the bank after he pays his rent?	**34.**
35. The Thomas triplets want to buy some oranges. Justin has 23 cents, Jarrod has 45 cents, and Jeremy has 52 cents. How much money do the triplets have?	**35.**
36. A school lunch costs $1.55. Sean has $2.45. How much money will he have left after buying lunch?	**36.**
37. Fred bought 7 games on clearance for $104.65 total. Each game was on sale for the same price. How much did each game cost?	**37.**
38. Gas costs $2.64 a gallon. Elaine spent $38.28 at the gas station. How many gallons of gas did she buy?	**38.**
39. There are 2.5 servings in a can of tuna fish. How many servings are there in 7 cans?	**39.**
40. There are 5.28 cups of pudding to be divided into 6 dishes. How much pudding should be put into each dish to make them equal?	**40.**

Fractions and Division

Fractions tell how items are divided. When you see a fraction written like this, $\frac{1}{2}$, that means something has been divided into 2 equal parts, and the fraction shows one of those parts. The division problem $1 \div 2$ gives the same result.

Solve: Gillian wants to share a pie equally with her two brothers. How much pie will each person receive? Write the answer as a fraction and as a division problem.

First, draw a circle to help you figure out the answer. The pie needs to be divided between 3 people, so divide the circle into 3 equal parts (thirds).

Then, find the answer as a fraction and as a division problem.

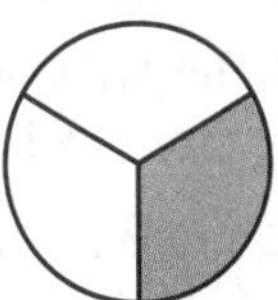

Fraction: Each person will receive 1 of the 3 equal parts, or $\frac{1}{3}$ of the pie.

Division problem: Each person will receive 1 whole divided by 3, or $1 \div 3$.

Practice

Read each problem and then answer the questions.

1. If you have 3 pizzas, and you want to split them between 4 people, how much pizza will each person receive?

   Each pizza will be cut into ___________ pieces.

   Each person will receive ___________ of a pizza or 3 pieces each.

2. A 45-pound bag of rice is going to be split between 5 families. How much rice will each family receive?

   The way to write this as a division problem is ___________.

   The way to write this as a fraction is ___________.

   Each family will receive ___________ pounds of rice.

Math

Changing Improper Fractions to Mixed Numbers

An improper fraction has a numerator that is equal to or greater than the denominator. Sometimes you will need to express an improper fraction as a mixed number that has the same value.

Solve: Rewrite the improper fraction $\frac{5}{3}$ as a mixed number.

First, draw a diagram to show $\frac{5}{3}$. The denominator, 3, shows the number of equal parts. Draw a circle, divide it into 3 equal parts and shade all 3. Since the numerator, 5, is greater than the denominator, 3, there is more than one whole. Draw a second circle, divide it into 3 equal parts, and shade 2 more parts so $\frac{5}{3}$ is shaded.

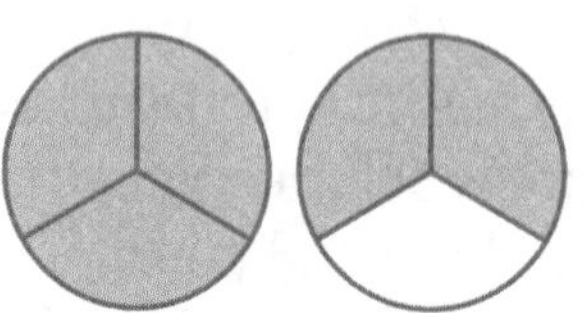

$$\frac{3}{3} + \frac{2}{3} = \frac{5}{3}$$

Then, use the diagram to write the mixed number. Write the whole number part and the fractional part.

$\frac{5}{3}$ = 1 whole

The diagram shows 1 whole plus $\frac{2}{3}$ shaded.

So, $\frac{5}{3} = 1\frac{2}{3}$.

Practice

Write each illustrated fraction as an improper fraction and as a mixed number.

1. 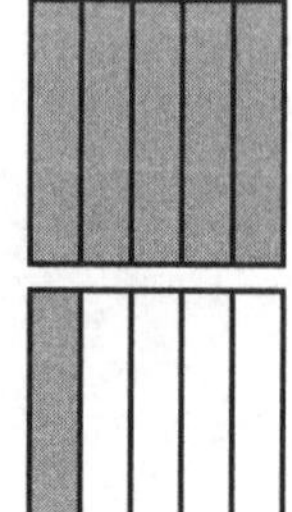 ________ or ________

2. 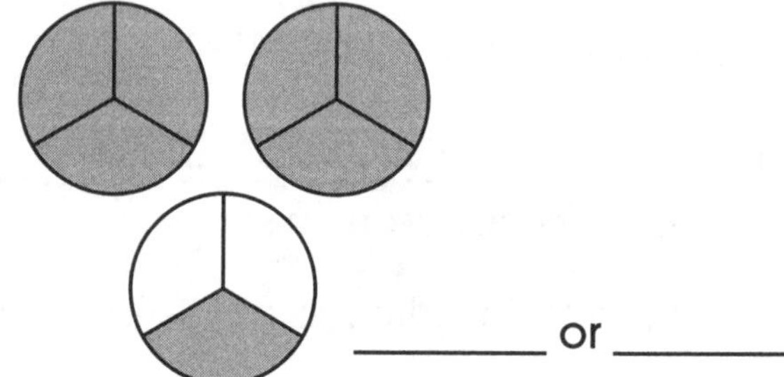 ________ or ________

Math

Changing Improper Fractions to Mixed Numbers

You can also use long division to convert improper fractions to mixed numbers.

Solve: Rewrite $\frac{14}{3}$ as a mixed number.

First, write $\frac{14}{3}$ as a division problem. The numerator is the dividend. The denominator is the divisor.

$\frac{14}{3}$ can be written as

$14 \div 3$ or $3\overline{)14}$.

Next, divide. Then, write the whole number part of the quotient as the whole number part of the mixed number. Write the remainder over the original denominator (the divisor). This shows the fractional part.

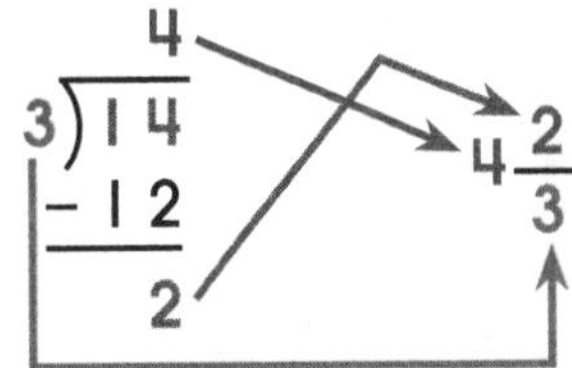

Practice

Use division to change each improper fraction to a whole number.

1. $\frac{15}{2}$ ________
2. $\frac{7}{4}$ ________
3. $\frac{20}{7}$ ________
4. $\frac{11}{3}$ ________
5. $\frac{13}{6}$ ________
6. $\frac{14}{5}$ ________
7. $\frac{21}{4}$ ________
8. $\frac{17}{7}$ ________
9. $\frac{22}{9}$ ________
10. $\frac{19}{8}$ ________
11. $\frac{9}{2}$ ________
12. $\frac{13}{3}$ ________

Changing Mixed Numbers to Improper Fractions

You can also change mixed numbers to improper fractions.

Solve: Rewrite $4\frac{3}{5}$ as an improper fraction.

First, multiply the denominator by the whole number to get a product. Add the numerator to the product to get the new numerator. Keep the denominator the same.	$4\frac{3}{5}$ $= \frac{(4 \times 5) + 3}{5}$ $= \frac{20 + 3}{5}$
Then, write the improper fraction.	$4\frac{3}{5} = \frac{23}{5}$

Math

Practice

Change each mixed number to an improper fraction.

1. $4\frac{2}{5}$ ________
2. $3\frac{5}{6}$ ________
3. $2\frac{4}{9}$ ________
4. $4\frac{5}{12}$ ________
5. $1\frac{2}{7}$ ________
6. $4\frac{4}{9}$ ________
7. $3\frac{1}{8}$ ________
8. $5\frac{2}{3}$ ________
9. $6\frac{2}{5}$ ________
10. $7\frac{2}{9}$ ________
11. $8\frac{1}{6}$ ________
12. $9\frac{3}{4}$ ________

Changing Mixed Numbers to Improper Fractions

When changing a mixed number to an improper fraction, sometimes you will be asked to write the fraction in its simplest form.

Solve: Write $1\frac{9}{12}$ as an improper fraction in its simplest form.

First, convert the mixed number to an improper fraction. Multiply the denominator by the whole number to get a product. Add the numerator to the product to get the new numerator. Keep the denominator the same.

$$1\frac{9}{12} = \frac{(12 \times 1) + 9}{12} = \frac{12 + 9}{12} = \frac{21}{12}$$

Then, simplify the improper fraction. The greatest common factor of 12 and 21 is 3, so divide both the numerator and denominator by 3.

$$\frac{21}{12}\frac{\div 3}{\div 3} = \frac{7}{4}$$

$$1\frac{9}{12} = \frac{7}{4}$$

Math

Practice

Change each mixed number to an improper fraction. Write the fraction in its simplest form.

1. $3\frac{6}{8}$ ______
2. $4\frac{10}{15}$ ______
3. $4\frac{4}{8}$ ______
4. $3\frac{10}{4}$ ______
5. $1\frac{2}{6}$ ______
6. $2\frac{4}{8}$ ______
7. $3\frac{2}{14}$ ______
8. $2\frac{10}{16}$ ______
9. $5\frac{10}{12}$ ______
10. $4\frac{4}{18}$ ______
11. $6\frac{12}{16}$ ______
12. $3\frac{8}{10}$ ______

Lowest Common Denominators

Math

To add or subtract fractions, you will need to know how to find the lowest common denominator.

Solve: Find the lowest common denominator of $\frac{1}{4}$ and $\frac{3}{8}$. Then, rewrite each fraction using the lowest common denominator (LCD).

First, list the multiples of the denominators, 4 and 8. The lowest number in both lists is 8. So, the lowest common denominator is 8.

Multiples of 4: 4, 8, 12, 16, 20, 24,...
Multiples of 8: 8, 16, 24,...

Next, rewrite the first fraction using 8 as the denominator. Multiply the numerator and denominator of $\frac{1}{4}$ by the same factor, 2, to get the fraction $\frac{2}{8}$.

$\frac{1}{4} = \frac{}{8}$ ← The LCD of 4 and 8

$$\frac{1}{4} = \frac{1 \times 2}{4 \times 2} = \frac{2}{8}$$

$$\frac{1}{4} = \frac{2}{8}$$

Finally, rewrite the second fraction using 8 as the denominator. Multiply the numerator and denominator of $\frac{3}{8}$ by the same factor, 1. The result is the same fraction, because $\frac{3}{8}$ already has a denominator of 8.

$\frac{3}{8} = \frac{}{8}$ ← The LCD of 4 and 8

$$\frac{3}{8} = \frac{3 \times 1}{8 \times 1} = \frac{3}{8}$$

$$\frac{3}{8} = \frac{3}{8}$$

Practice

Find the lowest common denominator of each pair of fractions. Then, rewrite each fraction using the new common denominator.

1. $\frac{7}{10}, \frac{1}{5}$

   LCD ______

   ______, ______

2. $\frac{5}{6}, \frac{1}{2}$

   LCD ______

   ______, ______

3. $\frac{1}{6}, \frac{2}{9}$

   LCD ______

   ______, ______

Lowest Common Denominators

Practice

Find the lowest common denominator of each pair of fractions. Then, rewrite each fraction using the new common denominator.

1. $\frac{2}{3}, \frac{5}{6}$

   LCD ______

   ______ , ______

2. $\frac{1}{2}, \frac{1}{4}$

   LCD ______

   ______ , ______

3. $\frac{2}{5}, \frac{1}{10}$

   LCD ______

   ______ , ______

4. $\frac{1}{10}, \frac{3}{5}$

   LCD ______

   ______ , ______

5. $\frac{2}{3}, \frac{1}{2}$

   LCD ______

   ______ , ______

6. $\frac{3}{4}, \frac{3}{5}$

   LCD ______

   ______ , ______

7. $\frac{5}{8}, \frac{1}{2}$

   LCD ______

   ______ , ______

8. $\frac{2}{3}, \frac{2}{9}$

   LCD ______

   ______ , ______

9. $\frac{1}{2}, \frac{4}{5}$

   LCD ______

   ______ , ______

10. $\frac{3}{4}, \frac{7}{8}$

    LCD ______

    ______ , ______

11. $\frac{2}{3}, \frac{1}{5}$

    LCD ______

    ______ , ______

12. $\frac{1}{4}, \frac{5}{6}$

    LCD ______

    ______ , ______

Finding Equivalent Fractions

Equivalent fractions are fractions that are equal in value. To find equivalent fractions, multiply the numerator and denominator by the same number. This is the same as multiplying by 1, so the value does not change. Four fractions, each equivalent to $\frac{1}{2}$, are shown.

$\frac{1}{2}$ 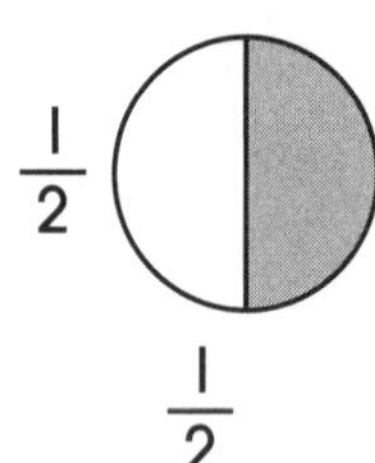

$\frac{1}{2}$

$\frac{2}{4}$

$\frac{1}{2} \times \frac{2}{2} = \frac{2}{4}$

$\frac{3}{6}$

$\frac{1}{2} \times \frac{3}{3} = \frac{3}{6}$

$\frac{4}{8}$

$\frac{1}{2} \times \frac{4}{4} = \frac{4}{8}$

Solve: $8 = \frac{\square}{4}$

First, rewrite the whole number as a fraction with a denominator of 1.

$$8 = \frac{\square}{4}$$

$$\frac{8}{1} = \frac{\square}{4}$$

Next, decide which number can be multiplied by the denominator, 1, to get 4. Since 1 × 4 = 4, multiply by 4.

$$\frac{8}{1} = \frac{8}{1} \times \frac{4}{4} = \frac{32}{4}$$

So, $8 = \frac{32}{4}$.

Practice

Rewrite each fraction in simplest form.

1. $3 = \frac{\square}{6}$
2. $\frac{1}{5} = \frac{\square}{10}$
3. $11 = \frac{\square}{4}$
4. $\frac{7}{2} = \frac{\square}{6}$
5. $\frac{3}{8} = \frac{\square}{24}$
6. $\frac{6}{5} = \frac{\square}{15}$

Finding Equivalent Fractions

Practice

Find the equivalent fraction.

1. $\frac{1}{4} = \frac{\square}{8}$

2. $\frac{3}{5} = \frac{\square}{15}$

3. $\frac{2}{9} = \frac{\square}{27}$

4. $7 = \frac{\square}{5}$

5. $\frac{5}{8} = \frac{\square}{24}$

6. $1 = \frac{\square}{6}$

7. $3 = \frac{\square}{9}$

8. $\frac{8}{11} = \frac{\square}{33}$

9. $\frac{5}{6} = \frac{\square}{30}$

10. $9 = \frac{\square}{4}$

11. $\frac{3}{10} = \frac{\square}{30}$

12. $4 = \frac{\square}{12}$

13. $\frac{11}{4} = \frac{\square}{28}$

14. $\frac{4}{7} = \frac{\square}{28}$

15. $8 = \frac{\square}{6}$

Math

Review

Use everything you have learned so far about fractions to solve the problems.

Read each problem and then answer the questions.

1. Cherie has 3 days to read a 21-page chapter for homework. How many pages will she need to read each day?

   The way to write this as a division problem is __________.

   The way to write this as a fraction is __________.

   Cherie will need to read __________ pages of the chapter each day.

2. John bought two 5-pound bags of baby carrots to share with his classmates. If there are 25 students in John's class, how many pounds of carrots will each student receive?

   The two bags of carrots will be split __________ ways.

   Each person will receive __________ pounds of carrots.

Write each fraction as an improper fraction and as a mixed number.

3. 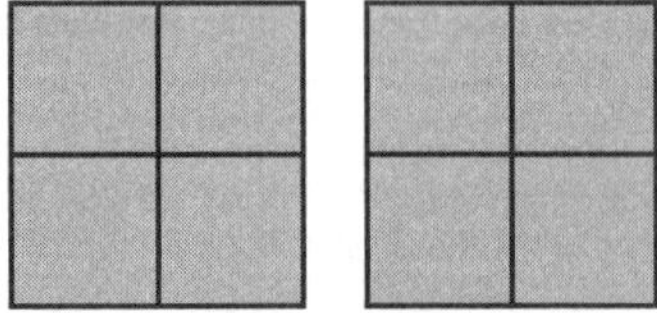

   _____ or _____

4. 

   _____ or _____

5. 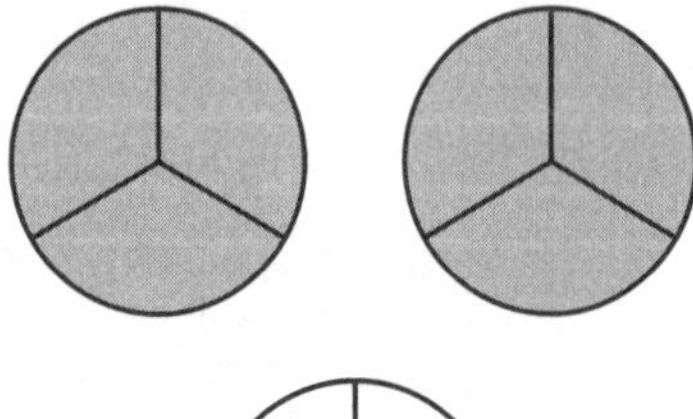

   _____ or _____

6. 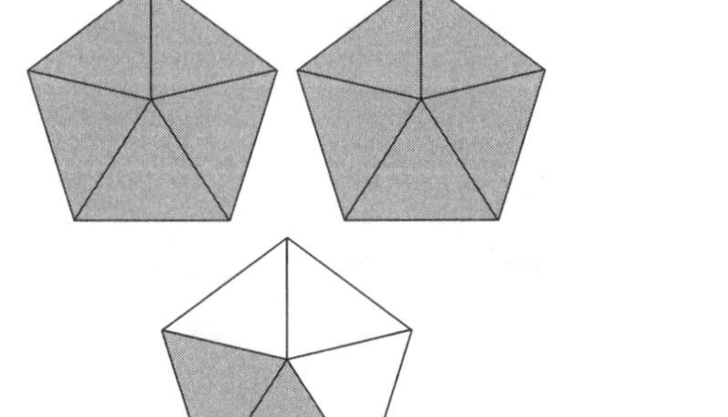

   _____ or _____

Change each improper fraction to a mixed number.

7. $\frac{43}{5}$ ______

8. $\frac{23}{8}$ ______

9. $\frac{21}{5}$ ______

10. $7\frac{1}{6}$ ______

11. $9\frac{2}{5}$ ______

12. $11\frac{1}{3}$ ______

Find the lowest common denominator of each pair of fractions. Then, rewrite each fraction using the new common denominator.

13. $\frac{3}{4}, \frac{1}{12}$

LCD ______

______ , ______

14. $\frac{1}{7}, \frac{2}{14}$

LCD ______

______ , ______

15. $\frac{6}{9}, \frac{1}{3}$

LCD ______

______ , ______

Find the number that completes the equivalent fraction.

16. $\frac{6}{7} = \frac{\square}{14}$

17. $2 = \frac{\square}{3}$

18. $5 = \frac{\square}{7}$

Simplifying Fractions

A factor of a number divides it evenly. To reduce a fraction to its simplest form, find the greatest common factor for the numerator and the denominator. Divide them by that number.

Solve: Rewrite $\frac{12}{16}$ in simplest form.

First, find the factors of 12 and 16. Circle the greatest common factor.

Factors of 12: 1, 2, 3, (4), 6, 12
Factors of 16: 1, 2, (4), 8, 16

Next, divide the numerator and denominator by 4.

$$\frac{12}{16} = \frac{12 \div 4}{16 \div 4} = \frac{3}{4}$$

Solve: Rewrite $\frac{36}{72}$ in simplest form.

First, find the factors of 36 and 72. Circle the greatest common factor.

Factors of 36: 1, 2, 3, 4, 6, 9, 12, 18, (36)
Factors of 72: 1, 2, 3, 4, 6, 8, 9, 12, 18, 24, (36), 72

Next, divide the numerator and denominator by 36.

$$\frac{36}{72} = \frac{36 \div 36}{72 \div 36} = \frac{1}{2}$$

Practice

Rewrite each fraction in simplest form.

1. $\frac{3}{6}$ ________
2. $\frac{5}{10}$ ________
3. $\frac{9}{18}$ ________
4. $\frac{6}{24}$ ________
5. $\frac{4}{12}$ ________
6. $\frac{2}{10}$ ________

Math

Simplifying Mixed Numbers

A mixed number is in simplest form if its fractional part is in simplest form and names a number less than 1.

Solve: Rewrite $3\frac{12}{8}$ in simplest form.

First, consider the whole number and fraction separately.	$3\frac{12}{8} = 3 + \frac{12}{8}$
Next, simplify the fraction. Find the greatest common factor of 12 and 8. Divide both the numerator and denominator by the greatest common factor, 4.	$\frac{12}{8} = \frac{12 \div 4}{8 \div 4} = \frac{3}{2}$
Then, rewrite the improper fraction so that it is a mixed number.	$\frac{3}{2} = 1\frac{1}{2}$
Finally, write the original mixed number in simplest form.	$3\frac{12}{8} = 3 + 1\frac{1}{2} = 4\frac{1}{2}$

Practice

Rewrite each mixed number in simplest form.

1. $4\frac{16}{10}$ ________
2. $2\frac{8}{12}$ ________
3. $6\frac{9}{6}$ ________
4. $5\frac{21}{8}$ ________
5. $7\frac{17}{6}$ ________
6. $11\frac{18}{20}$ ________
7. $3\frac{22}{17}$ ________
8. $6\frac{12}{20}$ ________
9. $4\frac{13}{8}$ ________

Math

Simplifying Mixed Numbers

Math

Practice

Rewrite each mixed number in simplest form.

1. $2\frac{8}{5}$ ________
2. $3\frac{15}{4}$ ________
3. $1\frac{7}{3}$ ________
4. $2\frac{5}{2}$ ________
5. $2\frac{10}{3}$ ________
6. $4\frac{6}{5}$ ________
7. $3\frac{15}{7}$ ________
8. $2\frac{20}{9}$ ________
9. $2\frac{20}{9}$ ________
10. $11\frac{3}{2}$ ________
11. $3\frac{19}{5}$ ________
12. $7\frac{17}{4}$ ________
13. $2\frac{9}{7}$ ________
14. $1\frac{16}{9}$ ________
15. $3\frac{11}{6}$ ________

Comparing and Ordering Fractions

You can use your knowledge of simplifying, finding common denominators, and finding equivalent fractions to compare two fractions.

Solve: Compare $\frac{4}{6}$ and $\frac{5}{9}$ using <, >, or =.

First, rewrite both fractions so they have a common denominator.

$$\frac{4}{6}\frac{\times 9}{\times 9} = \frac{36}{54}$$

$$\frac{5}{9}\frac{\times 6}{\times 6} = \frac{30}{54}$$

Then, compare the numerators to compare the fractions.

$36 > 30$, so $\frac{4}{6} > \frac{5}{9}$

Practice

Compare each pair of fractions using <, >, or =.

1. $\frac{2}{8}$ ______ $\frac{1}{3}$
2. $\frac{3}{5}$ ______ $\frac{6}{10}$
3. $1\frac{2}{3}$ ______ $\frac{9}{6}$
4. $\frac{4}{7}$ ______ $\frac{3}{14}$
5. $\frac{5}{9}$ ______ $\frac{11}{18}$
6. $2\frac{1}{2}$ ______ $\frac{7}{2}$
7. $\frac{19}{5}$ ______ $3\frac{4}{5}$
8. $\frac{5}{6}$ ______ $\frac{3}{4}$
9. $\frac{7}{12}$ ______ $\frac{2}{3}$
10. $\frac{3}{9}$ ______ $\frac{4}{12}$
11. $\frac{5}{7}$ ______ $\frac{4}{6}$
12. $2\frac{3}{7}$ ______ $\frac{19}{7}$

Math

Comparing and Ordering Fractions

Practice

Compare each pair of fractions using <, >, or =.

1. $\frac{4}{7}$ ______ $\frac{21}{11}$

2. $\frac{29}{9}$ ______ $2\frac{1}{6}$

3. $\frac{26}{11}$ ______ $\frac{22}{11}$

4. $\frac{11}{12}$ ______ $\frac{21}{24}$

5. $2\frac{7}{10}$ ______ $\frac{58}{20}$

6. $\frac{9}{13}$ ______ $\frac{21}{26}$

Write the fractions in order from least to greatest.

7. $\frac{1}{7}, \frac{6}{7}, 1\frac{2}{3}, 1\frac{8}{9}, 1\frac{1}{7}$

____

8. $1\frac{3}{8}, 1\frac{7}{12}, 1\frac{10}{12}, 1\frac{1}{4}, 1\frac{7}{8}$

____

9. $2\frac{2}{5}, 2\frac{3}{5}, 2\frac{7}{10}, 2\frac{9}{20}, 2\frac{1}{10}$

____

10. $3\frac{2}{9}, \frac{8}{9}, 3\frac{1}{3}, 3\frac{5}{6}, 3\frac{7}{9},$

____

Math

Changing Fractions to Decimals

To rewrite a fraction as a decimal, you can write an equivalent fraction with a denominator that is a power of 10.

Solve: Rewrite $\frac{1}{4}$ as a decimal.

First, rewrite $\frac{1}{4}$ as a fraction with a denominator that is a power of 10. Multiply the numerator and the denominator by the same factor to make an equivalent fraction.

4 is a factor of 100, so ¼ can be written as an equivalent fraction with a denominator of 100.

$$\frac{1}{4} = \frac{1 \times 25}{4 \times 25} = \frac{25}{100}$$

Then, rewrite the new fraction as a decimal to the hundredths place.

$\frac{25}{100}$ = 25 hundredths = 0.25

Solve: Rewrite $3\frac{1}{250}$ as a decimal.

First, rewrite $3\frac{1}{250}$ as a fraction with a denominator that is a power of 10. Multiply the numerator and the denominator by the same factor to make an equivalent fraction.

250 is a factor of 1,000, so 1/250 can be written as an equivalent fraction with a denominator of 100.

$$\frac{1}{250} = \frac{1 \times 4}{250 \times 4} = \frac{4}{1000}$$

Then, rewrite that fraction as a decimal to the thousandths place. Remember to include the whole number in the answer.

$3\frac{1}{250} = 3\frac{4}{1000}$

= 3 and 4 thousandths = 3.004

Math

Changing Fractions to Decimals

Math

Practice

Change each fraction to a decimal as indicated.

1. Change $\frac{2}{5}$ to tenths. ________

2. Change $\frac{2}{5}$ to hundredths. ________

3. Change $\frac{2}{5}$ to thousandths. ________

4. Change $3\frac{1}{2}$ to tenths. ________

5. Change $\frac{3}{25}$ to hundredths. ________

6. Change $\frac{17}{25}$ to thousandths. ________

7. Change $2\frac{1}{5}$ to tenths. ________

8. Change $\frac{17}{50}$ to hundredths. ________

9. Change $1\frac{27}{100}$ to thousandths. ________

10. Change $2\frac{9}{25}$ to hundredths. ________

Changing Decimals to Fractions

To rewrite a decimal as a fraction, you can write everything before the decimal point as a whole number and everything after the decimal point as the numerator over the appropriate power of ten.

Solve: Rewrite 0.2 as a fraction in simplest form.

First, write 0.2 as a fraction with a denominator of 10.	$0.2 = 2 \text{ tenths} = \frac{2}{10}$
Then, rewrite that fraction in simplest form. Divide the numerator and denominator by 2.	$\frac{2}{10} = \frac{2 \div 2}{10 \div 2} = \frac{1}{5}$

Solve: Rewrite 0.125 as a fraction in simplest form.

First, write 0.125 as a fraction with a denominator of 1000.	$0.125 = 125 \text{ thousandths} = \frac{125}{1000}$
Then, rewrite that fraction in simplest form. Divide the numerator and denominator by 125.	$\frac{125}{1000} = \frac{125 \div 125}{1000 \div 125} = \frac{1}{8}$

Practice

Write each decimal as a fraction or mixed number in simplest form.

1. 0.25 ________ **2.** 1.3 ________ **3.** 4.15 ________

4. 2.2 ________ **5.** 3.125 ________ **6.** 0.16 ________

7. 8.4 ________ **8.** 2.5 ________ **9.** 3.24 ________

Math

Review

Use everything you have learned so far about fractions to solve the problems.

Rewrite each fraction in simplest form.

1. $\frac{4}{20}$ ________

2. $\frac{12}{15}$ ________

3. $\frac{8}{32}$ ________

Rewrite each mixed numeral in simplest form.

4. $5\frac{6}{9}$ ________

5. $8\frac{12}{20}$ ________

6. $7\frac{4}{16}$ ________

Compare each pair of fractions using <, >, or =.

7. $\frac{19}{9}$ ______ $\frac{1}{10}$

8. $1\frac{1}{12}$ ______ $10\frac{1}{3}$

9. $2\frac{1}{9}$ ______ $10\frac{1}{2}$

Write the fractions in order from least to greatest.

10. $\frac{7}{8}$, $\frac{4}{7}$, $1\frac{1}{2}$, $\frac{2}{7}$, $1\frac{1}{4}$

____

Change each fraction to a decimal as indicated.

11. Change $2\frac{3}{5}$ to tenths.

____

12. Change $\frac{9}{20}$ to hundredths.

____

Math

Answer the questions.

1. A farmer harvested 32 tons of potatoes and is going to split them among 4 different warehouses. How many tons of potatoes will each warehouse receive?

   The way to write this as a division problem is __________ .

   The way to write this as a fraction is __________ .

   Each warehouse will receive __________ tons of potatoes.

Change each improper fraction to a mixed number in simplest form.

2. $\frac{22}{4}$ ________
3. $\frac{9}{8}$ ________
4. $\frac{17}{6}$ ________
5. $\frac{23}{9}$ ________
6. $\frac{26}{12}$ ________
7. $\frac{19}{3}$ ________

Change each mixed number to an improper fraction in simplest form.

8. $3\frac{6}{8}$ ________
9. $9\frac{8}{12}$ ________
10. $4\frac{7}{14}$ ________
11. $6\frac{3}{8}$ ________
12. $2\frac{9}{8}$ ________
13. $7\frac{6}{9}$ ________

Math

Chapter Review

Find the lowest common denominator of each pair of fractions. Then, rewrite each fraction using the new common denominator.

14. $\frac{1}{4}$ and $\frac{2}{3}$

LCD _____

_____ and _____

15. $\frac{3}{8}$ and $\frac{7}{10}$

LCD _____

_____ and _____

16. $\frac{4}{7}$ and $\frac{2}{3}$

LCD _____

_____ and _____

Find the equivalent fraction.

17. $6 = \frac{\square}{3}$

18. $\frac{7}{9} = \frac{\square}{18}$

19. $8 = \frac{\square}{6}$

Rewrite each fraction in simplest form.

20. $\frac{18}{36}$ _______

21. $\frac{26}{28}$ _______

22. $\frac{17}{68}$ _______

Rewrite each mixed number in simplest form.

23. $3\frac{3}{2}$ _______

24. $7\frac{8}{12}$ _______

25. $5\frac{3}{9}$ _______

Math

Compare each pair of fractions using <, >, or =.

26. $\frac{20}{8}$ ______ $\frac{12}{8}$

27. $\frac{4}{9}$ ______ $7\frac{1}{4}$

28. $2\frac{11}{12}$ ______ $1\frac{1}{5}$

29. $\frac{4}{2}$ ______ $\frac{29}{9}$

30. $3\frac{7}{9}$ ______ $\frac{37}{9}$

31. $\frac{14}{3}$ ______ $1\frac{1}{7}$

Write the fractions in order from least to greatest.

32. $\frac{5}{6}$, $1\frac{4}{7}$, $\frac{1}{6}$, $1\frac{1}{3}$, $1\frac{7}{8}$

____

Change each fraction to a decimal as indicated.

33. Change $2\frac{1}{5}$ to tenths.

______

34. Change $\frac{17}{50}$ to hundredths.

______

35. Change $1\frac{27}{100}$ to thousandths.

______

36. Change $\frac{9}{20}$ to hundredths.

______

Math

Adding Fractions with Unlike Denominators

To add fractions with like denominators, just add the numerators and keep the denominators the same. When adding fractions with unlike denominators, find the lowest common denominator (LCD) and rename the fractions. Then, add. Reduce to simplest form as needed.

Solve: $\frac{1}{7} + \frac{2}{3}$

First, list the multiples of the denominators, 7 and 3. The lowest number in both lists is 21. So, the lowest common denominator (LCD) is 21.

Multiples of 7: 7, 14, 21, 28, 35, ...
Multiples of 3: 3, 6, 9, 12, 15, 18, 21, ...

Next, rewrite the fractions so that 21 is the denominator. To give $\frac{1}{7}$ that denominator, multiply the numerator and denominator by 3. To give $\frac{2}{3}$ that denoninator, multiply the numerator and denominator by 7.

$$\frac{1}{7} = \frac{1 \times 3}{7 \times 3} = \frac{3}{21}$$

$$\frac{2}{3} = \frac{2 \times 7}{3 \times 7} = \frac{14}{21}$$

Finally, add the fractions by adding the numerators. Keep the common denominator. The sum is already in simplest form.

$$\frac{1}{7} = \frac{3}{21}$$

$$+\ \frac{2}{3} = \frac{14}{21}$$

$$\frac{17}{21}$$

Practice

Add. Write the answers in simplest form.

1. $\frac{1}{6} + \frac{1}{3}$

2. $\frac{1}{2} + \frac{3}{4}$

3. $\frac{2}{5} + \frac{7}{10}$

4. $\frac{1}{7} + \frac{1}{6}$

Adding Fractions with Unlike Denominators

Math

Practice

Add. Write the answers in simplest form.

1. $\frac{3}{5} + \frac{1}{4}$

2. $\frac{2}{3} + \frac{2}{7}$

3. $\frac{1}{5} + \frac{1}{7}$

4. $\frac{3}{8} + \frac{1}{6}$

5. $\frac{1}{2} + \frac{1}{3}$

6. $\frac{2}{9} + \frac{5}{8}$

7. $\frac{6}{7} + \frac{1}{3}$

8. $\frac{2}{5} + \frac{5}{7}$

9. $\frac{7}{10} + \frac{1}{3}$

10. $\frac{3}{7} + \frac{1}{8}$

11. $\frac{2}{3} + \frac{1}{5}$

12. $\frac{4}{7} + \frac{5}{9}$

13. $\frac{3}{4} + \frac{3}{10}$

14. $\frac{7}{8} + \frac{2}{5}$

15. $\frac{8}{9} + \frac{6}{7}$

16. $\frac{3}{5} + \frac{17}{20}$

Subtracting Fractions with Unlike Denominators

When subtracting fractions with unlike denominators, rename the fractions to have a common denominator. Then, subtract the fractions and write the difference in simplest form.

Solve: Subtract $\frac{1}{3}$ from $\frac{8}{9}$.

First, list the multiples of the denominators, 3 and 9. The lowest number in both lists is 9. So, the lowest common denominator (LCD) is 9.

Multiples of 3: 3, 6, 9, 12, 15, 18, 21, 24, 27...

Multiples of 9: 9, 18, 27, 36, 45 ...

Note: 18 and 27 are also common multiples, but not the LCD.

Next, rewrite the fractions so that 9 is the denominator. To give 3 that denominator, multiply the numerator and denominator by 3. The fraction $\frac{8}{9}$ already has that denominator.

$$\frac{1}{3} = \frac{1 \times 3}{3 \times 3} = \frac{3}{9}$$

Finally, subtract the fractions by subtracting the numerators. Keep the common denominator. The difference is already in simplest form.

$$\frac{8}{9} = \frac{8}{9}$$

$$-\ \frac{1}{3} = \frac{3}{9}$$

$$\frac{5}{9}$$

Practice

Subtract. Write the answers in simplest form.

1. $\frac{5}{6} - \frac{2}{9}$

2. $\frac{7}{10} - \frac{2}{3}$

3. $\frac{4}{5} - \frac{4}{7}$

4. $\frac{2}{5} - \frac{1}{4}$

Subtracting Fractions with Unlike Denominators

Practice

Subtract. Write the answers in simplest form.

1. $\frac{3}{4} - \frac{1}{2}$

2. $\frac{5}{6} - \frac{1}{3}$

3. $\frac{9}{10} - \frac{2}{5}$

4. $\frac{4}{7} - \frac{1}{8}$

5. $\frac{5}{9} - \frac{1}{3}$

6. $\frac{2}{5} - \frac{1}{9}$

7. $\frac{3}{5} - \frac{2}{7}$

8. $\frac{2}{3} - \frac{3}{8}$

9. $\frac{5}{6} - \frac{1}{3}$

10. $\frac{3}{4} - \frac{2}{9}$

11. $\frac{7}{10} - \frac{3}{6}$

12. $\frac{8}{9} - \frac{1}{4}$

13. $\frac{7}{8} - \frac{5}{12}$

14. $\frac{7}{10} - \frac{1}{4}$

15. $\frac{4}{5} - \frac{3}{7}$

16. $\frac{7}{9} - \frac{5}{12}$

Math

Adding Mixed Numbers

To add mixed numbers, first make sure that the fractional parts have a common denominator. Then, add from right to left and simplify as needed.

Solve: $3\frac{5}{8} + 2\frac{1}{2}$

First, give both fractional parts the same denominator. The least common multiple of 8 and 2 is 8, so that is the lowest common denominator (LCD). The fraction $\frac{5}{8}$ already has that denominator. Give $\frac{1}{2}$ that denominator by multiplying the numerator and denominator by 4.	$\frac{1}{2} = \frac{1}{2}\frac{\times 4}{\times 4} = \frac{4}{8}$
Next, rewrite the problem. Add the fractions. To do this, add the numerators and keep the same denominator. Then, add the whole numbers.	$3\frac{5}{8} = 3\frac{5}{8}$ $+\ 2\frac{1}{2} = 2\frac{4}{8}$ $5\frac{9}{8}$
Finally, rewrite the sum in simplest form. To do this, rewrite the improper fraction $\frac{9}{8}$ as a mixed number. Then, add.	$\frac{9}{8} = 1\frac{1}{8}$ $5\frac{9}{8} = 5 + 1\frac{1}{8} = 6\frac{1}{8}$

Practice

Add. Write the answers in simplest form.

1. $2\frac{1}{2} + 3\frac{2}{5}$ = ______

2. $1\frac{2}{3} + 6\frac{1}{5}$ = ______

3. $4\frac{2}{7} + 3\frac{3}{4}$ = ______

4. $5\frac{1}{4} + 2\frac{1}{5}$ = ______

Adding Mixed Numbers

Practice

Add mixed numbers to solve the problems. Write the answers in simplest form.

1. Caroline needs $3\frac{1}{7}$ cups of sugar for her first batch of brownies and $2\frac{8}{9}$ cups of sugar for a second batch. How much sugar does she need in all?	1.
2. Robert's gas tank has $5\frac{3}{5}$ gallons of gas in it. If he adds $7\frac{2}{3}$ gallons, how much gas will be in the tank?	2.
3. A hamburger weighs $\frac{1}{3}$ pound, and an order of french fries weighs $\frac{1}{4}$ pound. How many pounds total will a meal of hamburger and french fries weigh?	3.
4. John is $5\frac{6}{10}$ feet tall and Jamar is $\frac{5}{8}$ feet taller than John. How tall is Jamar?	4.
5. Mrs. Stevenson has used $4\frac{2}{3}$ inches of string. She needs $1\frac{6}{7}$ inches more. How much string will Mrs. Stevenson have used when she is done?	5.

Math

Math

Problem Solving

To subtract mixed numbers, first make sure that the fractional parts have a common denominator. Then, subtract from right to left. Be sure the difference is in simplest form.

Solve: $6\frac{5}{7} - 5\frac{1}{4}$

First, give both fractional parts the same denominator. The least common multiple of 7 and 4 is 28, so that is the lowest common denominator (LCD). Give $\frac{5}{7}$ that denominator by multiplying the numerator and denominator by 4. Give $\frac{1}{4}$ that denominator by multiplying the numerator and denominator by 7.

$$\frac{5}{7} = \frac{5}{7}\frac{\times 4}{\times 4} = \frac{20}{28}$$

$$\frac{1}{4} = \frac{1}{4}\frac{\times 7}{\times 7} = \frac{7}{28}$$

Next, rewrite the problem. Subtract the fractions. To do this, subtract the numerators and keep the same denominator. Then, subtract the whole numbers. The difference is already in simplest form.

$$\begin{array}{rr} 6\frac{5}{7} = & 6\frac{20}{28} \\ -\ 5\frac{1}{4} = & 5\frac{7}{28} \\ \hline & 1\frac{13}{28} \end{array}$$

Practice

Subtract. Write the answers in simplest form.

1. $\begin{array}{r} 4\frac{2}{3} \\ -\ 2\frac{1}{6} \\ \hline \end{array}$

2. $\begin{array}{r} 7\frac{7}{8} \\ -\ 2\frac{3}{4} \\ \hline \end{array}$

3. $\begin{array}{r} 8\frac{9}{10} \\ -\ 6\frac{2}{5} \\ \hline \end{array}$

4. $\begin{array}{r} 8\frac{3}{4} \\ -\ 4\frac{3}{8} \\ \hline \end{array}$

Subtracting Mixed Numbers

Practice

Subtract mixed numbers to solve the problems. Write the answers in simplest form.

1. Eric needs $\frac{1}{2}$ of a deck of playing cards for a magic trick. He only has $\frac{2}{7}$ of a deck. What fraction of a deck does Eric still need?

   Eric still needs ______ of a deck.

2. Randy ran $1\frac{3}{4}$ miles. Natasha ran $\frac{9}{10}$ miles. How many more miles did Randy run than Natasha?

   Randy ran ______ miles more than Natasha.

3. In January, employees at Home Real Estate Company worked $6\frac{3}{4}$ hours a day. In February, employees worked $7\frac{1}{8}$ hours a day. How many more hours did employees work daily during February than during January?

   Employees worked ______ hours more during February.

4. Peter's hat size is $7\frac{3}{8}$ units. Cal's hat size is $6\frac{7}{12}$ units. How many units larger is Peter's hat size than Cal's?

   Peter's hat size is ______ units larger than Cal's.

5. Mrs. Anderson uses $3\frac{1}{5}$ cups of apples for her pies. Mrs. Woods uses $4\frac{2}{3}$ cups of apples for her pies. How many more cups of apples does Mrs. Woods use than Mrs. Anderson?

   Mrs. Woods uses ______ more cups of apples.

1.
2.
3.
4.
5.

Review

Use everything you have learned so far about operations with fractions to solve the problems.

Add or subtract. Write the answers in simplest form.

1. $\frac{7}{12} + \frac{3}{5}$

2. $4 - \frac{5}{6}$

3. $\frac{2}{5} + \frac{9}{10}$

4. $6\frac{2}{3} - 4\frac{1}{3}$

5. $8\frac{3}{10} + 9\frac{2}{4}$

6. $\frac{5}{8} - \frac{1}{4}$

7. $\frac{5}{6} - \frac{7}{12}$

8. $5\frac{2}{7} - 4\frac{1}{4}$

9. $5\frac{2}{5} + 7\frac{2}{3}$

10. $2\frac{1}{2} - 1\frac{1}{12}$

11. $4\frac{3}{8} + 2\frac{11}{24}$

12. $9\frac{1}{8} - 8\frac{1}{16}$

13. $3\frac{3}{10} + 3\frac{2}{3}$

14. $6\frac{3}{5} - 2\frac{1}{4}$

15. $6\frac{1}{7} + 2\frac{3}{5}$

16. $3\frac{4}{5} - 1\frac{3}{10}$

Math

Add or subtract mixed numbers to solve the problems. Write the answers in simplest form.

17. Lauren practiced tennis twice last week. On Tuesday, she practiced $2\frac{4}{8}$ hours. On Thursday, she practiced $1\frac{2}{6}$ hours. How much longer did Lauren practice on Tuesday?

17.

18. Mr. Daniels' chili recipe calls for 5 cups of diced tomatoes and $\frac{1}{4}$ cup of diced green chilies. How many cups of tomatoes and green chilies does Mr. Daniels need altogether?

18.

19. Ben watched a baseball game for $2\frac{1}{5}$ hours. Drew watched a football game for $2\frac{2}{8}$ hours. How much time altogether did Ben and Drew spend watching the games?

19.

20. The Rizzos' farm has $9\frac{1}{2}$ acres of corn. The Johnsons' farm has $7\frac{1}{3}$ acres of corn. How many more acres of corn does the Rizzo's farm have?

20.

21. Jeremy cleans his house in $4\frac{1}{2}$ hours. Hunter cleans his house in $3\frac{1}{4}$ hours. How much longer does it take Jeremy to clean his house than Hunter?

21.

Multiplying Fractions

Sometimes, you will need to multiply two fractions. To do this, multiply the numerators. Then, multiply the denominators. Write the product in simplest form.

Solve: $\frac{3}{4} \times \frac{1}{6}$

First, multiply the numerators. Then, multiply the denominators.	$\frac{3}{4} \times \frac{1}{6} = \frac{3 \times 1}{4 \times 6} = \frac{3}{24}$
Finally, simplify if possible. Divide the numerator and the denominator by 3.	$\frac{3}{24} = \frac{3 \div 3}{24 \div 3} = \frac{1}{8}$

Practice

Multiply the fractions. Write the answers in simplest form.

1. $\frac{1}{3} \times \frac{1}{7} =$
2. $\frac{2}{5} \times \frac{1}{2} =$
3. $\frac{3}{4} \times \frac{7}{9} =$
4. $\frac{2}{9} \times \frac{1}{4} =$
5. $\frac{4}{5} \times \frac{3}{8} =$
6. $\frac{1}{7} \times \frac{3}{5} =$
7. $\frac{1}{2} \times \frac{11}{12} =$
8. $\frac{5}{6} \times \frac{2}{7} =$
9. $\frac{4}{11} \times \frac{1}{4} =$
10. $\frac{2}{3} \times \frac{5}{6} =$
11. $\frac{3}{13} \times \frac{1}{3} =$
12. $\frac{7}{8} \times \frac{8}{9} =$
13. $\frac{5}{7} \times \frac{3}{5} =$
14. $\frac{9}{10} \times \frac{4}{5} =$
15. $\frac{11}{12} \times \frac{3}{8} =$

Math

Multiplying Fractions

You can also use visual models to multiply fractions.

Solve: $\frac{1}{2} \times \frac{1}{4}$

First, draw a rectangle, divide it in half, and shade the upper $\frac{1}{2}$. Next, divide the rectangle into fourths and shade the leftmost $\frac{1}{4}$. Note the purple area where the shaded regions overlap.

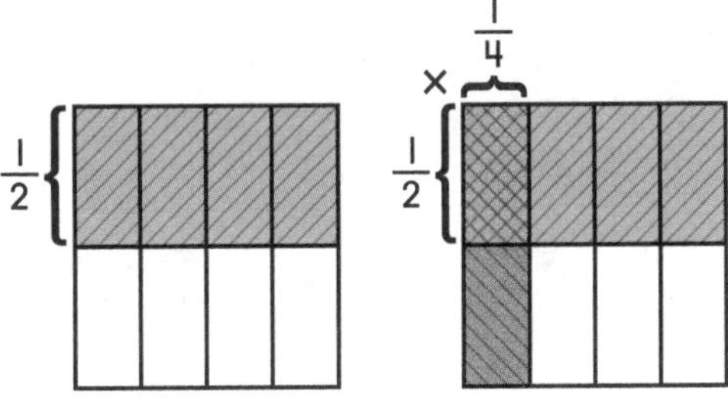

Finally, identify the product. The rectangle is now divided into 8 parts, so 8 is the denominator. The shaded areas overlap in 1 part, or $\frac{1}{8}$ of the rectangle.

$$\frac{1}{2} \times \frac{1}{4} = \frac{1}{8}$$

Solve: $\frac{2}{3} \times \frac{4}{5}$

First, draw a rectangle, divide it into thirds, and shade the upper $\frac{2}{3}$. Next, split the rectangle into fifths and shade the leftmost $\frac{4}{5}$.

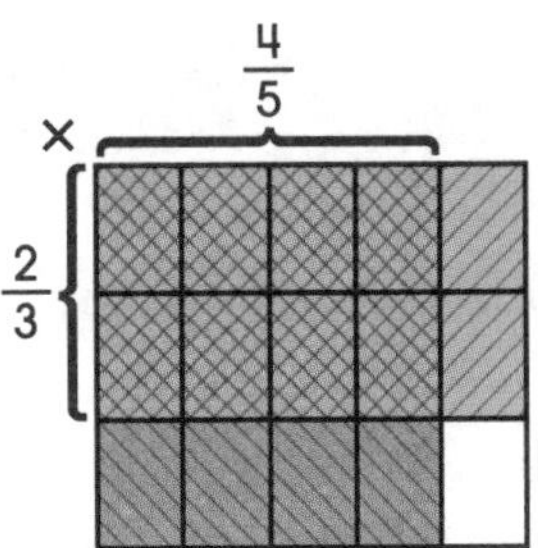

Finally, identify the product. The rectangle is now divided into 15 parts, so 15 is the denominator. The shaded areas overlap in 8 parts, or $\frac{8}{15}$ of the rectangle.

$$\frac{2}{3} \times \frac{4}{5} = \frac{8}{15}$$

Math

Multiplying Fractions

Math

Practice

Multiply. If needed, use the space to draw a visual model. Write the answers in simplest form.

1. $\frac{1}{2} \times \frac{3}{4} =$

2. $\frac{2}{3} \times \frac{1}{5} =$

3. $\frac{2}{5} \times \frac{1}{4} =$

4. $\frac{1}{4} \times \frac{3}{8} =$

5. $\frac{5}{12} \times \frac{1}{2} =$

6. $\frac{1}{2} \times \frac{5}{7} =$

Multiplying Mixed Numbers

Before multiplying mixed numbers, rewrite the mixed numbers as improper fractions. Then, multiply as you would multiply any fractions. Write the product in simplest form.

Solve: $2\frac{1}{5} \times 1\frac{1}{4}$

First, rewrite the mixed numbers as improper fractions.

$$2\frac{1}{5} = \frac{(5 \times 2) + 1}{5} = \frac{11}{5}$$

$$1\frac{1}{4} = \frac{(4 \times 1) + 1}{4} = \frac{5}{4}$$

Next, multiply as you would multiply any fractions. Multiply the numerators and then the denominators.

$$\frac{11}{5} \times \frac{5}{4} = \frac{11 \times 5}{5 \times 4} = \frac{55}{20}$$

Finally, simplify if possible. Divide the numerator and the denominator by 5. Then, rewrite as a mixed number.

$$\frac{55}{20} = \frac{55 \div 5}{20 \div 5} = \frac{11}{4}$$

$$\frac{11}{4} = 2\frac{3}{4}$$

Practice

Multiply. Write the answers in simplest form.

1. $3\frac{3}{4} \times 2\frac{2}{3} =$

2. $1\frac{1}{4} \times 2\frac{1}{2} =$

3. $2\frac{1}{5} \times 2\frac{1}{4} =$

4. $1\frac{1}{5} \times 2\frac{1}{6} =$

5. $1\frac{3}{5} \times 1\frac{2}{5} =$

6. $2\frac{1}{2} \times 3\frac{1}{3} =$

7. $1\frac{7}{8} \times 2\frac{3}{5} =$

8. $1\frac{9}{10} \times 1\frac{1}{4} =$

9. $2\frac{5}{6} \times 2\frac{1}{5} =$

Math

Dividing Fractions by Whole Numbers

When dividing, you are splitting a piece or a total into smaller parts. When dividing fractions, you are splitting one fraction into smaller parts. You can use drawings to help you visualize how to divide fractions.

Solve: If 5 people evenly split $\frac{1}{3}$ of a pan of brownies, how much will each person receive?

First, draw the problem. The shaded area shows $\frac{1}{3}$.

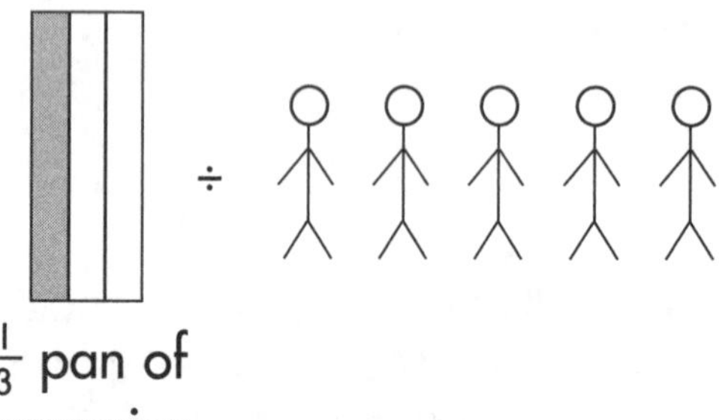

$\frac{1}{3}$ pan of brownies

Next, divide the third into 5 pieces. Doing this divides the entire pan into 15 pieces.

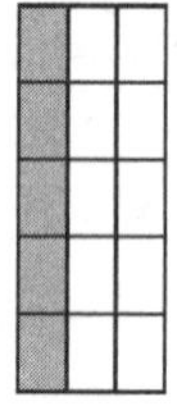

Each person receives one of the shaded pieces, or $\frac{1}{15}$ of the original pan of brownies.

Practice

Create a drawing to help you solve the division problem.

1. $\frac{1}{4} \div 7 =$

2. $\frac{1}{3} \div 3 =$

Math

Dividing Fractions by Whole Numbers

You can also divide a fraction by a whole number using computation. Multiply the dividend (the first fraction) by the reciprocal of the divisor (the second fraction). When a number and its reciprocal are multiplied, the product is 1. To find a reciprocal of a fraction, flip the numerator and the denominator.

Solve: $\frac{4}{5} \div 8$

First, write the whole number as a fraction over 1.

$$\frac{4}{5} \div 8 = \frac{4}{5} \div \frac{8}{1}$$

Next, find the reciprocal of the divisor, $\frac{8}{1}$. To do this, flip the numerator and the denominator.

The reciprocal of $\frac{8}{1}$ is $\frac{1}{8}$.

Then, rewrite the problem as multiplication. Multiply the dividend by the reciprocal of the divisor. Multiply as you would multiply any fractions. Multiply the numerators and then the denominators.

$$\frac{4}{5} \div \frac{8}{1} = \frac{4}{5} \times \frac{1}{8} = \frac{4 \times 1}{5 \times 8} = \frac{4}{40}$$

Finally, simplify if possible. Divide the numerator and the denominator by 4.

$$\frac{4}{40} = \frac{4}{40}\frac{\div 4}{\div 4} = \frac{1}{10}$$

Practice

Divide the fractions. Write the answers in simplest form.

1. $\frac{2}{3} \div 4 =$

2. $\frac{1}{9} \div 3 =$

3. $\frac{6}{7} \div 2 =$

4. $\frac{2}{7} \div 4 =$

5. $\frac{5}{6} \div 5 =$

6. $\frac{4}{5} \div 6 =$

Math

Dividing Fractions by Whole Numbers

Math

Practice

Divide. Write the answers in simplest form.

1. $\frac{3}{5} \div 4 =$
2. $\frac{5}{8} \div 5 =$
3. $\frac{9}{4} \div 6 =$
4. $\frac{5}{3} \div 4 =$
5. $\frac{4}{3} \div 5 =$
6. $\frac{8}{5} \div 5 =$
7. $\frac{3}{8} \div 4 =$
8. $\frac{9}{10} \div 3 =$
9. $\frac{11}{12} \div 3 =$
10. $\frac{7}{5} \div 2 =$
11. $\frac{8}{5} \div 4 =$
12. $\frac{7}{9} \div 7 =$
13. $\frac{9}{5} \div 3 =$
14. $\frac{8}{9} \div 2 =$
15. $\frac{5}{4} \div 4 =$
16. $\frac{9}{7} \div 3 =$
17. $\frac{2}{15} \div 4 =$
18. $\frac{9}{2} \div 12 =$

Dividing Whole Numbers by Fractions

You can also divide a whole number by a fraction using computation. Write the whole number dividend as a fraction over 1. Then, multiply by the reciprocal of the divisor. Simplify if possible.

Solve: $5 \div \frac{3}{4}$

First, write the whole number as a fraction over 1.	$5 \div \frac{3}{4} = \frac{5}{1} \div \frac{3}{4}$
Next, take the reciprocal of the divisor, $\frac{3}{4}$. To do this, flip the numerator and the denominator.	The reciprocal of $\frac{3}{4}$ is $\frac{4}{3}$.
Then, rewrite the problem as multiplication. Multiply the dividend by the reciprocal of the divisor. Multiply as you would multiply any fractions. Multiply the numerators and then the denominators.	$\frac{5}{1} \div \frac{3}{4} = \frac{5}{1} \times \frac{4}{3} = \frac{5 \times 4}{1 \times 3} = \frac{20}{3}$
Finally, simplify. Rewrite the improper fraction as a mixed number.	$\frac{20}{3} = 6\frac{2}{3}$

Practice

Divide. Write the answers in simplest form.

1. $2 \div \frac{1}{7} =$

2. $3 \div \frac{2}{5} =$

3. $6 \div \frac{3}{8} =$

4. $4 \div \frac{6}{5} =$

5. $2 \div \frac{5}{3} =$

6. $4 \div \frac{1}{6} =$

Math

Dividing Whole Numbers by Fractions

Practice

Divide. Write the answers in simplest form.

1. $5 \div \frac{1}{3} =$
2. $6 \div \frac{1}{8} =$
3. $9 \div \frac{1}{4} =$
4. $10 \div \frac{1}{6} =$
5. $4 \div \frac{1}{5} =$
6. $5 \div \frac{1}{9} =$
7. $8 \div \frac{2}{5} =$
8. $3 \div \frac{4}{11} =$
9. $6 \div \frac{5}{6} =$
10. $3 \div \frac{5}{4} =$
11. $7 \div \frac{3}{5} =$
12. $4 \div \frac{3}{7} =$
13. $2 \div \frac{6}{11} =$
14. $9 \div \frac{2}{7} =$
15. $4 \div \frac{2}{9} =$
16. $7 \div \frac{5}{8} =$
17. $8 \div \frac{5}{6} =$
18. $2 \div \frac{7}{12} =$

You can use the multiplying and dividing with fractions strategies you have learned so far to solve more difficult problems.

First, underline the important information that you will need to solve the problem.

During Year 2, the size of a pond decreases to $\frac{1}{3}$ of what it was in Year 1. Assume that the same decrease occurs during Year 3. What fraction of the pond will remain after Year 3?

Next, determine which operation is best for solving the problem.

The size of the pond decreases by $\frac{1}{3}$ each year So, we can multiply by $\frac{1}{3}$ two times to find the answer.

Then, draw diagrams and write multiplication problems to represent the size of the pond in Year 1, Year 2, and Year 3.

Draw a rectangle to show the 1 whole pond in Year 1.

Year 1

After Year 2, the pond is $\frac{1}{3}$ the size it was in Year 1. Divide the rectangle into thirds and shade $\frac{1}{3}$.

Year 2

After Year 3, the pond is $\frac{1}{3}$ the size it was in Year 2. Divide each third into thirds and shade $\frac{1}{3}$ of the region showing Year 2.

Year 3

Finally, solve the problem.

The diagram for Year 3 is $\frac{1}{9}$ shaded and

$$\frac{1}{3} \times \frac{1}{3} = \frac{1}{9}.$$

After Year 3, only $\frac{1}{9}$ of the pond remains.

Math

Problem Solving

Practice

Multiply or divide to solve each problem. Show your work by drawing models or using computation. Write the answers in simplest form.

1. Simon bought $\frac{2}{3}$ pounds of cookies. He ate $\frac{4}{5}$ of the cookies he bought. What was the weight of the cookies that Simon ate?

1.

2. Students must take their tests home to be signed. Two-thirds of the class took home their tests. Only $\frac{1}{8}$ of the students who took their tests home got them signed. What fraction of the entire class got their tests signed?

2.

3. One serving of pancakes calls for $\frac{1}{3}$ cup of milk. How many cups of milk are needed for 4 servings of pancakes?

3.

4. If Carlos works $\frac{5}{12}$ of a day every day, how much will Carlos have worked after 5 days?

4.

Math

Use everything you have learned so far about fractions to solve the problems.

Multiply. Write the answers in simplest form.

1. $\frac{11}{12} \times \frac{2}{3} =$

2. $2\frac{7}{8} \times 2 =$

3. $3 \times \frac{5}{8} =$

4. $\frac{1}{6} \times 4 =$

5. $3\frac{3}{5} \times \frac{3}{7} =$

6. $2\frac{1}{8} \times 2\frac{2}{3} =$

Divide. Write the answers in simplest form.

7. $\frac{1}{5} \div 6 =$

8. $5 \div \frac{1}{3} =$

9. $\frac{1}{3} \div 7 =$

10. $5 \div \frac{1}{10} =$

11. $3 \div \frac{4}{7} =$

12. $\frac{17}{5} \div 3 =$

Solve each problem. Write the answers in simplest form.

13. Five new dresses have been sewn. Chelsea did $\frac{1}{7}$ of the total sewing. What fraction of each dress did Chelsea sew?

13.

14. Roberto studied $1\frac{2}{5}$ hours every day for 7 days. How many hours did Roberto study in 7 days?

14.

Math

Chapter Review

Add or subtract. Write the answers in simplest form.

1. $\frac{1}{2} + \frac{3}{4}$

2. $\frac{3}{3} + \frac{1}{10}$

3. $\frac{7}{10} - \frac{3}{6}$

4. $\frac{8}{9} - \frac{1}{4}$

5. $8\frac{1}{6} + 1\frac{4}{7}$

6. $2\frac{5}{6} + 6\frac{3}{5}$

7. $8\frac{8}{12} - 2\frac{3}{4}$

8. $9\frac{3}{10} - 6\frac{1}{8}$

9. $6\frac{4}{5} + 2\frac{1}{15}$

10. $7\frac{5}{9} - 3\frac{1}{3}$

11. $12\frac{7}{10} - 3\frac{1}{20}$

12. $\frac{9}{12} + \frac{2}{6}$

13. $2\frac{7}{8} - 1\frac{11}{16}$

14. $8\frac{8}{10} - 6\frac{2}{5}$

15. $\frac{7}{9} - \frac{1}{3}$

16. $\frac{9}{10} + \frac{11}{20}$

Math

Multiply or divide. Write the answers in simplest form.

17. $1\frac{5}{7} \times \frac{2}{3} =$

18. $7 \div \frac{2}{5} =$

19. $2\frac{8}{5} \times 1\frac{3}{8} =$

20. $\frac{2}{7} \div 5 =$

21. $\frac{9}{11} \times 1\frac{1}{4} =$

22. $6 \div \frac{3}{8} =$

23. $1\frac{3}{6} \times 3\frac{4}{8} =$

24. $\frac{4}{9} \div 6 =$

25. $2\frac{8}{9} \times \frac{2}{7} =$

26. $8 \div \frac{3}{5} =$

27. $\frac{1}{2} \times \frac{1}{3} =$

28. $6 \div \frac{1}{10} =$

29. $\frac{3}{4} \times \frac{2}{7} =$

30. $3 \div \frac{1}{5} =$

31. $2\frac{3}{4} \times 2 =$

32. $\frac{1}{8} \div 14 =$

33. $1\frac{3}{8} \times 3 =$

34. $\frac{1}{3} \div 8 =$

Chapter Review

Solve each problem by adding, subtracting, multiplying, or dividing fractions. Write the answers in simplest form.

35. It takes Lacy $8\frac{1}{3}$ seconds to climb up the slide and $2\frac{1}{4}$ seconds to go down the slide. How many seconds is Lacy's trip up and down the slide?

35.

36. A soccer ball weighs 6 ounces when fully inflated. Raymundo has inflated the ball to $4\frac{2}{3}$ ounces. How many more ounces must be added before the ball is fully inflated?

36.

37. A race track is $\frac{1}{4}$ mile long. If Martha ran around the race track $5\frac{1}{9}$ times, how many miles did Martha run?

37.

38. Andrew cut a $\frac{1}{7}$-yard long rope into 8 equal pieces. How long will each piece of rope be?

38.

Math

Line plots help you show information or data. A line plot can make it easier to see number patterns and how data are related.

Solve: Use the data in the tally chart to make a line plot. Then, identify how many books are 6 inches or shorter.

Lengths of Books on a Shelf	
inches	Number of Books
5	||||
$5\frac{1}{2}$	|||
6	||
$6\frac{1}{2}$	~~||||~~
7	~~||||~~

First, draw a number line and label it with the lengths in the chart. Title the plot.

Draw a number line with 5 tick marks, one for each length in the tally chart. Title it with the tally chart's title.

Next, draw an X to represent each tally in the table. For example, draw 4 Xs for 5 in., 3 Xs for $5\frac{1}{2}$ in., 2 Xs for 6 in., 5 Xs for $6\frac{1}{2}$ in., and 5 Xs for 7 in.

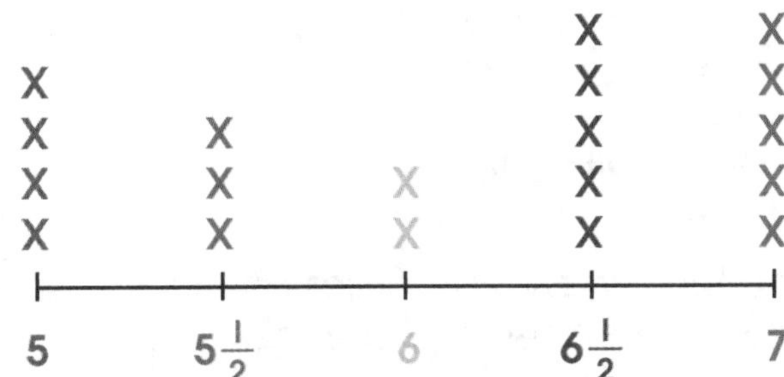

Finally, answer the question. To find how many books are 6 inches or shorter, count the Xs that show 6 inches or shorter.

The X's above 6 in., $5\frac{1}{2}$ in., and 5 in. show lengths that are 6 inches or shorter.

$2 + 3 + 4 = 9$ books

There are 9 books that are 6 inches or shorter.

Practice

Use the line plot above to solve the problems.

1. What is the difference in length between the shortest and longest books? ________

2. How many books are 6 inches long or longer? ________________

Math

Number Patterns and Relationships

Sometimes, pairs of data are related. These pairs of data can be represented in different ways: in a table, as ordered pairs, as points on a graph, or in words. These points can be connected to show patterns and relationships. If the points form a line, you can extend a line to make predictions.

Solve: A new country artist sold 1 million copies of his first album, 3 million copies of his second album, and 5 million copies of his third album. If the pattern continues, how many copies will he sell when he makes his fifth album?

First, represent the data as ordered pairs in a table. The first number in each pair is the album number and the second number shows how many millions of copies were sold. We need to predict how many copies of album 5 will be sold based on the pattern.

Album Number	Copies Sold (in Millions)	Ordered Pairs
1	1	(1, 1)
2	3	(2, 3)
3	5	(3, 5)
4	?	(4, ?)
5	?	(5, ?)

Next, create a graph to see the pattern in a different way. Plot the ordered pairs you know and connect them with a line. Then, extend the line.

Then, find the two missing ordered pairs. The first numbers are increasing by 1s and the second numbers are increasing by 2s. So, the next ordered pairs would be:

(4, 7)
(5, 9)

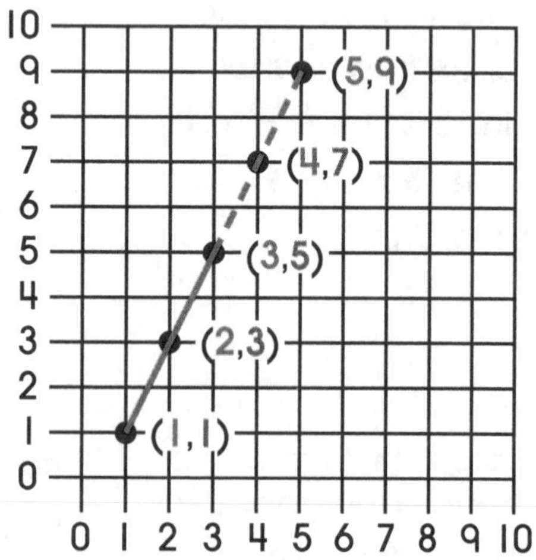

Finally, express the pattern in words.

For each new album, the artist sells 2 million more copies than the last album.

If the pattern continues, he will sell 9 million copies of album 5.

Number Patterns and Relationships

Practice

Use the information to complete each section of the table.

Long-distance swimmers generally need to take more breaths as they near the end of a race. Mark took 2 breaths on lap 2, he took 3 breaths on lap 4, and he took 4 breaths on lap 6. If the pattern continues, how many breaths will Mark take on lap 10?

1. Explain the pattern in words. ______________________________

____

2. Use the pattern to fill in the table with ordered pairs. The first one has been done for you.

Lap Number	Breaths
2	2
4	
6	
8	
10	

3. Graph your points on the coordinate plane below. The first pair has been done for you.

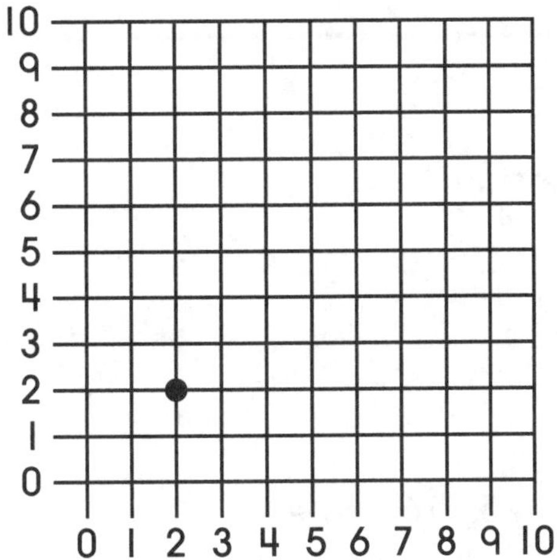

4. How many breaths will Mark take on lap 10? ______________

Math

Using Parentheses and Brackets

Parentheses and brackets are grouping symbols. They can be used to show that one part of a mathematical expression should be evaluated before the rest of the equation.

Solve: $3 \times (5 + 4)$

First, do the operation inside the parentheses.	$3 \times (5 + 4)$ 3×9
Next, multiply.	3×9 27

Solve: $100 - [4 \times (3 + 7)]$

The problem has a combination of grouping symbols. Since parentheses are inside brackets, do the operation inside parentheses first.	$100 - [4 \times (3 + 7)]$ $100 - [4 \times 10]$
Next, do the operation inside the brackets.	$100 - [4 \times 10]$ $100 - 40$
Finally, subtract.	$100 - 40 = 60$

Practice

Find the value of each expression.

1. $20 \div (4 + 6)$
2. $(8 + 1) \times 5$
3. $12 + [8 \div (4 - 2)]$
4. $22 \times [(5 - 3) \times 2]$
5. $(6 + 6) \div 3$
6. $(9 + 5) \div (9 - 2)]$

Using Parentheses and Brackets

Practice

Find the value of each expression.

1. $2 \times (4 - 2)$
2. $(3 + 13) - (2 + 8)$
3. $(452 - 448) \times 6$
4. $500 - [3 \times (20 + 80)]$
5. $25 \div (2 + 1 + 2)$
6. $[4 \times (13 - 4)] \times 3$
7. $(19 - 12) \times (3 + 1) \div 4$
8. $(11 + 11 + 11) \div 11$
9. $48 + [(19 + 3) \div 2]$
10. $3 \times [21 \times (4 - 2)]$
11. $56 \div (6 + 1)$
12. $(250 - 110) \div [7 \times (2 + 3)]$
13. $(7 + 1) \times (3 + 1) \times (2 + 1)$
14. $36 \div [(6 + 2) - (3 + 1)]$
15. $(9 + 3 + 6) \div (8 + 2 + 8)$
16. $210 - [90 \div (7 + 3)]$
17. $(18 + 4 + 3) \times (2 + 3)$
18. $(32 + 32) \div (4 + 4)$

The Order of Operations

The order of operations is used to find the value of an expression with more than one operation.

Solve: $3 \times (4 + 5) + 6 \div 3$

First, do all operations within **parentheses** or other grouping symbols.	$3 \times (4 + 5) + 6 \div 3$ $3 \times 9 + 6 \div 3$
Second, **multiply** and **divide** in order, from left to right.	$3 \times 9 + 6 \div 3$ $27 + 6 \div 3$ $27 + 6 \div 3$ $27 + 2$
Finally, **add** and **subtract** in order, from left to right.	$27 + 2 = 29$

Practice

Find the value of each expression.

1. $5 \times (5 - 3) =$ ________
2. $5 + 4 \times 3 \div 6 =$ ________
3. $20 - 4 \times 3 =$ ________
4. $20 \div 5 \times 2 =$ ________
5. $(7 \times 8) - (4 \times 9) =$ ________
6. $6 \times 5 - 5 \times 4 =$ ________
7. $7 + 6 \div 2 - 2 =$ ________
8. $5 \times 3 \div 5 + 12 =$ ________

Math

Writing Simple Expressions

Sometimes you may need to translate words into a mathematical expression. Finding key words can help you do this.

Solve: Write an expression to represent these words: 5 more than 3 times the sum of 4 and 2

First, underline the **key words** that indicate the operations. Circle the numbers.

(5) more than (3) times the sum of (4) and (2)

Next, translate.

More than means **addition.**

Times means **multiplication.**

Sum of means **addition.**

You are not finished until you check to see if **grouping symbols** are needed.

(5) more than (3) times the sum of (4) and (2)

5 + 3 × 4 + 2

Finally, add grouping symbols. In the expression shown, 3 should be multiplied by the sum of 4 and 2, not by 4. Add parentheses so that the 3 is multiplied by the sum.

(5) more than (3) times the sum of (4) and (2)

5 + 3 × (4 + 2)

Practice

Write the expression for each phrase.

1. 5 times the sum of 3 and 3 ________________

2. 6 increased by 14 divided by 7 ________________

3. 2 times 3 plus 9 ________________

Math

Writing Simple Expressions

Math

Practice

Write the expression for each phrase.

1. 2 less than 5 ________________

2. 3 times the sum of 4 and 12 ________________

3. 10 more than the quotient of 15 and 3 ________________

4. 2 increased by 6 times 4 ________________

5. $\frac{2}{3}$ of 30 minus 11 ________________

6. Twice the difference between 8 and 2 ________________

7. 6 times 4 plus 3 times 4 ________________

8. $\frac{1}{4}$ times 8 increased by 11 ________________

9. The sum of 10 and 12 divided by 2 ________________

10. $\frac{1}{2}$ of 8 minus 2 ________________

11. Three times the difference between 7 and 1 ________________

12. Four divided by 2 plus 2 times 4 ________________

1. Complete the table. Then, use the information from the table to complete the graph.

In 2017, Ella will be 10 years old. How old will she be in 2021? ____________________

Year	Ella's Age
2017	10
2018	

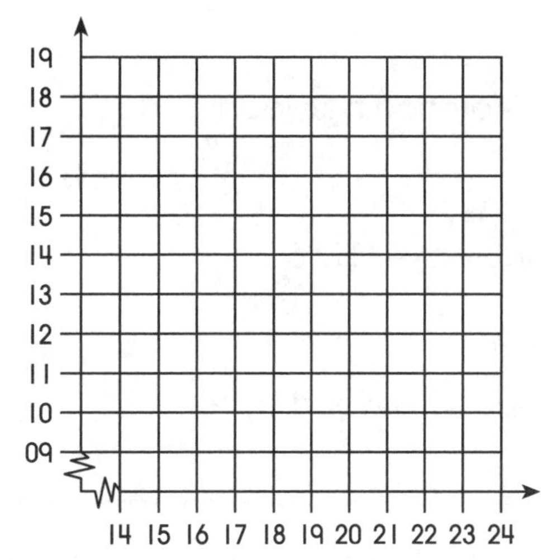

Find the value of each expression.

2. (6 − 1) × 3 = ________

3. (9 + 5) − (3 × 2) = ________

4. [(4 × 3) − 1] − 4 = ________

5. {[6 × (1 + 2) + 4] − 5} × 3 = ________

6. [(9 × 5) − 3] ÷ 6 = ________

7. (7 × 4) + (8 × 2) = ________

Chapter Review

Write the expression for each phrase.

8. eleven times the sum of 8 and 5 ____________

9. six times the difference between 16 and 2 ____________

10. one half of 8 increased by 6 ____________

11. the sum of 8 and 12 divided by 4 ____________

Write the expression needed and solve each problem.

12. Maria paints pictures and sells them at a gift shop. She charges $62.00 for a large painting and $25.50 for a small painting. Last month she sold eight large paintings and four small paintings. How much did she make in all?

Expression: ____________

12.

13. Brandon and Cole were playing touch football against Austin and Greg. Touchdowns were worth 7 points. Brandon and Cole scored 4 touchdowns. Austin and Greg's team scored 8 touchdowns. How many more points did Austin and Greg have than Brandon and Cole?

Expression: ____________

13.

Math

Metric Conversions

In many countries, and in the United States only for specific purposes, people use the metric system to measure length, mass, and volume. The metric system is based on units of 100. This table shows metric conversions for converting from one unit to another.

Length	*Mass*	*Volume*
1 kilometer (k) = 1,000 meters (m)	1 kilogram (kg) = 1,000 grams (g)	1 kiloliter (kL) = 1,000 liters (L)
1 meter (m) = 0.001 kilometers (km)	1 gram (g) = 0.001 kilograms (kg)	1 liter (L) = 0.001 kiloliters (kL)
1 meter (m) = 100 centimeters (cm)	1 gram (g) = 100 centigrams (cg)	1 liter = 100 centiliters (cL)
1 centimeter (cm) = 0.01 meters (m)	1 centigram (cg) = 0.01 grams (g)	1 centiliter (cL) = 0.01 liters (L)
1 meter (m) = 1,000 millimeters (mm)	1 gram (g) = 1,000 milligrams (mg)	1 liter (L) = 1,000 milliliters (mL)
1 millimeter (mm) = 0.001 meter (m)	1 milligram (mg) = 0.001 gram (g)	1 milliliter (mL) = 0.001 liters (L)

Solve: 6 grams = __________ milligrams

First, find the metric conversion you need.

Grams are units of mass.

A useful metric conversion is:
1 g = 1,000 mg

Next, decide if you should multiply or divide. Since you are converting from a larger unit, grams, to a smaller unit, milligrams, multiply.

6 g = (6 × 1,000) mg = 6,000 mg

Practice

Complete the following metric conversions.

1. 2 m = __________ cm
2. 500 mL = __________ L
3. 472 g = __________ mg
4. 1,200 mm = __________ m
5. 20 kg = __________ g
6. 5,100 m = __________ km
7. 15 cL = __________ L
8. 4,220 L = __________ kL

Math

Metric Conversions

Math

Practice

Complete the following metric conversions.

1. 5 g = __________ mg
2. 117,000 g = __________ kg
3. 4,000 L = __________ kL
4. 51,000 mL = __________ L
5. 600 mm = __________ cm
6. 4 kL = __________ L
7. 42 m = __________ mm
8. 2 g 150 mg = __________ mg
9. 438 L = __________ mL
10. 500 cm = __________ mm
11. 2,500 g = __________ kg
12. 48 m = __________ mm
13. 1 kg, 520 mg = __________ mg
14. 482 cg = __________ g
15. 380 mm = __________ m
16. 59,600 mL = __________ L

Standard Measurement Conversions

In the U.S. and some other countries, standard measurements are used. This table shows useful unit conversions in this measurement system.

Length	*Volume*	*Weight*
1 mile (mi.) = 1,760 yards (yd.)	1 gallon (gal.) = 4 quarts (qt.)	1 pound (lb.) = 16 ounces (oz.)
1 mile (mi.) = 5,280 feet (ft.)	1 gallon (gal.) = 8 pints (pt.)	
1 yard (yd.) = 36 inches (in.)	1 quart (qt.) = 2 pints (pt.)	
1 yard (yd.) = 3 feet (ft.)	1 quart (qt.) = 4 cups (c.)	2,000 pounds (lb.) = 1 ton (T.)
1 foot (ft.) = 12 inches (in.)	1 pint (pt.) = 2 cups (c.)	

Solve: 28,000 lb. = __________ T.

First, find the standard conversion you need.	Pounds are units of weight. A useful conversion is: 2,000 lb. = 1 T.
Next, decide if you multiply or divide. Since you are converting from a smaller unit, pounds, to a larger unit, tons, divide.	28,000 lb = (28,000 ÷ 2,000) T. = 14 T.

Practice

Complete the following metric conversions.

1. 12 qt. = __________ pt.
2. 3 mi. = __________ yd.
3. 3 ft., 6 in. = __________ in.
4. 8 oz. = __________ lb.
5. 3 gal. = __________ pints
6. 2 qt., 1 c. = __________ c.
7. 48 in. = __________ ft.
8. 6.5 T. = __________ lb.

Math

Standard Measurement Conversions

Math

Practice

Complete the following standard conversions.

1. 12 ft. = __________ yd.
2. 10 pt. = __________ qt.
3. 80 oz. = __________ lb.
4. 7 qt. = __________ c.
5. 14,000 lb. = __________ T.
6. 8 ft. 2 in. = __________ in.
7. 1 T. 5 oz. = __________ oz.
8. 8 gal. = __________ pt.
9. 7 yd. = __________ in.
10. 2 mi. 3,241 ft. = __________ ft.
11. 15 yd. = __________ in.
12. 30,000 lb. = __________ T.
13. 2 gal. 2 pt. = __________ qt.
14. 6 lb. 7 oz. = __________ oz.
15. 12 c. = __________ pt.
16. 1 mi. 372 yd. = __________ yd.

Using Line Plots

A line plot is used to show how many times something occurs in a data set. Line plots can be used to organize information to solve word problems.

Solve: A pitcher holds 2 quarts of iced tea. There are several glasses being filled that hold various amounts—2 glasses hold $\frac{1}{8}$ qt., 1 glass holds hold $\frac{1}{4}$ qt., and 3 glasses hold $\frac{1}{3}$ qt. How much iced tea will be left in the pitcher?

First, draw a line plot to organize the information.

Put 2 Xs above $\frac{1}{8}$ for "2 glasses hold $\frac{1}{8}$ qt."

Put 1 X above $\frac{1}{4}$ for "1 glasses holds $\frac{1}{4}$ qt."

Continue with the rest of the data.

Number of Glasses

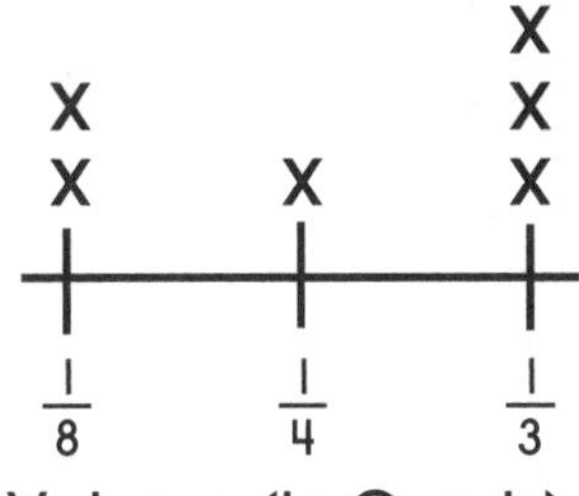

Volume (in Quarts)

Next, use the data in the line plot to write an expression. Multiply the number of X's by the volume below it. Add those volumes to show the total volume of iced tea in the glasses.

Then, subtract the sum from 2 quarts to find how much iced tea will be left in the pitcher.

$$2 - [(2 \times \frac{1}{8}) + \frac{1}{4} + (3 \times \frac{1}{3})]$$

Then, evaluate the expression. First, complete the operations inside grouping symbols, working from left to right.

$$2 - [(2 \times \frac{1}{8}) + \frac{1}{4} + (3 \times \frac{1}{3})]$$

$$2 - [\frac{1}{4} + \frac{1}{4} + (3 \times \frac{1}{3})]$$

$$2 - [\frac{1}{4} + \frac{1}{4} + (3 \times \frac{1}{3})]$$

$$2 - [\frac{1}{4} + \frac{1}{4} + 1]$$

$$2 - [\frac{1}{4} + \frac{1}{4} + 1]$$

$$2 - [1\frac{2}{4}]$$

Finally, subtract.

$$2 - 1\frac{2}{4} = \frac{2}{4} = \frac{1}{2}$$

There is $\frac{1}{2}$ quart of iced tea left in the pitcher.

Using Line Plots

Practice

Draw a line plot to organize the information. Then, write expressions to solve the problems.

1. Alexis is building a track for her toy train. She needs 3 more feet of track to reach the train station. She has 2 pieces of track that are each $\frac{1}{4}$ foot long, 1 piece of track that is $\frac{1}{2}$ foot long, and 1 piece of track that is $1\frac{1}{3}$ feet long. Are the pieces of track long enough to reach the station?

2. Getting ready for a science experiment, Mr. Yip poured water into 8 1-pint beakers. Two beakers hold $\frac{1}{4}$ pint, 3 beakers hold $\frac{3}{8}$ pint, 1 beaker holds $\frac{5}{8}$ pint, and 2 beakers hold $\frac{5}{6}$ pint. If Mr. Yip wants to split the water equally between the 8 beakers, how much water will be in each beaker?

Math

Volume

The volume of a rectangular solid can be found by figuring out how many cubes of a particular unit size will fit inside the shape. Diagrams can help you visualize this.

Solve: Find the volume of a rectangular solid with a length of 8 units, a width of 4 units, and a height of 6 units.

First, divide the figure into its given length units, 8 units.

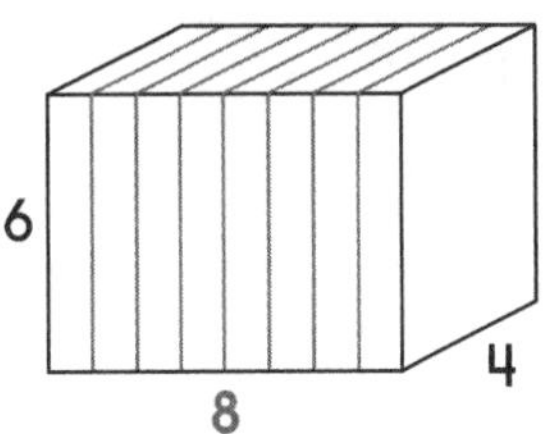

Second, divide the figure into its given width units, 4 units.

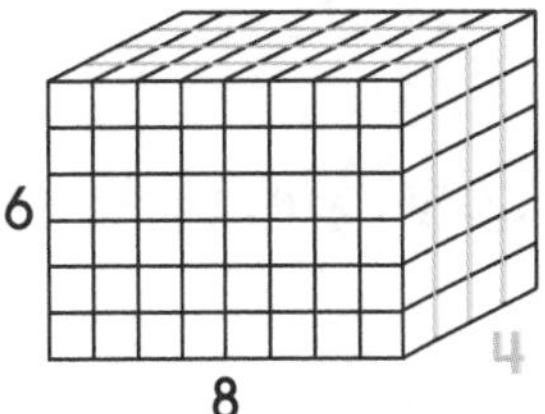

Next, divide the figure into its given height units, 6 units.

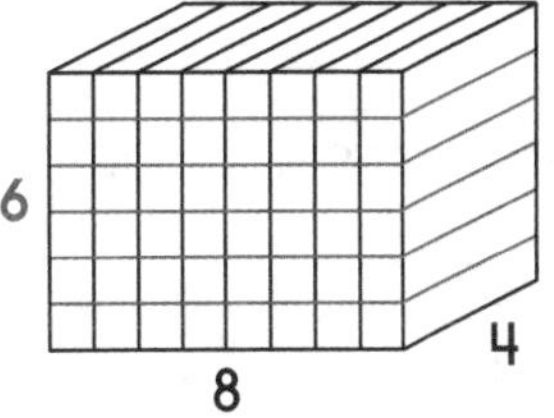

Finally, multiply the length, width, and height to find the total number of cubes inside the figure. This is the volume.

Volume = 8 × 4 × 6 = 192 cubic units

Practice

Use the diagrams to find out how many units are in each figure.

1.

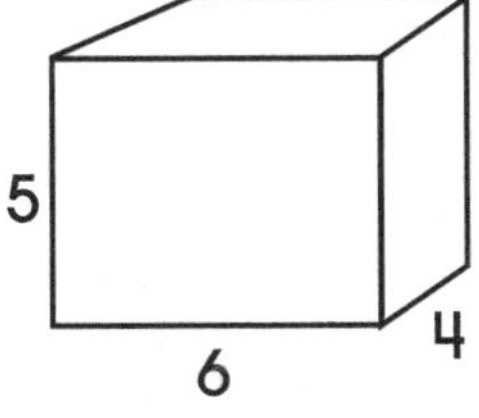

____ × ____ × ____ = ______ cubic units

2.

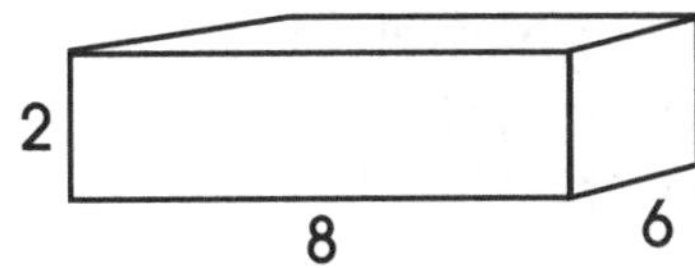

____ × ____ × ____ = ______ cubic units

Math

Volume

Volume is the number of cubic units needed to fill a given solid. Examples of cubic units include cubic meters, cubic inches, and cubic feet. To find the volume of a rectangular prism, use this formula:

Volume (*V*) = length (*l*) x width (*w*) x height (*h*)

V = *l* x *w* x *h*

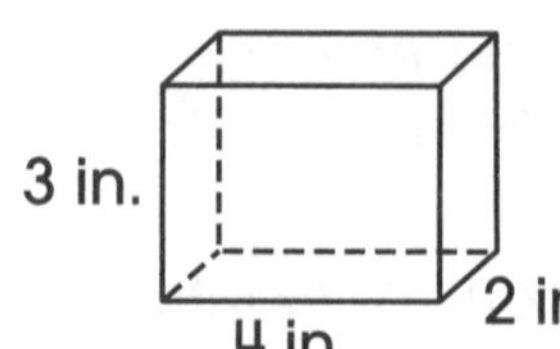

Length: 4 in.
Width: 2 in.
Height: 3 in.

Solve: Find the volume of the rectangular prism.

First, substitute the **length**, **width**, and **height** into the volume formula.	*V* = l × w × h = (4 in.) × (2 in.) × (3 in.)
Next, multiply to find the volume.	*V* = (4 in.) × (2 in.) × (3 in.) = 24 cubic inches

---

Practice

Find the volume of each rectangular prism.

1. 2 in. 2 in. 2 in.

   V = ________ cu. in.

2. 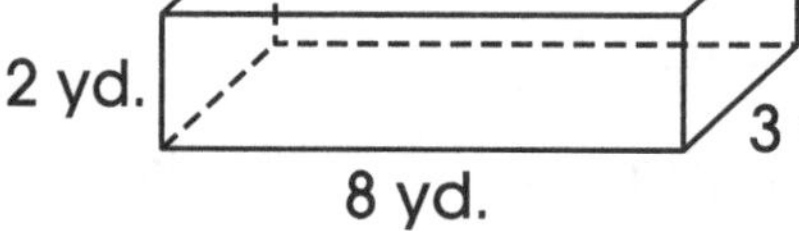

   V = ________ cu. yd.

3. 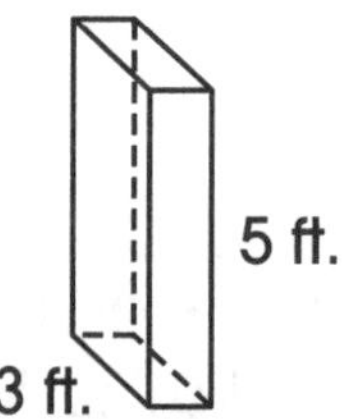

   V = ________ cu. ft.

Use the dimensions given to find the volume of each figure.

4. Length = 12 centimeters
   Width = 4 centimeters
   Height = 6 centimeters

   V = ________ cu. cm

5. Length = 4 meters
   Width = 10 meters
   Height = 5 meters

   V = ________ cu. m

Volume

Some solids are made up of two or more solid figures. You can find the volumes of these figures by breaking them into smaller figures, finding the volume of each smaller figure and adding those volumes.

Solve: Find the volume of the figure shown.

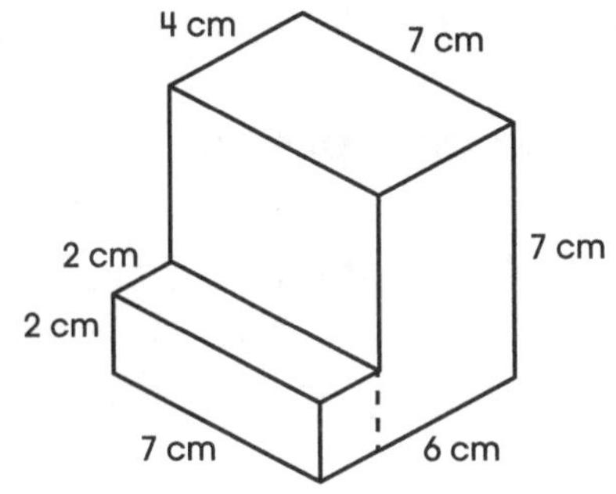

First, break the figure into two smaller, rectangular prisms.

It can be divided into two rectangular prism:

One is 7 cm by 2 cm by 2 cm.

The other is 7 cm by 4 cm by 7 cm.

Next, find the volume of each smaller prism.

One prism:
(7 cm) × (2 cm) × (2 cm) = 28 cu. cm

Other prism:
(7 cm) × (4 cm) × (7 cm) = 196 cu. cm

Finally, add the volumes of the two smaller prisms to find the total volume of the figure.

Volume = (28 cu. cm) + (196 cu. cm)
= 224 cu. cm

Math

Practice

Find the volume of each figure.

1.

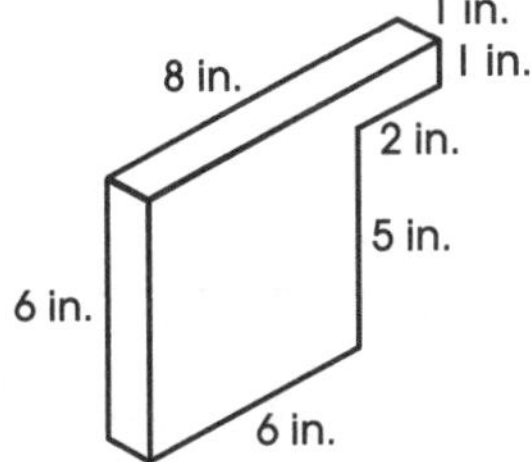

$V =$ ________ cu. in.

2.

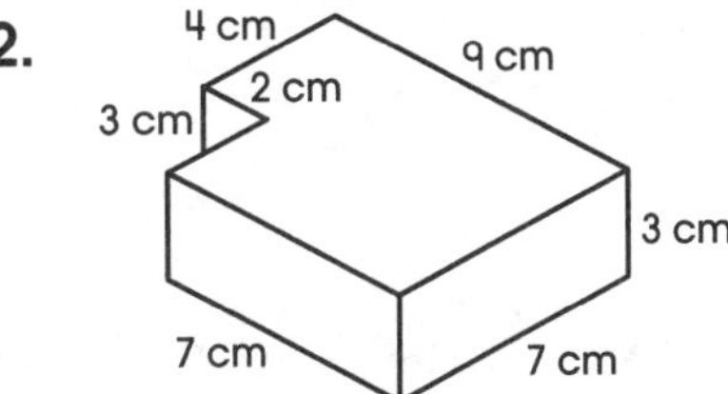

$V =$ ________ cu. cm

Volume

Math

Practice

Solve each problem.

1. Ms. Ferris owns a barn 12 yards long, 11 yards wide, and 9 yards high. If Ms. Ferris' barn is rectangular, what is the volume of her barn?	1.
2. A toy doll was sent to Lucy in a box 8 inches long, 5 inches wide, and 15 inches high. What is the volume of the box?	2.
3. A swimming pool is 8 meters in length, 6 meters in width, and 3 meters in depth. What is the volume of the swimming pool?	3.
4. An aquarium is shaped like a rectangular prism and is 15 inches long, 20 inches wide, and 15 inches tall. How many cubic inches of water can the aquarium hold?	4.
5. A moving box is $\frac{1}{2}$ meter long, 1 meter wide, and $\frac{3}{4}$ meter tall. How many cubic meters can the box hold?	5.

Use everything you have learned so far about measurement to solve the problems.

Complete the following.

1. 9 yd. = __________ ft.
2. 7 ft. 9 in. = __________ in.
3. 17 pt. = __________ c.
4. 8 gal. 2 qt. = __________ qt.
5. 12 lb. = __________ oz.
6. 14 T. = __________ lb.
7. 16 km = __________ m
8. 6 m 36 cm = __________ cm
9. 7 kL = __________ mL
10. 8 g 942 mg = __________ mg

Draw a line plot to organize the data. Then, write an expression to solve the problem.

11. Joanna needs 4 cups of milk to make pudding. She has $\frac{3}{4}$ cup of milk at home. She goes to borrow milk from her neighbors. One neighbor has $\frac{3}{4}$ cup, and two other neighbors give her $\frac{1}{2}$ cup. How much more milk will she need?

Find the volume of each rectangular solid.

12.

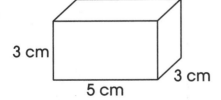

3 cm

3 cm

5 cm

$V =$ ________ cu. cm

13.

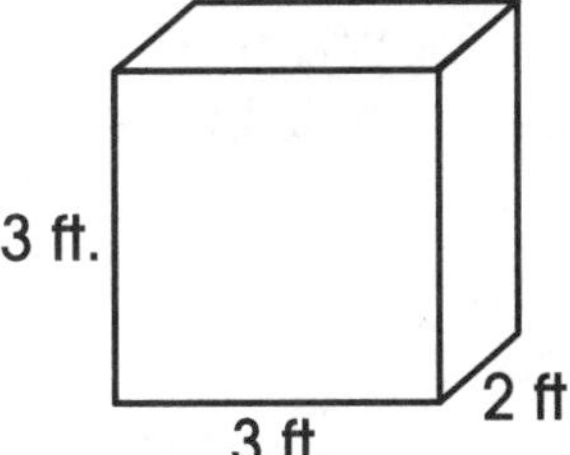

$V =$ ________ cu. ft.

Math

Review

Use the dimensions given to find the volume of each figure.

14. Length = 8 inches
Width = 5 inches
Height = 3 inches

$V =$ ________ cu. in.

15. Length = 12 meters
Width = 8 meters
Height = 3 meters

$V =$ ________ cu. m

Find the volume of each figure.

16.

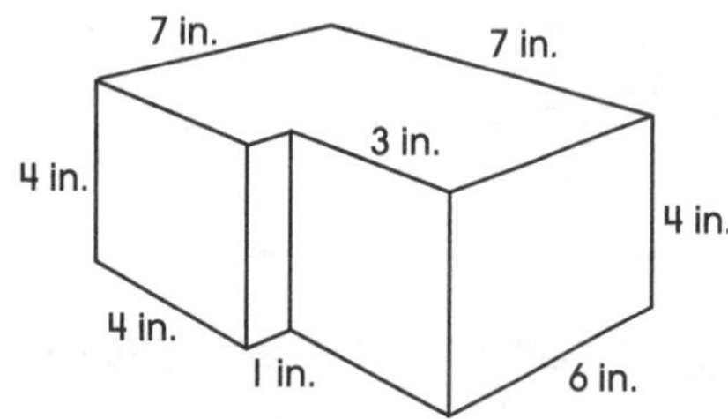

$V =$ ________ cu. in.

17.

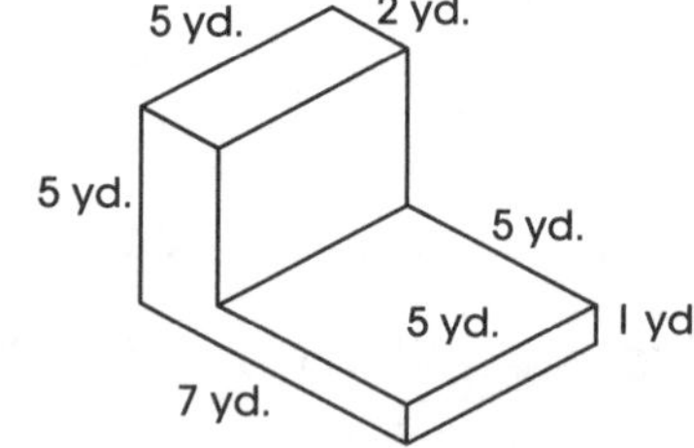

$V =$ ________ cu. yd.

Solve each problem.

18. A water tank is 5 meters long, 3 meters wide, and 2 meters tall. The water tank is a rectangular solid. What is its volume?

18.

19. A rectangular bathtub has dimensions of 5 feet long by 2 feet wide by 2 feet deep. If you only fill the bathtub to a depth of 18 inches, how many cubic inches of water is in the tub?

19.

Math

Classifying Quadrilaterals

Polygons are closed figures with all straight sides. A quadrilateral is one type of polygon. The different quadrilaterals are defined below.

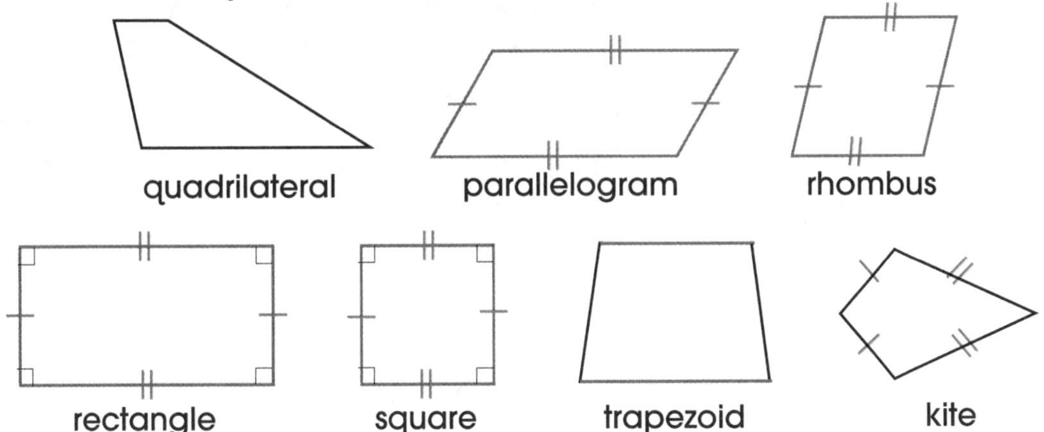

A **quadrilateral** has four sides.

A **parallelogram** has four sides, and both sets of opposite sides are parallel.

A **rhombus** has two pairs of parallel sides and four sides that are congruent, or the same length.

A **rectangle** has four right angles, two pairs of parallel sides, and two pairs of congruent sides.

A **square** has four right angles and four congruent sides.

A **trapezoid** has one pair of parallel sides.

A **kite** has two pairs of congruent sides but no parallel sides.

Solve: Identify the figures that are rectangles.

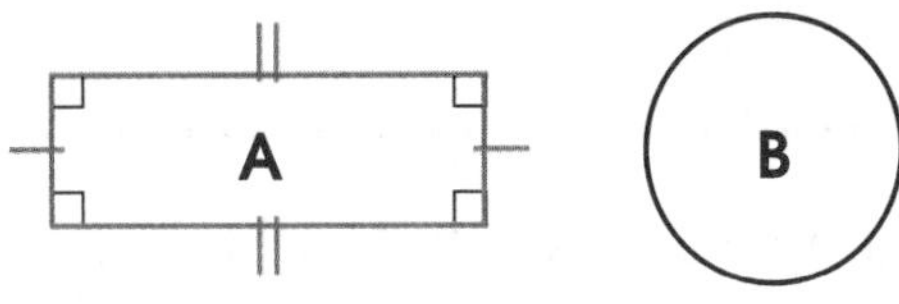

B

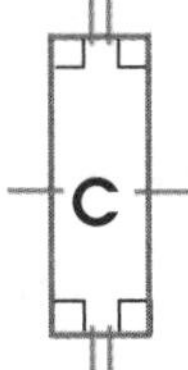

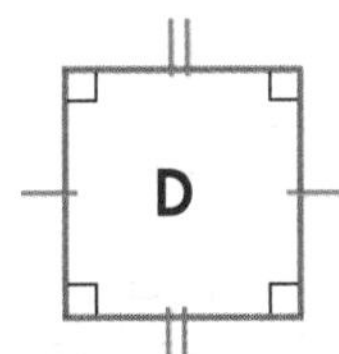

First, describe the characteristics of a rectangle.

A rectangle has four right angles, two pairs of parallel sides, and two pairs of congruent sides.

Next, identify the rectangles.

Figures A, C, and D have four right angles.

Figures A and C each have two pairs of sides that are parallel and congruent. Figure D has four congruent sides, and two pairs of parallel sides. Figure B is a circle.

Figures A, C, and D are rectangles.

Classifying Quadrilaterals

Math

Practice

Use the figures below to answer each question. Letters may be used more than once. Some questions will have more than one answer. Some letters may not be used.

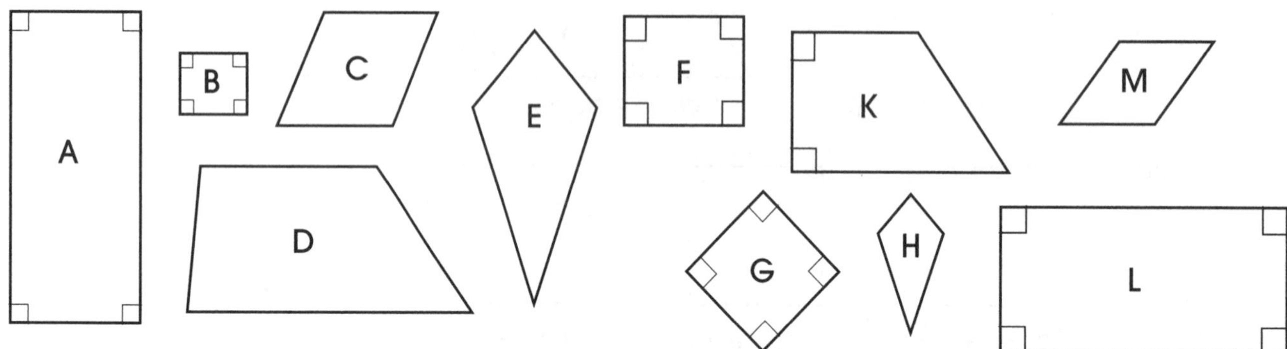

1. Which figure is a rectangle? ______________________________
2. Which figure is a rhombus? ______________________________
3. Which figure is a trapezoid? ______________________________
4. Which figure is a square? ______________________________
5. Which figure is a kite? ______________________________
6. Which figure is both a rhombus and a rectangle? ______________________________

Complete the hierarchy of quadrilaterals. Fill in the blank bubbles with terms from the chart of quadrilaterals.

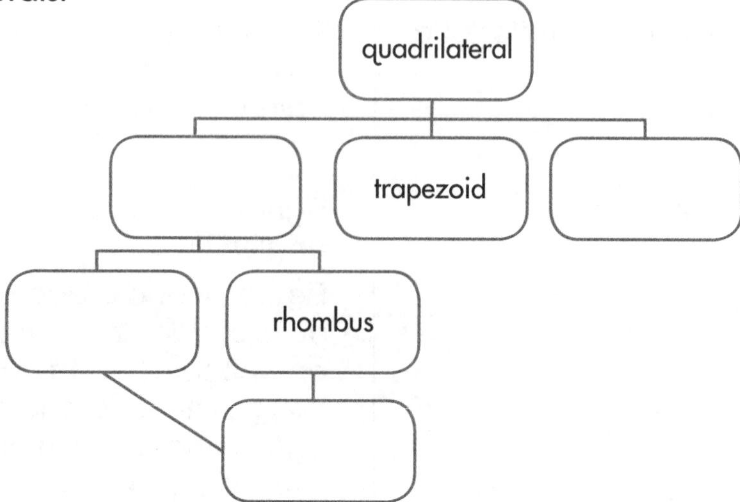

Classifying Figures

In addition to quadrilaterals, there are many other types of polygons.

regular polygon a closed plane figure formed from line segments that meet only at their endpoints; it has all sides equal in length and all angles equal in measure.

pentagon a polygon with 5 sides and 5 angles

triangle a polygon with 3 sides and 3 angles

hexagon a polygon with 6 sides and 6 angles

quadrilateral a polygon with 4 sides and 4 angles

octagon a polygon with 8 sides and 8 angles

Solve: Identify the figures that are hexagons.

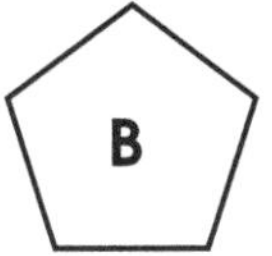

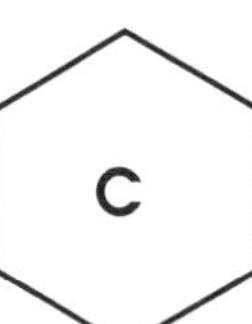

First, describe the characteristics of a hexagon.

A hexagon is a polygon with 6 sides and 6 angles.

Next, identify the hexagons.

Figure A is not closed, so it is not a polygon.

Figure B has 5 sides. It is a pentagon.

Figure C appears to be a regular hexagon.

Figure D is an irregular polygon, but it has 6 straight sides. Figures C and D are hexagons.

Math

Classifying Figures

Math

Practice

1. Circle all of the regular polygons.

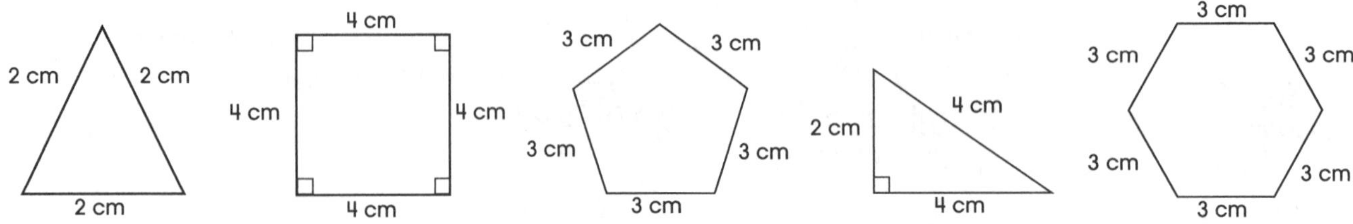

2. Circle all of the rectangles.

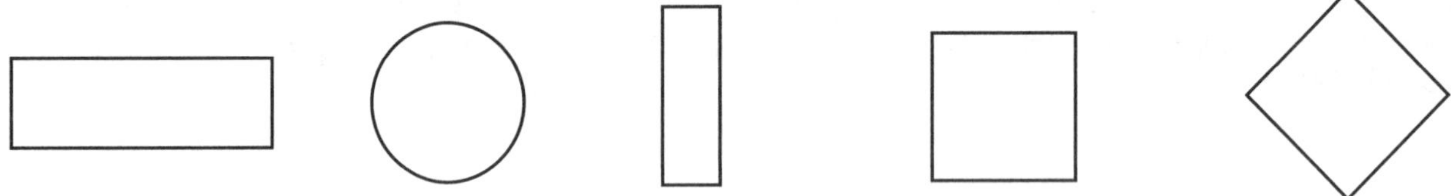

3. Circle all of the triangles.

4. Circle all of the octagons.

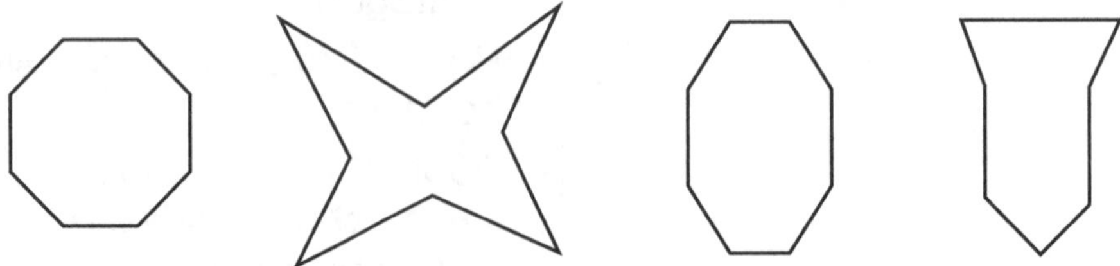

Classifying and Measuring Angles

A **protractor** is used to measure an angle. An angle is measured in degrees.

A **right angle** measures exactly 90°.

An **acute angle** measures less than 90°.

An **obtuse angle** measures greater than 90° but less than 180°.

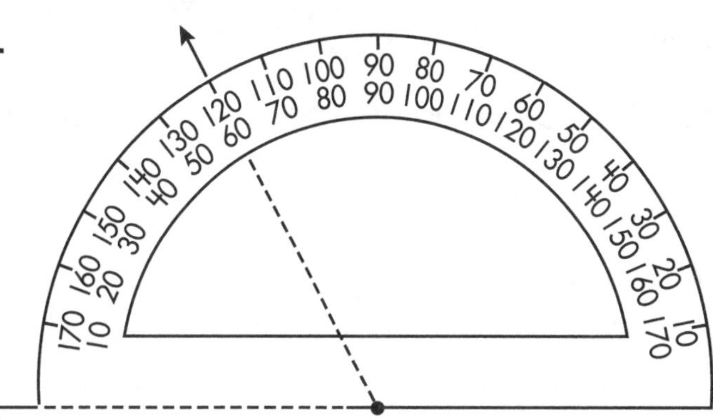

An angle is made up of two rays that share an endpoint. The shared endpoint is called the vertex. The angle is named using the vertex and the two points on the rays. The vertex is the middle point listed in the name.

This angle is made up of ray BA and ray BC. Its name is ABC.

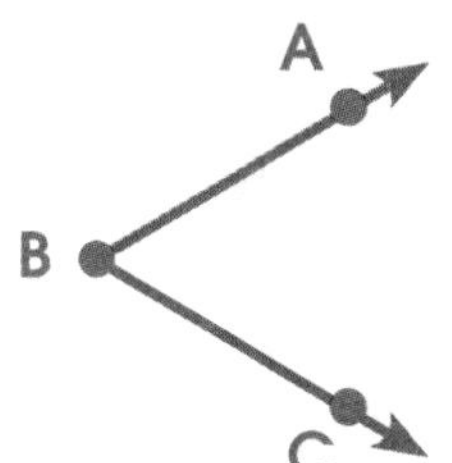

The angle is made up of ray BA ($\overrightarrow{BA}$) and ray BC ($\overrightarrow{BC}$).

The angle is named ABC (∠ABC)

Since angle JKL is obtuse, its measure cannot be 60°.

Its measure is 120°.

Solve: Use a protractor to classify and measure angle *JKL*.

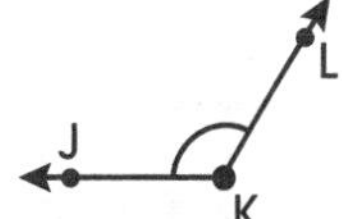

First, classify angle *JKL*.

Next, measure angle *JKL* To do this, align ray *KJ* with the bottom of the protractor, using the mark at the center.

Its measure is greater than 90°. It is an obtuse angle.

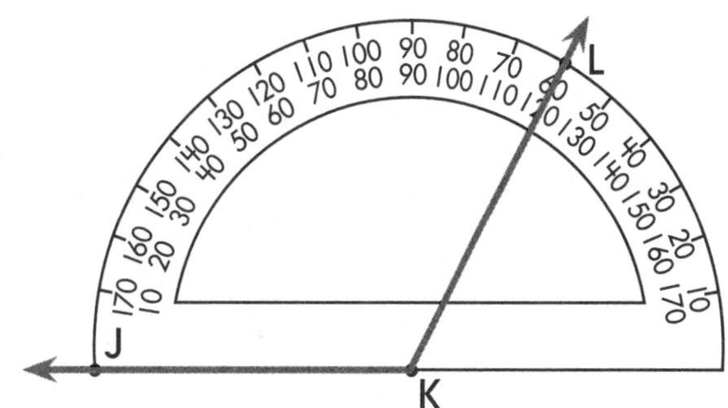

Finally, look at ray *KL* and decide which measurement is appropriate for the angle.

Ray *KL* crosses the numbers 60 and 120. Since angle *JKL* is obtuse, its measure cannot be 60°.

Angle *JKL*'s measure is 120°.

Math

Classifying Angles

Math

Practice

Identify each angle as **right**, **acute**, or **obtuse**.

1. 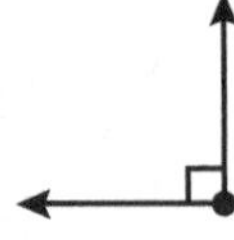

____

2. 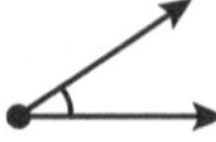

____

3. 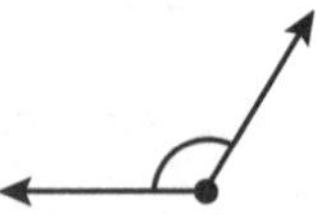

____

Name each angle. Use a protractor to measure each angle. Then, label each angle **right**, **acute**, or **obtuse**.

4. 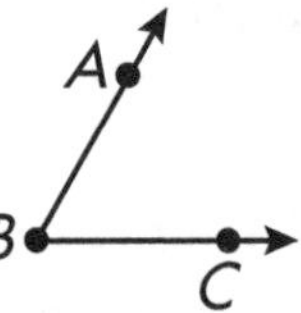

∠__________ = __________

____

5. 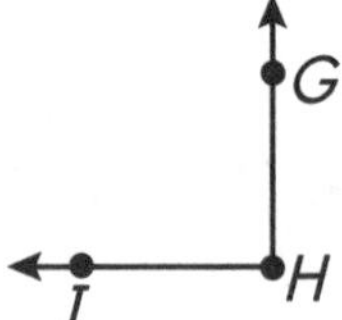

∠__________ = __________

____

6. 

∠__________ = __________

____

Name each angle. Find the measure of each angle of the given triangle. Then, label each angle as **right**, **acute**, or **obtuse**.

7. 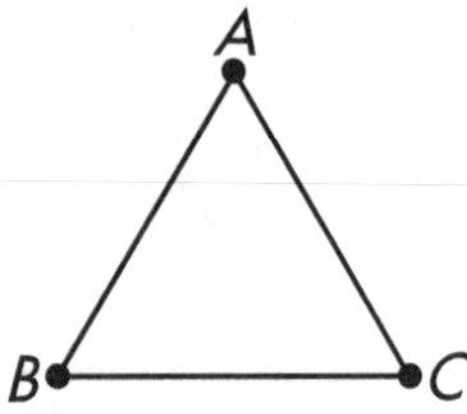

∠__________ = __________

It is ______________________.

∠__________ = __________

It is ______________________.

∠__________ = __________

It is ______________________.

Understanding Circles

The **origin** of a circle is a point inside the circle that is at the center, or the same distance from any point on the circle. A circle is named by its origin. The circle below is named *X*.

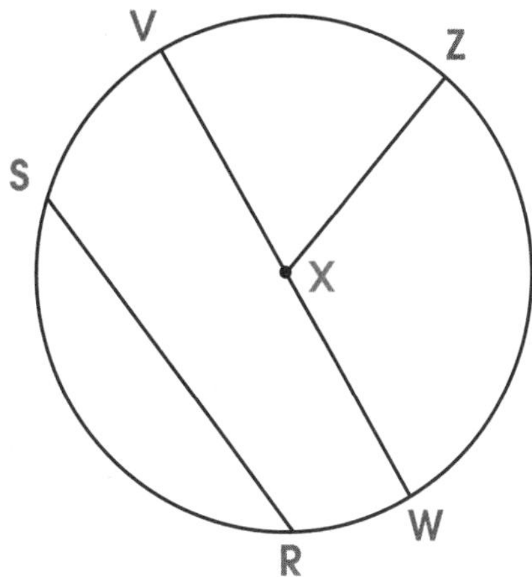

A **radius** of a circle is a line segment with one endpoint at the origin and the other endpoint on the circle. What is a radius of circle *X*?

The line segments *XZ*, *XV*, and *XW* all have one endpoint at the origin of the circle and another endpoint on the circle. Each is a **radius**.

A **chord** is a line segment with both endpoints on the circle. What is a chord of circle *X*?

Both endpoints of the line segments *VW* and *SR* are on the circle. Each is a **chord**.

A **diameter** is a chord that passes through the origin of the circle. What is a diameter of circle *X*?

The chord *VW* passes through the origin of the circle. It is a **diameter**.

Math

Understanding Circles

Math

Practice

Identify each line segment as **radius**, **chord**, or **diameter**.

1. 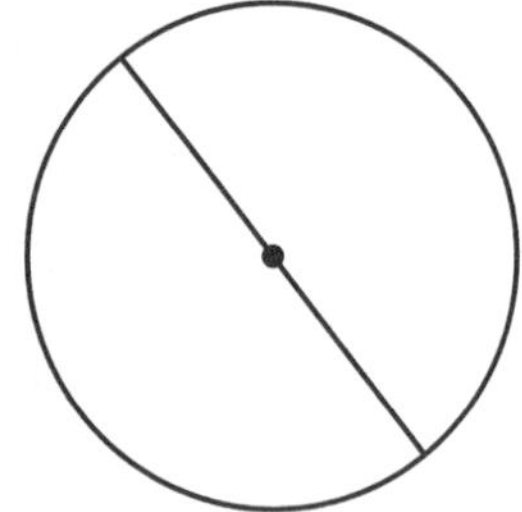

____

2. 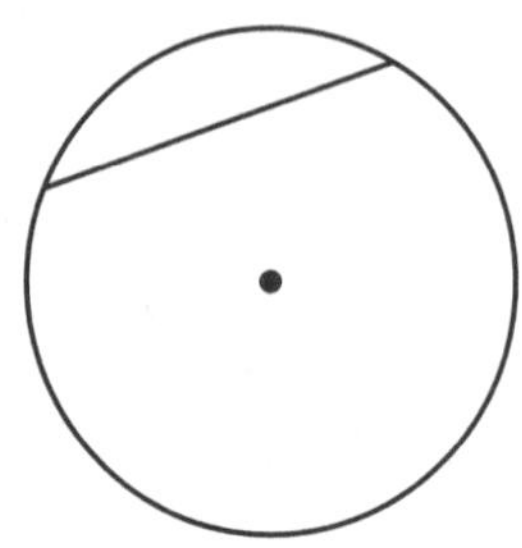

____

3. 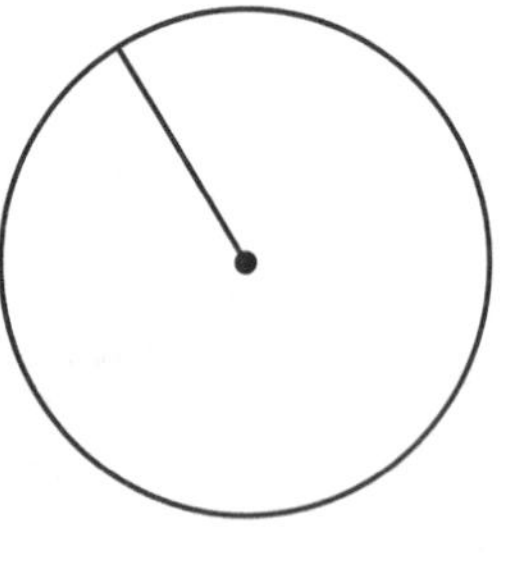

____

4. 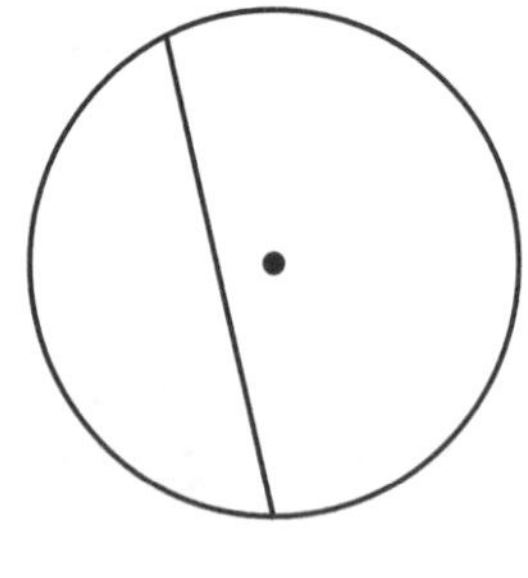

____

Use the circle at the right to answer the questions.

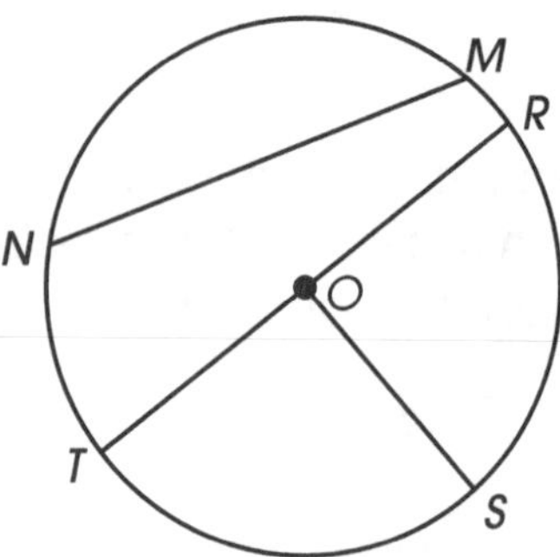

5. Name the circle. _______________
6. Name the origin. _______________
7. Name a radius. _______________
8. Name a chord. _______________
9. Name a diameter. _______________
10. Draw circle *F*, with radius $\overline{FG}$, diameter $\overline{HK}$, and chord $\overline{LM}$.

The Coordinate System

A point on a grid is plotted by using an ordered pair. An ordered pair is two numbers written in (x, y) order. The first number in an ordered pair represents its point on the x-axis, or the horizontal axis. The second number represents the point on the y-axis, or the vertical axis. Points located on the same grid are called coordinate points, or coordinates.

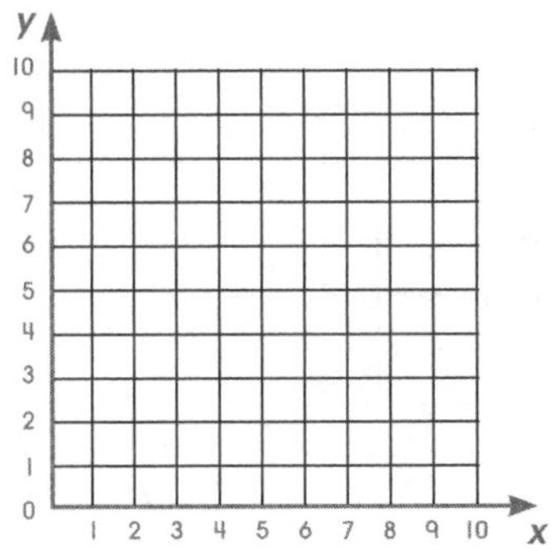

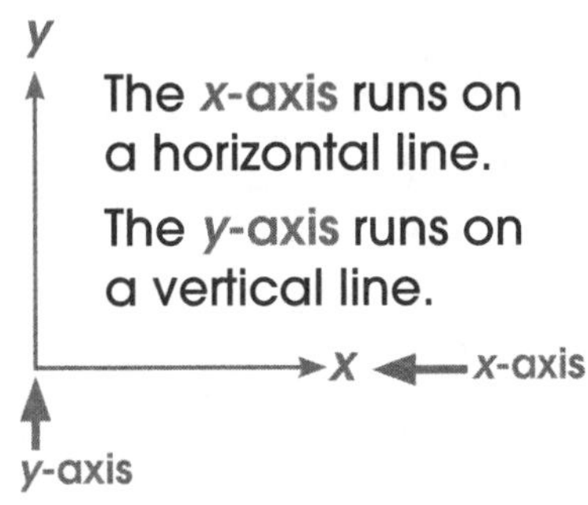

Solve: Plot the ordered pair (10, 3) on a coordinate plane.

First, start at the origin, or 0, where the x-axis and the y-axis meet. Then, move 10 units right along the x-axis.

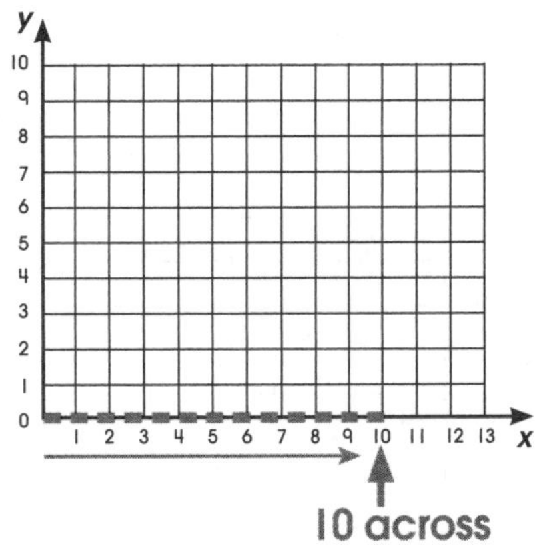

Next, move 3 units up along the *y*-axis. Plot a point to represent (10, 3).

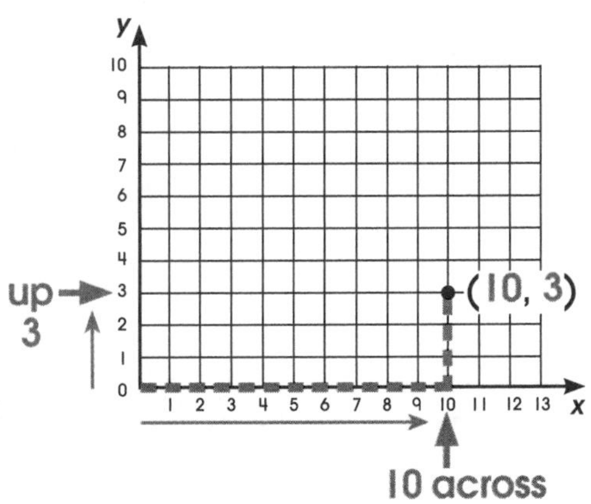

The Coordinate System

Practice

Identify the ordered pairs from each grid.

1.

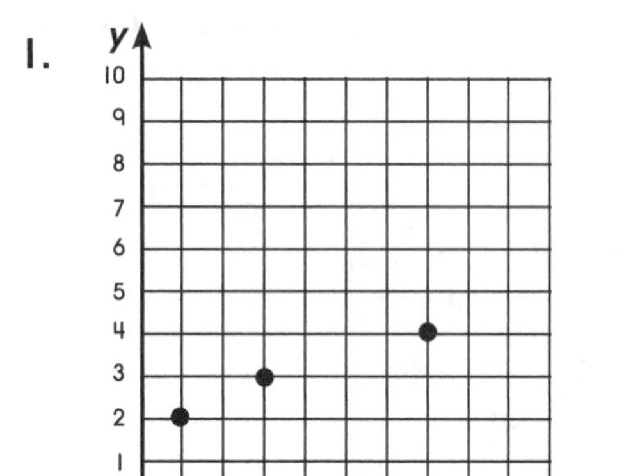

____

2.

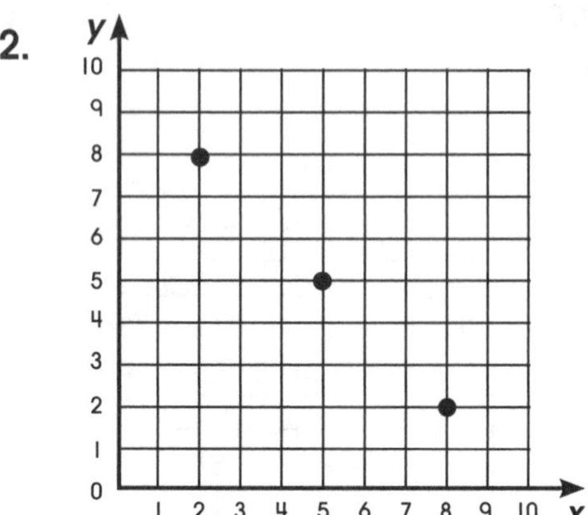

____

Plot each ordered pair.

3.

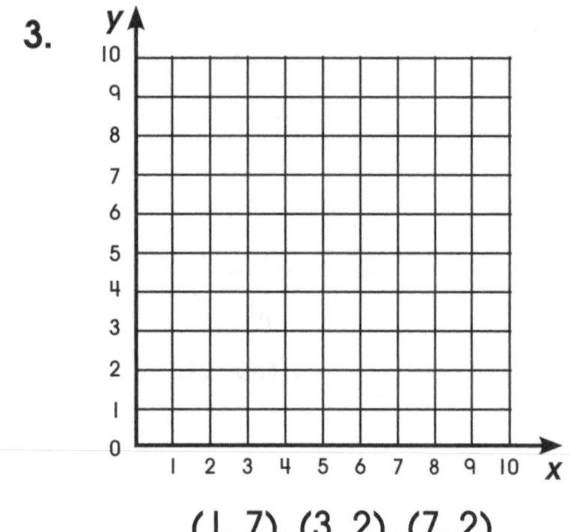

(1, 7), (3, 2), (7, 2)

4.

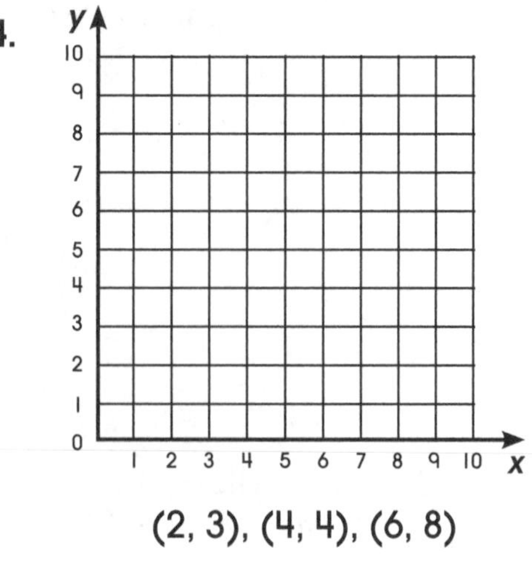

(2, 3), (4, 4), (6, 8)

Ordered Pairs

You can name a point on a grid by using an ordered pair.

Point A on the grid at the right is named by the ordered pair (3, 2). It is located at 3 on the horizontal scale (*x*) and at 2 on the vertical scale (*y*).

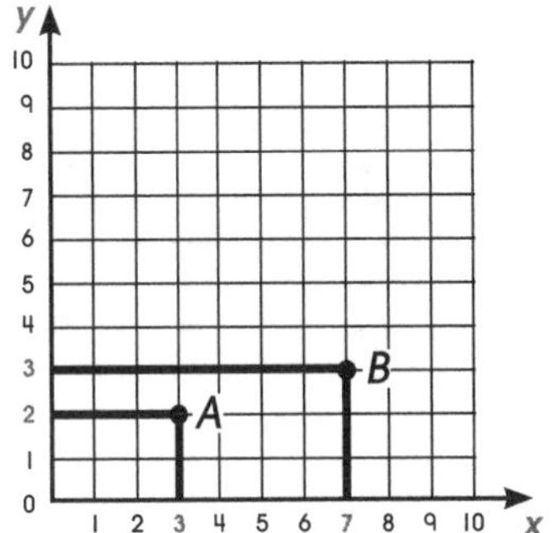

Point B is named by the ordered pair (7, 3). It is located at 7 on the horizontal scale (*x*) and at 3 on the vertical scale (*y*).

Solve: Name the point that is located at (2, 5). Then, name the point located at (5, 2).

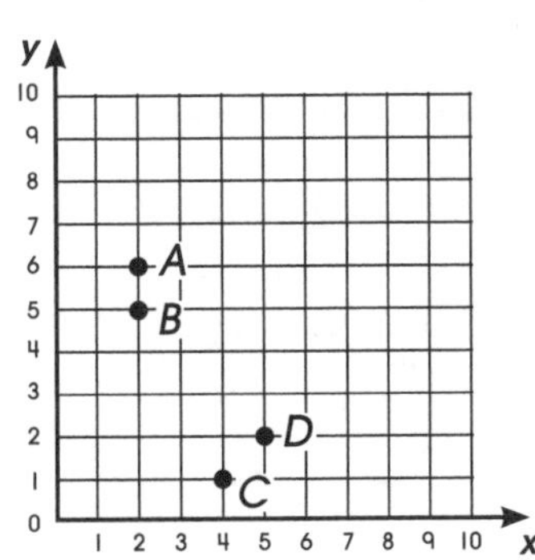

First, look at the first number in (2, 5).	The first number is 2. The point will be aligned with 2 on the horizontal scale (*x*).
Next, look at the second number in (2, 5).	The point will be aligned with 5 on the vertical scale (*y*). It is located at point B, which is aligned with 2 on the horizontal scale and 5 on the vertical scale.
Finally, repeat the process to locate (5, 2).	(5, 2) is located at point D.

Math

Ordered Pairs

Practice

Use Grid 1 to name the point for each ordered pair.

1. (1, 2) ________
2. (2, 4) ________
3. (3, 6) ________
4. (9, 3) ________
5. (9, 0) ________
6. (5, 5) ________
7. (2, 8) ________
8. (4, 3) ________
9. (7, 7) ________
10. (6, 2) ________

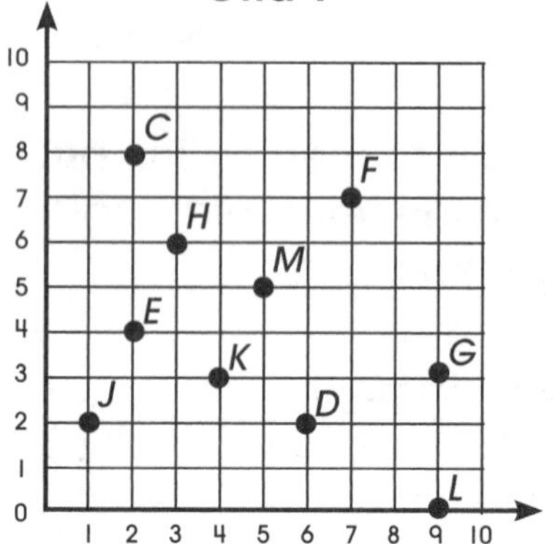

Use Grid 2 to find the ordered pair for each point.

11. *B* ________
12. *V* ________
13. *S* ________
14. *A* ________
15. *W* ________
16. *N* ________
17. *T* ________
18. *R* ________
19. *Z* ________
20. *P* ________

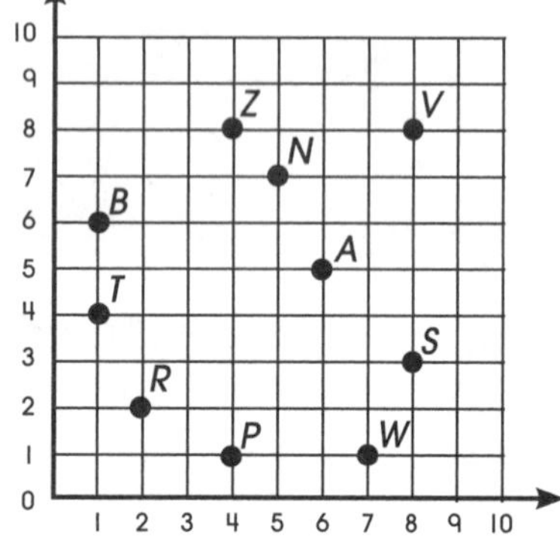

Plot the four points shown on Grid 3. Label the points.

21. *A* (2, 4)
22. *D* (3, 5)
23. *C* (5, 1)
24. *Z* (6, 3)

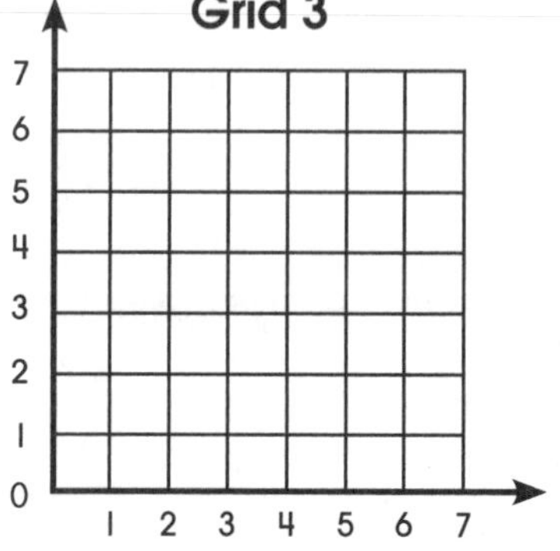

Math

Practice

Use the grids to complete the items below.

Grid 1

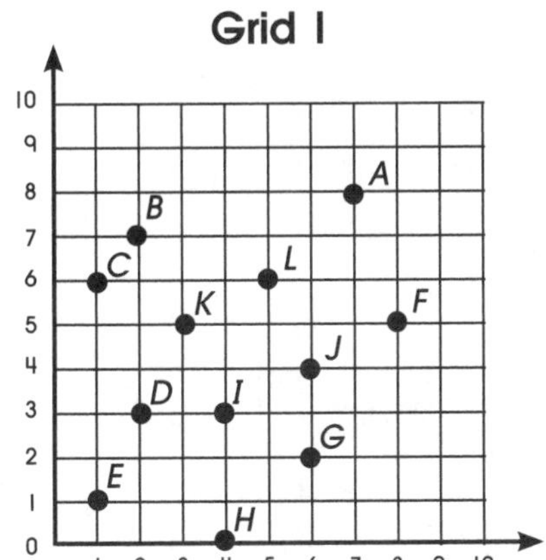

Grid 2

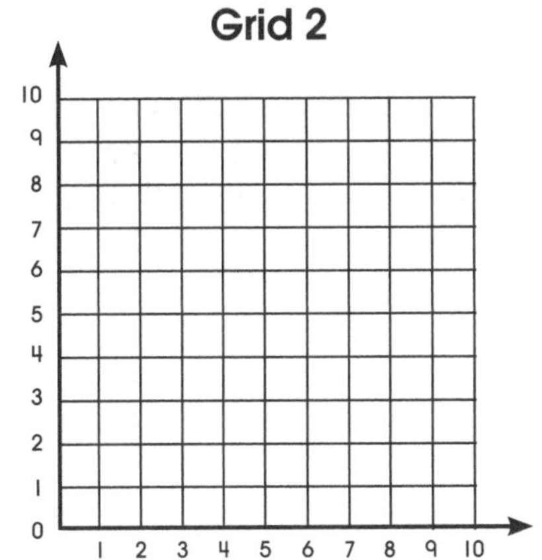

Refer to Grid 1. Name the point located at each ordered pair.

1. (3, 5) ________ 2. (4, 0) ________ 3. (8, 5) ________

Refer to Grid 1. Write the ordered pair for each point.

4. *A* (________) 5. *C* (________) 6. *D* (________)

Plot the points on Grid 1. Label the points.

7. Plot point *M* at (3, 2).
8. Plot point *N* at (6, 5).
9. Plot point *O* at (1, 8).
10. Plot point *P* at (2, 6).
11. Plot point *Q* at (7, 4).
12. Plot point *R* at (4, 8).

Ordered Pairs

You can use coordinate grids to solve problems.

Solve: A line segment runs from (3, 2) to (7, 2). How long is that line segment?

First, draw the line segment on a coordinate grid. Plot points at (3, 2) and (7, 2) and connect them.

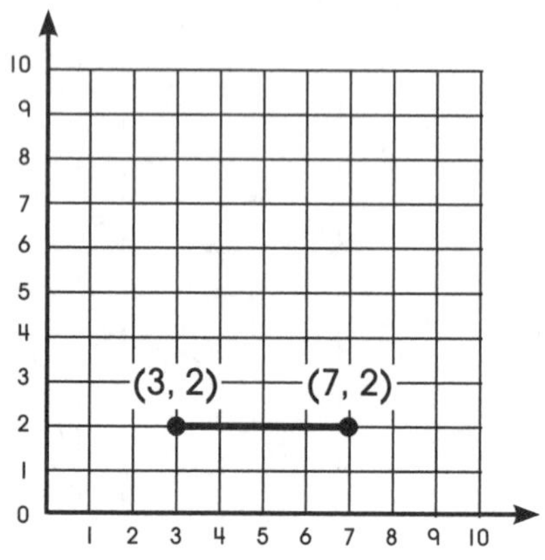

Next, count the number of horizontal units between the end points of the segment. For a vertical line, you would count the number of vertical units between end points.

There are 4 units (spaces) between (3, 2) and (7, 2).

The length of the line segment is 4 units.

Practice

Use the coordinate grid to solve the problems.

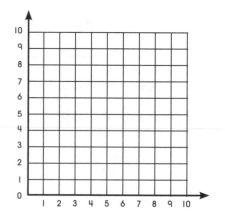

1. A line segment runs from (2, 8) to (4, 8).

   How long is the line segment?

   ____

2. A line segment runs from (3, 1) to (3, 7).

   How long is the line segment?

   ____

3. A rectangle has points at (4, 2), (6, 2), (6, 7), and (4, 7).

   What is the perimeter of the rectangle?

   ____

You can use the coordinate grid strategies you have learned about so far to solve more difficult problems.

First, underline the important information that you will need to solve the problem.	Bob rides his bike from his home which is located at (6, 2) on the grid. He rides 4 blocks north, 3 blocks west, and then 4 blocks south. How many blocks will he have to ride to get home?
Next, determine which strategy is best for solving the problem.	Draw Bob's route on a coordinate grid. Then, determine the distance from his ending point to his home.
Then, represent Bob's route on a coordinate grid.	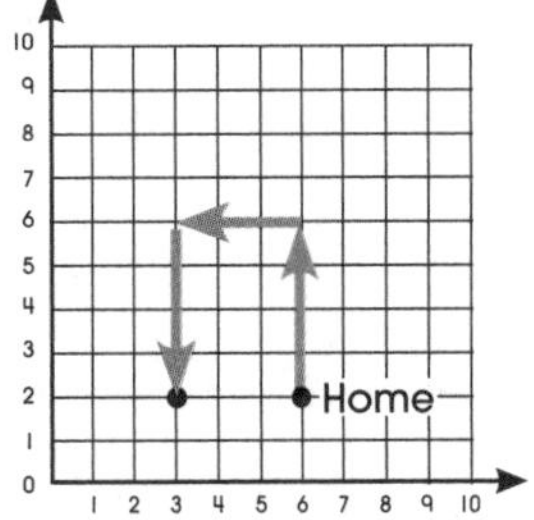
Finally, solve the problem. Count the distance between the ending point and Bob's home.	Bob's home is at (6, 2). He ends at (3, 2). There are 3 horizontal units between those points. Each unit shows 1 block, so Bob has to ride 3 blocks to get home.

Practice

Use the coordinate grid to solve the problems.

1. Carmen's mom drives from her home 8 blocks north to the store. Then, they go 4 blocks west for lunch and 6 blocks south for dessert. How far will they have to drive to get back home?

2. On her way to school, Tisha walked 2 blocks east to her friend's house. Then, they walked together 5 blocks north to buy snacks. Finally, they walked 3 blocks east and 1 block south to get to school. How far will Tisha have to walk to get home from school if she makes no stops?

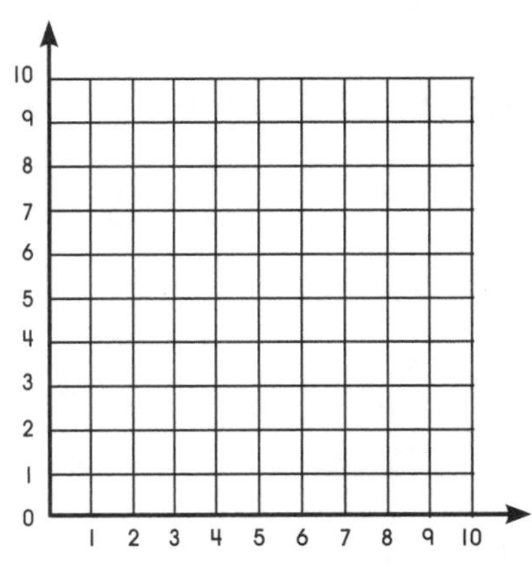

Math

Review

Use everything you have learned so far about shapes and coordinates to solve the problems.

Identify each type of polygon. Then, circle all of the quadrilaterals.

1. 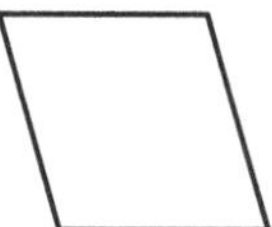 ____________

2. 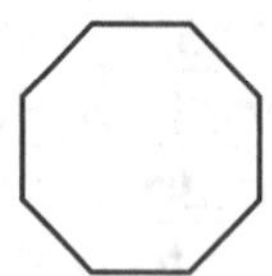 ____________

3. 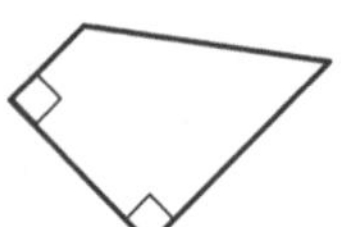 ____________

4. 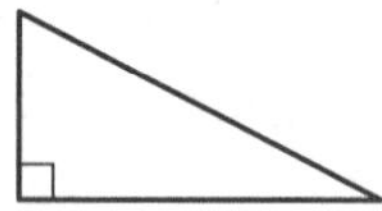 ____________

Name the quadrilateral or quadrilaterals described.

5. I have 4 sides and 4 right angles. ____________________

6. I have 4 sides and only 1 pair of parallel sides. ____________________

7. I have 4 sides, 2 obtuse angles, and 2 acute angles. ____________________

Name each angle. Use a protractor to measure each angle. Then, label each angle right, acute, or obtuse.

8. 

∠________ = ________

____

9. 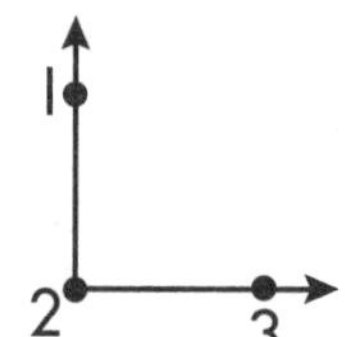 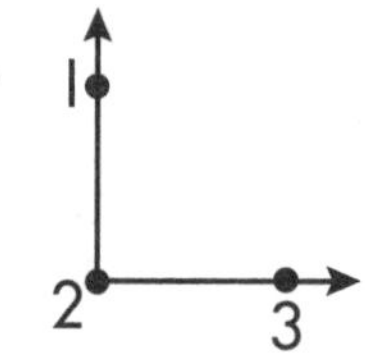

∠________ = ________

____

10. 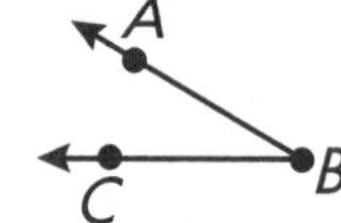

∠________ = ________

____

Use the circle to answer the questions.

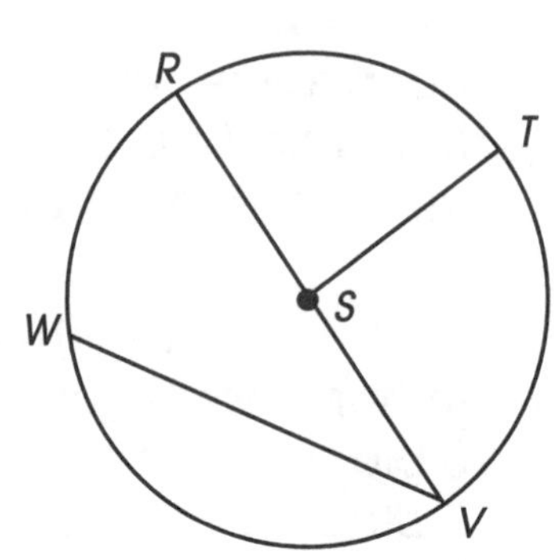

11. Name the circle. ____________

12. Name the origin of the circle. ____________

13. Name a radius. ____________

14. Name a diameter. ____________

15. Name a chord that is not a diameter. ____________

Math

Identify the ordered pair from the grid.

16. ________

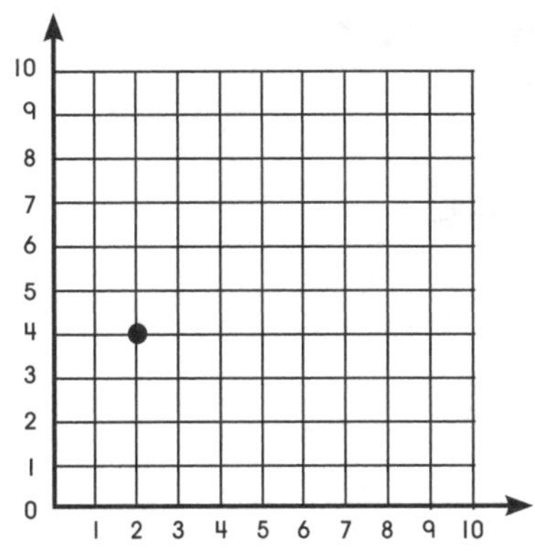

Plot the ordered pair.

17. (5, 5)

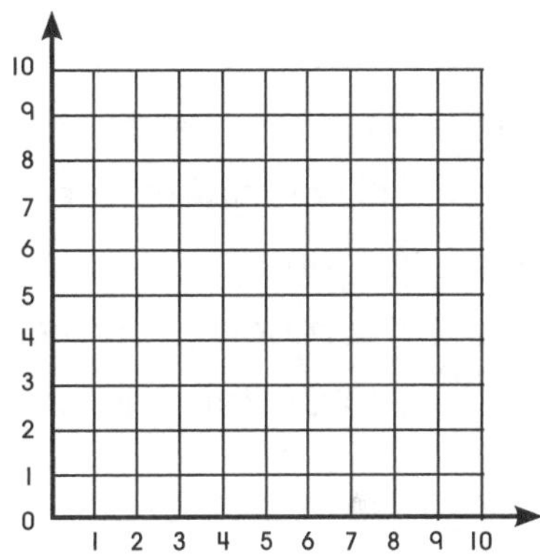

Use the grid to name the point for each ordered pair.

18. (3, 6) ________

19. (9, 3) ________

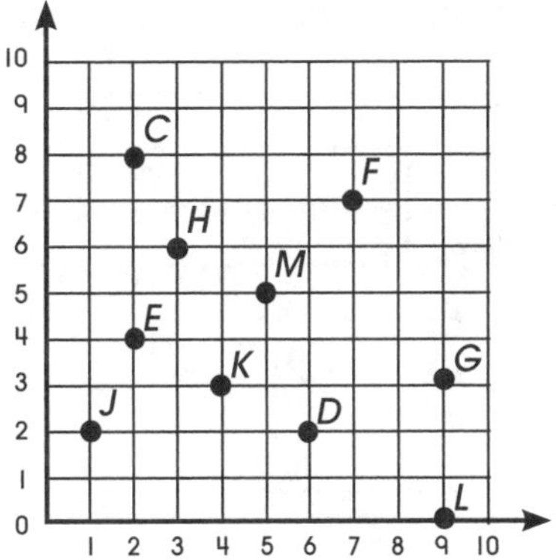

Use the coordinate grid to solve the problem.

20. Shane and Wesley want to meet and play baseball halfway between both of their houses. Shane lives at (4, 1) and Wesley lives at (10, 1). Plot both boys' houses on the grid. At which point should Shane and Wesley meet to play baseball?

They should meet at point ________.

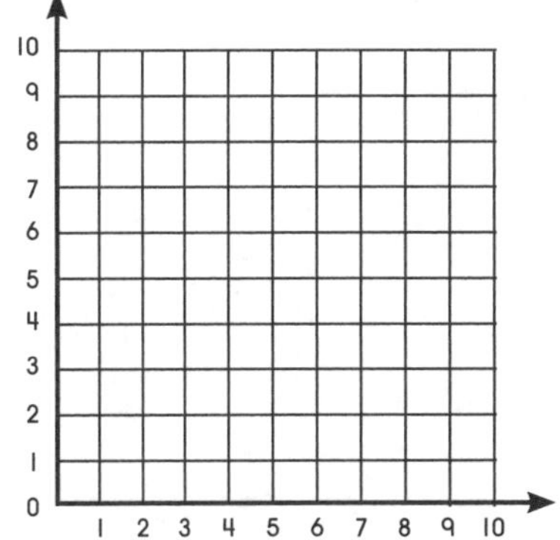

Chapter Review

Complete the following.

1. 6 ft. = ____________ yd.
2. 3 mi. = ____________ ft.
3. 4 qt. = ____________ pt.
4. 5 gal. = ____________ qt.
5. 3 lb. = ____________ oz.
6. 500 mm = ____________ cm
7. 6 L = ____________ mL
8. 8 kg = ____________ g

Draw a line plot to organize the data. Then, solve the problem.

9. Joseph needs to run 3 miles during his workout for the soccer team. He begins practice by running $\frac{1}{2}$ mile. Then, he takes 3 breaks during practice to run $\frac{1}{4}$ mile each time. How much more will he need to run at the end of practice to finish his 3 miles?

____

Find the volume of each rectangular solid.

10.

3 in.

2 in.

6 in.

$V =$ ____________________

11.

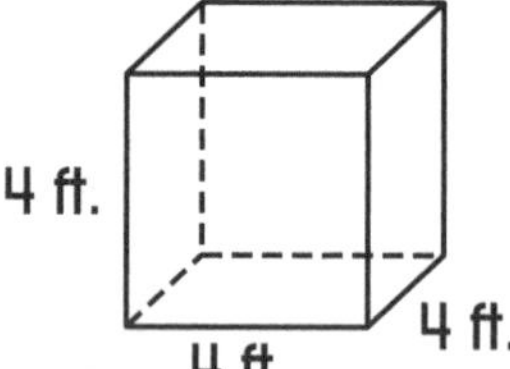

$V =$ ____________________

Find the volume of each figure.

12.

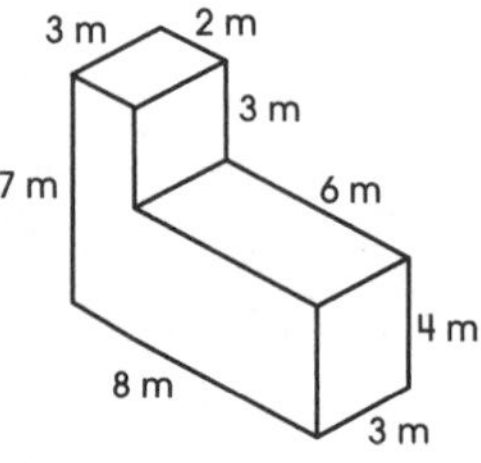

$V =$ ____________________

13.

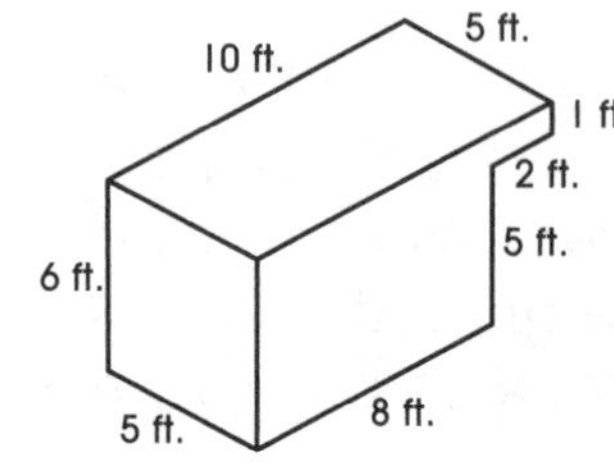

$V =$ ____________________

Identify each type of polygon.

14. 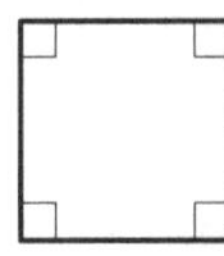
____

15. 
____

16. 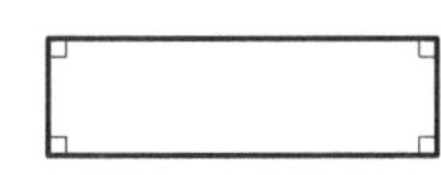
____

17. 
____

Classify the following quadrilaterals. Some shapes may have more than one correct classification.

(A) quadrilateral (B) trapezoid (C) parallelogram (D) square

18. 
____

19. 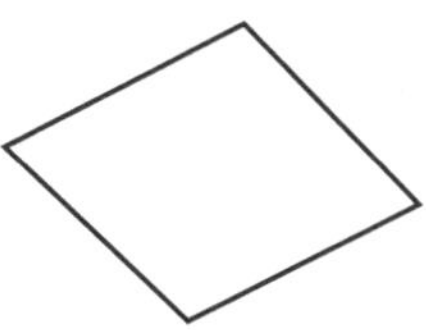
____

20. 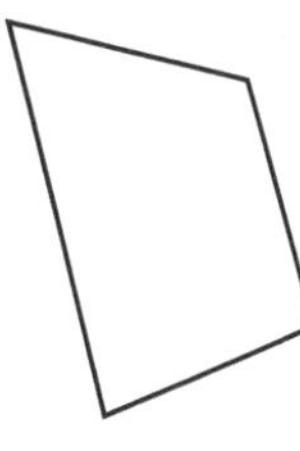
____

21. 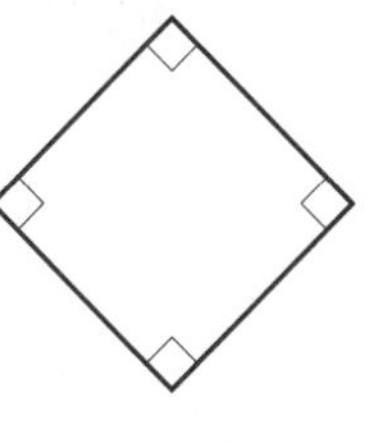
____

Use a protractor to measure each angle. Label each angle **right**, **acute**, or **obtuse**.

22. 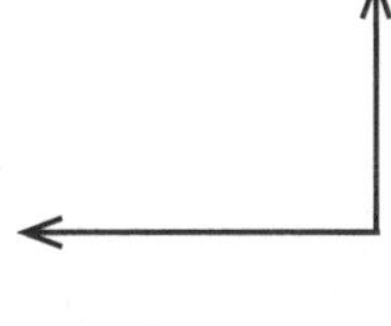
____
____

23. 
____
____

24. 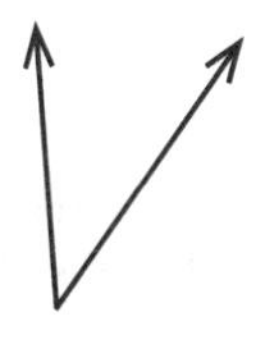
____
____

Use the circle to answer the questions.

25. Name the circle. ________________

26. Name the origin of the circle. ________________

27. Name a radius. ________________

28. Name a chord. ________________

29. Name a diameter. ________________

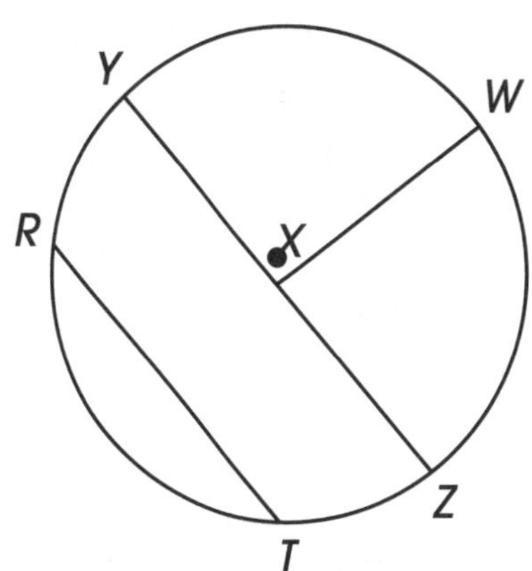

Chapter Review

Tell what point on the grid is located at each ordered pair.

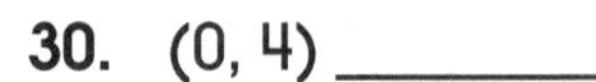

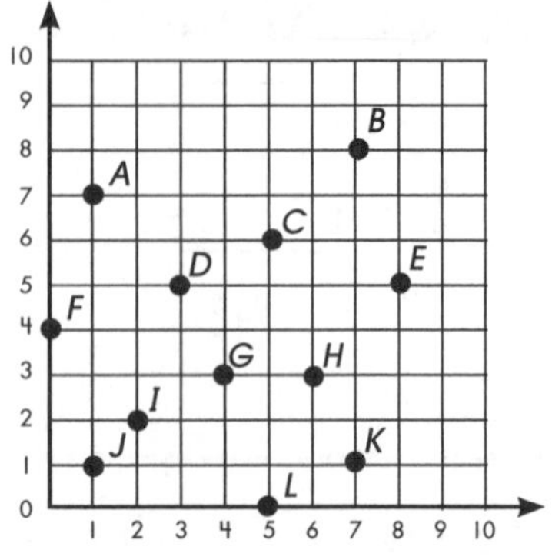

30. (0, 4) ________ **31.** (3, 5) ________

32. (5, 0) ________ **33.** (5, 6) ________

34. (7, 8) ________ **35.** (6, 3) ________

Use the coordinate grid to solve each problem.

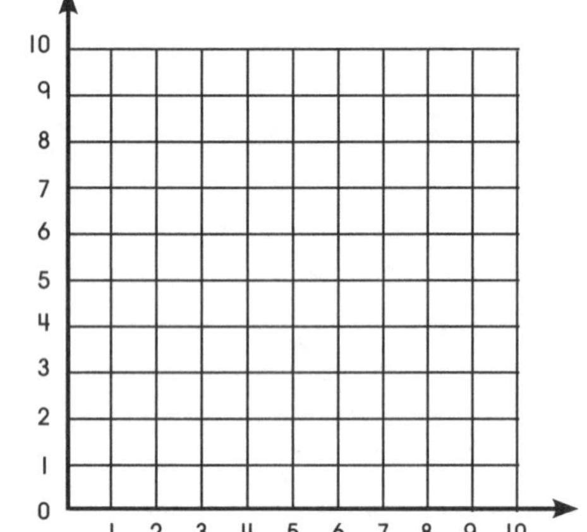

36. A line runs from point (4, 3) to (10, 3).

How long is the line? ________ units

37. A rectangle has points (1, 1), (5, 1), (5, 3), and (1, 3).

What is the perimeter of the rectangle? ________

38. Ross's mom tells him to walk to his Aunt Sally's house to bring her some chicken soup. Because Aunt Sally's house is so far away, Ross takes a break halfway at the park. If Ross's house is at (3, 1) and Aunt Sally's house is at (3, 9), at what point is the park? ________

Plot the points to show Ross's house, Aunt Sally's house, and the park.

39. Audrey is meeting her friend at the playground at (1, 7). Audrey lives at (4, 1). Audrey is planning to travel west rst and then north. How far does Audrey have to walk to get to the playground?

Audry has to walk ________ units.

Math

Add, subtract, multiply, or divide.

1. $\begin{array}{r} 22.92 \\ \times\ 2.64 \\ \hline \end{array}$

2. $\begin{array}{r} \$67.52 \\ +\ 20.18 \\ \hline \end{array}$

3. $\begin{array}{r} \$16.52 \\ -\ 6.93 \\ \hline \end{array}$

4. $7.9\overline{)64.78}$

Multiply or divide by the power of ten to find the product.

5. $6.07 \times 1{,}000 =$ ________

6. $3.457 \div 100 =$ ________

7. $1 \times 10^4 =$ ________

Write the number in expanded form.

8. 3,465 ____

Write the numbers in order from least to greatest.

9. 1.5, 1.7, $\frac{1}{150}$, $\frac{8}{3}$ ______________________

Round each number to the place of the underlined digit.

10. $\underline{1}$,785,302 __________

11. 7.3$\underline{2}$22 __________

12. 4.$\underline{3}$97 __________

Solve the problem.

13. Sami started with 5 pounds of flour. He used 2.25 pounds for bread and 1.5 pounds for cookies. How much did he use? He needs 1.15 lbs for pie. Does he have enough left?

Find the equivalent fraction.

14. $6 = \frac{\square}{3}$

15. $\frac{7}{9} = \frac{\square}{18}$

16. $8 = \frac{\square}{6}$

Change each fraction to a decimal as indicated.

17. Change $2\frac{1}{5}$ to tenths. ________

18. Change $\frac{17}{50}$ to hundredths. ________

Math Review

Write each decimal as a fraction or mixed number in simplest form.

19. 0.4 ________ 20. 0.75 ________ 21. 3.1 ________

Add, subtract, multiply, or divide. Write the answers in simplest form.

22. $\frac{7}{12} + \frac{1}{10}$

23. $2\frac{1}{2} + 3\frac{6}{7}$

24. $\frac{5}{8} - \frac{1}{8}$

25. $7\frac{1}{4} - 3\frac{1}{3}$

26. $\frac{7}{12} \times \frac{3}{8} =$ ________

27. $\frac{1}{9} \div 4 =$ ________

28. $4\frac{1}{5} \times 3 =$ ________

Solve the following problems.

29. $[4 + 1 + (2 \times 2)] \times 3 =$ ________

30. $5 + 7 \times 3 \div 7 - 2 + 4 =$ ________

31. 5 more than 3 times the sum of 4 and 2 = ________

32. 120 in. = ________ ft. 33. 9 pt. = ________ c. 34. 3 m = ________ cm

35. Pedro has a stack of coins that weighs 85 grams. Conner has a stack of coins that weighs 64,300 milligrams. Whose stack of coins weighs more? How much more?

35.

Math

Find the volume of each rectangular solid.

36. 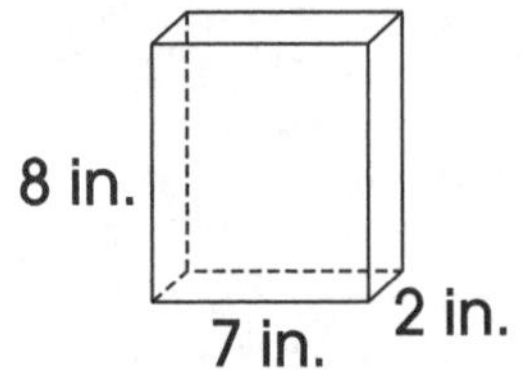

$V =$ ________ cu. in.

37. Length = 3 feet
Width = 2 feet
Height = 6 feet

$V =$ ________ cu. ft.

Classify the following quadrilaterals. Some shapes may have more than one correct classification.

(A) parallelogram (B) quadrilateral (C) rectangle

38. 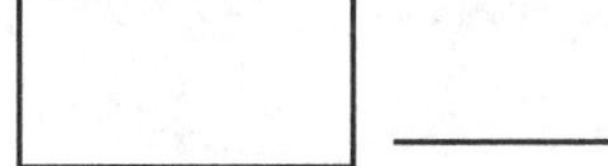 ________

39. 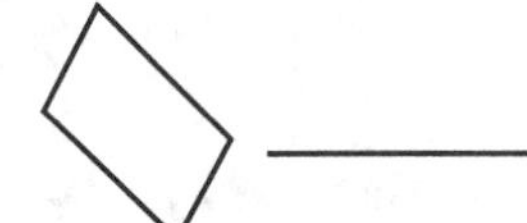 ________

40. 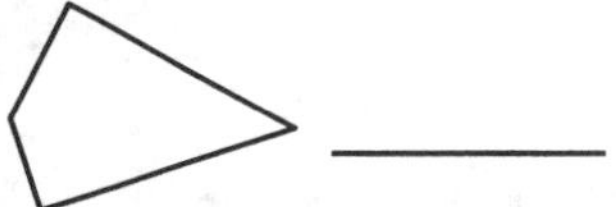 ________

Identify each angle as **right**, **acute**, or **obtuse**.

41. 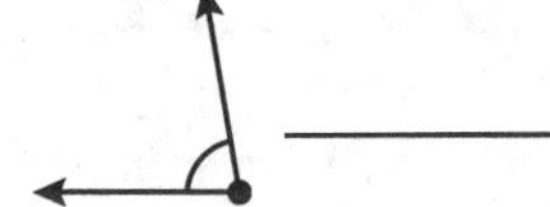 ________

42. 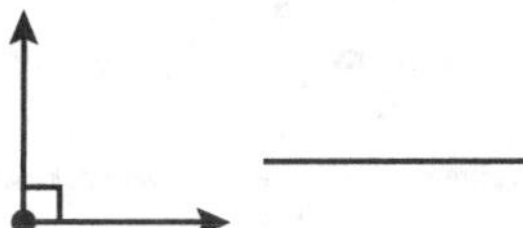 ________

43.  ________

Use the grid to name the point for each ordered pair.

44. (6, 4) ________

45. (1, 8) ________

46. (1, 4) ________

47. (3, 5) ________

48. (8, 7) ________

49. (4, 2) ________

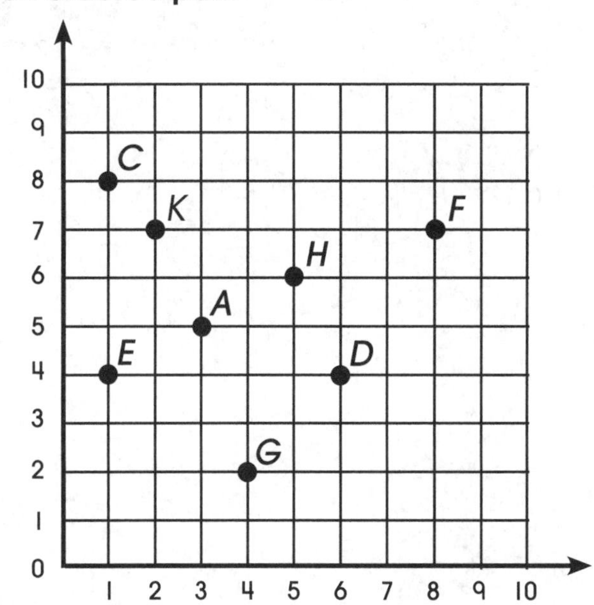

LANGUAGE ARTS

Simple Steps for Fifth Grade uses a combination of sentence examples and color coding designed to build students' language arts skills and deepen their understanding of language arts concepts.

Instructions

The instructional sections of this book are organized around examples. In these sections, key language arts concepts and terms are assigned colors. This can help students visualize a connection between the skill they are learning and the way that it is applied.

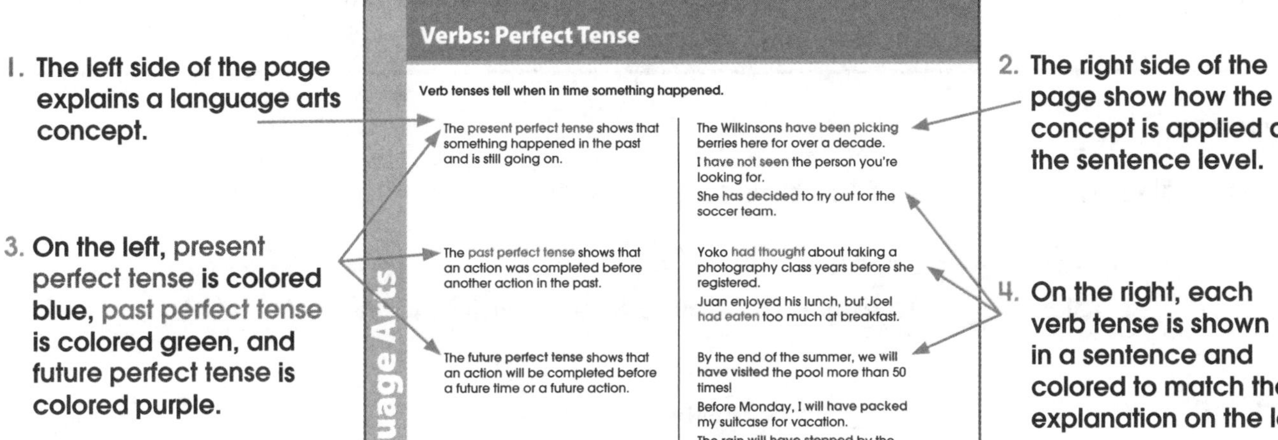

1. The left side of the page explains a language arts concept.
3. On the left, present perfect tense is colored blue, past perfect tense is colored green, and future perfect tense is colored purple.
Verbs: Perfect Tense
Verb tenses tell when in time something happened.
The present perfect tense shows that something happened in the past and is still going on.
The past perfect tense shows that an action was completed before another action in the past.
The future perfect tense shows that an action will be completed before a future time or a future action.
The Wilkinsons have been picking berries here for over a decade.
I have not seen the person you're looking for.
She has decided to try out for the soccer team.
Yoko had thought about taking a photography class years before she registered.
Juan enjoyed his lunch, but Joel had eaten too much at breakfast.
By the end of the summer, we will have visited the pool more than 50 times!
Before Monday, I will have packed my suitcase for vacation.
The rain will have stopped by the time we arrive at the picnic.
Language Arts
2. The right side of the page show how the concept is applied at the sentence level.
4. On the right, each verb tense is shown in a sentence and colored to match the explanation on the left.

Practice

Practice problems follow the concepts after they are explained, giving students an opportunity to work with what they have just learned.

Review

Review sections are included throughout each chapter, along with a chapter review section at the end of each chapter and an overall math review at the end of the math section.

Language Arts

Common and Proper Nouns

Common nouns name people, places, and things. They are general nouns. They do not name specific people, places, or things. Common nouns usually begin with lower-case letters.

a person: uncle	My uncle is visiting.
a place: park	The park is a nice place to play.
a thing: tree	Many trees grow in this forest.

Practice

Use the common nouns from the box below to complete the following sentences.

aunt	firefighters	dog	sailors	house
books	flowers	post office	telephone	track

1. The flowers look pretty in the vase.
2. The telephone rang and rang.
3. My aunt is visiting from Colorado.
4. The students run on the track beside the school.
5. firefighters must not be afraid of smoke and fire.
6. My dog loves to chase after sticks that I throw.
7. books on many subjects can be found in the library.
8. sailors must like living on the sea.
9. The post office sells stamps.
10. Our house is just down the street.

Common and Proper Nouns

Proper nouns also name people, places, and things. However, they are not general like common nouns. Proper nouns name specific people, places, and things. They usually begin with capital letters.

a specific person: Mrs. Jackman	Mrs. Jackman is my favorite teacher.
a specific place: Brazil	I want to visit the country of Brazil.
a specific thing: Lincoln Memorial	Her favorite monument is the Lincoln Memorial.

Practice

Write the correct words from the box to complete Patrick's journal entry. Use only proper nouns.

Uncle Rich	Principal Ron	my principal	planet
my school	tomorrow	The Lord of the Rings	national park
Grand Canyon	Venus	the playground	my uncle
book	Saturday	Highland Park	Pierce School

I love Satardax mornings. I go to Highland park to walk the trails and read The Lord of the Rings. Later, Aunt Pat and Uncle Rich come to my house. We plan our trip to the Grang Canyon. We use the telescope to look at Vehus when it gets dark. On Monday, it's back to Pierre School. I like Principal Ron. He is a good principal. But I still look forward to the weekend.

Language Arts

Regular and Irregular Plural Nouns

A regular plural noun **names more than one person, place, or thing. To form a regular plural noun, add the letter s to the end of a word.**

birds carrots cups spiders

Irregular plural nouns can be formed in different ways.

Nouns ending in the letters **s**, **x**, or **z**, or in a **ch** or **sh** sound, need es.	bosses	taxes	waltzes
If a word ends in the letter **y**, then the **y** is changed to an i before adding the es.	countries	cities	flies
However, words that end in **y** with a vowel before the **y** only require an s.	boys	keys	donkeys
If a noun ends in **f** or **fe**, and the **f** sound can still be heard in the plural form, add s.	roofs	cuffs	chiefs
If the final sound of the plural form is **v**, then change the **f** to ve and add an s.	calves	leaves	wives

Practice

Circle the correct spelling of the plural nouns in the following letter.

Dear Mom and Dad,

Camp is great. I made a lot of (friendes/friends). Two (foxes/foxs) ran by camp today. Tomorrow, we are going hiking. Don't worry, we won't go too close to the (cliffs/clives). The (leaves/leafs) are turning colors. I found a leaf that is the color of (cherrys/cherries). I have to go practice for the (playes/plays) now. I miss you.

Taylor

Regular and Irregular Plural Nouns

Here are some other kinds of irregular plural nouns.

Irregular plural nouns do not have a pattern for changing from singular to plural. These nouns and their plural spellings have to be learned.	child (children) goose (geese) ox (oxen)	tooth (teeth) foot (feet)
Some irregular nouns do not change at all when they are in the plural form. These forms also have to be learned.	cod wheat deer	fish sheep series

Practice

Find the following irregular plurals in the word search puzzle. The words can be forward, backward, vertical, horizontal, or diagonal.

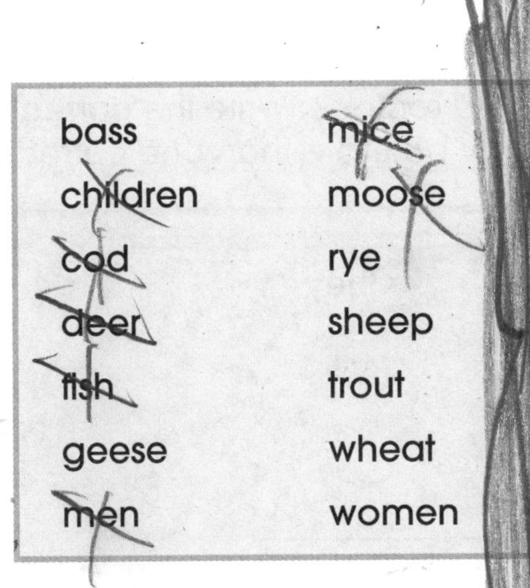

c	h	i	l	d	r	e	n	a	z
o	s	b	y	c	y	w	d	v	e
d	i	u	f	t	e	g	s	h	r
i	f	q	j	p	m	l	o	n	a
b	z	y	c	d	x	i	w	d	e
f	v	e	g	h	t	s	c	e	i
w	o	m	e	n	e	s	e	e	g
h	j	e	q	r	k	p	l	r	p
e	o	n	l	m	n	e	m	a	x
a	m	s	u	c	n	e	o	c	c
t	o	h	t	t	k	h	r	i	i
e	i	r	u	n	e	s	o	o	m
g	d	o	r	e	e	b	s	g	b
i	r	e	d	r	a	w	j	a	m
t	t	n	t	c	a	h	s	i	b

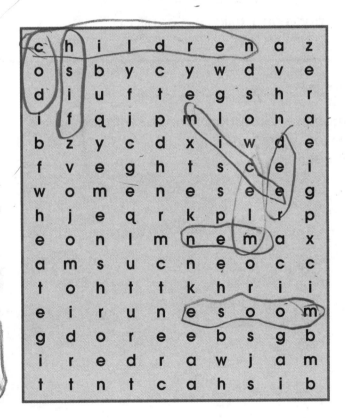

Language Arts

Subject and Object Pronouns

A pronoun is a word used in place of a noun. A subject pronoun replaces a noun that is the subject of a sentence. I, you, he, she, and it are subject pronouns.

> Pancakes are great for breakfast. Pancakes taste good with syrup.
> Pancakes are great for breakfast. They taste good with syrup.

Singular subject nouns	Singular subject pronouns
Dominique likes cats.	I like cats.
Lynn likes to run.	You like to run.
Ellis works for a newspaper.	He works for a newspaper.
Carol is a teacher.	She is a teacher.
Bicycling is their favorite sport.	It is their favorite sport.

Plural subject nouns	Plural subject pronouns
Gavin and Gabriel are brothers.	We are brothers.
Lisa and Chang are friends.	You are friends.
Jenna and Julia are tennis partners.	They are tennis partners.

Practice

Match the following pronouns with the nouns they could replace. Write the correct answer or answers to Column A in Column B. There may be more than one correct answer.

I	he	it	they
you	she	we	

Column A	Column B
Jack and Jennifer	we they
Nicole	he I
ball	it
Josh	you
cars	it

Subject and Object Pronouns

Practice

Write the correct subject pronouns to complete the following passage. Some words may be used more than once.

I	he	it	they
you	she	we	

"Chris, are __________ awake?" Mrs. Johnson called from downstairs.

"__________ can't find my shoes. Do __________ know where __________ are?" Chris shouted.

"Ask your sister. Maybe __________ has seen them," answered Mrs. Johnson.

Chris knocked on Kendra's door. "Have __________ seen my shoes?"

"__________ saw one earlier. __________ was in the dog's mouth," Kendra replied.

"Mom, where's Toby?" Chris scrambled downstairs. "__________ are going to be late for school!"

Mr. Johnson answered, "Toby's out back, and it looks like that little guy is digging a hole. Wait, __________ is definitely covering something up. __________ better get out there!"

Subject and Object Pronouns

An object pronoun replaces a noun that is the receiver, or object, of the action in the sentence. Me, you, him, her, and it are object pronouns.

In this example, the object pronoun her is a substitute for the object noun Kaylen.

Tyrone bought a gift for Kaylen.
Tyrone bought a gift for her.

Singular object nouns	Singular object pronouns
Mom cooked dinner for Henri.	Mom cooked dinner for me.
Kerry handed the serving bowl to Miranda.	Kerry handed the serving bowl to you.
Joey sat next to Ivan.	Joey sat next to him.
Ivan asked Mom for the recipe.	Ivan asked her for the recipe.
Mom gave the recipe to Ivan.	Mom gave it to Ivan.

Plural object nouns	Plural object pronouns
It was nice of Mom to cook dinner for the family.	It was nice of Mom to cook dinner for us.
Mom even let Henri invite his friends.	Mom even let Henri invite you.
A special dessert was served to the guests.	A special dessert was served to them.

Practice

Circle the errors in object pronoun use in the following school note. Write the correct object pronoun above the mistake. Not all object pronouns used in this note are mistakes.

Attached is a permission slip for your child to go on a field trip to the Science Museum on February 9. Please sign her and return it to you by Friday, February 4. Your child will write a report about the visit. I will read all of the reports and will display it in the school.

Thank you,

Mrs. Jones

Language Arts

Pronoun Agreement

A pronoun replaces a noun in a sentence. The noun that the pronoun refers to is called the antecedent. All pronouns have antecedents.

Pronouns must agree in gender with their antecedents and what their antecedents refer to.

Tony must bring his own lunch to the picnic.	He must bring his own lunch to the picnic. (agrees in gender) Not: He must bring her own lunch to the picnic. (does not agree in gender)

Pronouns must also agree in number with their antecedents and what their antecedents refer to.

Armando must bring three lunches to the picnic.	Armando must bring them to the picnic. (agrees in number) Not: Armando must bring it to the picnic. (does not agree in number)

Practice

Circle the correct pronoun in parentheses. Remember that pronouns must agree in both gender and number.

1. Adam did well on (her, his) English report.
2. Adam didn't do well on (his, its) math test.
3. He missed eight problems. (He, They) were hard.
4. Charlotte did well on (her, his) math test.
5. Charlotte didn't do well on (her, them) English report.
6. She made six mistakes in grammar. (They, She) were spelling and punctuation errors.

Language Arts

Language Arts

Pronoun Agreement

Practice

Choose pronouns from the box to fill in the blanks.

his	it
her	them

1. Who ate the pizza with pepper?

   Who ate the pizza with __________________?

2. Charlotte ate the pizza with pepper.

   She ate __________________ pizza with __________________.

3. Who ordered a salad with tomatoes?

   Who ordered a salad with __________________?

4. Jose ordered the salad with tomatoes.

   He ordered __________________ salad with __________________.

5. I like pizza with __________________. (fill in your favorite topping)

   I like pizza with __________________. (pronoun from the box)

   I like salad with __________________. (fill in your favorite topping)

   I like salad with __________________. (pronoun from the box)

Write a letter to your best friend telling about a recent event at school. Include at least four pronouns and antecedents in your letter.

____

____

____

____

____

____

____

Review

Language Arts

Use everything you have learned so far about nouns and pronouns to answer the questions.

Answer the following questions by circling the letter of the best answer.

1. Which sentence contains a common noun?
   - **a.** I visited Yellowstone National Park.
   - **b.** I liked seeing the animals.
   - **c.** I heard that you went to Everglades National Park.

2. Which sentence contains a proper noun?
   - **a.** The U.S. Capitol is in Washington, D.C.
   - **b.** History is one of my favorite subjects.
   - **c.** I like to study science.

3. Which sentence contains a regular plural noun?
   - **a.** I liked seeing the moose at the park.
   - **b.** The geese were in the pond and then they flew overhead.
   - **c.** The cats liked playing together.

4. Which sentence contains an irregular plural noun?
   - **a.** The dogs loved playing in the water.
   - **b.** Rabbits make great pets.
   - **c.** The mice scurried under the floorboards.

5. Which sentence contains a subject pronoun?
   - **a.** Ava went on a science field trip.
   - **b.** She went on a science field trip.
   - **c.** Aaron went on a science field trip.

6. Which sentence contains an object pronoun?
   - **a.** The team captain picked me.
   - **b.** The team captain picked Sandy to play.
   - **c.** He picked the best player to be on his side.

7. Which sentence has an incorrect use of pronoun agreement?
   - **a.** The brothers left his jackets on the field.
   - **b.** Diane picked up her books at the library.
   - **c.** Jason forgot his books at the library.

Regular and Irregular Verbs

A **verb** is a word that tells the action or the state of being in a sentence. Add **ed** to the present tense of a regular verb to make it past tense. If the word already ends in the letter **e**, just add the letter **d**.

Present-tense verb	Past-tense verb
The dogs sniff the flowers.	The dogs **sniffed** the flowers.

Present-tense verb	Past-tense verb
The girls like to play baseball.	The girls **liked** to play baseball.

Irregular verbs do not follow the same rules as regular verbs when forming their past tense. They must be learned. Below are some common irregular verbs in their present-tense and **past-tense** forms. Some irregular verbs do not change at all when they are in the past-tense form.

Present-tense verbs	Past-tense verbs
I am excited.	I **was** excited.
We begin the lesson.	We **began** the lesson.
I get good grades.	I **got** good grades.
You do that well.	You **did** that well.
I sleep heavily.	I **slept** heavily.
The sandwich is delicious.	The sandwich **was** delicious.
You bring the drinks.	You **brought** the drinks.
We eat cereal for breakfast.	We **ate** cereal for breakfast.
I rise early on Sundays.	I **rose** early on Sundays.
I think best in the morning.	I **thought** best in the morning.
I let the dog out.	I **let** the dog out.
I put away the dishes.	I **put** away the dishes.

Regular and Irregular Verbs

Practice

Use a present- or past-tense verb to complete each sentence below. There is more than one correct answer.

1. Quinten ____________________ a good question in science class earlier.
2. As they look at the picture, the ladies ____________________ at its beauty.
3. I ____________________ at the stars as I walk through the planetarium.
4. Kelly and Taylor, please ____________________ that in your report.
5. Shelly and Dylan ____________________ when they are late.
6. The spectators ____________________ and cheered many times during the game last night.
7. Jim fell on the ice. But he ____________________ about it later.
8. ____________________ the luggage.
9. May I have some milk? I want to ____________________ it to my coffee.
10. Carl ____________________ waffles for breakfast.

Choose four present- and four past-tense irregular verbs from the list on page 158. Write a fictional paragraph using these verbs.

____

____

____

____

____

____

____

Language Arts

Helping Verbs

A helping verb is not a main verb. A helping verb helps form some of the tenses of a main verb.

The forms of the verb to be are helping verbs.	is are was were am been
Helping verbs often help express express time and mood.	She could run for miles and miles. She will run for miles and miles.
Here are some examples of helping verbs.	shall may will must have could had did would has should can do

Practice

Circle the letter of the sentence that contains a helping verb. Remember, helping verbs help to set the time and mood of sentences.

1. a. We shall all go to the movies.
   b. We went to the movies.
   c. They ran to the movies.

2. a. Jake helped me with my homework.
   b. Jake will help me with my homework.
   c. Jake helps me with my homework every day.

3. a. I could study all night for the test.
   b. I studied for the test.
   c. I studied with Carol.

Language Arts

Helping Verbs

Helping verbs are often used with main verbs that end with ing.

An ing verb is a clue that there is a verb phrase or helping verb in the sentence.	She was running for miles and miles.
Sometimes, more than one helping verb is used in a sentence. This is called a verb phrase.	She had been running for miles and miles.

Practice

Choose a helping verb or verb phrase from the box to complete each sentence. Then, circle the main verb of the sentence. Sometimes there is a word between the helping and main verbs.

have	is	were
had	are	am
has	was	been

1. We ___________ ___________ planning our vacation for many months.
2. I ___________ looking forward to it.
3. We ___________ traveling by ship.
4. We ___________ to visit a travel agent last week to get our tickets.
5. It ___________ fun choosing the ship.

Linking Verbs

Linking verbs do not name an action. Linking verbs connect, or link, a subject to a noun or adjective. They do not express an action. A noun or adjective will follow a linking verb in a sentence.

The most common linking verbs are the forms of the verb to be.

It is time for bed.
We are outside.
That sound was loud!
Many people were there.
I have been sick.
I am tired, Dad.

Some linking verbs express the five senses.

Do you smell that?
You look beautiful.
The milk tastes funny.
I don't feel too well.
That plan sounds good.

Other linking verbs reflect a state of being.

You appear ready.
I seem better today.
You have become tall.
Tom and Tammy grow happier every day.
He remains at home.

Practice

Circle the linking verb and underline the noun or adjective that is linked to the subject.

1. The book is good.
2. The flowers smell sweet.
3. The team appears disorganized.
4. The apples are bad.
5. Sharon looks fantastic tonight.
6. We were late.
7. The pear was tasty.
8. I am cold.

Practice

Rewrite each of the sentences with a linking verb or more than one linking verb from the box. Notice how using other forms of linking verbs adds variety to your sentences.

grows	been	sounds
has	remained	tastes

1. The water from the faucet is bad.

____

2. The older woman in the play is weary.

____

3. The trip is long.

____

4. Walking, instead of riding, is great.

____

5. The team is disorganized after half time.

____

Write a paragraph using at least five of the linking verbs on page 162. Remember, linking verbs link the subject of the sentence to either a noun or an adjective.

____

____

____

____

____

____

____

Language Arts

Verbs: Perfect Tense

Verb tenses tell when in time something happened.

The present perfect tense shows that something happened in the past and is still going on.	The Wilkinsons have been picking berries here for over a decade. I have not seen the person you're looking for. She has decided to try out for the soccer team.
The past perfect tense shows that an action was completed before another action in the past.	Yoko had thought about taking a photography class years before she registered. Juan enjoyed his lunch, but Joel had eaten too much at breakfast.
The future perfect tense shows that an action will be completed before a future time or a future action.	By the end of the summer, we will have visited the pool more than 50 times! Before Monday, I will have packed my suitcase for vacation. The rain will have stopped by the time we arrive at the picnic.

Practice

Read each sentence. If the underlined verb is in the past perfect tense, write **PP** on the line. If it is in the present perfect tense, write **PR**. If it is in the future perfect tense, write **FP**.

1. ____________________ Soon, I <u>will have finished</u> reading this book.

2. ____________________ I <u>have enjoyed</u> the first several chapters.

3. ____________________ Until now, I <u>had not read</u> any other books by the author.

4. ____________________ By next summer, I <u>will have read</u> all of her books.

Practice

Underline the perfect tense in each sentence below.

1. I have watched backyard birds for many years.
2. I had noticed that my yard was very quiet during the winter.
3. The birds had gone elsewhere to find food.
4. I have been excited to see who comes to visit me now.
5. I have been adding new feeders to my yard every year.
6. By next winter, I will have built three more wooden feeders.
7. I also will have stocked each one with a different kind of bird seed.
8. These tiny visitors have added a touch of color to my days.

Write three sentences of your own about a place you have volunteered or might like to volunteer. Write one in the past perfect, one in the present perfect, and one in the future perfect tense.

Verbs: Perfect Tense

Language Arts

Practice

Read each sentence. On the line, write the boldface verb in the past, present, or future perfect tense. The words in parentheses will tell you which tense to use.

1. Audrey **volunteer** at Lakeside Waterfowl Rescue. (present perfect)

   ____

2. Aisha **work** with Audrey for the last six months. (present perfect)

   ____

3. They **rescue** dozens of ducks, geese, herons, and other birds every month. (past perfect)

   ____

4. The rescue **provide** fresh food and water every day, rain or shine. (past perfect)

   ____

5. They **raise** lots of money every year. (past perfect)

   ____

6. The rescue **rely** on its volunteers to take care of the animals since its doors first opened. (present perfect)

   ____

7. At the end of the summer, Audrey **earn** an award for hours donated. (future perfect)

   ____

8. By next fall, Aisha **receive** the same award. (future perfect)

   ____

Verb Tense Shifts

Verb tense shifts happen when a writer changes from one tense to another in the same sentence. Being consistent with the time frame of a piece of writing is important. It helps the reader follow what is happening.

In this example, the verb rolled is in the past tense, and the verb starts is in the present tense.	The gardener rolled up his sleeves and starts working.
The sentence can be corrected in two ways.	The gardener rolls up his sleeves and starts working. The gardener rolled up his sleeves and started working.

Practice

Complete each sentence below with the word in parentheses in the correct tense. Make sure that the verb tense you choose agrees with the rest of the sentence.

1. My family pulled up to the cabin and ________________ the car. (unload)
2. We ________________ at the same cabin every year, and I love it. (stay)
3. In the 1960s, Grandpa Leo ________________ all of the logs by hand and built it himself. (chop)
4. The inside is not fancy, but it ________________ homey and cozy. (is)
5. Mom filled the fridge with groceries, and Dad ________________ a fire in the fireplace. (start)
6. Since the fireplace is huge, it ________________ the small cabin quickly. (warm)
7. When I was six, I ________________ my hand roasting marshmallows in the fireplace. (burn)
8. Next year, we will come in June, and we ________________ my cousins here. (meet)

Verb Tense Shifts

Language Arts

Practice

Read the selection below. There are seven places where the verb tense shifts. Use proofreading marks to correct the errors. Write the correct tense of each incorrect verb above it.

ⅇ	**delete a word or letter**
^	**insert a word or letter**

Have you ever heard of the artist Andy Goldsworthy? He is probably not what you picture when you thought of an artist. Andy doesn't use a canvas and paints, and he didn't sculpt metal or clay. Andy was an artist who uses the elements of nature to create art. For example, he connects and arranges colorful leaves in a brook and then photographed them. He made a star out of icicles and an arch out of sea pebbles and then photographs it. Sometimes, creating art can be frustrating. Andy has carefully arranged scenes and watches the wind knock down his work. The weather has ruined pieces and changes his plans many times. However, none of this slows Andy Goldsworthy down. He loves his work and his interactions with nature—snow, feathers, pebbles, flowers, and branches.

Place a check mark next to the sentences that use verb tense shifts correctly.

1. _______ Elena drew a picture of her cat and painted a picture of her dog.

2. _______ Right now, she is taking sculpture lessons and learned photography.

3. _______ She might be a famous artist when she grew up.

Subject-Verb Agreement

A verb must agree in number with the subject of the sentence. This is known as subject-verb agreement.

- If the subject is singular, the verb must be singular.
- If the subject is plural, the verb must be plural.

The shirts fits just right.	Shirts is a plural subject. Fits is a singular verb. The subject and the verb do not agree.
The shirt fits just right. Or: The shirts fit just right.	This sentence is now written correctly.
The movie were sold out.	Movie is a singular subject. Were is a plural verb. The subject and the verb do not agree.
The movie was sold out. Or: The movies were sold out.	This sentence is now written correctly.

Practice

Circle the correct verb for each sentence.

1. Troy (help, helps) his sister with her homework after school.
2. They both (try, tries) to be as helpful as possible around the house.
3. Sometimes, their little brother even (pitch, pitches) in.
4. After dinner, they all (clear, clears) the table.
5. This (make, makes) their parents very happy.

Subject-Verb Agreement

Here are some rules related to subject-verb agreement.

If the subject is a compound subject and includes the word **and**, a plural verb is needed.	Erika **and** Chris photograph the birds.
If the subject is a compound subject and includes the words **or** or **nor**, then the verb must agree with the subject that is closer to the verb.	Neither Juanita **nor** Susan likes chocolate pie. Either the dog **or** the kids are making a lot of noise.
If the subject and the verb are separated by **a word or words**, make sure that the verb still agrees with the subject.	Susan, **as well as her coworkers**, wants to complete the project.

Practice

Circle the correct verb for each sentence.

1. Either she or her friends (know, knows) who has the book.
2. Neither they nor Amal (like, likes) cake.
3. Tara and Brendan (eat, eats) pizza and salad every week
4. Bella, along with her sister, (play, plays) basketball after school.
5. Neither Anna nor Austin (like, likes) going to parties.
6. My brother and I (argue, argues) about which team is better.
7. Either today or tomorrow (seem, seems) to be the best time for our club meeting.

Subject-Verb Agreement

Here are more rules related to subject-verb agreement.

When using the phrases **there is**, **there are**, **here is**, and **here are**, make sure that the subjects and verbs agree.

Singular:
There is one piece of pizza left.
Here is the right path to take.

Plural:
There are many pieces left.
Here are the bikes we are supposed to use.

Sometimes, a subject is a collective noun. A collective noun is a singular word that represents a group, like **family** and **team**. A singular verb is usually used with a collective noun.

The family is ready to go.
The team runs one mile every day.

Practice

Circle the correct verb for each sentence.

1. There (is, are) one store that I like at that mall.
2. Here (is, are) the books on that subject.
3. The news (is, are) on at six.
4. A thousand dollars (is, are) the prize.
5. The team (play, plays) in the championship game tonight.
6. The group (travel, travels) to the chess tournament every year.
7. Here (is, are) the puppy that I told you about.
8. There (is, are) too many cars in the driveway.

Review

Use everything you have learned so far about nouns and verbs to answer the questions.

Draw a line from the word or phrase in Column A to the word or phrase that it describes in Column B.

Column A	Column B
1. sound	Regular Verb
2. whispered.	Irregular Verb
3. should	Helping Verb
4. taught	Linking Verb

Read each sentence. If the underlined verb is in the past perfect tense, write **PP** on the line. If it is in the present perfect, write **PR**, and if it is in the future perfect, write **FP**.

6. ______ Lola had dreamed the same dream three nights last week.
7. ______ By the end of our trip, we will have visited more than ten state parks.
8. ______ Emilio has been getting his hair cut here for his entire life.
9. ______ Aaron will have made twelve new paintings at the end of this semester.
10. ______ Dr. Mohammed had thought that Mom had shingles before the examination.

Write two sentences about your favorite activities to do with friends or family. Make sure the subjects and the verbs agree.

11. ____

____

12. ____

____

In the following paragraph, there are four incorrect shifts in verb tense. Circle and correct each one you find.

13. After college, Molly plans to join the Peace Corps. She applies last year and was accepted. Mom and Dad knew how important it was to her, so they throw her a big party. It will be strange to have my big sister go so far away, and I know I missed her a lot. I am looking forward to hearing about all of her experiences in Africa. I saved all of her letters to me.

---

14. **Write a paragraph about what you did last summer and what you plan to do this summer. Be careful to use verb tenses correctly.**

Adjectives

An adjective is a word that describes a noun or pronoun. Using colorful, lively adjectives makes writing and speaking more interesting. There are two kinds of adjectives: common adjectives and proper adjectives.

Most adjectives are common adjectives and are not capitalized. They can be found before or after the noun they describe.	It was a breezy day. The day was breezy. I will wear a red shirt. My shirt is red.

Practice

Unscramble the words to reveal adjectives that might describe a butterfly.

1. e b f a u t u l i ____________________

2. r o f c l o l u ____________________

3. t e r p t y ____________________

4. g r h i t b ____________________

Write a list of eight adjectives that describe your two favorite animals.

Animal: ____________________

5. ____________________ 6. ____________________

7. ____________________ 8. ____________________

Animal: ____________________

9. ____________________ 10. ____________________

11. ____________________ 12. ____________________

Nouns and pronouns can also be described by proper adjectives.

Proper adjectives are formed from proper nouns. They are always capitalized.

The chef likes baking his pizzas in the Italian oven.

My civics class was invited to attend a Congressional hearing in Washington, D.C.

Practice

Circle only the proper adjectives in each sentence.

1. Pacific waves are often perfect for surfing.
2. It was a beautiful February day for downhill skiing.
3. A diet of double cheeseburgers and French fries is bad for your health.
4. The little children waved as the enormous plane flew over the Alaskan village.
5. She liked many types of Asian food, including Thai curry, Japanese sushi, and Chinese dumplings.

Write a paragraph about places you would like to visit. Use at least three proper adjectives.

6. ______________________________

____

____

____

____

____

Adverbs

An adverb is a word used to describe a verb, an adjective, or another adverb. An adverb can tell how, why, when, where, how often, and how much. How much?

How?	John drove carefully on the slick road.
Where?	It was a good day to stay inside.
How often?	The rain seemed like it would never stop.
How much?	The puddle completely covered the sidewalk.
When?	The weather might be better tomorrow.

Practice

Circle the letter of the sentence that contains an adverb. Remember, adverbs modify verbs, adjectives, and other adverbs.

1. a. Lisa quickly finished work so she could go to dinner.
   b. Lisa finished work so she could go to dinner.
   c. Lisa did not finish her work.

2. a. Fruit makes a delicious dessert.
   b. Fruit often makes a delicious dessert.
   c. Fruit is dessert.

3. a. You take the biggest slice of pizza.
   b. You always take the biggest slice of pizza.
   c. May I take the biggest slice of pizza?

Practice

Circle each adverb in the following paragraph. Then, underline the verb, adjective, or other adverb it describes.

The Emperor's New Clothes and *The Little Mermaid* are just a couple of the fairy tales written by a remarkably famous writer, Hans Christian Andersen. He was born poor in 1805 in Denmark. What extra money the family had they eagerly spent at the theatre. When they didn't have money for tickets, Hans would quietly sit outside the theatre actively reading the playbill. He knew he would definitely follow his love of literature and the theatre as a career. Hans went to the University of Copenhagen and became a writer. He wrote more than 150 fairy tales. They have been translated into more than 100 languages. Hans Christian Andersen remains one of the world's best known and most translated authors.

Write five sentences using adverbs.

1. ____

2. ____

3. ____

4. ____

5. ____

Conjunctions

Conjunctions are words that connect individual words or groups of words in sentences. There are three kinds of conjunctions: coordinating conjunctions, correlative conjunctions, and subordinating conjunctions.

Coordinating conjunctions connect words, phrases, or clauses using words like and, but, and or.	The snow is cold and fluffy. Chris likes soccer, but Samantha likes football.
Correlative conjunctions are used with pairs and are used together. Both/and, either/or, and neither/nor are examples of correlative conjunctions.	Either Tammy or Tara will wash the dishes.

Practice

Complete the following sentences with a conjunction or pair of conjunctions from the box.

and	**but**	**or**
both/and	**either/or**	**neither/nor**

1. Tabitha wanted to have pretzels for a snack ______________ Kisha wanted snowcones.
2. ______________ Ivan ______________ Jose wanted to tell Chang the bad news.
3. We were going to see a movie, ______________ we went out to eat instead.
4. Do you want apple pie ______________ blueberry pie?
5. We can ______________ run ______________ ride our bikes to get there on time.
6. ______________ William ______________ Esther will need to work together to complete the project.

Language Arts

Conjunctions

Subordinating conjunctions connect two clauses that are not equal. They connect dependent clauses to independent clauses.

Examples

after	as long as
since	while

In this example sentence, They ran home is the independent clause because it is a complete sentence by itself. The dependent clause is after the sun went down, because it is not a complete sentence without the independent clause.

They ran home after the sun went down.

Practice

Complete the following sentences with a conjunction from the box.

as long as	**while**	**until**
because	**after**	

1. Linda practiced jumping ________________ she could before her legs got too tired.
2. Trevor wanted to stay inside and play board games ________________ it was still raining.
3. Hugo sets the table ________________ Miranda finishes cooking.
4. We will eat dessert ________________ the main course.
5. The dog waited by the door ________________ her owner returned home.

Conjunctions

Practice

Identify the conjunctions in the following sentences as coordinate, correlative, or subordinate. Write **CD** for coordinating, **CR** for correlative, or **S** for subordinate before each sentence.

1. ______ Are we going to go biking or hiking on Saturday?
2. ______ Neither pasta nor pizza was offered on the menu.
3. ______ As long as it's raining, we may as well get our homework done.
4. ______ Either Rachel or Carrie will be voted president of the class.
5. ______ Let's walk to school since it is a sunny, warm day.
6. ______ Todd wants to play baseball this weekend, but he has a class in the morning.
7. ______ While we are waiting in line, let's get some popcorn.
8. ______ Both the girls' and the boys' teams are going to the championship.

Write four sentences of your own using conjunctions. Use two conjunctions from each category.

9. ______________________________

____

10. ______________________________

____

11. ______________________________

____

12. ______________________________

____

Interjections

An interjection is a one or two-word phrase used to express surprise or strong emotion.

Here is a list of common interjections.

ah	ouch	eh	hi
hooray!	aw	uh-uh	wow
aha	uh	hey	huh
oh	uh-huh	well	yeah

Practice

Underline the interjection in each sentence.

1. Ouch! I hate when that happens.
2. Oh! That's why your phone was in the refrigerator.
3. Aw, this little baby is as cute as a button.
4. Hey, how are you doing?
5. Wow! This is a good book.
6. Aha! I've found the answer.
7. Will I go to the store with you? Yeah, sure.
8. Uh, I don't know how to fix this.
9. Hurray! Our team finally won a game.
10. Uh-uh, that's the wrong answer.

Interjections

Interjections can be used with exclamation marks, commas, or question marks.

An exclamation mark is usually used after an interjection to separate it from the rest of the sentence.	Oh! I'm so happy that you can make the trip.
If the feeling isn't quite as strong, a comma is used in place of the exclamation mark.	Oh, it's too bad he won't be joining us.
Sometimes question marks are used as an interjection's punctuation.	Eh? Is that really true?

Practice

Use each interjection in a sentence.

1. aha

 ____

2. hey

 ____

3. oh

 ____

4. huh

 ____

5. ah

 ____

Language Arts

Prepositions

A preposition is a word or groups of words that shows the relationship between a noun or pronoun (the object of the sentence) and another word in the sentence.

In this sentence, across is the preposition, and street is the object of the preposition.	The students walked across the street.
In this sentence, through is the preposition, and yard is the object of the preposition.	The dog ran through the yard.

Here is a list of common prepositions.

above	away	beside	for	off	under
across	because	between	from	on	until
after	before	by	in	outside	up
along	behind	down	inside	over	with
around	below	during	into	to	within
at	beneath	except	near	toward	without

Practice

Underline the preposition in each sentence. Circle each object.

1. Many planets revolve around the sun.
2. Our planet has one moon in orbit.
3. The moon orbits near Earth.
4. The Phoenix landed on Mars.
5. Sometimes, you can see Venus at night.
6. Jupiter is the largest planet in the solar system.

Language Arts

Prepositions

A prepositional phrase includes a preposition and the object that follows. It can also include adjectives or adverbs that modify the object. Prepositional phrases often tell when or where something is happening.

The prepositional phrase in this sentence includes the preposition beneath, the object the waves, and the modifier frothing.	The ship sank beneath the frothing waves.
The prepositional phrase in this sentence includes the preposition around, the object the room, and the modifiers crowded and noisy.	The dancers whirled around the crowded, noisy room.

Practice

Write a journal entry about what you did yesterday. Use at least five prepositional phrases. After you have written your entry, underline all of the prepositional phrases you used.

Practice

Identify the preposition, object, and modifier in each of the following sentences. Write **P** above the preposition, **O** above the object, and **M** above the modifier.

1. The students played outside at the late recess.
2. The horse jumped over the high fence.
3. Alice walked out of the scary movie.
4. Timmy looked down the deep well.
5. The paper fell underneath the small bookcase.
6. The salad greens were piled high in the chilled bowl.
7. He parked his bike beside my shiny new car.
8. Want to hike up that steep hill?
9. It's cold, so I'm going to put two blankets on my bed.
10. He pointed the flashlight toward the dark stairway.

Articles

An article is a specific word that serves as an adjective before a noun. A, an, and the are articles. There are two types of articles: definite and indefinite articles.

The is a definite article. This means it names a specific noun.

The article the shows that the person wants to go to a specific park.	I want to go to the park where everyone else went.

A and an are indefinite articles. They do not name a specific noun.

The article a shows that the person wants to go to any park, and it doesn't matter which one.	I would like to go to a park this weekend.
a dress a book bag a one-way street	Use a when the noun it precedes begins with a consonant or a consonant sound.
an eyebrow an honest person	Use an when the noun it precedes begins with a vowel or a vowel sound.

Practice

Circle the correct article.

1. She got (the, an) A on the test.
2. I'll order (the, a) same sandwich he ordered.
3. Austin gave me (a, an) extra pencil.
4. Make a right turn here at (the, a) traffic light.
5. Jessie poured herself (the, a) glass of milk.
6. I bought this toy for only (a, an) dollar.

Practice

Match the object in each set with the article that goes with it. Draw a line from Column A to the correct article in Column B. In Column C, write the article and noun together.

Column A	Column B	Column C
nonspecific play	a	__________
specific play	an	__________
nonspecific envelope	the	__________

Column A	Column B	Column C
specific beach	a	__________
nonspecific beach	an	__________
nonspecific art piece	the	__________

Column A	Column B	Column C
nonspecific hero	a	__________
nonspecific umbrella	an	__________
specific umbrella	the	__________

Review

Use everything you have learned so far about adjectiives, adverbs, conjunctions, prepostions interjections and articles to answer the questions.

Read each sentence below. When you see **(adj.)**, fill in the blank with an adjective. When you see **(adv.)**, fill in the blank with an adverb.

1. The twins (adv.) ____________________ crept up the stairs.
2. As the children watched, the (adj.) ____________________ panda sat down to munch on a stalk of bamboo.
3. Isaiah took a sip of the (adj.) ____________________ soup.
4. The crowd cheered (adv.) ____________________ in the stands.
5. Clementine plucked (adj.) ____________________ apples from the trees in the orchard.
6. Both my brothers (adv.) ____________________ agreed to clean their room in exchange for their allowances.
7. The (adj.) ____________________ waves soothed Jack's sunburn.
8. Make sure you drive (adv.) ____________________ on the frozen roads!

In each sentence, circle the preposition or prepositions. Underline the object of each preposition.

9. Can you imagine living in the Arctic and hunting for mussels under a layer of ice?
10. At low tide, an Inuit might carve a hole in the ocean ice.
11. He can walk along the ocean floor.
12. A thick layer of ice lies above his head.

Language Arts

Circle the conjunction in each sentence. On the line, write whether it is a coordinate, correlative, or subordinate conjunction.

13. The dragonfly and the bumblebee circled the flower. ________________

14. Both Chestnut and Blaze like to spend the day in the pasture. ________________

15. While her mom is at the library, Minh will play at the park. ________________

16. Irina wants to go to the play, but Ivan hopes to see a movie. ________________

17. Neither Eddie nor Dante has been sick at all this summer. ________________

18. Since Tasha has moved to Oregon, I have not had a best friend.

____

---

19. **Write the part of speech above the words in bold. Write ADJ for adjectives, ADV for adverbs, CONJ for conjunctions, INT for interjections, PREP for prepositions, and ART for articles.**

Hooray! Happy Birthday!

In ancient Rome, they celebrated **the** birthdays **of** their **favorite** gods **and** **important** people, like **the** emperor. **In** Britain, they celebrate **the Queen's** birthday. **In** **the** United States, **the** birthdays **of** presidents **and important** leaders, like Martin Luther King, Jr., are celebrated. **In** Japan, Korea, **and** China, the **sixtieth** birthday marks **a** transition **from an active** life **to** one **of** contemplation. **Many Eastern** cultures don't even recognize **the actual** date **of** birth. When **the first** moon **of the new** year arrives, everyone is **one year** older.

Chapter Review

Write the correct words from the box to complete this excerpt from Elena's journal. Use only proper nouns.

national park	Mount Rushmore	Pierce School
school	South Dakota	states

My family is planning a trip to (1.) ________________________. We will drive through the state of (2.) ________________________ to get there. On Monday the 17th, it's back to (3.) ________________________.

Give an example for each of the rules below about regular and irregular plural nouns.

4. Rule: Nouns ending in the letters **s**, **x**, or **z**, or in a **ch** or **sh** sound, add **es**.

   Example: ____

5. Rule: If a word ends in the letter **y**, then the **y** is changed to an **i** before adding the **es**.

   Example: ____

Rewrite the following sentences. Replace the underlined subject and object nouns with the correct subject and object pronouns.

6. <u>My cousin and I</u> wanted to go the movies. Dad drove <u>my cousin and me</u>.

   ____

7. <u>Cathy and Marie</u> won the game. The trophy goes to <u>Cathy and Marie</u>.

   ____

Circle the correct pronoun for each sentence.

8. Janice tutored Renata in (its, her) grammar skills.

9. Renata tutored the twins in (his, their) math skills.

Chapter Review

Use a present-tense or past-tense verb to complete each sentence below.

10. The spectators ________________ and cheered many times during the game.

11. Carl ________________ waffles for breakfast.

Circle the letter of the sentence that contains a helping verb.

12. a. Cheryl accepted only the best.
    b. Cheryl would accept nothing less.

13. a. I will think about it.
    b. I think you are correct.

Circle the linking verb and underline the noun or adjective that is linked to the subject.

14. Carrion flowers smell like rotten meat.

15. Sharon's voice sounds fantastic tonight.

Read each sentence. On the line, write the boldface verb in the past, present, or future perfect tense. The words in parentheses will tell you which tense to use.

16. Tara **learn** to play the guitar. (present perfect) ________________

17. She **want** to start her own band. (past perfect) ________________

18. After next week, Tara play her first show! (future perfect)) ________________

Complete each sentence below with the word in parentheses. Make sure that the verb tense you choose is consistent with the rest of the sentence.

19. Amber pounded her drums, and Ben ________________ his electric bass. (pound)

20. After Tara plugged in her guitar, the band ________________ to practice a new song. (start)

Language Arts

Chapter Review

Add an adjective that describes each noun in bold.

21. Candice and Danny were twins and wanted a ________________ **pet** for their birthday.

22. Their mother said, "Pets are a ________________ **responsibility**. Are you ready for this?"

Circle the adverb in each sentence.

23. My dog happily gobbled its dinner.

24. Let's go inside and play a board game.

Circle the conjunctions in the following sentences. On the line, write whether the conjunction is coordinate, correlative, or subordinate.

25. Do you want tomatoes or pickles on your sandwich? ________________

26. We carried umbrellas because it was a soggy, cloudy day.

    ____

27. Neither dogs nor cats are allowed in the building. ________________

Underline the interjection in each sentence.

28. Well, we are learning about Egyptian pyramids.

29. Wow! The first pyramid was built in 2780 BC.

Identify the preposition, object, and modifier in each of the following sentences. Write P above the preposition, O above the object, and M above the modifier.

30. We ducked under the low-hanging branches.

31. The hikers made their way up the steep mountain trail.

Declarative Sentences

A declarative sentence is a sentence that makes a statement.

Declarative sentences say something about a place, person, thing, or idea. When punctuating a declarative sentence, use a period at the end of the sentence.

Richard Pough was the founder of The Nature Conservancy.

Salad is my favorite food.

Practice

Write a dialogue between two people. Write 10 declarative sentences they say about a place they are visiting. Be sure to use periods when you are making writing declarative sentences.

Language Arts

Language Arts

Interrogative Sentences

An interrogative sentence is a sentence that asks a question.

When punctuating an interrogative sentence, use a question mark.

Was that lightning in the sky?

Do you like sunflower seeds in on your salad?

Practice

A farmer is taking a student on a tour of her garden. The student has many questions. The farmer's answers are given below, but the student's questions are missing. Write the question with the appropriate punctuation in the space provided.

Example: How many vegetables do you grow?	I grow almost 30 varieties of vegetables!
1. ______________________	Garlic is my biggest crop.
2. ______________________	My favorite is Delicata squash.
3. ______________________	To become a farmer, you should study science and math, read a lot, and do farming apprenticeships.
4. ______________________	I sell my vegetables at a roadside stand and at farmers markets around the region.
5. ______________________	I grew up on a farm, so I've been doing this my whole life.

Exclamatory Sentences

An exclamatory sentence expresses urgency, surprise, or strong emotion.

When punctuating an exclamatory sentence, use an exclamation mark.

I can't believe you ate the whole pie!

I think I smell a skunk!

Practice

Identify which sentences are exclamatory by putting an exclamation mark at the end of the sentence. If the sentence is not exclamatory, do not add any punctuation.

1. Watch out for the ice
2. Ouch! I can't believe I stubbed my toe on the table again
3. Where are you having dinner tonight
4. The storm is quickly coming our way
5. I'm not sure if I want to go to the movies or not
6. It is so cold that I think I have frostbite
7. Don't you like the cold weather
8. Ah! The sunset is gorgeous
9. You're it
10. Oh no! The bridge is out
11. What time is it
12. Oranges are my favorite fruit
13. Watch out! The oranges fell off the display
14. The *Lord of the Rings* is my favorite series of books
15. That author really inspires me

Imperative Sentences

An imperative sentence makes an order or a demand. It is often written in the present tense. The subjects of imperative sentences are usually not expressed, because it is usually understood that the subject is you.

Look at the rabbit behind the trees.	(You look at the rabbit behind the trees.)
Write the note here.	(You write the note here.)
Throw me the ball!	(You throw me the ball!)

Practice

Choose a verb from the box to complete each imperative sentence. Remember, the subject *you* is implied in the sentences.

carry	drive	pick	swing	vote
drink	pass	shoot	throw	yell

1. ____________________ for Simon for president!
2. ____________________ the potatoes, please.
3. ____________________ up the paper from the floor.
4. ____________________ that bag for your aunt.
5. ____________________ the ball to second base!
6. ____________________ slowly when on ice.
7. ____________________ the racket higher.
8. ____________________ the cheers louder!
9. ____________________ all of your tomato juice.
10. ____________________ the basketball through the hoop!

Language Arts

Review

Use everything you have learned so far about sentences to answer the questions.

On each line, write whether the sentence is declarative, interrogative, exclamatory, or imperative.

1. Walk up the steps and then turn left. ____________________
2. Anne took a risk and accepted the new job. ____________________
3. Was that statue priceless? ____________________
4. Our team won the game in the final two seconds! ____________________
5. San Diego has a very temperate climate. ____________________
6. Carry that bag for your aunt. ____________________
7. It is so cold that I think I have frostbite! ____________________
8. Did the poem inspire your artwork? ____________________
9. Ouch, I bumped my elbow again! ____________________
10. Are those chestnuts I smell roasting? ____________________
11. Oh goodness, the sunset is gorgeous! ____________________
12. Walk slowly across the ice. ____________________
13. Where are you going after school? ____________________
14. If you order pizza, make sure to get onions. ____________________
15. I can't wait to meet my favorite author! ____________________
16. Wear your helmet when you ride your bike. ____________________

Language Arts

Simple Sentences

A simple sentence is a sentence with one independent clause. A simple sentence does not have any dependent clauses.

An independent clause is a complete thought that can stand alone as a sentence.	Chantal brushed her teeth.
A dependent clause is not a complete thought and cannot stand alone as a sentence.	after washing her face

Practice

The following sentences contain both independent and dependent clauses. Rewrite each of the following sentences as two simple sentences.

Example:
Sarah wanted to go swimming, but it rained.

Sarah wanted to go swimming. It rained.

1. The car broke down, so I took a taxi.

____

2. The boy started a new painting while his first painting was drying.

____

3. The baby cried because she was hungry.

____

4. I watered the plant after it wilted.

____

Simple Sentences

Simple subjects can take different forms.

Simple sentences can have one or more **subjects**.	The **costumes** glittered. The **costumes** and the **jewelry** glittered.
Simple sentences can have one or more **verbs** or **verb phrases**.	The costumes **glittered**. The costumes **glittered** and **sparkled**.
Simple sentences can have more than one **subject** and more than one **verb** or **verb phrase**.	The **costumes** and the **jewelry** **glittered** and **sparkled**.

Practice

Underline the subjects and circle the verbs or verb phrases in the following simple sentences.

1. Elsa liked baking cookies and liked cooking spaghetti.
2. Elsa and her grandmother liked baking and liked cooking together.
3. Tanya liked eating her grandmother's cookies.
4. Grandma liked eating Tanya's spaghetti.
5. Aaron washed and dried the dishes.
6. My brother and I walked and fed the dog.
7. Fire trucks and ambulances surrounded the burning building.
8. The firefighters saved our lives.

Language Arts

Compound Sentences

A compound sentence is a sentence with two or more independent clauses joined by a coordinate conjunction, punctuation, or both. Compound sentences express more than one complete thought.

A compound sentence can be two simple sentences joined by a comma and a coordinate conjunction.	The costumes glittered, but the jewelry was dull.
A compound sentence can also be two simple sentences joined by a semicolon.	The costumes glittered; the jewelry was dull.

Practice

Match simple sentences in Column A with simple sentences in Column B to create compound sentences. Add either a comma with a coordinate conjunction or a semicolon.

	Column A	Column B
1.	The seats were bad. ___________	The snack bar line was long.
2.	The actors were funny. ___________	We can stay late.
3.	The intermission was short. ___________	The show was good.
4.	The ushers were nice. ___________	The ticket takers were rude.
5.	We can leave early. ___________	The orchestra played well.
6.	The theater lights were low. ___________	The actors were serious.
7.	The audience laughed. ___________	The audience applauded.
8.	The actors' voices were loud. ___________	The seats were sold out.
9.	The play had good reviews. ___________	The music was soft.
10.	The actors bowed. ___________	The stage lights were bright.

Practice

Combine each pair of simple sentences into a compound sentence.

1. Rashad likes apples. Jenna likes pears.

   ____

2. Jenna likes skating. Rashad likes running.

   ____

3. Rashad likes dancing. Jenna likes singing.

   ____

4. Jenna likes summer. Rashad likes winter.

   ____

5. Rashad likes math. Jenna likes science.

   ____

Continue to write about what Rashad and Jenna each like and don't like. Write two more sentences for each character. Then, combine the sentences to form compound sentences.

Rashad

____

____

Jenna

____

____

Compound Sentences

____

____

Complex Sentences

A complex sentence has one independent clause and one or more dependent clauses joined together. It expresses more than one complete thought.

Remember, a dependent clause does not express a complete thought and cannot stand alone as a sentence. The dependent clause can be anywhere in the sentence.

While he waited for the train, Skylar listened to the street musician sing the blues.

Practice

Circle the letter of the sentence that best answers each question.

1. Which of the following sentences contains two **simple** sentences?
   - **a.** He is wearing his baseball uniform. He is holding his baseball bat.
   - **b.** He is wearing his baseball uniform and holding his baseball bat.
   - **c.** He is wearing his baseball uniform, although the game was cancelled.

2. Which of the following sentences contains a **compound** sentence?
   - **a.** She is eating a salad. She is drinking lemonade.
   - **b.** She is eating a salad, and she is drinking lemonade.
   - **c.** She is drinking lemonade since she is thirsty.

3. Which of the following sentences contains a **complex** sentence?
   - **a.** Mary went jogging. Rose went jogging.
   - **b.** Mary and Rose went jogging.
   - **c.** Before breakfast, Mary and Rose went jogging.

Language Arts

Complex Sentences

In a complex sentence, the independent clause and dependent clause are connected with a subordinate conjunction or a relative pronoun.

Common subordinate conjunctions

after	although	as
because	before	if
since	when	where
while	until	unless

Ashton's grades have improved since he got a math tutor.

Relative pronouns

who whose which that

Ashton is tutored by Mr. Addy, who is a math teacher.

Practice

Write a paragraph about an event at your school using compound and complex sentences. Include at least two complex and two compound sentences.

____

____

____

____

____

____

____

____

____

____

____

____

____

Language Arts

Combining Sentences

Combining sentences that are short and choppy makes text easier to read. It also creates sentence variety, which makes writing more interesting.

Compound subjects and compound verbs	Combined
Brad went on a hiking trip. **C.J.** went on a hiking trip.	**Brad** and **C.J.** went on a hiking trip.
We **hiked** on our long weekend away. We **biked** on our long weekend away.	We **hiked** and **biked** on our long weekend away.
Adjectives and nouns I ate an **orange** for breakfast. The orange was sweet.	I ate a sweet **orange** for breakfast.
Adverbs and verbs Abby walked through the foggy forest. Abby walked **slowly**.	Abby walked **slowly** through the foggy forest.
Subordinate conjunctions The class is going on a camping trip. The class is going on the trip **unless** it rains.	The class is going on a camping trip **unless** it rains.

Combining Sentences

Practice

Rewrite these simple sentences as compound or complex sentences.

1. Rachel went to the carnival on Saturday. Dan went to the carnival on Saturday.

   ____

2. The popcorn crackled as it popped. The popcorn snapped as it popped.

   ____

3. Nancy investigated the old trunk. The trunk was brown.

   ____

4. Carson excitedly spoke about his journey. Carson loudly spoke about his journey.

   ____

5. We can stop for breakfast. We can stop if we do it quickly.

   ____

6. My ice cream melted. My ice cream fell off the cone.

   ____

7. We are going to see a movie. We are going soon.

   ____

8. Let's play football in the backyard. Let's play football until it rains.

   ____

9. I saw a spider crawl under the couch. The spider was furry.

   ____

Sentence Fragments

A sentence fragment is not a complete sentence. It is a group of words that is missing either a subject, a predicate, or both. A sentence fragment is also a group of words that does not express a complete thought, as in a dependent clause.

Sentence fragment	Complete sentence
Takes a walk every day at lunch. (no subject)	Sandy takes a walk every day at lunch.
A walk every day at lunch. (no subject and no verb)	Sandy takes a walk every day at lunch.
Because the line was so long. (not a complete thought)	We went to a different restaurant because the line was so long.

Practice

When is your birthday? Write five complete sentences about the month of your birth. Make sure all of your sentences are complete. They should each have a subject and a verb, and should express complete thoughts. Once you have completed your sentences, circle the subjects and underline the predicates.

1. ____________________________

2. ____________________________

3. ____________________________

4. ____________________________

5. ____________________________

6. ____________________________

Sentence Fragments

Language Arts

Practice

The sentences in Column A are sentence fragments. Choose a group of words from Column B that will complete each sentence and make it whole. Write the new sentences on the line.

	Column A	Column B
1.	is the twelfth month of the year.	December has two birthstones,
2.	Until 46 B.C.,	December
3.	Several European countries	Orville Wright made the first heavier-than-air flight at Kitty Hawk, North Carolina,
4.	turquoise and zircon.	
5.	on December 17, 1903.	celebrate December 6th as the Feast of Saint Nicholas.
		December had only 29 days.

1. ____

2. ____

3. ____

4. ____

5. ____

Review

Use everything you have learned so far about sentences to answer the questions.

After each sentence, write whether it is a simple sentence, a compound sentence, a complex sentence, or a sentence fragment. If the sentences are simple sentences or sentence fragments, rewrite them as compound or complex.

1. Edward and Cynthia wrapped and delivered the presents. ____________________

____

2. Although it was a sunny day, ____________________

____

3. The coach challenged her team. The coach inspired her team. ____________________

____

4. Grill the peaches until they are slightly brown. ____________________

____

5. The ocean was blue. The ocean was warm. ____________________

____

6. After the hike, ____________________

____

7. Our parents cheered for us. Our parents danced after every goal.

____

____

8. Whether or not you go, ____________________

____

Language Arts

On each line, write whether the sentence is declarative, interrogative, exclamatory, or imperative.

1. Walk up the steps and then turn left. ____________________
2. The weather is fantastic! ____________________
3. Three bridges cross the Grand Canal. ____________________
4. Did your dad make chicken and rice for dinner last night? ____________________
5. What a beautiful bridge that is! ____________________
6. How warm does it get in Venice in the summer? ____________________

On each line, write whether the sentence is simple, compound, or complex.

7. She jogged through the mist. ____________________
8. The chefs cooked and baked in the competition. ____________________
9. After dinner, I'm going for a walk. ____________________
10. Farm Sanctuary rescues and protects farm animals. ____________________
11. Mr. Baum, who is also the baseball coach, is my favorite teacher. ____________________
12. He didn't think he was a fan of Shakespeare, yet he enjoyed the play. ____________________
13. You can go to the movies if you finish your homework. ____________________
14. Before the party, she will pick up Maria. ____________________
15. Mike, who loved animals, was learning about moose and caribou at school. ____________________

Chapter Review

16. **Rewrite the paragraph by combining simple sentences and correcting sentence fragments.**

Recycling is important to our environment. It is important for many reasons. Recycling saves trees. If we recycle the paper products we use. Fewer trees will have to be cut down. It also protects our natural habitats. When we cut down trees, birds and squirrels lose their homes. Rabbits and many other forest animals lose their homes. Recycling greatly reduces our need for landfills. If we recycle what would be trash. There will be less garbage to put into the landfills. It also reduces curbside pollution. Less garbage means less trash on our streets. Less garbage means less pollution on our streets. These are excellent reasons why we should encourage our friends to recycle. These are excellent reasons why we should encourage our families to recycle. We should all be committed to a recycling program.

Draw a line to match the sentences on the left with the type of combined sentences they are on the right.

17. So that the birthday party remains a surprise, we must get there on time.
18. Helen and Tammy brought sweaters as presents.
19. Helen brought a purple, knit sweater.

compound subjects

combining adjectives

complex sentence

Choose a sentence fragment from the box to complete each sentence.

It was presented
Construction began
is "Liberty Enlightening the World."
stands on Liberty Island in the New York Harbor.

20. The Statue of Liberty ____________________ (look for a verb phrase)

21. ____________________ in France in 1875. (look for a subject and a verb)

22. ____________________ to the United States on July 4, 1884. (look for a subject and verb)

23. The official name of the Statue of Liberty____________________. (look for a verb phrase)

Capitalizing Proper Nouns

Proper nouns are specific people, places, and things. They always begin with a capital letter.

Capitalize names of cities.	Anchorage, Los Angeles, Detroit, Kona, Columbus, New York
Capitalize names of states.	Maine, Florida, Ohio, Alaska, Hawaii, Michigan
Capitalize names of countries.	United States, Brazil, Senegal, Japan, Israel, Denmark

---

Practice

Circle the correct answer that completes each of the following sentences .

1. California is the most populated (State, state) in the United States.
2. The least populated state in the United States is (Wyoming, wyoming).
3. China is the most populated (Country, country).
4. Australia is the only continent that is its own (Country, country).
5. The capital of California is (Sacramento, sacramento).
6. This (City, city) has a population of approximately 485,000.
7. (Los Angeles, los Angeles), has the largest population in California.
8. The city in the United States with the largest population is (New York, new york).
9. The (City, city) of New York has a population of approximately 22 million.
10. The capital city of the state of (New York, new york) is Albany.
11. Albany, (New York, new york) has a population of approximately 98,500.

Capitalizing Proper Nouns

Proper nouns include the days of the week and the months of the year. They always begin with a capital letter.

Capitalize days of the week.	Sunday, Monday, Tuesday, Wednesday, Thursday, Friday, Saturday
Capitalize days of the year.	January, February, March, April, May, June, July, August, September, October, November, December

---

Practice

Complete the following sentences by writing the correct month of the year on the line. Remember to capitalize the month when you write it in. Use an encyclopedia or the Internet if you need help.

1. The chrysanthemum is the flower for ________________, the eleventh month of the year.
2. The United States celebrates Independence Day on ________________ 4th.
3. ________________ is the shortest month of the year.
4. In the Northern Hemisphere, summer begins in the month of ________________.
5. ________________ was named for the Roman emperor, Augustus.
6. Fools come out to play on this ________________ day.
7. The month of ________________ was named for the Roman god, Janus.
8. Cinco de Mayo is a holiday celebrated in Mexico on the fifth day of

   ________________.
9. The sapphire is the birthstone for ________________.
10. Farmers start to bring in their crops, including pumpkins, in the month of

    ________________.

Capitalizing Proper Nouns

The names of specific streets, places, and people are proper nouns and are capitalized.

Capitalize the names of specific streets.	Blue Street, Ohio Avenue, Wind Boulevard
Nonspecific words like **street** and **road** are not capitalized.	I live one street over from you.
Capitalize the names of specific places.	Rocky Mountain National Park
Capitalize first and last names of people, including special titles, initials, and abbreviations that go with the names.	President Barack Obama
Do not capitalize nonspecific street names, places, or titles.	My best friend is our class president.

Practice

Circle the proper nouns.

1. Our neighbors stayed at Water's Edge Hotel near the beach.
2. Cross the highway and then turn right on Riverbend Drive.
3. The veterinarian, Dr. Green, vaccinated all of the dogs in town.
4. Her soccer practices are at Barry Field.
5. Hawaii Volcanoes National Park is located on the island Hawaii.
6. Karl lives on Lane Road.

Capitalizing Proper Nouns

Correct the mistakes in the use of capitalization with proper nouns. Use the proofreading marks explained in the box to the right.

≡ capitalize a letter
/ lowercase a letter

Do you believe in haunted houses? How about haunted hotels? Granville, Ohio, is home to the buxton inn. The buxton inn, located on broadway street, has a haunting reputation. The Hotel was built in 1812 by orrin granger, founder of the City of Granville. The Hotel was named after major buxton, who ran the inn from 1865 to 1905. So whose ghosts have supposedly appeared in this Inn? orrin granger was first seen in the 1920s eating a piece of pie in the kitchen. major buxton has been seen by Guests, mostly in the Dining Room. The ghosts of other Owners have also been spotted. Even a kitty of days gone by has been seen roaming throughout the buxton inn. Of course the ghost cat now has a name—Major Buxton.

Write a short autobiography. Write about the city where you were born, the name of the first street where you lived, your parents' and siblings' names, and the name of your first school and your first teacher. Write about a few of your favorite memories growing up. Make sure that all of the proper nouns in your autobiography are capitalized.

Capitalizing Proper Nouns

Language Arts

Words like **mother, father, aunt,** and **uncle** can be used as proper nouns or common nouns. When they are used as proper nouns, they should be capitalized.

Mother and Father can be used in place of names. If they are, capitalize them.	Dear Mother, where did I leave my jacket?
In the following instance, father is not used as a replacement of a name.	My father took me to the hockey game.
This is also true for the words **aunt, uncle, grandmother,** and **grandfather**.	This saxophone belongs to Uncle Ali. My aunt likes to hike in the mountains.
Official names, such as those of businesses and their products, are capitalized.	Papa's Pizza (business name)
Nonspecific names of products are not capitalized, even if they follow the business or product name.	I like Papa's Pizza's pizza. (business name followed by product name)

Practice

Circle the letter that matches each description.

1. the word *mother* not used to replace a name
   - a. Mother, please pass the beans.
   - b. My mother was the pitcher on her softball team.
2. the word *grandfather* used as a name
   - a. Grandfather Clarence was a veterinarian.
   - b. My grandfather is a good cook.
3. official business name followed by product type
   - a. Oat Crisps cereal
   - b. Oat Crisps

Capitalizing Proper Nouns

Titles are proper nouns and are capitalized.

Always capitalize the first and last words of titles.	*Watership Down*
Don't capitalize articles (**a**, **an**, **the**), short prepositions (**in**, **of**, **at**), or short conjunctions (**and**, **but**) except when they are the first word in the title.	*The Lord of the Rings*
Capitalize school subjects only if they name a specific course.	She is taking Nanotechnology 101 in college.
Do not capitalize the names of general subjects.	I am studying physics.
Exception: Language subjects are all proper nouns, so they should all be capitalized.	I am doing my homework for Spanish.
Titles of long works are underlined or italicized in text.	book: *Walk Two Moons* magazine: *National Geographic* movie: *The Lightning Thief*
Titles of most short works are put in quotation marks, not underlined.	poem: "Jabberwocky" short story: "The Tortoise and the Hare" article: "Being Jane Goodall"

Capitalizing Proper Nouns

Practice

Circle the correct answer that completes each of the following sentences.

1. I read (*Island of the Blue Dolphins, Island of The Blue Dolphins*) this summer.
2. I like doing the crossword puzzle in the (*Chicago tribune, Chicago Tribune*).
3. My favorite song is ("Wagon Wheel", "wagon wheel").
4. Have you ever seen (*night At the museum, Night at the Museum*)?
5. I have gym class after (spanish, Spanish).
6. Mr. Howard is the best (history, History) teacher.
7. Mr. Selhi teaches a course called (Introduction to Geometry, introduction to geometry).
8. Can I walk with you to (Math, math) class?
9. My sister is studying (American poetry, american poetry) in college.
10. The poem ("Dawn", "dawn") by Paul Lawrence Dunbar is one of Dylan's favorites.

Write the titles of your favorites below. Don't forget to capitalize when necessary and underline or use quotes correctly.

1. book ______________________________
2. movie ______________________________
3. song ______________________________
4. magazine ______________________________

Capitalizing Sentences

Here are the rules for capitalizing sentences and quotations.

The first word of every sentence is capitalized.	**Build** the parfait by sprinkling the berries on the yogurt.
The first word in a direct quotation is capitalized. (Quotation marks are placed before and after the exact words.)	Our teacher said, **"Please go to the board and write your answer."**
Indirect quotations are not capitalized. An indirect quotation does not use the speaker's exact words or use quotation marks.	The coach said he wanted to have practice three nights a week.
If a **quotation is split and the second half continues**, do not capitalize the second half.	**"I think my puppy is the cutest,"** said the boy, **"and the best trained."**
If a new sentence begins after a split, then capitalize it as you would with any sentence.	**"We went to the shelter to find a kitten,"** said Candy. **"We** got one!"

Practice

One of the sentences in each of the following pairs is not capitalized correctly. Write **X** on the line before the sentence that is capitalized correctly.

1. _____ "Check out the exercise room," said Maria. "It has everything we use."

   _____ "Check out the exercise room," said Maria. "it has everything we use."

2. _____ The agent John said that The pool will open in the spring.

   _____ The agent John said that the pool will open in the spring.

3. _____ "Rob," said Regina, "the view is fantastic!"

   _____ "Rob," said Regina, "The view is fantastic!"

Language Arts

Capitalizing Sentences

Language Arts

Practice

Use the proofreading marks to correct the mistakes in capitalization.

≡ capitalize a letter
/ lowercase a letter

1. "Hey, Mom!" hollered Matt. "guess what I learned about in school today?"
2. Matt knew his mother wouldn't guess. he pulled a picture out of his backpack.
3. "Here it is, Mom," said Matt. "it's a snot otter!"
4. "Oh my," exclaimed his mom, "What exactly is a snot otter?"
5. "I knew you would ask," Matt gleefully replied. "snot otters are a type of salamander."
6. "they live in cool, fast-moving streams with big rocks. But their habitats are declining."
7. "That is sad," replied Matt's mother. "why are they in danger?"
8. "Water pollution and sediment build-up in streams are a couple of reasons," answered Matt. "if you find a snot otter, you should put it back in the stream. They are not pets."
9. "well, I'm glad to hear that," Matt's mom said, smiling.

Capitalizing Personal Letters

A personal letter has five parts: the heading, salutation, body, closing, and signature.

The heading has the letter writer's address and the date that it was written. The street, city, state, and month are capitalized.	3126 Milly Dr. Marblehead, MI 20000 October 5, 2016
The salutation is the greeting. Dear and the recipient's name are capitalized. Place a comma after the name.	Dear Eddy,
The body is the main part of the letter and is capitalized in the standard way.	How are you? Mother and Alva are in Denmark visiting Grandma!
The closing can be written many ways. Only the first word is capitalized. Place a comma after the closing.	With love, All the best,
The signature is usually only your first name. It is always capitalized.	Adel

Language Arts

Capitalizing Personal Letters

Practice

Proofread the following personal letter. Make all of the necessary capitalization corrections.

≡ capitalize a letter
/ lowercase a letter

5711 eastwind loop
anchorage, AK 20000
february 26, 2016

dear aunt Linda,

How have you been? I've been great. school is going very well this year. I really like social studies and english. However, I've had a little trouble with math. my best friend is helping me with that.

I'm playing on the junior varsity basketball team. I love it. I think I will try out for the track team this spring.

I can't wait to see you on your next visit. Please tell uncle Ray that I said hello.

With Love,
Kay

Use everything you have learned so far about capitalization to proofread the following personal letter. Make all of the necessary capitalization corrections.

≡ capitalize a letter
/ lowercase a letter

4064 palm tree lane
oakdale, FL 20000
March 19, 2016

dear Perry,

How do you like anaheim, California, and your new school? things are about the same here. I'm getting ready for baseball season. Our first game is next thursday. coach Washington says That I can start as pitcher.

The basketball team won the division, but we didn't get very far in state. I think the baseball team will do well. we already have a sponsor for the team. Fast Feet Sporting Goods has already signed on. I like Fast Feet Shoes, but I'm still going to buy my gloves from your Uncle's store.

My family is going on vacation this summer. We're going to chicago, illinois. My Grandpa and Grandma are going too. We are going to visit aunt Christina. We're also going to navy pier and the sears tower. Did you know that the Sears Tower used to be the tallest Building in the world?

Are you trying out for the track team this year? Aren't tryouts in march? I hope you get to come back to visit soon. maybe we can meet somewhere in the middle next winter break? Write when you can.

your Friend,
Denny

Periods

A period is placed at the end of different kinds of sentences.

Place a period at the end of a declarative sentence.	They left for their trip on Friday.
Place a period at the end of an imperative sentence when the statement is not urgent.	Take this coffee to your father, please.

Practice

Add the correct punctuation mark in each sentence.

1. Diedre lives in the house on the right _____
2. I'm so excited to visit her this weekend _____
3. Look at the bright plants her mom planted _____
4. Lilac bushes were growing under the window _____
5. Have you ever been here before _____

Write two declarative sentences and two imperative sentences. Make sure to use periods at the end of each sentence.

6. ______________________________
7. ______________________________
8. ______________________________
9. ______________________________

Periods

A period is placed at the end of a direct-quotation sentence when it is declarative or imperative.

The period usually goes inside the final quotation mark.	Lori said, "I'll give the ticket to the agent."
In direct-quotation sentences when the quote comes at the beginning of the sentence, use a comma at the end of the direct quotation instead of a period.	"I'll give the ticket to the agent," said Lori.

Practice

Rewrite the following sentences by adding punctuation marks where necessary.

1. "Richard and I are going to plant the field tomorrow" Martha said

   ____

2. Martha added "We are going to plant oats to the left here"

   ____

Interview a friend about his or her pet (real or imaginary). Then, write a paragraph about it. Be sure to include direct quotations that are punctuated correctly.

____

____

____

____

____

____

____

Periods

Periods are also used in abbreviations, initials, and titles before names.

Use a period after each part of an abbreviation. Do not leave a space between the period and the following letter.	B.C. A.D. P.M.
Use a period after each letter of an initial.	J.R.R. Tolkien
Use a period with abbreviated titles before names.	Dr. Ms.
Do not use periods if the abbreviation is an acronym. Acronyms are words formed from the first letters of words in a phrase.	ASAP (as soon as possible)

Practice

The following people were either misidentified or are not pleased with how their names appeared in a recent magazine article. Rewrite them as they request.

1. Donna Kay Dell — "I prefer my middle name to be an initial."

   ____

2. Melissa Sarah Oliver — "I prefer first and middle initials."

   ____

3. M. L. Roberts — "I am a doctor."

   ____

Practice

Draw a line to match the following abbreviations, titles, and acronyms in Column A with their meanings in Column B.

Column A	Column B
1. P.O.	Public Broadcasting System
2. PBS	Also Known As
3. Mr.	Post Office
4. LOL	Avenue
5. M.D.	Medical Doctor
6. Ave.	United Sates of America
7. J. K. Rowling	Joanne Kathleen Rowling
8. AKA	Laugh Out Loud
9. U.S.A.	Mister

You are having a formal party. Make a formal list of 10 people you would like to invite. Include their titles and abbreviations, like Mr., Dr., and Mrs.

______________________________ ______________________________

______________________________ ______________________________

______________________________ ______________________________

______________________________ ______________________________

______________________________ ______________________________

Question Marks

Question marks are used in interrogative sentences (sentences that ask a question).

Ending a sentence with a question mark shows that a question is being asked.	How many students are in the class? Can I play too?

When used in quotations, questions marks can be placed either inside or outside of the closing quotation mark depending on the meaning of the sentence.

When the question mark is punctuating the quotation itself, it is placed inside the quotation mark.	The customer asked, "How much does the car cost?"
When the question mark is punctuating the entire sentence, it is placed outside the quotation mark.	Did the sales person say, "It's the most expensive car on the lot"?
For indirect quotations, a period is used instead of a question mark.	I asked my sister if she would help us with our math homework.

Language Arts

Practice

Place a question mark in the appropriate place in the sentences that need one. Add quotation marks where needed. In the sentences that do not need a question mark, place a period at the end of the sentence.

1. Did you hear back from the admissions office__
2. Jason said he saw the movie 12 times__
3. My mom asked, "How much homework do you have tonight__
4. Did your teacher say, "Finish the entire chapter tonight__
5. I asked Jill if she had a good day__
6. There must have been 200 people in the theatre__

Practice

Proofread the following dialogue. Use the proofreading marks to correct the mistakes in question mark use.

ꝑ	delete letters, words, punctuation
∧	insert letters, words, punctuation
⤻	move punctuation from one place to another

Patrick was doing a report on the Milky Way Galaxy. He asked the director of the local observatory if he could ask him some questions?

Patrick asked, "How many planets orbit the sun in our solar system"?

The director answered, "We have eight planets that orbit the sun."

Patrick asked, "Was my teacher right when she said that planets are divided into two categories?"

"Yes, Patrick, Mrs. Sanchez was right," said the director. "Mercury, Venus, Earth, and Mars belong to the terrestrial planets." The director asked, "Do you know the name of the other category"?

"The other category is the Jovian planets?" answered Patrick.

The director said, "You are correct!"

Patrick had a good time and learned a lot about the Milky Way Galaxy. He asked the director if he could come back again?

Language Arts

Exclamation Marks

Exclamation marks are used with exclamatory sentences and interjections.

Exclamation marks help exclamatory sentences express surprise or a strong emotion.	I'm so excited that you made it into the first college on your list!
Exclamation marks also help interjections express surprise or a strong emotion.	Oh, no! I left my homework at home.

Practice

Place an ! at the end of each sentence that needs an exclamation mark.

1. Watch out The stove is hot _____
2. The soup should be on medium high _____
3. Thank you for my beautiful flowers _____
4. Tulips are my favorite flower _____
5. Ouch My fingers were still in the door _____
6. After all of my hard work, I finally got an A on the test _____
7. I have a lot of homework to do tonight _____
8. I won the race _____
9. Oh, no The rain is coming down really hard now _____
10. I like the sound of rain on the rooftop _____
11. The cars are coming fast _____
12. My favorite color is green _____

Commas

Commas have a variety of uses. Three uses for commas are to set off items in a series, in direct address, and with multiple adjectives.

A series is at least three items listed together in a sentence. The items can be words, phrases, or clauses. Commas are used to separate them.

I must clean the kitchen, the bathroom, and the family room this weekend.

When multiple adjectives are used to describe a noun, they are separated by commas.

The sweet, cool apple tasted good on the hot day.

Make sure each adjective describes the noun.

The piping hot pizza was ready to come out of the oven.

There is no comma because the pizza is not piping. The adverb **piping** describes the adjective hot.

When the name of a person being spoken to is used in a sentence, it is called direct address. A comma is used to separate the name from the rest of the sentence.

Ming, after our chores are done, we can go to the park.

Pass the ball here, Ming!

Practice

Write three sentences describing your favorite foods. In each sentence, use commas in a series or with multiple adjectives.

1. ______________________________

2. ______________________________

3. ______________________________

Commas

Practice

Draw a line to match the following sentences in Column A to the type of commas they require in Column B.

Column A	Column B
1. The soft, sweet, loving kitten purred.	commas in a series
2. They stayed out of the biting cold water.	commas in direct address
3. Daphne, please answer the door.	commas separating adjectives
4. I worked out on the treadmill, bike, and	no comma necessary between adverb and adjective elliptical cycle.

Column A	Column B
5. The sizzling hot sauce was too hot to eat.	commas in a series
6. Stephanie, please pass the strawberries.	commas in direct address
7. The sweet, juicy, ripe peaches were perfect.	commas separating adjectives
8. The tennis players grabbed their towels, bags, and balls on their way off the court.	no comma necessary between adverb and adjective

---

Rewrite the following sentences by adding commas where necessary.

9. John wanted pasta vegetables and rolls for dinner.

____

10. Tiffany make the reservation for 7:30.

____

11. The new black car was just what he wanted.

____

12. I checked in on the slowly boiling water.

____

Practice

Make a list of five of your favorite things. Then, make a list of words that describe these things. Write five sentences about your favorite things using the words that describe them. Be sure to include commas in the appropriate places.

1. __________ ____________________

2. __________ ____________________

3. __________ ____________________

4. __________ ____________________

5. __________ ____________________

Language Arts

Commas

Commas are also used to combine sentences, set off prepositional phrases, and punctuate dialogue.

Use a **comma** to combine two independent clauses with a **coordinate conjunction** and create a compound sentence.	The players must be well trained, **and** they must train for at least six months.
If a sentence begins with a **prepositional phrase**, set it off with a **comma**.	**After he finishes his homework**, he can talk with his friends.
Commas are also used when setting off **dialogue** from the rest of the sentence.	The tour guide said, "Today's walking tour will take us past several museums." "Then, we will eat in a cafe," she promised.

Practice

Complete the following sentences by adding commas where necessary. Not all of the sentences need commas.

1. The Teton Mountain Range is a beautiful sight and it is a challenge for rock climbers.
2. The Teton Mountain Range is located in Wyoming and the range is in part of the Grand Teton National Park.
3. Because of its beauty more than 3 million people visit each year.
4. Rock climbers come from all over the world to climb Grand Teton.
5. "The view from the mountain is breathtaking" said one climber too.
6. While Grand Teton's highest peek is 13,700 feet other peaks attract climbers.
7. "Wildlife viewing is amazing here" said another tourist.

Practice

Proofread the following paragraph. Use a proofreading mark to add commas where necessary.

∧ **inserts letter, words, punctuation**

What is a marathon? Most runners know that a marathon is a foot race of 26.2 miles but not everyone knows how the marathon began. Now popular worldwide the marathon has its roots in Greece. We are familiar with bicycle couriers but ancient Greeks used foot couriers. Many of them had to run city to city to make deliveries. In 490 B.C. Persia was at war with Greece. A Persian army landed 25 miles from Athens at the city of Marathon. After a mighty battle the Greeks were victorious. A runner was sent from Marathon to Athens to spread the news of the victory. Pheidippides ran the 25 miles from Marathon to Athens. When he reached the city legend says he said "Rejoice, we conquer." Then, Pheidippides fell dead. Although the facts are not known for sure the legend prevails. The modern race got a name and the marathon was born.

Write a paragraph explaining your favorite sport or hobby, how it got its beginning, and why you like it. Use a variety of sentences. Add a quotation of your own.

____

____

____

____

____

____

____

Commas

The five parts of a personal letter are: the heading, salutation (greeting), body, closing, and signature. Commas appear in four of the five parts of the personal letter.

A **comma** follows the city and the date in the heading.	3151 Stuckey Lane Chicago, IL 30000 March 7, 2008
A **comma** follows the name in the salutation.	Dear Mimi,
Follow the normal rules for using **commas** in sentences in the body of the letter.	Mama, Papa, and Didi all send their love.
A **comma** follows the last word in the closing.	Your big brother,

---

Practice

Write a short, friendly letter. Pay attention to your use of commas.

____

____

____

____

____

____

____

____

____

____

____

Language Arts

Practice

Proofread the following friendly letter. Use proofreading marks to insert commas where necessary.

ɥ	**deletes letter, words, punctuation**
∧	**inserts letter, words, punctuation**

5512 Alpine Lane

Ridgeview CO 55214

April 26 2015

Dear Marina

How are you? Are you getting excited for summer? I am going to volunteer at the local animal shelter and I am going to learn all about the different kinds of animals there. I am sure that it will be a hard job but it will be rewarding too.

What are your plans for summer? Will you be going camping with your parents like you did last year? That sounds like so much fun! After you get back I want to hear all about it.

I need to get back to reading about animal care but I hope to hear from you soon!

Your friend

Sharon

Quotation Marks

Quotation marks are used to show the exact words of a speaker. This is called a direct quotation.

Quotation marks are placed before and after the exact words.	"I must make it to the post office before 5:00," said Sharon. "I want to get my invitations in the mail today."

Single quotation marks are used when a direct quotation is made within a direct quotation.

Single quotation marks set off what the coach said. Double quotation marks show what Dylan said.	Dylan said, "Michael, the coach said, 'Practice will be at 4:00 instead of 3:00.'"

Quotation marks are used with some titles, including short stories, poems, songs, and articles in magazines and newspapers.

Quotation marks are placed before and after the exact words.	Short story: "A White Heron"
If a title is quoted within a direct quotation, then single quotation marks are used.	Hannah said, "I hope the DJ plays my favorite song, 'Call Me Maybe.'"

Practice

Draw a line to match the following sentences or titles from Column A to the type of quotation in Column B.

	Column A	Column B
1.	Susan said, "Let's go to lunch at 12:30."	direct quotation
2.	"Right," Connie answered. "My boss said, 'Our lunch meeting is scheduled for 12:00 sharp.'"	quote within a quote
3.	"Mary Had a Little Lamb"	title

	Column A	Column B
4.	"Cinderella"	direct quotation
5.	My sister said, "The coach said 'Eat a good dinner the night before the game.'"	quote within a quote
6.	"I'm heading for the beach," Sheryl said.	title

Practice writing sentences with quotation marks. Write two sentences that are direct quotations, two that are quotes within quotes, and two that include titles.

7. ______________________________

8. ______________________________

9. ______________________________

10. ______________________________

11. ______________________________

12. ______________________________

Apostrophes

Apostrophes are used to form contractions and possessives.

Apostrophes are used in contractions, which are shortened forms of words. The words are shortened by leaving out letters. An apostrophe takes the place of the omitted letters.	I am = I'm let us = let's
Apostrophes are also used to form possessives, which show possession, or ownership. To form the possessive of a singular noun, add an apostrophe and an s.	I have Walt's books.
To form the possessive of plural nouns ending in s, simply add an apostrophe.	The boys' uniforms will be ready on Friday.
If the plural noun does not end in an s, add both the apostrophe and an s.	The children's puppet show will be performed on Wednesday.
If you are writing about more than one letter of the alphabet or number, an apostrophe is not needed to form the plural. Only add **s** at the end.	My name has two B**s** in it. I have two page 4**s** in my book.

Practice

Choose a contraction from the box to replace each phrase in parentheses and complete each sentence.

We're	It's	He'd
I'm	We've	let's

1. (I am) ____________________ hungry and thirsty.
2. (We are) ____________________ on our way to the café.
3. (It is) ____________________ not too far away, and it has the best muffins.
4. Do you think we should take something back for Pablo? (He would) ____________ appreciate it.
5. (We have) ____________________ been eating for almost an hour.
6. Come on, (let us) ____________________ hurry.

Rewrite the following sentences, adding apostrophes where necessary.

1. Myras grades really improved after she started studying with her two older sisters.

   ____

2. With her sisters help and her parents encouragement, she is now a much better student.

   ____

3. Math isnt her best subject, but she was determined to work hard.

   ____

4. Much to her teachers surprise, Myra got an A on the years final test.

   ____

Colons

A colon is used to introduce a series, to set off a clause, for emphasis, and in time.

Colons are used to introduce a series in a sentence. Usually, but not always, the list is proceeded by the words **following**, **these**, or **things**.	The chef does the following: washes the vegetables, chops the vegetables, and steams the vegetables.
Colons are sometimes used instead of a comma in more formal cases to set off a clause.	The weather reporter said: "We can expect six more inches of snow overnight."
Colons are used to set off a word or phrase for emphasis.	We hoped to see some activity in the night sky. And then we saw it: a shooting star.
Colons are used when writing the time.	Are we meeting at 9:00 or 10:00?

Practice

Identify why the colon is used in each sentence. Write **S** for series, **C** for clause, **E** for emphasis, or **T** for time.

1. _____ One of the most violent types of storms occurs primarily in the United States: tornados.
2. _____ A tornado is defined as the following: "a violent rotating column of air extending from a thunderstorm to the ground."
3. _____ Thunderstorms that develop in warm, moist air in advance of a cold front can produce these things: hail, strong wind, and tornados.
4. _____ Staying aware is very important for safety. During storms, look for the following: dark, greenish skies; large hail; loud roars; and flash floods.
5. _____ You can prepare for tornados by doing the following: developing a safety plan, practicing house drills, and listening to weather reports.

Practice

Rewrite the following passage, adding colons where needed.

I would like to apply for the following position Latin Cultural Food Writer. I graduated from the Culinary Art Institute in New York. I have cooked dishes from many cultures Latin, French, and Middle Eastern.

I have expertise in Mexican food history, culture, and cooking. When the Spanish explorer Cortez first came to America, he found many culinary surprises chocolate, peanuts, vanilla, beans, squash, avocados, coconuts, corn, and tomatoes. I have created many dishes which incorporate many of these foods and flavors.

Included with this letter are the following my resume, school transcripts, and references.

You can reach me weekdays between 700 am and 300 pm.

Write four sentences, one for each type of colon use: series, clause, emphasis, and time.

1. __________

2. __________

3. __________

4. __________

Semicolons

A semicolon is a cross between a period and a comma. Semicolons can be used to join two independent clauses, to separate clauses containing commas, and to separate groups in a series that contain commas.

Semicolons join two independent clauses when a coordinate conjunction is not used.	The loud thunder scared me; I hid under my covers.
Semicolons are used to separate clauses when they already contain commas.	Although the thunder was loud, it did no harm; I emerged from my bed safe and sound.
Semicolons are also used in lists or series to separate words or phrases that already contain commas.	We are looking for a home with these features: land with a field, a garden, and an orchard; a house with a nice kitchen, a solid foundation, and a studio; and a barn or garage.

Practice

Match the first half of the sentences in Column A with the second half in Column B. Then, circle all of the semicolons in the sentences.

Column A	Column B
1. Donna was close to home;	I went to the doctor instead.
2. After the game was over, my team went for pizza;	it wasn't important anyway.
3. The long shopping list included the following:	she had traveled a long way.
4. I didn't go to school;	check the spelling, facts, and names; call your references; and verify the address.
5. Because we were on vacation, we weren't home to get the letter;	we were all starving.
6. Before sending the resume, do the following:	rye, pumpernickel, and wheat bread; lettuce, carrots, and onions for salad; and cranberry, grapefruit, and tomato juice.

Language Arts

Practice

Proofread the following magazine. Use the proofreading marks to correct the mistakes in semicolon use, including out-of-place semicolons and commas used instead of semicolons.

ℓ	**delete letters, words, punctuation**
^;	**insert semicolon**

Who is Sue? Sue is a Tyrannosaurus rex she is the largest and best preserved T. rex ever discovered. Although she was discovered in South Dakota, Sue now resides in Chicago, Illinois, at The Field Museum, she is on display for the public to see. Visitors can see Sue's features up close: ribs, forelimbs, and mouth bones, a CT scan of her skull the braincase as well as; many other parts. Sue is quite special she is the most complete T. rex fossil ever discovered. While we have a lot to learn about our past from Sue, we may also learn about our present and future Sue has given us much to explore.

Write four complete sentences, each including two independent clauses joined by a semicolon.

Hyphens

Hyphens are used to divide words at the end of a line and to create new words. They are also used between numbers.

Use a hyphen to divide a word between lines or into syllables.	sanc-tu-ary de-po-sit
Do not divide one-syllable words with fewer than six letters.	ball, toy, cedar, book
Divide syllables after the vowel if a vowel is a syllable by itself.	cele-brate not: cel-ebrate
Do not divide one letter from the rest of the word.	ele-phant not: e-lephant
Hyphens can be used to create new words when combined with words and word parts such as *self*, *ex*, or *great*.	My great-grandfather worked on the railroad.

Practice

How many hyphenated words can you think of that include *self*, *ex*, or *great*? Write at least two of each. Use a dictionary if you need help.

______________________________ ______________________________

______________________________ ______________________________

______________________________ ______________________________

______________________________ ______________________________

Language Arts

Practice

Solve the following puzzle. Write the words from the box in the appropriate spaces. The words must be divided correctly in order to fit into the spaces.

basket	compose	dinosaur	graduate	puppy
bicycle	crocodile	embankment	personal	television

1. ___ ___ ___ ___ - ___ ___ ___ ___ ___ ___

2. ___ ___ ___ - ___ ___ ___

3. ___ ___ ___ - ___ ___ ___ ___ ___

4. ___ ___ ___ ___ ___ - ___ ___ ___ ___

5. ___ ___ ___ ___ ___ - ___ ___ ___

6. ___ ___ ___ - ___ ___ ___ ___

7. ___ ___ ___ ___ ___ ___ - ___ ___ ___ ___

8. ___ ___ ___ ___ - ___ ___ ___

9. ___ ___ ___ ___ ___

10. ___ ___ ___ ___ - ___ ___ ___ ___

Parentheses

Parentheses are used to show extra material, to set off phrases in a stronger way than commas, and to enclose numbers.

Parentheses show supplementary, or extra, material. Supplementary material is a word or phrase that gives additional information.

Those apples (the ones in the basket) are good for baking in cobblers.

Sometimes, words or phrases that might be set off with commas are set off with parentheses instead. This gives the information more emphasis for a stronger phrase.

The television program, the one that was canceled, was my favorite.

The television program (the one that was canceled) was my favorite.

Parentheses are also used to enclose numbers in a series.

I do not want to go to the movie because (1) it is showing too late, (2) the theater is all the way across town, and (3) it is too scary.

Practice

Write two sentences that have supplemental material in parentheses, two sentences that set off information in parentheses for emphasis, and two sentences that have numbers in parentheses.

1. ______________________________

2. ______________________________

3. ______________________________

4. ______________________________

5. ______________________________

6. ______________________________

Language Arts

Practice

Complete the following sentences by adding parenthetical phrases from the box. Add the parentheses where they belong. The first one is done for you.

(1) (2) (3) with four doors	(1) (2) (3) my best friend	my great-great-grandmother's see key

1. The road on this map looks like a two-lane road.

   The road on this map (see key) looks like a two-lane road.

2. The recipe is the best!

   ____

3. Andy is moving to another state.

   ____

4. I love to exercise because it is good for my heart, it gives me energy, and I feel good afterward.

   ____

   ____

5. The new, blue car is the one I want.

   ____

6. Pigs are my favorite animal because they are intelligent, they are cute, and they make "oinking" sounds.

   ____

   ____

Language Arts

Review

Use everything you have learned so far about sentences to answer the questions.

1. Proofread the following letter. Use a proofreading mark to insert the missing periods and commas.

∧ inserts letter, words, punctuation

575 Grant Mountain Road

Snowyville ME 04900

February 12 2016

Dear Mrs. Terry

Thanks for allowing me to turn in assignments by mail until I recover from this horrible flu. Here is my essay topic proposal in sample format.

The British poet Rupert C Brooke said "Cities, like cats, reveal themselves at night" How true his statement is! Some cats save lives when they reveal themselves at night

Take for example Aggie a cat rescued from a shelter Aggie was a curious playful cat but she was not aggressive That is until one evening when she heard an intruder climbing through the window Before her owner even made it downstairs she pounced attacked and scared away the intruder. Her owner exclaimed "Aggie now you have saved me!"

Cats also rescue and save their own. One particular cat Mrs Mimi lived in an abandoned building in the US with her five kittens When the building caught on fire she had to save her family. One by one she carried her kittens out of the burning building to safety She was burned and blistered but she got every one of her kittens out

Sincerely

Matty Parsons

Add question marks and exclamation marks where they are needed.

2. May I go with you to the baseball game

3. Wait for me

4. We won! We won

5. The hiker asked, "Is this as far as the trail goes"

6. Did the coach say, "Run three more laps"

Use proofreading marks to insert single and double quotation marks, apostrophes and semicolons.

7. Claude Monet lived in France from 1840 to 1926 and was the founder of impressionism. Many of Monet's paintings were landscapes said Mrs. Konikow.

8. "Did Mrs. Konikow say, Many of Monet's paintings were landscapes?" Patricia asked Doug.

9. Someday, I would like to go to France, said Patricia, but for now I think I'll just take a trip to the library.

10. This summer, I learned how to swim played baseball, soccer, and tennis and ate lots of fresh corn, tomatoes, and cucumbers.

11. Before I go back to school, I have one thing left on my summer to-do list a cookout at my best friends house.

Chapter Review

I. Proofread the following personal letter. Make all of the necessary capitalization corrections.

≡ capitalize a letter
/ lowercase a letter

1505 oak ridge drive

Pleasant Grove, MI 48000

september 8, 2016

dear aunt Angelina,

How are you? I enjoyed reading Your letter and seeing the pictures from your Vacation to the bahamas. Do you want to go back next year?

I'm looking forward to your visit in november. You are really going to enjoy pleasant grove! It will be nice to show you our neighborhood and eat at milo's sundaes, my favorite ice-cream Store. mom and Dad said you can stay in my room if you want. If it's still warm enough, i might camp in the backyard.

Last week, I tried out for the school play. I got the part! I will be playing the role of dorothy in the wizard of Oz. Rehearsals start next week. It will be a lot of fun, but I'm sad that our performance won't be until after your visit.

Love,

Miranda

The following sentences are missing punctuation. Add periods, question marks, and exclamation where needed.

2. Don't forget to stop by the store and pick up bread on your way home from school

3. What time is Gillian stopping over

4. Look out

5. E B White is my favorite author.

6. My dentist is Dr Guten.

---

7. **Proofread the following letter. Use proofreading marks to add commas where necessary.**

^ **insert commas**

6919 Muirfield Rd.

Bloomfield MI 30000

September 29 2014

Dear Vijay

This weekend I went to the Ryder Cup and I saw my favorite players! The Ryder Cup is a golf match between the United States and Europe. I got to see Bubba Watson Sergio Garcia and Rickie Fowler. Although you can't say anything during the course of play I yelled out "Rickie you're the best!" between holes. It was great. I bought you a hat at the gift shop and I'll give it to you when I see you after winter break. I hope you are well.

Your friend

Mindy

Chapter Review

Rewrite each sentence. Add punctuation where necessary.

8. My great grandmother played softball in college, said Aidan.

9. The doctor said "You'll be fine!"

10. I want to take Ms. Roses class because 1 she teaches a lot of geography, 2 she takes her classes on field trips, and 3 she is nice.

11. "Charlotte, did our teacher say, the bus for the museum leaves at 900?"

12. I am excited about going to the museum of art I want to be an artist someday.

13. Susan got what she had been hoping for a new job.

14. I didnt read the <u>Hunger Games</u> series but I loved the movies.

Using Tenses with Irregular Verbs

When they change tenses, irregular verbs do not follow the same rules as regular verbs.

The **present tense** of a verb tells that the action is taking place now or continuously.

I **do** the crossword puzzles on Sunday.

The **past tense** of a verb tells that the action took place in the past.

Renee and Kristen **went** on an archaeological dig last semester.

The **past participle** of a verb tells that the action began in the past and was completed in the past. In order to form the past participle, the verb must be preceded by one of the following verbs: **was**, **were**, **has**, **had**, or **have**.

Yuki, Lori, and Blair **had come** with us on our vacation three years in a row, but last year they didn't.

Practice

Complete the following sentences by circling the correct verb in parentheses.

1. Timmy (come, has come) over for dinner every night this week.
2. I can (did, do) my homework now.
3. The class (go, had gone) to the same exhibit last year.
4. Bianca and Nicole (gone, went) to see the butterflies at the butterfly house.
5. Please (came, come) and pick up your order.
6. Andrea (do, has done) that assignment many times before.

Using Tenses with Irregular Verbs

Practice

Proofread the following paragraphs. Use the proofreading marks to correct mistakes with the use of the verbs **run, see,** and **sit.** Use clues from the rest of the sentence to determine what the tense of the sentence should be.

ꝭ delete letters, words, punctuation
^ insert letters, words, punctuation

They have ran, follow, sniff, have seen, and sometimes they sat. They are important members of many teams. Who are they? They are rescue dogs. Rescue dogs are important to police departments, fire departments, and many rescue organizations. Rescue dogs can saw and smell things that human beings can't. Human rescuers saw these dogs had run through wildernesses looking for missing persons, sniffing for clues along the way. Some dogs ran up snowy mountains to find fallen hikers and skiers. Sometimes they have sat for hours waiting for their turn to seek and rescue. And when they are called, they are ready to go.

Rescue dogs and their guardians are well trained teams. They work together, ran together, play together, and rescue together. These teams go through many hours of intensive training and see and experienced many types of challenging situations. We owe a lot to these hard-working dogs and those who train and love them.

Many believe that rescue dogs run with their noses to the ground in order to pick up scents. That's not necessarily true; rescue dogs can be trained to receive scents from the air and can ran with their noses up!

Comparative and Superlative Adjectives

All types of adjectives describe nouns.

Regular adjectives describe one noun.	**cute/cuter/cutest** Phoebe has a **cute** puppy.
Comparative adjectives compare two nouns.	**big/bigger/biggest** Joe's sandwich is **bigger** than Barney's.
Superlative adjectives compare three or more nouns.	**light/lighter/lightest** This windbreaker is the **lightest** jacket in my closet.
The word **more** before an adjective means it is **comparative**, comparing two nouns.	Students in the morning class are **more energetic** than students in the afternoon class.
The word **most** before an adjective means it is **superlative**, comparing three or more nouns.	Please sign the three yellow forms first; they are the **most important**.

The words **more** and **most** are normally used instead of **er** and **est** with adjectives that have more than two syllables.

Practice

Complete the following sentences by circling the correct word or words in parentheses.

1. Of the three bats, Henry's is the (light, lightest).
2. Christina has a very (cute, cuter) kitten.
3. My notebook is (bigger, biggest) than yours.
4. (Light, Lightest) rain fell on the roof.
5. Every mother thinks her child is the (cute, cutest) in the class.

Language Arts

Language Arts

Comparative and Superlative Adjectives

Practice

Identify each of the following sentences as either a comparative sentence or a superlative sentence. Write **C** for comparative and **S** for superlative. Then, underline the adjectives (including the words **more** or **most**) in the sentences.

1. ______ The most challenging sports competition in the world is the Tour de France.
2. ______ The Tour de France can be ridden in some of the worst weather conditions.
3. ______ One of the best shirts to earn in the Tour de France is the polka-dot jersey.
4. ______ The world's most famous bicyclers come to France to compete.
5. ______ Athletes now have more specialized training than they did years ago.
6. ______ The more training an athlete has, the more prepared they will be.

Write a paragraph describing a performance or sporting event you have seen. Use at least six comparative or superlative adjectives.

____

____

____

____

____

____

____

____

____

____

____

Adjective or Adverb?

Adjectives modify nouns. Adverbs modify verbs, adjectives, and other adverbs. Some adverbs are easily confused with adjectives.

Bad is an adjective, and badly is an adverb. Determine what you are modifying before using bad and badly.

Bad is used as an adjective modifying the noun **storm**. No **-ly** is added.	A bad storm is heading our way.
Badly is used as an adverb modifying the verb **sings**. Use the **-ly** form of bad.	Cami sings badly.

Good is an adjective, and well is an adverb. Determine what you are modifying before using good and well.

In this sentence, the adverb well modifies the verb **bakes**. The adjective good modifies the noun **cook**.	Claudia is a good cook and bakes well too.

The words very and really are both adverbs.

The adverb very modifies the adverb softly, which modifies the verb **talk**.	Please talk very softly in the library.
The adverb really modifies the adjective nervous, which modifies the noun Gina.	Gina is really nervous about her test.

Language Arts

Adjective or Adverb?

Practice

Complete the following sentences by circling the correct adjective or adverb in parentheses. Underline the verb, adjective, or adverb that it modifies. Then, identify what type of word the adjective or adverb modifies: write **V** for verb, **ADJ** for adjective, **ADV** for adverb, and **N** for noun.

1. ______ Jim was sick and ran (bad, badly) during the race.
2. ______ Amy had a great day and ran (good, well) in her race.
3. ______ The day I lost the race was a (bad, badly) day for me.
4. ______ I was a (bad, badly) beaten runner.
5. ______ But it was a (good, well) day for my friend.
6. ______ She accepted her praises (good, well).
7. ______ I will train harder so I do (good, well) in my next race.
8. ______ That will be a (good, well) day for the whole team.

Write a paragraph describing a school event in which some things went well, and some things didn't go so well. Use each of the words **bad**, **badly**, **good**, **well**, **really**, and **very** at least once.

Negatives and Double Negatives

A negative sentence states the opposite. Negative words include: not, no, never, nobody, nowhere, nothing, barely, hardly, scarcely, and contractions containing the word not.

Double negatives occur when two negative words are used in the same sentence. Don't use double negatives; doing so will make your sentence positive again, and it is poor grammar.

Correct	Incorrect
We do not have any soup in the pantry.	We do not have no soup in the pantry.
I have nothing to wear to the party this weekend.	I don't have nothing to wear to the party this weekend.
Greg can hardly put weight on his leg since his knee operation.	Greg can't hardly put weight on his leg since his knee operation.

Practice

Identify which of the following sentences have double negatives by writing an **X** on the line. Then, go back and correct the double negatives by crossing out one of the negatives or by changing the wording.

1. ______ The chef hardly uses any fat in his cooking.
2. ______ I don't like no green peppers on my pizza.
3. ______ I can barely see nothing in this fog.
4. ______ The instructions never say to use a hammer.
5. ______ Nobody hardly showed up at the premiere.

Language Arts

Negatives and Double Negatives

Practice

Rewrite this paragraph to correct the double negatives.

Firefighting is a brave and courageous job. If you can't imagine yourself not working hard, then this job isn't for you. Firefighters go through special training. They don't never take training lightly. Firefighters must wear special gear and use special equipment. It isn't easy to use the equipment. They spend many class hours learning about it and training with it. Firefighters must train in actual fires. Some trainees don't make it through this training. They may find they don't like climbing no ladders that are so high. Some may find they aren't scarcely strong enough. The firefighters who graduate are ready for the job. They don't never know what dangers each day will bring, but they are trained and ready. Firefighters keep us, our pets, and our homes safe. Firefighting is a brave and courageous career to explore.

Synonyms and Antonyms

Synonyms and antonyms are two types of word relationships. Synonyms describe things that are similar, and antonyms describe things that are different.

Synonyms are words that have the same, or almost the same, meaning. Using synonyms can help you avoid repeating words and can make your writing more interesting.

Here are some examples of synonyms:

clever/smart
reply/answer
wreck/destroy
applaud/clap

Antonyms are words that have opposite meanings. Using antonyms can help you show how people, places, situations, and things are different.

Here are some examples of antonyms:

wide/narrow
accept/decline
break/repair
borrow/lend

Practice

Read each sentence below. If the underlined words are synonyms, write **S** on the line. If they are antonyms, write **A** on the line.

1. ______ Do you know if the house at the end of the street is vacant or occupied?
2. ______ Although Tamika is shy now, I don't expect that she'll be timid her whole life.
3. ______ The hero of the story was courageous, and he was rewarded for being so brave.
4. ______ The plane departs at 11:00 and arrives at its destination at 2:30.
5. ______ The commander was well respected by his men, and they were happy to follow their leader.

Homophones

Homophones are words that sound the same but have different spellings and different meanings. There are hundreds of homophones in the English language.

allowed: to have permission	Are you allowed to go to the midnight movie?
aloud: in a speaking voice	Practice saying your multiplication tables aloud.
threw: propelled through the air with the hand and arm	Tomas threw the football to me.
through: movement into one point and out another	The tunnel goes through the mountain.

Practice

Read the following sentences. Circle the letter of the definition of the underlined homophone that fits the sentence. If you are unsure about which homophone to use, look up the meanings in a dictionary.

1. Taylor will have many books to buy when he starts college.
   a. to purchase
   b. to be near

2. The horse's mane glistened in the morning sunshine.
   a. the most important
   b. hair

3. Ellen lives by the pond with the ducks and geese.
   a. to purchase
   b. to be near

4. Please underline the sentence with the main idea in this paragraph.
   a. the most important
   b. hair

Multiple-Meaning Words

Multiple-meaning words, or homographs, are words that are spelled the same but have different meanings. They may also sometimes have different pronunciations.

The word permit can mean "allow," or it can mean "a license."

My mother will not permit us to eat junk food.	In North Carolina, you need a permit to go fishing.

Practice

Read each sentence. Then, choose the sentence in which the underlined word is used the same way as it is in the first sentence.

1. ______ Mom says that Yasmine has a <u>mind</u> for numbers.
   a. Do you mind if I try your dessert?
   b. A mind is a terrible thing to waste.

2. ______ Hudson earned extra points for good <u>conduct</u>.
   a. It takes years to learn how to conduct an orchestra.
   b. Micah's conduct at the performance made his parents proud.

3. ______ "I <u>object</u>, Your Honor!" shouted the attorney.
   a. If you don't object to eating late, we'll have dinner at 8:00.
   b. The object of the game is to get rid of all of your cards.

4. ______ I'd like you to take the <u>lead</u> during Monday's presentation.
   a. Paint in old houses sometimes contains lead.
   b. "Once we're on the trail," said Crosby, "you take the lead."

5. ______ Try not to <u>tear</u> the leaves when you plant the seedlings.
   a. How did you tear your jacket?
   b. A single tear dripped down Mrs. Romano's cheek.

6. ______ Did you <u>suspect</u> that Alfie planned a surprise party?
   a. The suspect in the robbery will be tried in court next week.
   b. I suspect that Camilla has candy hidden in her room.

Similes and Metaphors

Language Arts

Similes and metaphors are figures of speech that make writing more interesting and vivid for the reader.

A **simile** is a figure of speech that compares two things using the words like or as.

Ansel slept as soundly as a bear in winter.

The firecrackers boomed like thunder across the sky.

A **metaphor** is a figure of speech that compares two unlike things that are similar in some way.

The grass was a cool carpet beneath Marisa's feet.

Aunt Hattie was a mama bear when it came to protecting her children.

Practice

Read each sentence below. On the line, write **S** if the sentence contains a simile and **M** if it contains a metaphor.

1. ______ The full moon was a plump, friendly face peeking over the hill.
2. ______ In the middle of rush hour, the highway was a parking lot.
3. ______ Chase was excited to go, but his brother moved as slowly as molasses.
4. ______ The hail felt like tiny stinging bees as it pelted my skin.
5. ______ Rico is a night owl—he rarely goes to bed before midnight.
6. ______ The wildflowers by the side of the road were as colorful as a bag of confetti thrown into the air.

Similes and Metaphors

Practice

Read each item below. On the line, write a simile or metaphor to describe it.

1. the freshly fallen snow

 ____

2. the crowd in the stadium

 ____

3. the sand on the beach

 ____

4. the nervous girl

 ____

5. the fuzzy puppy

 ____

6. the sweet ice cream

 ____

On the lines below, describe an experience you've had or a trip you've taken. Use at least two similes and two metaphors.

____

____

____

____

____

____

____

Idioms and Proverbs

An idiom is an expression that doesn't actually mean what it says.

What it says	What it means
a heart of gold	to be very kind
a drop in the bucket	a small amount

A proverb is a saying, an observation, or a piece of advice.

What it says	What it means
A watched pot never boils.	When you are waiting or watching for something to happen, it seems to take a long time.
A picture is worth a thousand words.	A picture can communicate much more to a viewer than words do.

Practice

Read the proverbs. Then, write what you think each one means on the lines below.

1. A penny saved is a penny earned.

____

____

2. Don't put all of your eggs in one basket.

____

____

3. It is no use crying over spilled milk.

____

____

Language Arts

Practice

Read each idiom below. On the line, write the letter of the meaning.

1. _____ at a snail's pace
2. _____ to jump the gun
3. _____ down the drain
4. _____ couch potato
5. _____ under the weather
6. _____ get the ball rolling
7. _____ a needle in a haystack
8. _____ at the 11th hour
9. _____ to tighten your belt
10. _____ all ears

a. something is lost and can't be retrieved
b. to spend less money
c. to do something before it is time
d. to get things started
e. at the last minute
f. a person who watches lots of TV or is lazy
g. to be listening
h. to do something very slowly
i. hard to find
j. to feel sick

Imagine that you are writing a short e-mail to a friend. See how many idioms you can include. You may use idioms from the lesson or others that you are familiar with.

____

____

____

____

____

____

____

____

Language Arts

Chapter Review

Complete the following sentences by circling the correct verb tense in parentheses.

1. Members of the track team (ran, run) home from school before it gets dark.
2. Mitch (did, do) his homework before he ate dinner.
3. Lori and Darrin (saw, see) last year's parade, but didn't make it this year.
4. They (go, have gone) to the festival since they were children.
5. The birds (sit, have sat) in their nest since early morning.
6. I (do, had done) my chores when I first get home from school.
7. I can (saw, see) much better with my glasses than without.
8. Noah (go, went) with his mother to the store yesterday afternoon.
9. Last evening, I (ran, run) three laps around the track before going home.
10. The rain (come, had come) in downpours throughout the night.
11. They (see, had seen) the nurse long before the doctor arrived.

Read the sentences. On each line, write whether the sentence is a simile, a metaphor, an idiom, or a proverb.

12. Who let the cat out of the bag? ____________________
13. The Olympic jumper soared through the air like a bird. ____________________
14. Don't judge a book by its cover. ____________________
15. The early bird catches the worm. ____________________
16. The waterfall was a laughing giant roaring over the cliff. ____________________

Proofread the following sentences. Use the proofreading marks to correct mistakes with homophones and double negatives.

ℓ	**delete letters, words, punctuation**
∧	**insert letters, words, punctuation**

17. Diane was aloud to visit her friends after she finished her homework.

18. Lynn wants to by earrings with the money she earns from shoveling snow.

19. Elise brushes her horse's main every morning and every night.

20. Mr. and Mrs. Jones past the turn they were supposed to make into the school.

21. Andrew through the football the farthest.

22. Amy wanted to go to the game to.

Make up your own metaphor, simile, and proverb. Write one of each on the lines below.

23. ______________________________

____

24. ______________________________

____

25. ______________________________

____

Chapter Review

Complete the following sentences by circling the correct use of adjective or adverb in parentheses.

26. Stephanie thought *The Wizard of Oz* was the (cute, cutest) play she had seen all year.

27. We have to climb over one (big, biggest) rock in order to pass the test.

28. That is the (bigger, biggest) mountain I've ever seen.

29. Clint makes (more, most) money mowing lawns than Perry does selling lemonade.

30. The ice storm we had last night was (worse, worst) than the one we had last year.

31. The blizzard brought the (more, most) snow I had ever seen.

32. I think swimming in the lake in the winter is a (bad, badly) idea.

In each sentence below, a pair of words is underlined. On the line, write S if the words are synonyms, A if they are antonyms, or M if they are multiple-meaning words.

33. ______ Do you store your summer clothes in the <u>attic</u> or the <u>basement</u>?

34. ______ Be careful that when you <u>bow</u>, your <u>bow</u> doesn't slip out of your hair.

35. ______ The <u>presents</u> are on the table, and the guests can't wait for you to open your <u>gifts</u>.

36. ______ Did Rascal <u>eat</u> the entire bone, or did he <u>consume</u> only part of it?

37. ______ That bread is <u>stale</u>, but I did make some <u>fresh</u> bread today.

38. ______ Mom put Clare's <u>down</u> comforter <u>down</u> the laundry chute.

ll in each blank with a word that matches the part of speech indicated in parentheses and agrees with the rest of the sentence.

1. Many ____________________ (common noun) grow in this forest.
2. The school that I go to is called ____________________ (proper noun).
3. In cities, there are tons of ____________________ (regular plural noun).
4. ____________________ (irregular plural noun) love to play outside.
5. Lynn likes to run. ____________________ (subject pronoun) won a race.
6. I needed a pencil. Paul gave ____________________ (object pronoun) one of his.
7. She made six mistakes. ____________________ (agreeing pronoun) were spelling errors.
8. Grandmother ____________________ (regular verb) me old photos and told stories.
9. Carl ____________________ (irregular verb) waffles for breakfast.
10. Tonight, Hai ____________________ (helping verb) help me dress for the dance.
11. We ____________________ (linking verb) almost there.
12. Mom ____________________ (perfect tense verb) working in the garden a little bit every day.
13. Neither Jo nor Mahmoud ____________________ (verb that agrees with subject) meat.
14. Today was such a ____________________(adjective) day at the lake.
15. The kittens purr very ____________________(adverb) when they are cuddling.
16. Kari didn't go biking ____________________ (conjunction) it was raining.
17. Please fit your clothes neatly ____________________((preposition) the suitcase.

Language Arts Review

On each line, write whether the sentence declarative, interrogative, exclamatory, or imperative.

18. Oh no! The bridge is closed! ____________

19. I want to read my book all day tomorrow. ____________

20. Be nice to your sister. ____________

21. Did you hear the thunder? ____________

On each line, write whether the sentence is simple, compound, or complex.

22. Henry liked baking bread and making soup. ____________

23. We played a lot; we slept a lot. ____________

24. Frida, my best friend, wants to be a neuroscientist. ____________

Rewrite each pair of simple sentences and sentence fragments as one combined, complete sentence.

25. Mikaela jogged through the buggy forest. Mikaela jogged quickly.

____

26. Strawberries and blueberries. The earliest fruit to ripen.

____

Add periods, question marks, and exclamation points where needed.

27. When will you get home

28. Jamie said, "Mr Hammond said to do Lesson Eight for homework"

29. Careful, the path is very muddy

30. At the M L K School, everybody reads Isabelle Allende in sixth grade.

31. Proofread the following letter and add commas where necessary.

> 11B Jay St.
>
> Tewksbury MA 02000
>
> February 11 2015
>
> Hi Leti
>
> I have some sad news. On Monday our favorite restaurant burned down. I saw the huge thick black cloud of smoke. Leti have you ever seen a fire? Sasha was with me and she was crying "I want to go home!" Remember the owners? They must be so upset. I miss you!
>
> Sophia

Rewrite each sentence. Where necessary, add quotation marks, apostrophes, colons, semicolons, and hyphens.

32. My grandmothers sister had a daughter who lives in England now, said Janie.

____

33. On Mondays, Mom works at 900; on Tuesdays, 300 and on Fridays, 1100.

____

34. Her great grandfather was a famous musician he was a jazz pianist.

____

Identify whether each example is a simile, metaphor, idiom, or proverb.

35. Curiosity killed the cat. _______________

36. The skater was a graceful swan as she glided across the ice. _______________

37. The dinosaur's teeth shone like daggers. _______________

Answer Key

Multi-Digit Multiplication

Multiplication is the way to find sums of equal groups of numbers. Follow these steps to multiply numbers with more than one digit. Be careful to regroup as needed. Use zeros as placeholders to help you line up partial products correctly.

Solve: 54 × 37

First, write the problem vertically. Place the factor with the most digits on top. — 54 × 37 = 378

Next, use place value to break the smaller factor up. 37 can be broken up into 30 and 7. — 54 × 30; 54 × 7

Then, multiply 54 by 30 and by 7. Work right to left. — 54 × 30 = 1620; 54 × 7 = 378

Finally, add the results to find the final product. — 1620 + 378 = 1998; 54 × 37 = 1,998

Practice

1. 73 × 21 = 1,533
2. 45 × 44 = 1,980
3. 76 × 32 = 2,432
4. 93 × 39 = 3,627

Simple Steps • Fifth Grade — Multiplying and Dividing Whole Number 7

Page 7

Multi-Digit Multiplication

Follow these steps to multiply by larger numbers.

When you multiply by a three-digit number, you also add a row with two zeros to align your third product starting in the hundreds column. — 872 × 494: 3488 + 78480 + 348800 = 430,768

When you multiply by a four-digit number, you will also insert another row with three zeros to align your answer starting in the thousands column. — 2312 × 1341: 2312 + 92480 + 693600 + 2312000 = 3,100,392

Practice

Solve the following problems. Show your work.

1. 143 × 142 = 20,306
2. 1503 × 741 = 1,113,723
3. 4610 × 1239 = 5,711,790
4. 1225 × 242 = 296,450
5. 774 × 455 = 352,170
6. 1811 × 1021 = 1,849,031
7. 3789 × 532 = 2,015,748
8. 5925 × 1112 = 6,588,600
9. 596 × 589 = 351,044

8 Multiplying and Dividing Whole Number — Simple Steps • Fifth Grade

Page 8

Dividing by 2-Digit Numbers

To divide by two-digit numbers, set up the division problem using a long division symbol. Be careful to keep columns aligned correctly, and remember to write the remainder at the top when you finish.

Solve: 14)718

First, estimate to find the first digit in the quotient. Think: How many times does the divisor go into the hundreds and tens place of the dividend? — 14 goes into 71 at least 5 times. The tens digit of the quotient is 5.

Then, multiply the tens digit of the quotient by the divisor. Subtract the result from the hundreds and tens place of the dividend. Bring down the ones place from the dividend to get the total number of ones left in the dividend. — 14 x 5 = 71. 71 − 70 = 1. There are 18 ones left in the dividend.

Finally, repeat the process for the ones digit. Estimate how many times the divisor goes into the ones. Multiply the ones digit of the quotient by the divisor. Subtract the result from the total number of ones to get the remainder. Record the remainder with the rest of the quotient. — 51 r4. 14 goes into 18 at least 1 time. The ones digit of the quotient is 1. 14 x 1 = 14. 18 − 14 = 4. 14 cannot divide 4, so the remainder is 4.

Hint: The remainder must always be less than the divisor.

1. 17)770 — 45 r5
2. 29)850 — 29 r9
3. 52)989 — 19 r1

Simple Steps • Fifth Grade — Multiplying and Dividing Whole Number 9

Page 9

Dividing by 2-Digit Numbers

For longer dividends, continue repeating the steps of division until there are no digits left in the dividend to divide.

Solve: 32)7980

First, estimate how many times the divisor goes into the thousands and hundreds place of the dividend. Multiply the hundreds digit of the quotient by the divisor. Subtract the result from the thousands and hundreds place of the dividend. Bring down the tens place to get the total number of tens left in the dividend. — 32 goes into 79 at least 2 times. The hundreds digit of the quotient is 2. 32 x 2 = 64. 79 − 64 = 15. There are 158 tens left in the dividend.

Then, continue to estimate, multiply, subtract, and bring down until there are no digits left in the dividend to divide. Finally, write the remainder at the top. — 249 r12. 32 goes into 158 at least 4 times. 32 x 4 = 128. 158 − 128 = 30. There are 300 ones left in the dividend. 32 goes into 300 at least 9 times. 32 x 9 = 288. 300 − 288 = 12. The remainder is 12.

Practice

Solve the following problems.

1. 31)1893 — 61 r2
2. 33)1095 — 99 r6
3. 42)2792 — 53 r12

10 Multiplying and Dividing Whole Number — Simple Steps • Fifth Grade

Page 10

Dividing by 2-Digit Numbers

Practice

Solve the following problems.

1. 23)264 — 11 r11
2. 46)857 — 18 r29
3. 58)2439 — 42 r3
4. 32)571 — 17 r27
5. 28)635 — 22 r19
6. 21)4,670 — 222 r8
7. 21)491 — 23 r8
8. 19)412 — 21 r13
9. 17)4,990 — 293 r9
10. 38)1460 — 38 r16
11. 33)1812 — 54 r30
12. 42)2792 — 66 r20

Simple Steps • Fifth Grade — Multiplying and Dividing Whole Number 11

Page 11

Problem Solving

You can use the multiplication strategies you have learned so far to solve more difficult problems.

First, underline the important information that you will need to solve the problem. — Students in Thornton's schools are collecting cans and bottles for a charity drive. They are having a contest to see which students and which schools collect the most cans and bottles. The contest lasts 15 weeks. One student, Raul, collects 33 cans per week. How many cans does Raul collect during the contest?

Next, determine which operation is best for solving the problem. — Raul collects the same number of cans each week. So, we can multiply the number of cans collected per week, 33, by the number of weeks, 15. (33 × 15)

Then, write the problem, with the digits aligned. — Multiply by 5 ones and regroup 1 ten: 33 × 15 → 165. Multiply by 1 ten. Use a zero as a placeholder: 165 + 330 = 495

Finally, solve the problem. — Raul collected 495 cans.

Practice

Solve the problem. Show your work in the space provided.

1. Elmhurst has 328 students. Each student collects 28 cans during the charity drive contest. How many cans do the students collect? — 1. 9,184 cans

12 Multiplying and Dividing Whole Number — Simple Steps • Fifth Grade

Page 12

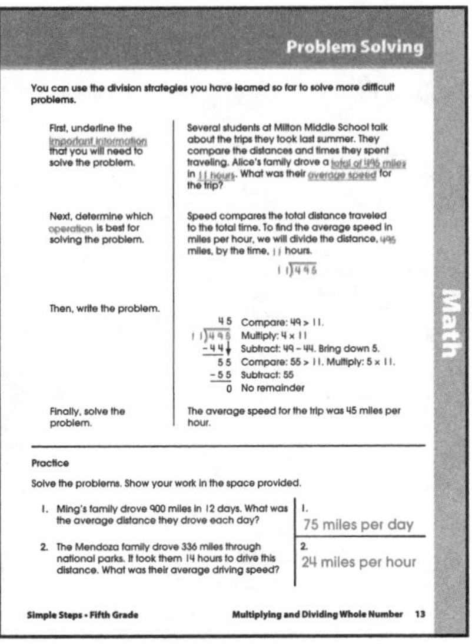

Problem Solving

You can use the division strategies you have learned so far to solve more difficult problems.

First, underline the important information that you will need to solve the problem.	Several students at Milton Middle School talk about the trips they took last summer. They compare the distances and times they spent traveling. Alice's family drove a total of 495 miles in 11 hours. What was their average speed for the trip?
Next, determine which operation is best for solving the problem.	Speed compares the total distance traveled to the total time. To find the average speed in miles per hour, we will divide the distance, 495 miles, by the time, 11 hours. $11\overline{)495}$
Then, write the problem.	45 Compare: 49 > 11. Multiply: 4 × 11. Subtract: 49 − 44. Bring down 5. Compare: 55 > 11. Multiply: 5 × 11. Subtract: 55. 0 No remainder
Finally, solve the problem.	The average speed for the trip was 45 miles per hour.

Practice

Solve the problems. Show your work in the space provided.

1. Ming's family drove 900 miles in 12 days. What was the average distance they drove each day? — 75 miles per day
2. The Mendoza family drove 336 miles through national parks. It took them 14 hours to drive this distance. What was their average driving speed? — 24 miles per hour

Simple Steps • Fifth Grade   Multiplying and Dividing Whole Number 13

Page 13

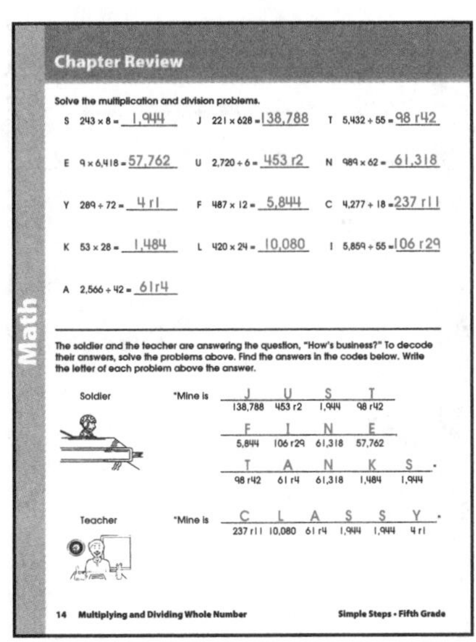

Chapter Review

Solve the multiplication and division problems.

S 243 × 8 = 1,944   J 221 × 628 = 138,788   T 5,432 ÷ 55 = 98 r42

E 9 × 6,418 = 57,762   U 2,720 ÷ 6 = 453 r2   N 989 × 62 = 61,318

Y 289 ÷ 72 = 4 r1   F 487 × 12 = 5,844   C 4,277 ÷ 18 = 237 r11

K 53 × 28 = 1,484   L 420 × 24 = 10,080   I 5,859 ÷ 55 = 106 r29

A 2,566 ÷ 42 = 61 r4

The soldier and the teacher are answering the question, "How's business?" To decode their answers, solve the problems above. Find the answers in the codes below. Write the letter of each problem above the answer.

Soldier "Mine is J U S T (138,788 453 r2 1,944 98 r42) F I N E (5,844 106 r29 61,318 57,762) T A N K S (98 r42 61 r4 61,318 1,484 1,944)."

Teacher "Mine is C L A S S Y (237 r11 10,080 61 r4 1,944 1,944 4 r1)."

14 Multiplying and Dividing Whole Number   Simple Steps • Fifth Grade

Page 14

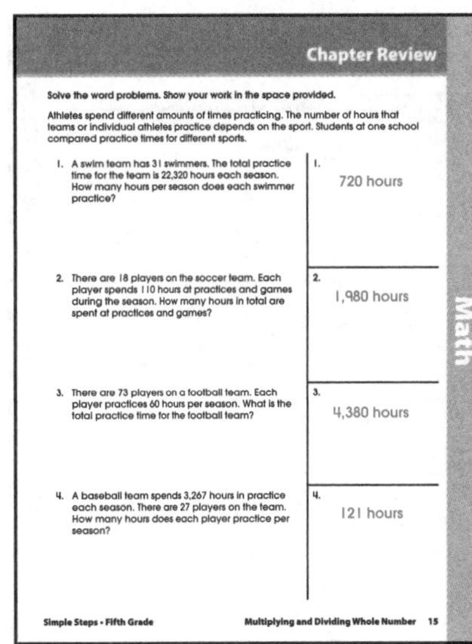

Chapter Review

Solve the word problems. Show your work in the space provided.

Athletes spend different amounts of times practicing. The number of hours that teams or individual athletes practice depends on the sport. Students at one school compared practice times for different sports.

1. A swim team has 31 swimmers. The total practice time for the team is 22,320 hours each season. How many hours per season does each swimmer practice? — 720 hours
2. There are 18 players on the soccer team. Each player spends 110 hours at practices and games during the season. How many hours in total are spent at practices and games? — 1,980 hours
3. There are 73 players on a football team. Each player practices 60 hours per season. What is the total practice time for the football team? — 4,380 hours
4. A baseball team spends 3,267 hours in practice each season. There are 27 players on the team. How many hours does each player practice per season? — 121 hours

Simple Steps • Fifth Grade   Multiplying and Dividing Whole Number 15

Page 15

Place Value

When you write a number, the position of a digit indicates the digit's value. The value of each place is 10 times the value of the place to the right.

Solve: Write the value of the underlined digit: 2,325,976

Visualize a place-value chart to see that 2 is in the ten thousands place. So, 2 has a value of 2 ten thousands, or 20,000.

Millions	Hundred Thousands	Ten Thousands	Thousands	Hundreds	Tens	Ones
2	3	2	5	9	7	6

Practice

Write the numerical value of the digit in the place named.

1. 5,363,246 hundred thousands — 300,000
2. 952,418 thousands — 2,000
3. 4,510,367 millions — 4,000,000
4. 8,123,405 hundreds — 400
5. 9,867,823 ten thousands — 60,000
6. 567,345 ones — 5
7. 1,328,976 tens — 70
8. 5,004,002 millions — 5,000,000
9. 2,982,023 ten thousands — 80,000

16 Understanding Place Value and Decimals   Simple Steps • Fifth Grade

Page 16

Place Value

You can also use place value to determine the value of decimals.

Solve: In 1,324.973, what is value of the 9?

Visualize a place-value chart to see that 9 is in the tenths place. So, 9 has a value of $\frac{9}{10}$, or 0.9.

thousands	hundreds	tens	ones	tenths	hundredths	thousandths
1	3	2	4 .	9	7	3

Practice

Write the place of the given digit.

1. 3 in $10.03 — hundredths
2. 7 in 7,000.2 — thousands
3. 9 in 691 — tens
4. 4 in 1.43 — tenths

Write the digit that is in the given place.

5. 731.045 ones — 1
6. 30.146 hundredths — 4
7. 2,910.42 ones — 0
8. 8.773 thousandths — 3
9. 16.51 hundredths — 1
10. 481.265 hundreds — 4

Simple Steps • Fifth Grade   Understanding Place Value and Decimals 17

Page 17

Powers of Ten

An exponent is a number that shows how many times a base number is to be used in multiplication. A power of 10 is a number with an exponent and the base number 10.

$10^1 = 10 = 10$
$10^2 = 10 \times 10 = 100$
$10^3 = 10 \times 10 \times 10 = 1{,}000$
$10^4 = 10 \times 10 \times 10 \times 10 = 10{,}000$

Solve: Convert 10^5 to a standard number.

First, look at the exponent to determine how many times the base number 10 is used in the number. Note how the exponent is equal to the number of zeros.	$10^5 = 10 \times 10 \times 10 \times 10 \times 10$
Next, multiply to determine the standard number.	$10 \times 10 \times 10 \times 10 \times 10 = 100{,}000$

Practice

Convert the powers of ten to standard numbers.

1. 10^3 = 1,000
2. 10^6 = 1,000,000
3. 10^7 = 10,000,000
4. 10^{12} = 1,000,000,000,000

Convert each value below to a power of ten.

5. 100 = 10^2
6. 100,000,000 = 10^8
7. 1,000,000,000 = 10^9
8. 10,000,000,000 = 10^{10}

18 Understanding Place Value and Decimals   Simple Steps • Fifth Grade

Page 18

Answer Key

Answer Key

Patterns of Zeros and Decimals

Math

To multiply a number by a power of 10, count the number of zeros in the power of 10. Move the decimal point in the product that many places to the right. Insert zeros as needed.

To multiply by 10, move the decimal point one place to the right.	0.4 → 4. 10 × 0.4 = 4
To multiply by 100, move the decimal point two places to the right.	0.40 → 40. 100 × 0.4 = 40
To multiply by 1,000, move the decimal point three places to the right.	0.400 → 400. 1,000 × 0.4 = 400

Practice

Multiply by the power of ten to find the product.

1. 21.48 × 10 = 214.8
2. 6.07 × 1,000 = 6,070
3. 7.58 × 100 = 758
4. 7.434 × 100,000 = 743,400
5. 4.43 × 10,000 = 44,300
6. 0.571 × 10 = 5.71

Simple Steps • Fifth Grade Understanding Place Value and Decimals 19

Page 19

Patterns of Zeros and Decimals

Math

To divide a number by a power of 10, count the number of zeros in the power of 10. Move the decimal point in the quotient that many places to the left. Insert zeros as needed.

To divide by 10, move the decimal point one place to the left.	265800. → 26580.0 265,800 ÷ 10 = 26,580
To divide by 100, move the decimal point two places to the left.	265800. → 2658.00 265,800 ÷ 100 = 2,658
To divide by 1,000, move the decimal point three places to the left.	265800. → 265.800 265,800 ÷ 1,000 = 265.8

Practice

Divide by the power of ten to find the quotient.

1. 13.4 ÷ 10 = 1.34
2. 27.65 ÷ 100 = 0.2765
3. 3.457 ÷ 100 = 0.03457
4. 726.9 ÷ 1,000 = 0.7269
5. 1,533,211 ÷ 10,000 = 153.3211
6. 27.75 ÷ 10 = 2.775

20 Understanding Place Value and Decimals Simple Steps • Fifth Grade

Page 20

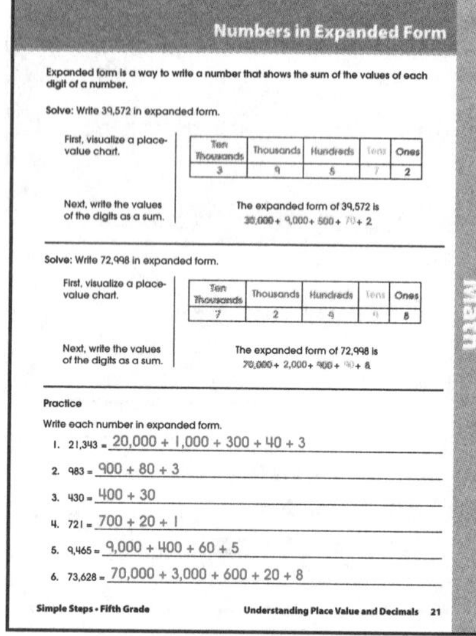

Numbers in Expanded Form

Math

Expanded form is a way to write a number that shows the sum of the values of each digit of a number.

Solve: Write 39,572 in expanded form.

First, visualize a place-value chart.

Ten Thousands	Thousands	Hundreds	Tens	Ones
3	9	5	7	2

Next, write the values of the digits as a sum.

The expanded form of 39,572 is 30,000 + 9,000 + 500 + 70 + 2

Solve: Write 72,998 in expanded form.

First, visualize a place-value chart.

Ten Thousands	Thousands	Hundreds	Tens	Ones
7	2	9	9	8

Next, write the values of the digits as a sum.

The expanded form of 72,998 is 70,000 + 2,000 + 900 + 90 + 8

Practice

Write each number in expanded form.

1. 21,343 = 20,000 + 1,000 + 300 + 40 + 3
2. 983 = 900 + 80 + 3
3. 430 = 400 + 30
4. 721 = 700 + 20 + 1
5. 9,465 = 9,000 + 400 + 60 + 5
6. 73,628 = 70,000 + 3,000 + 600 + 20 + 8

Simple Steps • Fifth Grade Understanding Place Value and Decimals 21

Page 21

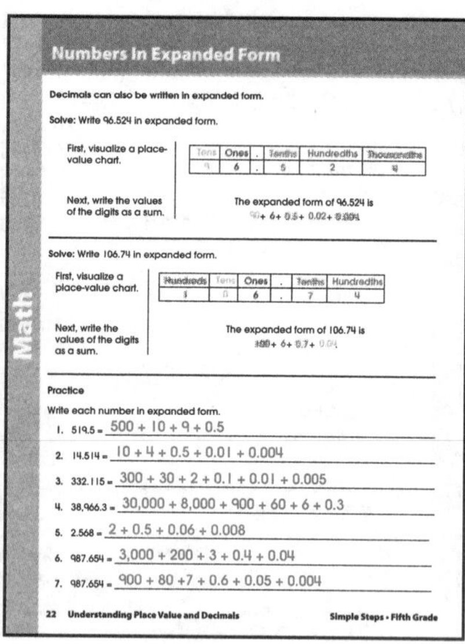

Numbers in Expanded Form

Math

Decimals can also be written in expanded form.

Solve: Write 96.524 in expanded form.

First, visualize a place-value chart.

Tens	Ones	.	Tenths	Hundredths	Thousandths
9	6	.	5	2	4

Next, write the values of the digits as a sum.

The expanded form of 96.524 is 90 + 6 + 0.5 + 0.02 + 0.004

Solve: Write 106.74 in expanded form.

First, visualize a place-value chart.

Hundreds	Tens	Ones	.	Tenths	Hundredths
1	0	6	.	7	4

Next, write the values of the digits as a sum.

The expanded form of 106.74 is 100 + 6 + 0.7 + 0.04

Practice

Write each number in expanded form.

1. 519.5 = 500 + 10 + 9 + 0.5
2. 14.514 = 10 + 4 + 0.5 + 0.01 + 0.004
3. 332.115 = 300 + 30 + 2 + 0.1 + 0.01 + 0.005
4. 38,966.3 = 30,000 + 8,000 + 900 + 60 + 6 + 0.3
5. 2.568 = 2 + 0.5 + 0.06 + 0.008
6. 987.654 = 3,000 + 200 + 3 + 0.4 + 0.04
7. 987.654 = 900 + 80 + 7 + 0.6 + 0.05 + 0.004

22 Understanding Place Value and Decimals Simple Steps • Fifth Grade

Page 22

Review

Math

Use everything you have learned so far about place value to answer the questions.

What is the place value of the underlined digit?

1. 83.764 tens
2. 328.367 thousandths

Write the digit that is in the given place.

3. 32,476—thousandths 6
4. 3,798.142—hundreds 7
5. 109,433—tens 3
6. 47.335—hundredths 5

Answer the following questions.

7. How many hundredths are in 0.4? 40
8. How many tens are in 215? 21.5

Convert each power of ten to a standard number.

9. 10^9 = 1,000,000,000
10. 10^5 = 100,000
11. 10^4 = 10,000
12. 10^2 = 100

Multiply or divide by the given power of ten.

13. 532.4 × 100 = 53,240
14. 12.22 ÷ 10 = 1.222
15. 7.217 × 1,000 = 7,217
16. 3356.7 ÷ 100 = 33.567

Write each number in expanded form.

17. 3,465 = 3,000 + 400 + 60 + 5
18. 83.926 = 80 + 3 + 0.9 + 0.02 + 0.006

Simple Steps • Fifth Grade Understanding Place Value and Decimals 23

Page 23

Comparing and Ordering Decimals

Math

Comparing decimals is similar to comparing whole numbers.

The symbol < means that the number on the left is less than the number on the right. The symbol > means that the number on the left is greater than the number on the right.

Solve: Compare 0.08 and 0.8 using <, >, or =.

0.08 ◯ 0.8

First, line up the digits by place value.	0.08 0.8
Next, compare the digits with the greatest place value.	0.08 0.8 Both numbers have 0 ones.
Finally, compare the digits in the next place value.	0.08 0.8 0 tenths < 8 tenths, so: 0.08 (<) 0.8

Practice

Compare using <, >, or =.

1. 0.94 (>) 0.84
2. 21.3 (<) 21.4
3. 1.03 (<) 1.06
4. 2.234 (<) 2.244
5. 19.75 (=) 19.750
6. 107.702 (>) 107.072
7. 14.64 (<) 14.7
8. 3.227 (>) 3.226

24 Understanding Place Value and Decimals Simple Steps • Fifth Grade

Page 24

Comparing and Ordering Decimals

Practice

Compare using <, >, or =.

1. 0.007 (<) 0.07
2. 0.9 (=) 0.90
3. 2.159 (<) 2.259
4. 101.05 (>) 101.005
5. 10.05 (>) 10.005
6. 9.50 (>) 7.05
7. 201.102 (<) 202.102
8. 1.230 (=) 1.23

Compare the numbers, and place them in order from least to greatest.

9. 0.7, 1.7, 0.07, 0.06 0.06, 0.07, 0.7, 1.7
10. 2.2, 2.3, 0.23, 0.3 0.23, 0.3, 2.2, 2.3
11. 3.032, 3.031, 4.032, 3.3 3.031, 3.032, 3.3, 4.032
12. 0.92, 0.902, 2.902, 0.95 0.902, 0.92, 0.95, 2.902
13. 5.7, 5.6, 5.06, 15.07 5.06, 5.6, 5.7, 15.07
14. 102.1, 101.2, 102.2, 101.1 101.1, 101.2, 102.1, 102.2
15. 7.89, 7.98, 8.99, 7.098 7.098, 7.89, 7.98, 8.99

Math

Simple Steps • Fifth Grade — Understanding Place Value and Decimals 25

Page 25

Rounding Whole Numbers and Decimals

Rounding a number means choosing a simpler number that is close to the original number's value.

Solve: Round 10.84 to the nearest whole number.

First, visualize 10.84 on a number line. It is between 10 and 11.	10 — 10.5 — 10.84 — 11
Next, round to the closer whole number.	10.84 is closer to 11. It rounds up to 11.

You can also round by looking at the digits in a number. Round 17.361 to the nearest whole number.

First, find the digit in the ones place. This is the place you are rounding to. Then, find the digit to the right of that place.	17.361 3 is to the right of the 7.
If that digit is 4 or less, round down. If it is 5 or more, round up.	3 is less than 4, so 17.361 rounds down to 17.

Practice

Round to the nearest whole number.

1. 8.4 = 8
2. 0.6 = 1
3. 2.24 = 2
4. 19.9 = 20
5. 4.449 = 4
6. 7.52 = 8
7. 91.121 = 91
8. 3.98 = 4
9. 22.7 = 23
10. 36.099 = 36

Math

26 Understanding Place Value and Decimals — Simple Steps • Fifth Grade

Page 26

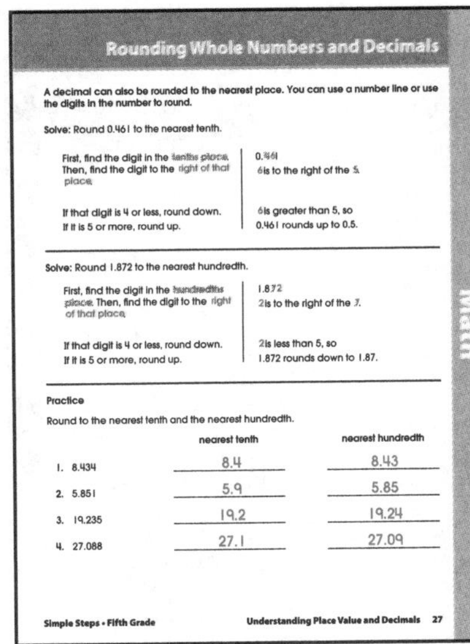

Rounding Whole Numbers and Decimals

A decimal can also be rounded to the nearest place. You can use a number line or use the digits in the number to round.

Solve: Round 0.461 to the nearest tenth.

First, find the digit in the tenths place. Then, find the digit to the right of that place.	0.461 6 is to the right of the 4.
If that digit is 4 or less, round down. If it is 5 or more, round up.	6 is greater than 5, so 0.461 rounds up to 0.5.

Solve: Round 1.872 to the nearest hundredth.

First, find the digit in the hundredths place. Then, find the digit to the right of that place.	1.872 2 is to the right of the 7.
If that digit is 4 or less, round down. If it is 5 or more, round up.	2 is less than 5, so 1.872 rounds down to 1.87.

Practice

Round to the nearest tenth and the nearest hundredth.

	nearest tenth	nearest hundredth
1. 8.434	8.4	8.43
2. 5.851	5.9	5.85
3. 19.235	19.2	19.24
4. 27.088	27.1	27.09

Math

Simple Steps • Fifth Grade — Understanding Place Value and Decimals 27

Page 27

Problem Solving

You can use the strategies you have learned about rounding to estimate measurements in real life.

First, underline the important information that you will need to solve the problem.	In Zion's science class, students are recording the masses of rocks they found during a nature walk. Ms. Essa wants each measurement rounded to the tenth of a unit. Zion's rock had a mass of 0.137 kilogram, according to the digital scale. What number should he record?
Next, determine which strategy is best for solving the problem.	To find a mass to the nearest tenth of a unit, round to the nearest tenth.
Then, represent the problem using a number line.	0.137 is between two tenths: 0.1 and 0.2. Plot those tenths on a number line. Then plot 0.137 on the same line. 0.1 — 0.137 — 0.15 — 0.2
Finally, the problem.	0.137 is closer to 0.1 than to 0.2. So, round down. Zion should record the mass as 0.1 kilogram.

Practice

Solve the problems. Show your work in the space provided.

1. Arturo will buy a sweater that costs $37.68. Arturo wants to know about how much money to bring. What is the cost of the sweater to the nearest dollar?	1. $38.00
2. The sign at a gas station says that regular gasoline costs $3.259 per gallon. What is the cost per gallon to the nearest hundredth of a dollar?	2. $3.26 per gallon

Math

28 Understanding Place Value and Decimals — Simple Steps • Fifth Grade

Page 28

Review

Use everything you have learned so far about comparing and rounding numbers to solve the problems.

Compare using <, >, or =.

1. 0.99 (>) 0.009
2. 214.01 (>) 214.001
3. 30.249 (<) 30.429
4. 9.008 (<) 9.08
5. 8.2 (=) 8.20
6. 23.4 (>) 2.34

Compare the numbers, and place them in order from least to greatest.

7. 0.7, 1.7, 0.07, 0.06 33.33, 33.34, 34.034, 34.33
8. 9.81, 9.081, 9.091, 9.082 9.081, 9.082, 9.091, 9.81

Round to the nearest whole number.

9. 95.945 96
10. 8.67 9
11. 99.198 99
12. 33.333 33

Round to the nearest tenth and the nearest hundredth.

	nearest tenth	nearest hundredth
13. 0.638	0.6	0.64
14. 1.454	1.5	1.45
15. 3.770	3.8	3.77
16. 6.923	6.9	6.92

Math

Simple Steps • Fifth Grade — Understanding Place Value and Decimals 29

Page 29

Chapter Review

What is the place value of the underlined digit?

1. 1,539.86 tens
2. 896,742 ten thousands
3. 35,263.8 thousands
4. 3,524,291.4 millions
5. 105.856 hundredths
6. 9,557.404 thousandths
7. 8,702,338 hundreds
8. 22.234 ones
9. 3,543.54 tenths
10. 777.73 tens

Write the digit that is in the given place.

11. 30.146—hundredths 4
12. 1,325.12—thousands 1
13. 1.325—tenths 3
14. 2,852.643—thousandths 3
15. 31,257,908—millions 1
16. 39.029—tens 3
17. 288,356—ten thousands 8
18. 4,900.007—thousandths 7

Answer the following questions.

19. How many ones are in 153? 153
20. How many hundreds are in 1,234? 12.34
21. How many tenths are in 15.03? 150.3
22. How many hundredths are in 0.3? 30
23. How many tens are in 227? 22.7

Math

30 Understanding Place Value and Decimals — Simple Steps • Fifth Grade

Page 30

Answer Key

Chapter Review

Convert each power of ten to a standard number.

24. 10^2 100
25. 10^8 100,000,000
26. 10^3 1,000
27. 10^6 1,000,000

Multiply by the given power of ten.

28. 8.75 × 1,000 = 8,750
29. 4.567 × 100 = 456.7
30. 91.95 × 10 = 919.5
31. 0.0377 × 10,000 = 377

Divide by the given power of ten.

32. 7,643 ÷ 100 = 76.43
33. 34,981 ÷ 1,000 = 34.981
34. 1,154,040 ÷ 10,000 = 115.404
35. 88.93 ÷ 10 = 8.893

Write each number in expanded form.

36. 592,682 = 500,000 + 90,000 + 2,000 + 600 + 80 + 2
37. 78.364 = 70 + 8 + 0.3 + 0.06 + 0.004
38. 97,933.4 = 90,000 + 7,000 + 900 + 30 + 3 + 0.4
39. 11.579 = 10 + 1 + 0.5 + 0.07 + 0.009
40. 1,523,899 = 1,000,000 + 500,000 + 20,000 + 3,000 + 800 + 90 + 9
41. 248.31 = 200 + 40 + 8 + 0.3 + 0.01
42. 2,202.477 = 2,000 + 200 + 2 + 0.4 + 0.07 + 0.007
43. 88,356.6 = 80,000 + 8,000 + 300 + 50 + 6 + 0.6

Simple Steps • Fifth Grade — Understanding Place Value and Decimals 31

Page 31

Chapter Review

Compare using <, >, or =.

44. 0.004 (<) 4.00
45. 614.05 (=) 614.05
46. 6.041 (<) 6.401
47. 8.26 (>) 8.026
48. 5.8 (<) 50.8
49. 2.9 (>) 2.009

Round to the nearest whole number.

50. 45.288 45
51. 97.5 98
52. 12.003 12
53. 72.71 73
54. 61.51 62
55. 34.598 35

Round to the nearest tenth and hundredth.

	nearest tenth	nearest hundredth
56. 7.953	8.0	7.95
57. 4.438	4.4	4.44
58. 5.299	5.3	5.30
59. 8.171	8.2	8.17
60. 0.562	0.6	0.56
61. 3.424	3.4	3.42

32 Understanding Place Value and Decimals — Simple Steps • Fifth Grade

Page 32

Adding Decimals to Hundredths

You can add decimals in the same way you add whole numbers. When writing the problem, be sure to keep the decimal points aligned and include the decimal point in the correct place in the sum.

Solve: 46.83 + 21.59

First, write the addition problem vertically, with decimal points aligned. Write the decimal point in the sum. — 46.83 + 21.59

Next, add the hundredths: 3 + 9 = 12. Write the 2 under the hundredths. Regroup 10 hundredths as 1 tenth. — 46.83 + 21.59 = ...2

Then, continue adding from right to left. Add the tenths, then the ones, and finally the tens. Regroup as needed. — 46.83 + 21.59 = 68.42

Practice

Solve the following problems.

1. 54.45 + 19.26 = 73.71
2. 732.84 + 21.25 = 754.09
3. 102.90 + 0.26 = 103.16
4. 103.36 + 34.21 = 137.57
5. 91.44 + 81.64 = 173.08
6. 217.77 + 109.47 = 327.24
7. 37.21 + 13.98 = 51.19
8. 455.16 + 80.28 = 535.44
9. 79.56 + 47.31 = 126.87

Simple Steps • Fifth Grade — Operations with Decimals 33

Page 33

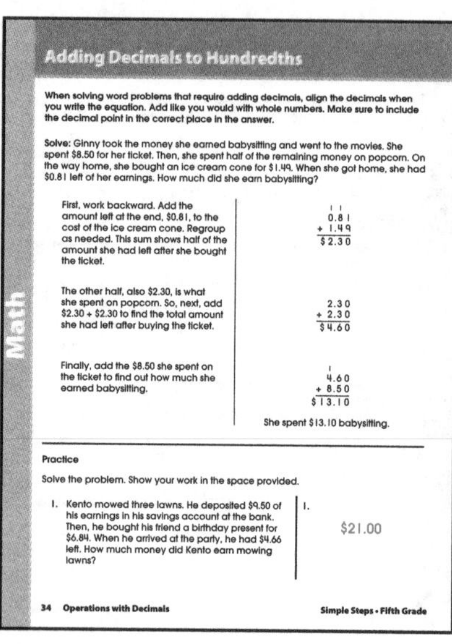

Adding Decimals to Hundredths

When solving word problems that require adding decimals, align the decimals when you write the equation. Add like you would with whole numbers. Make sure to include the decimal point in the correct place in the answer.

Solve: Ginny took the money she earned babysitting and went to the movies. She spent $8.50 for her ticket. Then, she spent half of the remaining money on popcorn. On the way home, she bought an ice cream cone for $1.49. When she got home, she had $0.81 left of her earnings. How much did she earn babysitting?

First, work backward. Add the amount left at the end, $0.81, to the cost of the ice cream cone. Regroup as needed. This sum shows half of the amount she had left after she bought the ticket. — 0.81 + 1.49 = $2.30

The other half, also $2.30, is what she spent on popcorn. So, next, add $2.30 + $2.30 to find the total amount she had left after buying the ticket. — 2.30 + 2.30 = $4.60

Finally, add the $8.50 she spent on the ticket to find out how much she earned babysitting. — 4.60 + 8.50 = $13.10

She spent $13.10 babysitting.

Practice

Solve the problem. Show your work in the space provided.

1. Kento mowed three lawns. He deposited $9.50 of his earnings in his savings account at the bank. Then, he bought his friend a birthday present for $6.84. When he arrived at the party, he had $4.66 left. How much money did Kento earn mowing lawns? — $21.00

34 Operations with Decimals — Simple Steps • Fifth Grade

Page 34

Adding Decimals to Hundredths

Practice

Solve the problems. Show your work in the space provided.

1. A pair of running shoes costs $22.29 for a store to buy from the manufacturer. The store owner wants to make a profit of $18.50. What should be the selling price of the shoes? — $40.79
2. Malcolm spent $48.74 on new speakers and $25.39 on computer games. After his purchases, he only had $0.58 left. How much money did Malcolm have before he went shopping? — $74.71
3. Opal is buying groceries for dinner. Salad costs $4.25, pasta costs $3.15, and bread costs $3.50. How much do Opal's groceries cost? — $10.90
4. Sheila bought three books for $12.63, $9.05, and $14.97. How much did she spend? — $36.65

Simple Steps • Fifth Grade — Operations with Decimals 35

Page 35

Subtracting Decimals to Hundredths

You can subtract decimals in the same way you subtract whole numbers. Be sure to align the decimal points and to include the decimal point in the correct place in the difference. Regroup as needed.

Solve: 79.62 − 38.89

First, write the subtraction problem vertically, with decimal points aligned. Write the decimal point in the sum. — 79.62 − 38.89

Start with the hundredths. Since 2 < 9, regroup 1 tenth in 6 tenths as 10 hundredths. Add 10 hundredths to the 2 hundredths to get 12 hundredths. Subtract hundredths. — ...3

Continue subtracting from right to left. Subtract the tenths, the ones, and the tens. Regroup as needed. — 40.73

Practice

Solve the following problems.

1. 8.86 − 5.29 = 3.57
2. 9.40 − 3.62 = 5.78
3. 75.13 − 23.21 = 51.92
4. 19.49 − 8.56 = 10.93
5. 83.94 − 22.47 = 61.47
6. 7.39 − 2.82 = 4.57
7. 41.72 − 31.34 = 10.38
8. 17.67 − 9.81 = 7.86
9. 95.09 − 27.21 = 67.88

36 Operations with Decimals — Simple Steps • Fifth Grade

Page 36

Answer Key

Subtracting Decimals to Hundredths

When solving word problems that require subtracting decimals, align the decimals when you write the equation. Subtract like you would with whole numbers. Make sure to include the decimal point in the correct place in your answer.

Solve: An owner of a clothing store bought a dress for $36.25 and sold it for $53.99. What was her profit?

First, write the problem vertically. Line up the decimal points and put the decimal point in the answer. — 53.99 − 36.25

Next, subtract the hundredths. — 53.99 − 36.25 = . 4

Continue subtracting from right to left. Subtract the tenths, the ones, and the tens. Regroup as needed. — 53.99 − 36.25 = 17.74

The store owner made $17.74 in profit.

Practice

Solve the problems. Show your work in the space provided.

1. A scale shows the mass of a box of books to be 12.79 kilograms. After removing a book, the mass is 10.98 kilograms. What is the mass of the removed book? — 1.81 kilograms
2. The height of the water in a barrel is 49.27 centimeters. After one month, due to evaporation, the height of water in the barrel is 29.52 centimeters. What is the decrease in water height during the month? — 19.75 centimeters

Math

Simple Steps • Fifth Grade — Operations with Decimals 37

Page 37

Subtracting Decimals to Hundredths

Practice

Solve the problems. Show your work in the space provided.

Pedro researches the amount of snowfall in a mountain town that is popular for skiing. The amount of snow measured last November was 21.23 inches. In December, the snowfall was 25.67 inches, and in January it was 24.78 inches. In February, the snowfall measured 22.17 inches.

1. Pedro compares the snowfall amounts in December and January. What is the difference between the two amounts? — 0.89 inch
2. How much more snow fell in December than in February? — 3.5 inches
3. What is the difference between the amount of snow measured in January and in February? — 2.61 inches

Math

38 Operations with Decimals — Simple Steps • Fifth Grade

Page 38

Inserting Zeros to Add and Subtract

When adding and subtracting decimals, you may need to insert zeros after the decimal point to help you keep the digits aligned. The value of a decimal does not change if you add zeros after the last nonzero digit. For example, 0.6 = 0.60 = 0.600 = 0.6000.

Solve: 0.6 + 0.39 + 1.23

First, write the problem vertically. Insert a zero as a placeholder in 0.6 to align the digits. Bring down the decimal point. — 0.60 + 0.39 + 1.23

Then, add from right to left. Add hundredths, tenths, and ones. Regroup as needed. — 0.60 + 0.39 + 1.23 = 2.22

Solve: 4.8 − 2.13

First, write the problem vertically. Insert a zero as a placeholder in 4.8. Bring down the decimal point. — 4.80 − 2.13

Then, subtract from right to left. Subtract hundredths, tenths, and ones. Regroup as needed. — 4.80 − 2.13 = 2.67

Practice

Add or subtract, inserting placeholder zeros as needed.

1. 2.1 + 0.25 = 2.35
2. 0.87 − 0.4 = 0.47
3. 14.37 + 3.1 = 17.47

Math

Simple Steps • Fifth Grade — Operations with Decimals 39

Page 39

Inserting Zeros to Add and Subtract

Practice

Solve the problems. Show your work in the space provided.

1. Nancy watched a video for 0.2 hours in the morning. At night, she continued watching the video for 0.87 hours. How much longer did she watch the video at night? — 0.67 hour
2. Kento spends 8.45 hours per week watching TV and 6.5 hours per week practicing the piano. Each week, how much more time does he spend watching TV? — 1.95 hours
3. Mr. Wilson just received his bill for $1,867.85 for the wedding dinner party for his daughter. His budget for the dinner was $2,000. How much less did the dinner cost than he expected? — $132.15 less than expected

Math

40 Operations with Decimals — Simple Steps • Fifth Grade

Page 40

Review

Use everything you have learned so far about adding and subtracting decimals to solve the problems.

Add or subtract, inserting placeholder zeros as needed.

1. 46.38 + 21.25 = 67.63
2. 64.81 + 7.3 = 72.11
3. 3.08 − 0.72 = 2.36
4. 78.6 − 38.89 = 39.71
5. 12.7 + 3.26 = 15.96
6. 8.81 + 0.13 = 8.94

Solve the word problems. Show your work in the space provided.

7. Chung's hat measures 6.37 units. His friend's hat measures 6.75 units. What is the difference in the hat sizes? — 0.38 units
8. In Benson Park, workers clear 1.64 acres of trash in an hour. At Alto Park, workers clear 1.77 acres in an hour. What total area is cleared in one hour? — 3.41 acres
9. Last month, Chou watched a movie that was 2.5 hours long. Yesterday, he watched a movie that was 1.38 hours long. How much longer was the movie he watched last month? — 1.12 hours
10. The Maxwells volunteered and pulled weeds at a playground. They worked 2.35 hours on Saturday and 1.8 hours on Sunday. How many hours altogether did they work? — 4.15 hours

Math

Simple Steps • Fifth Grade — Operations with Decimals 41

Page 41

Multiplying Decimals to Hundredths

To multiply decimals, first multiply as you would with whole numbers. Then, count the total number of decimal places in each factor. That is the number of decimal places to use in the product.

Solve: 8.7 × 0.3

First, multiply the numbers without their decimal points. Line up the numbers by place value. — 8.7 × 0.3. Think: 87 × 3 = 261.

Next, count the decimal places in each factor. — 8.7 → 1 decimal place; × 0.3 → 1 decimal place; 261

Then, add the number of decimal places to find out how many decimal places the product will have. This is how many numbers will be to the right of the decimal point in your answer. — 1 decimal place + 1 decimal place = 2 decimal places

Finally, write the decimal point in your product. — 8.7 × 0.3 = 2.61 → 2 decimal places

Practice

Underline the decimal places in each factor, then multiply.

1. 0.5 × 0.1 = 0.05
2. 0.9 × 0.3 = 0.27
3. 1.2 × 4.8 = 5.76
4. 2.6 × 7.7 = 20.02
5. 1.8 × 0.8 = 1.44
6. 3.4 × 3.6 = 12.24
7. 0.7 × 0.7 = 0.49
8. 9.6 × 0.9 = 8.64

Math

42 Operations with Decimals — Simple Steps • Fifth Grade

Page 42

Answer Key

Multiplying Decimals to Hundredths

Practice

Underline the decimal places in each factor, then multiply.

1. 199.6 × 8 = 1,596.8
2. 19.96 × 8 = 159.68
3. 199.6 × 0.8 = 159.68
4. 300.4 × 6 = 1,802.4
5. 30.04 × 6 = 180.24
6. 300.4 × 0.6 = 180.24
7. 250.2 × 5 = 1,251
8. 25.02 × 5 = 125.1
9. 250.2 × 0.5 = 125.10
10. 15.84 × 0.5 = 7.92
11. 42.6 × 0.6 = 25.56
12. 21.9 × 0.4 = 8.76
13. 21.7 × 4.2 = 91.14
14. 63.1 × 2.2 = 138.82
15. 3.41 × 6.2 = 21.142

Simple Steps • Fifth Grade   Operations with Decimals 43

Math

Page 43

Multiplying Decimals to Hundredths

Practice

Multiply. Underline the decimal places in the products.

1. 5.44 × 901.02 = 4,901.5488
2. 25.9 × 47.6 = 1,232.84
3. 291.23 × 4.34 = 1,263.9382
4. 3.08 × 608.8 = 1,875.104
5. 908.01 × 4.11 = 3,731.9211
6. 92.5 × 50.7 = 4,689.75
7. 901.3 × 8.2 = 7,390.66
8. 11.4 × 22.4 = 255.36
9. 109.21 × 32.2 = 3,516.562
10. 47.1 × 12.9 = 607.59
11. 81.75 × 2.7 = 220.725
12. 211.7 × 4.5 = 952.65
13. 18.08 × 18.7 = 338.096
14. 28.6 × 26.8 = 766.48
15. 727.3 × 7.0 = 5,091.10

44 Operations with Decimals   Simple Steps • Fifth Grade

Math

Page 44

Dividing Decimals to Hundredths

To divide a decimal by a whole number, determine the correct placement of the decimal point in your answer, then divide as usual.

Solve: 2.5 ÷ 4

First, write the decimal point in the quotient. Then, divide as you would divide whole numbers.
4 goes into 25 at least 6 times. 4 × 6 = 24. 25 − 24 = 1

Next, instead of writing 1 as the remainder, write a **zero** in the hundredths place and bring it down. Continue dividing.
Write a zero here. 4 goes into 10 at least 2 times. 4 × 2 = 8. 10 − 8 = 2

Finally, instead of writing 2 as the remainder, write a **zero** in the thousandths place and bring it down. Estimate, multiply, and subtract to get the final answer.
Write a zero here. 4 goes into 20 at least 5 times. 4 × 5 = 20. 20 − 20 = 0

Practice

Divide.

1. 5)2.7 = 0.54
2. 5)4.19 = 0.838
3. 4)0.31 = 0.0775

Simple Steps • Fifth Grade   Operations with Decimals 45

Math

Page 45

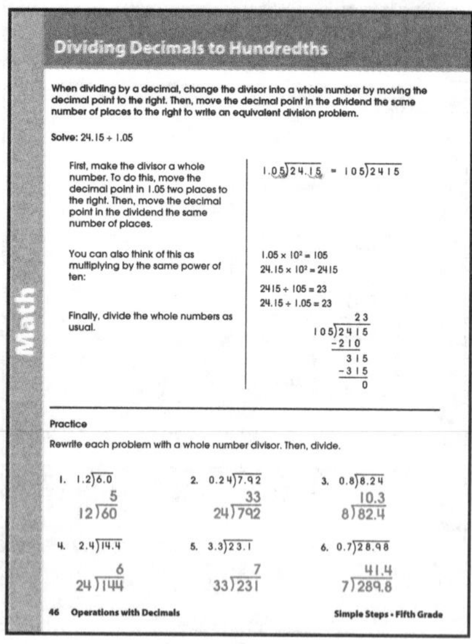

Page 46

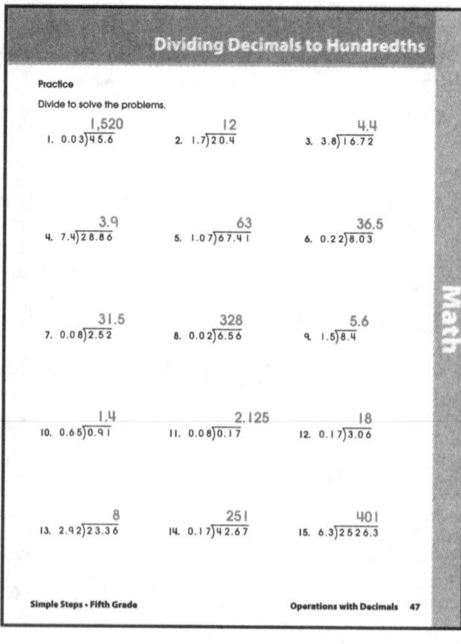

Page 47

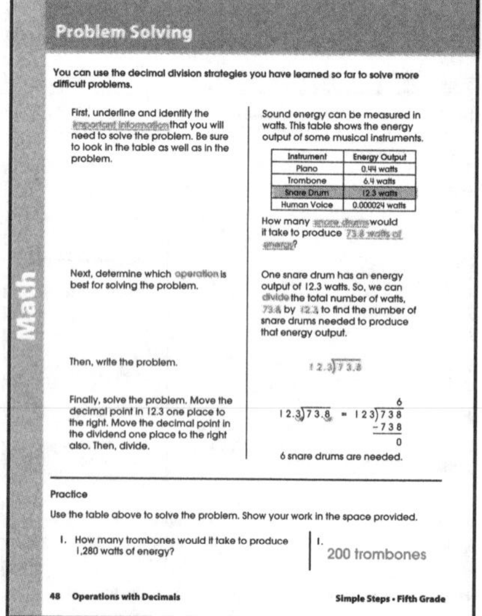

Page 48

Answer Key

Review

Use everything you have learned so far about decimal operations to solve the problems.

Multiply or divide.

1. 6.2 × 0.4 = 2.48
2. 3.05 × 2.83 = 8.6315
3. 5.73 × 2.83 = 16.2159
4. 4.03 × 1.1 = 4.433
5. 0.26)65 = 260
6. 0.04)19 = 475
7. 0.7)13.23 = 18.9
8. 1.3)2.86 = 2.2

Solve the problems. Show your work in the space provided.

9. Roberto bought a 12-pack of bottled water. Each bottle held 0.75 liters. How many liters of water did he buy? — 9 liters
10. A hike is 26.4 miles. Alicia wants to divide it equally over 3 days. How far does she need to hike each day? — 8.8 miles each day
11. There are 6.75 buckets of sand in a sandbox. If each full bucket holds 4.32 pounds of sand, how many pounds of sand are there in the sandbox? — 29.16 pounds

Math

Simple Steps • Fifth Grade — Operations with Decimals 49

Page 49

Chapter Review

Add or subtract.

1. 0.23 + 0.91 = 1.14
2. 78.07 + 1.34 = 79.41
3. 9.06 + 2.78 = 11.84
4. 48.78 + 9.03 = 57.81
5. 29.08 − 2.10 = 26.98
6. 13.73 − 8.64 = 5.09
7. 3.89 − 1.47 = 2.42
8. 33.04 − 6.75 = 26.29
9. 0.98 + 0.87 = 1.85
10. 26.32 + 1.14 = 27.46
11. 42.55 − 3.75 = 38.80
12. 81.12 + 56.29 = 137.41
13. Add 12.7 and 3.26. — 15.96
14. Subtract 2.21 from 8.3. — 6.09
15. Add 5.63 and 2.1. — 7.73
16. Add 26.3 and 5.25. — 31.55

Math

50 Operations with Decimals — Simple Steps • Fifth Grade

Page 50

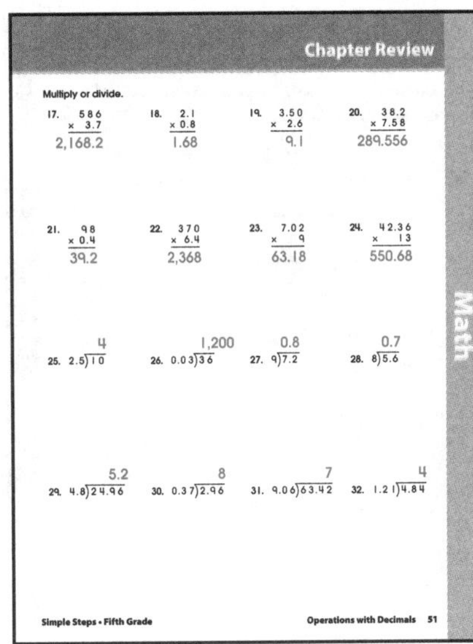

Chapter Review

Multiply or divide.

17. 586 × 3.7 = 2,168.2
18. 2.1 × 0.8 = 1.68
19. 3.50 × 2.6 = 9.1
20. 38.2 × 7.58 = 289.556
21. 98 × 0.4 = 39.2
22. 370 × 6.4 = 2,368
23. 7.02 × 9 = 63.18
24. 42.36 × 13 = 550.68
25. 2.5)10 = 4
26. 0.03)36 = 1,200
27. 9)7.2 = 0.8
28. 8)5.6 = 0.7
29. 4.8)24.96 = 5.2
30. 0.37)2.96 = 8
31. 9.06)63.42 = 7
32. 1.21)4.84 = 4

Math

Simple Steps • Fifth Grade — Operations with Decimals 51

Page 51

Chapter Review

Solve the problems. Show your work in the space provided.

33. Jeff wants to buy a vase for $32.75. He only has $25.15. How much does Jeff need to borrow from his brother to buy the vase? — $7.60
34. Booker needs to pay his rent. He has $1,252.45 in the bank. His rent is $672.30. How much money will Booker have left in the bank after he pays his rent? — $580.15
35. The Thomas triplets want to buy some oranges. Justin has 23 cents, Jarrod has 45 cents, and Jeremy has 52 cents. How much money do the triplets have? — $1.20
36. A school lunch costs $1.55. Sean has $2.45. How much money will he have left after buying lunch? — $0.90
37. Fred bought 7 games on clearance for $104.65 total. Each game was on sale for the same price. How much did each game cost? — $14.95
38. Gas costs $2.64 a gallon. Elaine spent $38.28 at the gas station. How many gallons of gas did she buy? — 14.5 gallons
39. There are 2.5 servings in a can of tuna fish. How many servings are there in 7 cans? — 17.5 servings
40. There are 5.28 cups of pudding to be divided into 6 dishes. How much pudding should be put into each dish to make them equal? — 0.88 cup

Math

52 Operations with Decimals — Simple Steps • Fifth Grade

Page 52

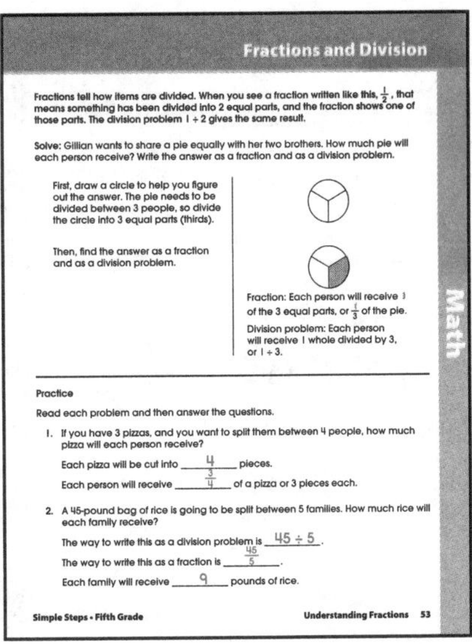

Fractions and Division

Fractions tell how items are divided. When you see a fraction written like this, $\frac{1}{2}$, that means something has been divided into 2 equal parts, and the fraction shows one of those parts. The division problem 1 ÷ 2 gives the same result.

Solve: Gillian wants to share a pie equally with her two brothers. How much pie will each person receive? Write the answer as a fraction and as a division problem.

First, draw a circle to help you figure out the answer. The pie needs to be divided between 3 people, so divide the circle into 3 equal parts (thirds).

Then, find the answer as a fraction and as a division problem.

Fraction: Each person will receive 1 of the 3 equal parts, or $\frac{1}{3}$ of the pie.

Division problem: Each person will receive 1 whole divided by 3, or 1 ÷ 3.

Practice

Read each problem and then answer the questions.

1. If you have 3 pizzas, and you want to split them between 4 people, how much pizza will each person receive?
   Each pizza will be cut into 4 pieces.
   Each person will receive $\frac{3}{4}$ of a pizza or 3 pieces each.
2. A 45-pound bag of rice is going to be split between 5 families. How much rice will each family receive?
   The way to write this as a division problem is 45 ÷ 5.
   The way to write this as a fraction is $\frac{45}{5}$.
   Each family will receive 9 pounds of rice.

Math

Simple Steps • Fifth Grade — Understanding Fractions 53

Page 53

Changing Improper Fractions to Mixed Numbers

An improper fraction has a numerator that is equal to or greater than the denominator. Sometimes you will need to express an improper fraction as a mixed number that has the same value.

Solve: Rewrite the improper fraction $\frac{5}{3}$ as a mixed number.

First, draw a diagram to show $\frac{5}{3}$. The denominator, 3, shows the number of equal parts. Draw a circle, divide it into 3 equal parts and shade all 3. Since the numerator, 5, is greater than the denominator, 3, there is more than one whole. Draw a second circle, divide it into 3 equal parts, and shade 2 more parts so $\frac{5}{3}$ is shaded.

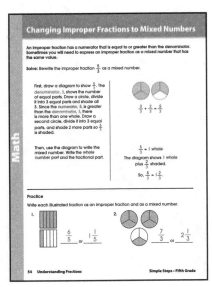

$\frac{3}{3} + \frac{2}{3} = \frac{5}{3}$

Then, use the diagram to write the mixed number. Write the whole number part and the fractional part.

$\frac{5}{3}$ = 1 whole

The diagram shows 1 whole plus $\frac{2}{3}$ shaded.

So, $\frac{5}{3} = 1\frac{2}{3}$.

Practice

Write each illustrated fraction as an improper fraction and as a mixed number.

1. $\frac{6}{5}$ or $1\frac{1}{5}$
2. $\frac{7}{3}$ or $2\frac{1}{3}$

Math

54 Understanding Fractions — Simple Steps • Fifth Grade

Page 54

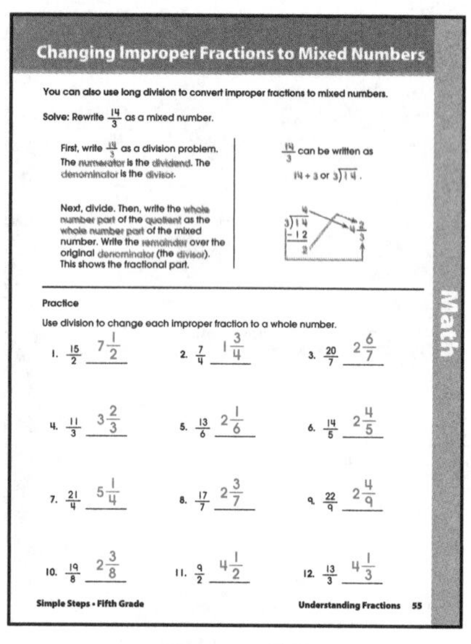

Changing Improper Fractions to Mixed Numbers

You can also use long division to convert improper fractions to mixed numbers.

Solve: Rewrite $\frac{14}{3}$ as a mixed number.

First, write $\frac{14}{3}$ as a division problem. The numerator is the dividend. The denominator is the divisor.

$\frac{14}{3}$ can be written as $14 \div 3$ or $3\overline{)14}$.

Next, divide. Then, write the whole number part of the quotient as the whole number part of the mixed number. Write the remainder over the original denominator (the divisor). This shows the fractional part.

$3\overline{)14}$ = 4 remainder 2 → $4\frac{2}{3}$

Practice

Use division to change each improper fraction to a whole number.

1. $\frac{15}{2}$ $7\frac{1}{2}$
2. $\frac{7}{4}$ $1\frac{3}{4}$
3. $\frac{20}{7}$ $2\frac{6}{7}$
4. $\frac{11}{3}$ $3\frac{2}{3}$
5. $\frac{13}{6}$ $2\frac{1}{6}$
6. $\frac{14}{5}$ $2\frac{4}{5}$
7. $\frac{21}{4}$ $5\frac{1}{4}$
8. $\frac{17}{7}$ $2\frac{3}{7}$
9. $\frac{22}{9}$ $2\frac{4}{9}$
10. $\frac{19}{8}$ $2\frac{3}{8}$
11. $\frac{9}{2}$ $4\frac{1}{2}$
12. $\frac{13}{3}$ $4\frac{1}{3}$

Math

Simple Steps • Fifth Grade Understanding Fractions 55

Page 55

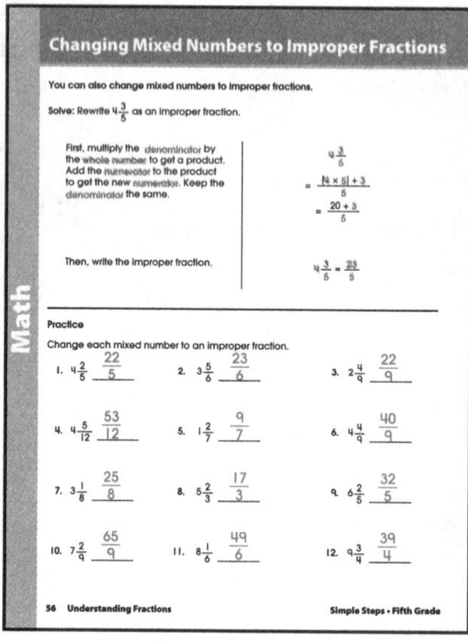

Changing Mixed Numbers to Improper Fractions

You can also change mixed numbers to improper fractions.

Solve: Rewrite $4\frac{3}{5}$ as an improper fraction.

First, multiply the denominator by the whole number to get a product. Add the numerator to the product to get the new numerator. Keep the denominator the same.

$4\frac{3}{5} = \frac{(4 \times 5) + 3}{5} = \frac{20 + 3}{5}$

Then, write the improper fraction.

$4\frac{3}{5} = \frac{23}{5}$

Practice

Change each mixed number to an improper fraction.

1. $4\frac{2}{5}$ $\frac{22}{5}$
2. $3\frac{5}{6}$ $\frac{23}{6}$
3. $2\frac{4}{9}$ $\frac{22}{9}$
4. $4\frac{5}{12}$ $\frac{53}{12}$
5. $1\frac{2}{7}$ $\frac{9}{7}$
6. $4\frac{4}{9}$ $\frac{40}{9}$
7. $3\frac{1}{8}$ $\frac{25}{8}$
8. $5\frac{2}{3}$ $\frac{17}{3}$
9. $6\frac{2}{5}$ $\frac{32}{5}$
10. $7\frac{2}{9}$ $\frac{65}{9}$
11. $8\frac{1}{6}$ $\frac{49}{6}$
12. $9\frac{3}{4}$ $\frac{39}{4}$

Math

56 Understanding Fractions Simple Steps • Fifth Grade

Page 56

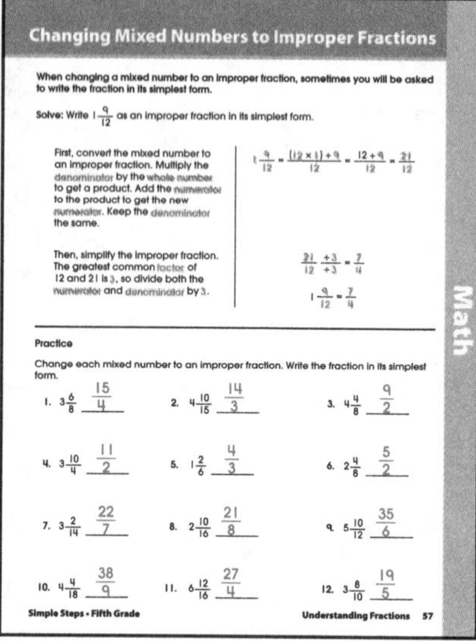

Changing Mixed Numbers to Improper Fractions

When changing a mixed number to an improper fraction, sometimes you will be asked to write the fraction in its simplest form.

Solve: Write $1\frac{9}{12}$ as an improper fraction in its simplest form.

First, convert the mixed number to an improper fraction. Multiply the denominator by the whole number to get a product. Add the numerator to the product to get the new numerator. Keep the denominator the same.

$1\frac{9}{12} = \frac{(12 \times 1) + 9}{12} = \frac{12 + 9}{12} = \frac{21}{12}$

Then, simplify the improper fraction. The greatest common factor of 12 and 21 is 3, so divide both the numerator and denominator by 3.

$\frac{21}{12} \frac{\div 3}{\div 3} = \frac{7}{4}$

$1\frac{9}{12} = \frac{7}{4}$

Practice

Change each mixed number to an improper fraction. Write the fraction in its simplest form.

1. $3\frac{6}{8}$ $\frac{15}{4}$
2. $4\frac{10}{15}$ $\frac{14}{3}$
3. $4\frac{4}{8}$ $\frac{9}{2}$
4. $3\frac{10}{4}$ $\frac{11}{2}$
5. $1\frac{2}{6}$ $\frac{4}{3}$
6. $2\frac{4}{8}$ $\frac{5}{2}$
7. $3\frac{2}{14}$ $\frac{22}{7}$
8. $2\frac{10}{16}$ $\frac{21}{8}$
9. $5\frac{10}{12}$ $\frac{35}{6}$
10. $4\frac{4}{18}$ $\frac{38}{9}$
11. $6\frac{12}{16}$ $\frac{27}{4}$
12. $3\frac{8}{10}$ $\frac{19}{5}$

Math

Simple Steps • Fifth Grade Understanding Fractions 57

Page 57

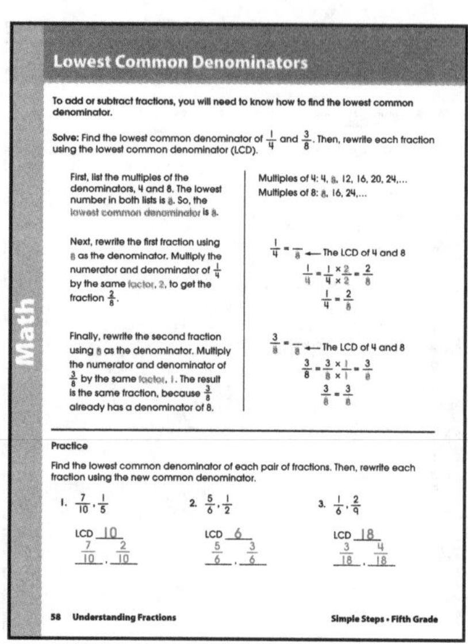

Lowest Common Denominators

To add or subtract fractions, you will need to know how to find the lowest common denominator.

Solve: Find the lowest common denominator of $\frac{1}{4}$ and $\frac{3}{8}$. Then, rewrite each fraction using the lowest common denominator (LCD).

First, list the multiples of the denominators, 4 and 8. The lowest number in both lists is 8. So, the lowest common denominator is 8.

Multiples of 4: 4, 8, 12, 16, 20, 24,...
Multiples of 8: 8, 16, 24,...

Next, rewrite the first fraction using 8 as the denominator. Multiply the numerator and denominator of $\frac{1}{4}$ by the same factor, 2, to get the fraction $\frac{2}{8}$.

$\frac{1}{4} = \frac{}{8}$ ← The LCD of 4 and 8

$\frac{1}{4} = \frac{1 \times 2}{4 \times 2} = \frac{2}{8}$

$\frac{1}{4} = \frac{2}{8}$

Finally, rewrite the second fraction using 8 as the denominator. Multiply the numerator and denominator of $\frac{3}{8}$ by the same factor, 1. The result is the same fraction, because $\frac{3}{8}$ already has a denominator of 8.

$\frac{3}{8} = \frac{}{8}$ ← The LCD of 4 and 8

$\frac{3}{8} = \frac{3 \times 1}{8 \times 1} = \frac{3}{8}$

$\frac{3}{8} = \frac{3}{8}$

Practice

Find the lowest common denominator of each pair of fractions. Then, rewrite each fraction using the new common denominator.

1. $\frac{7}{10}, \frac{1}{5}$ LCD 10; $\frac{7}{10}, \frac{2}{10}$
2. $\frac{5}{6}, \frac{1}{2}$ LCD 6; $\frac{5}{6}, \frac{3}{6}$
3. $\frac{1}{6}, \frac{2}{9}$ LCD 18; $\frac{3}{18}, \frac{4}{18}$

Math

58 Understanding Fractions Simple Steps • Fifth Grade

Page 58

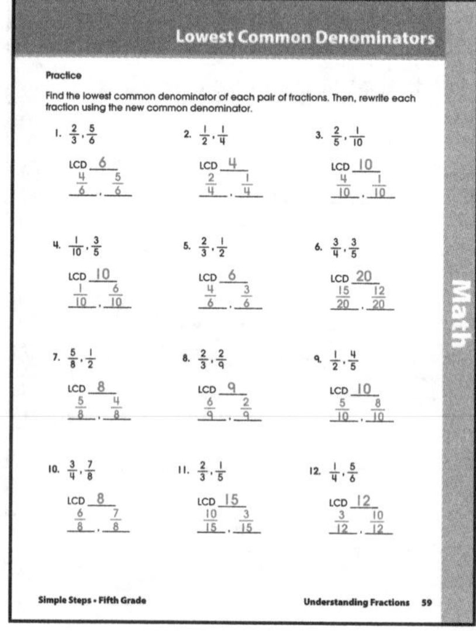

Lowest Common Denominators

Practice

Find the lowest common denominator of each pair of fractions. Then, rewrite each fraction using the new common denominator.

1. $\frac{2}{3}, \frac{5}{6}$ LCD 6; $\frac{4}{6}, \frac{5}{6}$
2. $\frac{1}{2}, \frac{1}{4}$ LCD 4; $\frac{2}{4}, \frac{1}{4}$
3. $\frac{2}{5}, \frac{1}{10}$ LCD 10; $\frac{4}{10}, \frac{1}{10}$
4. $\frac{1}{10}, \frac{3}{5}$ LCD 10; $\frac{1}{10}, \frac{6}{10}$
5. $\frac{2}{3}, \frac{1}{2}$ LCD 6; $\frac{4}{6}, \frac{3}{6}$
6. $\frac{3}{4}, \frac{3}{5}$ LCD 20; $\frac{15}{20}, \frac{12}{20}$
7. $\frac{5}{8}, \frac{1}{2}$ LCD 8; $\frac{5}{8}, \frac{4}{8}$
8. $\frac{2}{3}, \frac{2}{9}$ LCD 9; $\frac{6}{9}, \frac{2}{9}$
9. $\frac{1}{2}, \frac{4}{5}$ LCD 10; $\frac{5}{10}, \frac{8}{10}$
10. $\frac{3}{4}, \frac{7}{8}$ LCD 8; $\frac{6}{8}, \frac{7}{8}$
11. $\frac{2}{3}, \frac{1}{5}$ LCD 15; $\frac{10}{15}, \frac{3}{15}$
12. $\frac{1}{4}, \frac{5}{6}$ LCD 12; $\frac{3}{12}, \frac{10}{12}$

Math

Simple Steps • Fifth Grade Understanding Fractions 59

Page 59

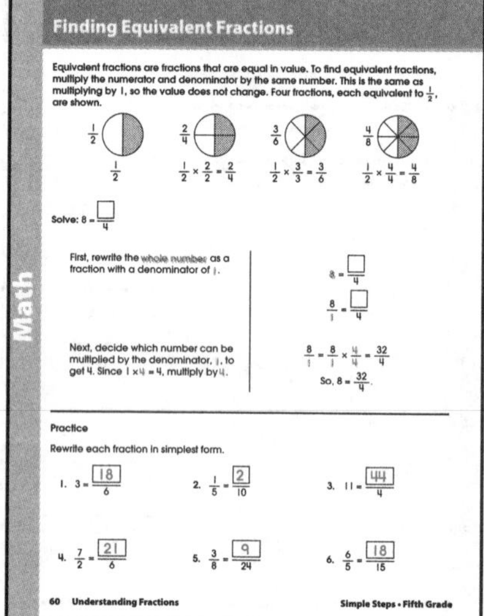

Finding Equivalent Fractions

Equivalent fractions are fractions that are equal in value. To find equivalent fractions, multiply the numerator and denominator by the same number. This is the same as multiplying by 1, so the value does not change. Four fractions, each equivalent to $\frac{1}{2}$, are shown.

$\frac{1}{2}$ $\frac{2}{4}$ $\frac{3}{6}$ $\frac{4}{8}$

$\frac{1}{2}$ $\frac{1}{2} \times \frac{2}{2} = \frac{2}{4}$ $\frac{1}{2} \times \frac{3}{3} = \frac{3}{6}$ $\frac{1}{2} \times \frac{4}{4} = \frac{4}{8}$

Solve: $8 = \frac{\square}{4}$

First, rewrite the whole number as a fraction with a denominator of 1.

$8 = \frac{\square}{4}$

$\frac{8}{1} = \frac{\square}{4}$

Next, decide which number can be multiplied by the denominator, 1, to get 4. Since $1 \times 4 = 4$, multiply by 4.

$\frac{8}{1} = \frac{8}{1} \times \frac{4}{4} = \frac{32}{4}$

So, $8 = \frac{32}{4}$.

Practice

Rewrite each fraction in simplest form.

1. $3 = \frac{18}{6}$
2. $\frac{1}{5} = \frac{2}{10}$
3. $11 = \frac{44}{4}$
4. $\frac{7}{2} = \frac{21}{6}$
5. $\frac{3}{8} = \frac{9}{24}$
6. $\frac{6}{5} = \frac{18}{15}$

Math

60 Understanding Fractions Simple Steps • Fifth Grade

Page 60

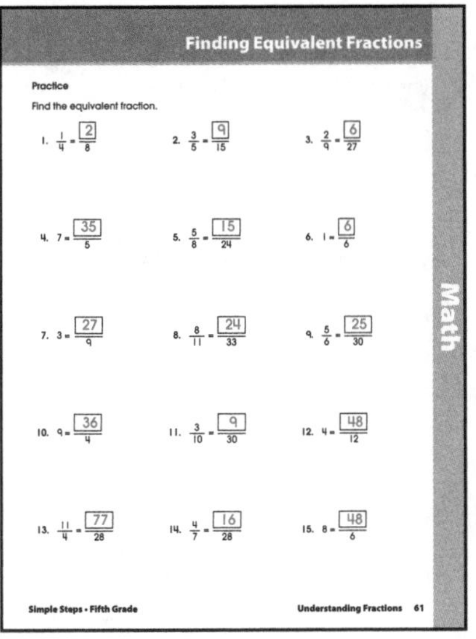

Finding Equivalent Fractions

Practice

Find the equivalent fraction.

1. $\frac{1}{4} = \frac{2}{8}$ 2. $\frac{3}{5} = \frac{9}{15}$ 3. $\frac{2}{9} = \frac{6}{27}$

4. $7 = \frac{35}{5}$ 5. $\frac{5}{8} = \frac{15}{24}$ 6. $1 = \frac{6}{6}$

7. $3 = \frac{27}{9}$ 8. $\frac{8}{11} = \frac{24}{33}$ 9. $\frac{5}{6} = \frac{25}{30}$

10. $9 = \frac{36}{4}$ 11. $\frac{3}{10} = \frac{9}{30}$ 12. $4 = \frac{48}{12}$

13. $\frac{11}{4} = \frac{77}{28}$ 14. $\frac{4}{7} = \frac{16}{28}$ 15. $8 = \frac{48}{6}$

Simple Steps • Fifth Grade Understanding Fractions 61

Math

Page 61

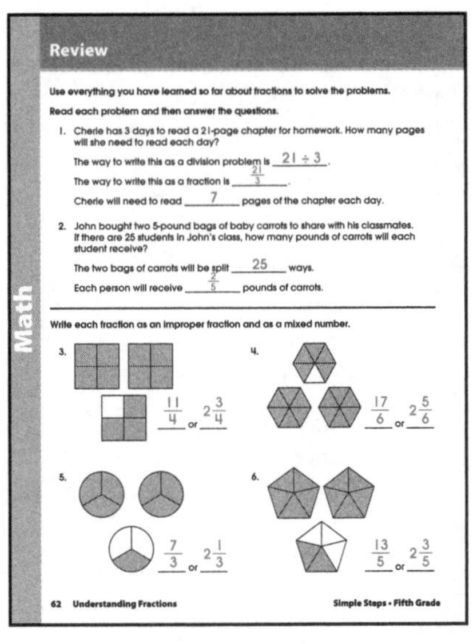

Review

Use everything you have learned so far about fractions to solve the problems.

Read each problem and then answer the questions.

1. Cherie has 3 days to read a 21-page chapter for homework. How many pages will she need to read each day?
   The way to write this as a division problem is $21 \div 3$.
   The way to write this as a fraction is $\frac{21}{3}$.
   Cherie will need to read 7 pages of the chapter each day.
2. John bought two 5-pound bags of baby carrots to share with his classmates. If there are 25 students in John's class, how many pounds of carrots will each student receive?
   The two bags of carrots will be split 25 ways.
   Each person will receive $\frac{2}{5}$ pounds of carrots.

Write each fraction as an improper fraction and as a mixed number.

3. $\frac{11}{4}$ or $2\frac{3}{4}$ 4. $\frac{17}{6}$ or $2\frac{5}{6}$

5. $\frac{7}{3}$ or $2\frac{1}{3}$ 6. $\frac{13}{5}$ or $2\frac{3}{5}$

62 Understanding Fractions Simple Steps • Fifth Grade

Math

Page 62

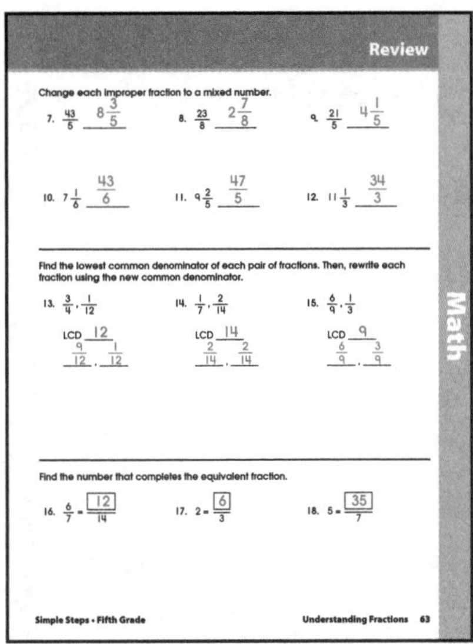

Review

Change each improper fraction to a mixed number.

7. $\frac{43}{5}$ $8\frac{3}{5}$ 8. $\frac{23}{8}$ $2\frac{7}{8}$ 9. $\frac{21}{5}$ $4\frac{1}{5}$

10. $7\frac{1}{6}$ $\frac{43}{6}$ 11. $9\frac{2}{5}$ $\frac{47}{5}$ 12. $11\frac{1}{3}$ $\frac{34}{3}$

Find the lowest common denominator of each pair of fractions. Then, rewrite each fraction using the new common denominator.

13. $\frac{3}{4}, \frac{1}{12}$ LCD 12 $\frac{9}{12}, \frac{1}{12}$ 14. $\frac{1}{7}, \frac{2}{14}$ LCD 14 $\frac{2}{14}, \frac{2}{14}$ 15. $\frac{6}{9}, \frac{1}{3}$ LCD 9 $\frac{6}{9}, \frac{3}{9}$

Find the number that completes the equivalent fraction.

16. $\frac{6}{7} = \frac{12}{14}$ 17. $2 = \frac{6}{3}$ 18. $5 = \frac{35}{7}$

Simple Steps • Fifth Grade Understanding Fractions 63

Math

Page 63

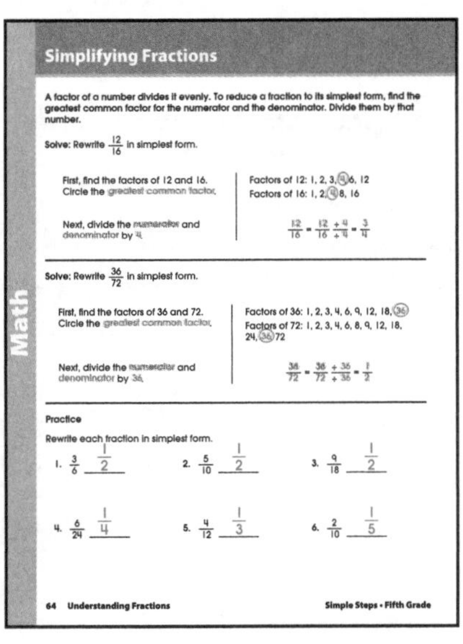

Simplifying Fractions

A factor of a number divides it evenly. To reduce a fraction to its simplest form, find the greatest common factor for the numerator and the denominator. Divide them by that number.

Solve: Rewrite $\frac{12}{16}$ in simplest form.

First, find the factors of 12 and 16. Circle the greatest common factor. — Factors of 12: 1, 2, 3, 4, 6, 12; Factors of 16: 1, 2, 4, 8, 16

Next, divide the numerator and denominator by 4. — $\frac{12}{16} = \frac{12 \div 4}{16 \div 4} = \frac{3}{4}$

Solve: Rewrite $\frac{36}{72}$ in simplest form.

First, find the factors of 36 and 72. Circle the greatest common factor. — Factors of 36: 1, 2, 3, 4, 6, 9, 12, 18, 36; Factors of 72: 1, 2, 3, 4, 6, 8, 9, 12, 18, 24, 36, 72

Next, divide the numerator and denominator by 36. — $\frac{36}{72} = \frac{36 \div 36}{72 \div 36} = \frac{1}{2}$

Practice

Rewrite each fraction in simplest form.

1. $\frac{3}{6}$ $\frac{1}{2}$ 2. $\frac{5}{10}$ $\frac{1}{2}$ 3. $\frac{9}{18}$ $\frac{1}{2}$

4. $\frac{6}{24}$ $\frac{1}{4}$ 5. $\frac{4}{12}$ $\frac{1}{3}$ 6. $\frac{2}{10}$ $\frac{1}{5}$

64 Understanding Fractions Simple Steps • Fifth Grade

Math

Page 64

Simplifying Mixed Numbers

A mixed number is in simplest form if its fractional part is in simplest form and names a number less than 1.

Solve: Rewrite $3\frac{12}{8}$ in simplest form.

First, consider the whole number and fraction separately.	$3\frac{12}{8} = 3 + \frac{12}{8}$
Next, simplify the fraction. Find the greatest common factor of 12 and 8. Divide both the numerator and denominator by the greatest common factor, 4.	$\frac{12}{8} = \frac{12}{8} \frac{\div 4}{\div 4} = \frac{3}{2}$
Then, rewrite the improper fraction so that it is a mixed number.	$\frac{3}{2} = 1\frac{1}{2}$
Finally, write the original mixed number in simplest form.	$3\frac{12}{8} = 3 + 1\frac{1}{2} = 4\frac{1}{2}$

Practice

Rewrite each mixed number in simplest form.

1. $4\frac{16}{10}$ $5\frac{3}{5}$ 2. $2\frac{8}{12}$ $2\frac{2}{3}$ 3. $6\frac{9}{6}$ $7\frac{1}{2}$

4. $5\frac{21}{8}$ $7\frac{5}{8}$ 5. $7\frac{17}{6}$ $9\frac{5}{6}$ 6. $11\frac{18}{20}$ $11\frac{9}{10}$

7. $3\frac{22}{17}$ $4\frac{5}{17}$ 8. $6\frac{12}{20}$ $6\frac{3}{5}$ 9. $4\frac{13}{8}$ $5\frac{5}{8}$

Simple Steps • Fifth Grade Understanding Fractions 65

Math

Page 65

Simplifying Mixed Numbers

Practice

Rewrite each mixed number in simplest form.

1. $2\frac{8}{5}$ $3\frac{3}{5}$ 2. $3\frac{15}{4}$ $6\frac{3}{4}$ 3. $1\frac{7}{3}$ $3\frac{1}{3}$

4. $2\frac{5}{2}$ $4\frac{1}{2}$ 5. $2\frac{10}{3}$ $5\frac{1}{3}$ 6. $4\frac{6}{5}$ $5\frac{1}{5}$

7. $3\frac{15}{7}$ $5\frac{1}{7}$ 8. $2\frac{20}{9}$ $4\frac{2}{9}$ 9. $2\frac{20}{9}$ $9\frac{1}{3}$

10. $11\frac{3}{2}$ $12\frac{1}{2}$ 11. $3\frac{19}{5}$ $6\frac{4}{5}$ 12. $7\frac{17}{4}$ $11\frac{1}{4}$

13. $2\frac{9}{7}$ $3\frac{2}{7}$ 14. $1\frac{16}{9}$ $2\frac{7}{9}$ 15. $3\frac{11}{6}$ $4\frac{5}{6}$

66 Understanding Fractions Simple Steps • Fifth Grade

Math

Page 66

Answer Key

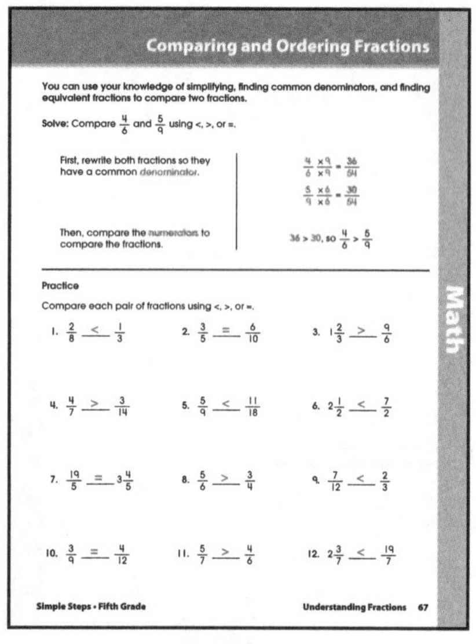

Comparing and Ordering Fractions

You can use your knowledge of simplifying, finding common denominators, and finding equivalent fractions to compare two fractions.

Solve: Compare $\frac{4}{6}$ and $\frac{5}{9}$ using <, >, or =.

First, rewrite both fractions so they have a common denominator.	$\frac{4}{6}\frac{\times 9}{\times 9} = \frac{36}{54}$ $\frac{5}{9}\frac{\times 6}{\times 6} = \frac{30}{54}$
Then, compare the numerators to compare the fractions.	$36 > 30$, so $\frac{4}{6} > \frac{5}{9}$

Practice

Compare each pair of fractions using <, >, or =.

1. $\frac{2}{8}$ < $\frac{1}{3}$
2. $\frac{3}{5}$ = $\frac{6}{10}$
3. $1\frac{2}{3}$ > $\frac{9}{6}$
4. $\frac{4}{7}$ > $\frac{3}{14}$
5. $\frac{5}{9}$ < $\frac{11}{18}$
6. $2\frac{1}{2}$ < $\frac{7}{2}$
7. $\frac{19}{5}$ = $3\frac{4}{5}$
8. $\frac{5}{6}$ > $\frac{3}{4}$
9. $\frac{7}{12}$ < $\frac{2}{3}$
10. $\frac{3}{9}$ = $\frac{4}{12}$
11. $\frac{5}{7}$ > $\frac{4}{6}$
12. $2\frac{3}{7}$ < $\frac{19}{7}$

Simple Steps • Fifth Grade — Understanding Fractions 67

Page 67

Comparing and Ordering Fractions

Practice

Compare each pair of fractions using <, >, or =.

1. $\frac{4}{7}$ < $\frac{21}{11}$
2. $\frac{29}{9}$ > $2\frac{1}{6}$
3. $\frac{26}{11}$ > $\frac{22}{11}$
4. $\frac{11}{12}$ > $\frac{21}{24}$
5. $2\frac{7}{10}$ < $\frac{58}{20}$
6. $\frac{9}{13}$ < $\frac{21}{26}$

Write the fractions in order from least to greatest.

7. $\frac{1}{7}, \frac{6}{7}, 1\frac{2}{3}, 1\frac{8}{9}, 1\frac{1}{7}$ — $\frac{1}{7}, \frac{6}{7}, 1\frac{1}{7}, 1\frac{2}{3}, 1\frac{8}{9}$
8. $1\frac{3}{8}, 1\frac{7}{12}, 1\frac{10}{12}, 1\frac{1}{4}, 1\frac{7}{8}$ — $1\frac{1}{4}, 1\frac{3}{8}, 1\frac{7}{12}, 1\frac{10}{12}, 1\frac{7}{8}$
9. $2\frac{2}{5}, 2\frac{3}{5}, 2\frac{7}{10}, 2\frac{9}{20}, 2\frac{1}{10}$ — $2\frac{1}{10}, 2\frac{2}{5}, 2\frac{9}{20}, 2\frac{3}{5}, 2\frac{7}{10}$
10. $3\frac{2}{9}, \frac{8}{9}, 3\frac{1}{3}, 3\frac{5}{6}, 3\frac{7}{9}$, — $\frac{8}{9}, 3\frac{2}{9}, 3\frac{1}{3}, 3\frac{7}{9}, 3\frac{5}{6}$

68 Understanding Fractions — Simple Steps • Fifth Grade

Page 68

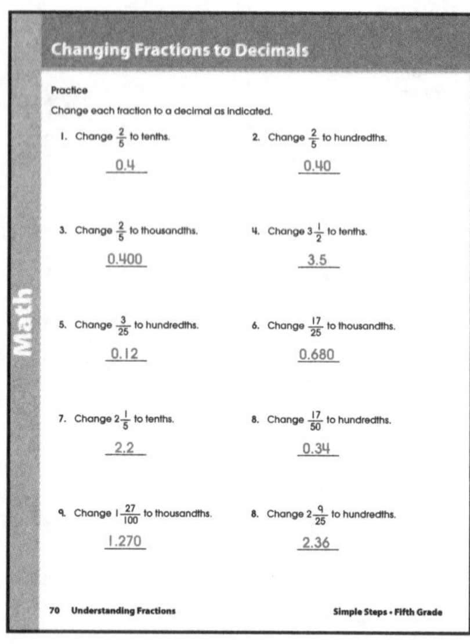

Changing Fractions to Decimals

Practice

Change each fraction to a decimal as indicated.

1. Change $\frac{2}{5}$ to tenths. 0.4
2. Change $\frac{2}{5}$ to hundredths. 0.40
3. Change $\frac{2}{5}$ to thousandths. 0.400
4. Change $3\frac{1}{2}$ to tenths. 3.5
5. Change $\frac{3}{25}$ to hundredths. 0.12
6. Change $\frac{17}{25}$ to thousandths. 0.680
7. Change $2\frac{1}{5}$ to tenths. 2.2
8. Change $\frac{17}{50}$ to hundredths. 0.34
9. Change $1\frac{27}{100}$ to thousandths. 1.270
8. Change $2\frac{9}{25}$ to hundredths. 2.36

70 Understanding Fractions — Simple Steps • Fifth Grade

Page 70

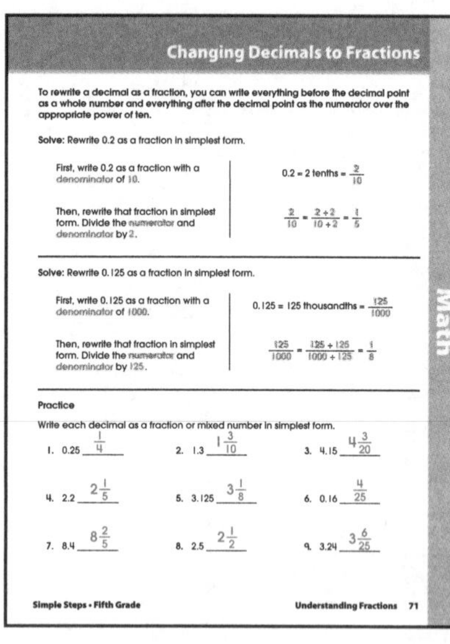

Changing Decimals to Fractions

To rewrite a decimal as a fraction, you can write everything before the decimal point as a whole number and everything after the decimal point as the numerator over the appropriate power of ten.

Solve: Rewrite 0.2 as a fraction in simplest form.

First, write 0.2 as a fraction with a denominator of 10.	$0.2 = 2 \text{ tenths} = \frac{2}{10}$
Then, rewrite that fraction in simplest form. Divide the numerator and denominator by 2.	$\frac{2}{10} = \frac{2 \div 2}{10 \div 2} = \frac{1}{5}$

Solve: Rewrite 0.125 as a fraction in simplest form.

First, write 0.125 as a fraction with a denominator of 1000.	$0.125 = 125 \text{ thousandths} = \frac{125}{1000}$
Then, rewrite that fraction in simplest form. Divide the numerator and denominator by 125.	$\frac{125}{1000} = \frac{125 \div 125}{1000 \div 125} = \frac{1}{8}$

Practice

Write each decimal as a fraction or mixed number in simplest form.

1. 0.25 $\frac{1}{4}$
2. 1.3 $1\frac{3}{10}$
3. 4.15 $4\frac{3}{20}$
4. 2.2 $2\frac{1}{5}$
5. 3.125 $3\frac{1}{8}$
6. 0.16 $\frac{4}{25}$
7. 8.4 $8\frac{2}{5}$
8. 2.5 $2\frac{1}{2}$
9. 3.24 $3\frac{6}{25}$

Simple Steps • Fifth Grade — Understanding Fractions 71

Page 71

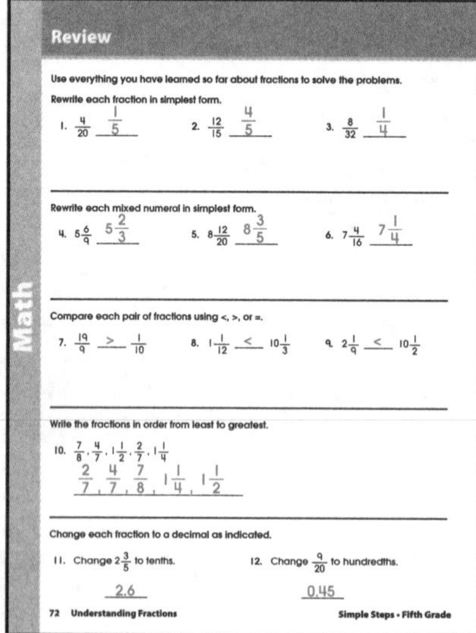

Review

Use everything you have learned so far about fractions to solve the problems.

Rewrite each fraction in simplest form.

1. $\frac{4}{20}$ $\frac{1}{5}$
2. $\frac{12}{15}$ $\frac{4}{5}$
3. $\frac{8}{32}$ $\frac{1}{4}$

Rewrite each mixed numeral in simplest form.

4. $5\frac{6}{9}$ $5\frac{2}{3}$
5. $8\frac{12}{20}$ $8\frac{3}{5}$
6. $7\frac{4}{16}$ $7\frac{1}{4}$

Compare each pair of fractions using <, >, or =.

7. $\frac{19}{9}$ > $\frac{1}{10}$
8. $1\frac{1}{12}$ < $10\frac{1}{3}$
9. $2\frac{1}{9}$ < $10\frac{1}{2}$

Write the fractions in order from least to greatest.

10. $\frac{7}{8}, \frac{4}{7}, 1\frac{1}{2}, \frac{2}{7}, 1\frac{1}{4}$ — $\frac{2}{7}, \frac{4}{7}, \frac{7}{8}, 1\frac{1}{4}, 1\frac{1}{2}$

Change each fraction to a decimal as indicated.

11. Change $2\frac{3}{5}$ to tenths. 2.6
12. Change $\frac{9}{20}$ to hundredths. 0.45

72 Understanding Fractions — Simple Steps • Fifth Grade

Page 72

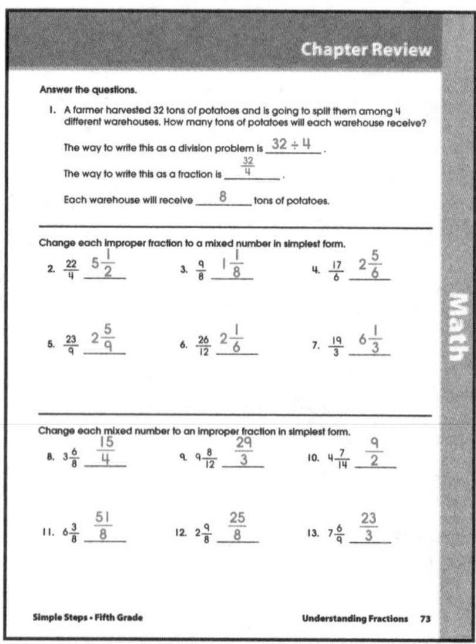

Chapter Review

Answer the questions.

1. A farmer harvested 32 tons of potatoes and is going to split them among 4 different warehouses. How many tons of potatoes will each warehouse receive?

   The way to write this as a division problem is $32 \div 4$.

   The way to write this as a fraction is $\frac{32}{4}$.

   Each warehouse will receive 8 tons of potatoes.

Change each improper fraction to a mixed number in simplest form.

2. $\frac{22}{4}$ $5\frac{1}{2}$
3. $\frac{9}{8}$ $1\frac{1}{8}$
4. $\frac{17}{6}$ $2\frac{5}{6}$
5. $\frac{23}{9}$ $2\frac{5}{9}$
6. $\frac{26}{12}$ $2\frac{1}{6}$
7. $\frac{19}{3}$ $6\frac{1}{3}$

Change each mixed number to an improper fraction in simplest form.

8. $3\frac{6}{8}$ $\frac{15}{4}$
9. $9\frac{8}{12}$ $\frac{29}{3}$
10. $4\frac{7}{14}$ $\frac{9}{2}$
11. $6\frac{3}{8}$ $\frac{51}{8}$
12. $2\frac{9}{8}$ $\frac{25}{8}$
13. $7\frac{6}{9}$ $\frac{23}{3}$

Simple Steps • Fifth Grade — Understanding Fractions 73

Page 73

Answer Key

Chapter Review

Find the lowest common denominator of each pair of fractions. Then, rewrite each fraction using the new common denominator.

14. $\frac{1}{4}$ and $\frac{2}{3}$ LCD 12; $\frac{3}{12}$ and $\frac{8}{12}$
15. $\frac{3}{8}$ and $\frac{7}{10}$ LCD 40; $\frac{15}{40}$ and $\frac{28}{40}$
16. $\frac{4}{7}$ and $\frac{2}{3}$ LCD 21; $\frac{12}{21}$ and $\frac{14}{21}$

Find the equivalent fraction.

17. $6 = \frac{18}{3}$
18. $\frac{7}{9} = \frac{14}{18}$
19. $8 = \frac{48}{6}$

Rewrite each fraction in simplest form.

20. $\frac{18}{36}$ $\frac{1}{2}$
21. $\frac{26}{28}$ $\frac{13}{14}$
22. $\frac{17}{68}$ $\frac{1}{4}$

Rewrite each mixed number in simplest form.

23. $3\frac{3}{2}$ $4\frac{1}{2}$
24. $7\frac{8}{12}$ $7\frac{2}{3}$
25. $5\frac{3}{9}$ $5\frac{1}{3}$

74 Understanding Fractions Simple Steps • Fifth Grade

Page 74

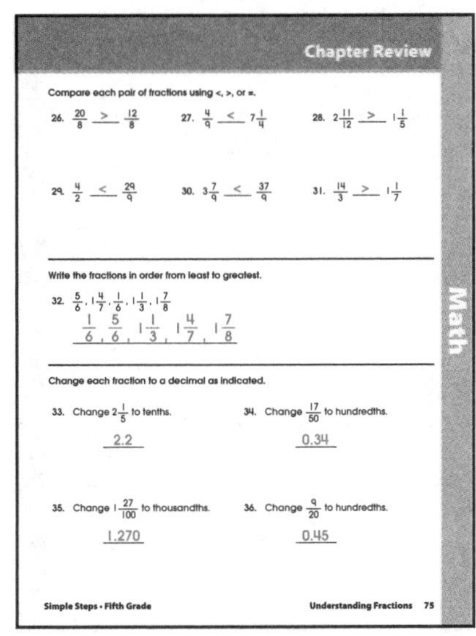

Chapter Review

Compare each pair of fractions using <, >, or =.

26. $\frac{20}{8} > \frac{12}{8}$
27. $\frac{4}{9} < 7\frac{1}{4}$
28. $2\frac{11}{12} > 1\frac{1}{5}$
29. $\frac{4}{2} < \frac{29}{9}$
30. $3\frac{7}{9} < \frac{37}{9}$
31. $\frac{14}{3} > 1\frac{1}{7}$

Write the fractions in order from least to greatest.

32. $\frac{5}{6}, 1\frac{4}{7}, \frac{1}{6}, 1\frac{1}{3}, 1\frac{7}{8}$ — $\frac{1}{6}, \frac{5}{6}, 1\frac{1}{3}, 1\frac{4}{7}, 1\frac{7}{8}$

Change each fraction to a decimal as indicated.

33. Change $2\frac{1}{5}$ to tenths. 2.2
34. Change $\frac{17}{50}$ to hundredths. 0.34
35. Change $1\frac{27}{100}$ to thousandths. 1.270
36. Change $\frac{9}{20}$ to hundredths. 0.45

Simple Steps • Fifth Grade Understanding Fractions 75

Page 75

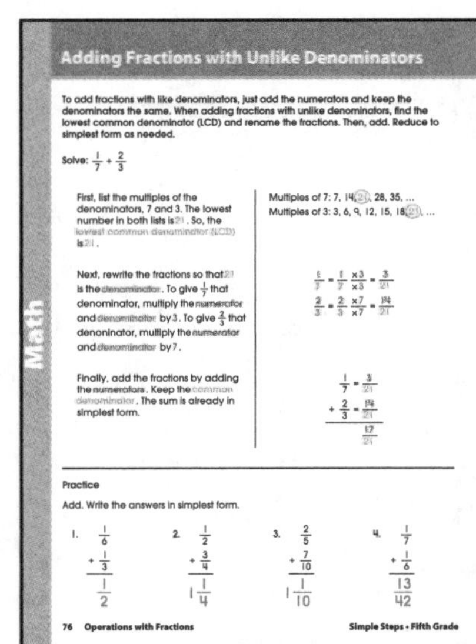

Adding Fractions with Unlike Denominators

To add fractions with like denominators, just add the numerators and keep the denominators the same. When adding fractions with unlike denominators, find the lowest common denominator (LCD) and rename the fractions. Then, add. Reduce to simplest form as needed.

Solve: $\frac{1}{7} + \frac{2}{3}$

First, list the multiples of the denominators, 7 and 3. The lowest number in both lists is 21. So, the lowest common denominator (LCD) is 21.

Multiples of 7: 7, 14, 21, 28, 35, ...
Multiples of 3: 3, 6, 9, 12, 15, 18, 21, ...

Next, rewrite the fractions so that 21 is the denominator. To give $\frac{1}{7}$ that denominator, multiply the numerator and denominator by 3. To give $\frac{2}{3}$ that denominator, multiply the numerator and denominator by 7.

$\frac{1}{7} = \frac{1}{7}\frac{\times 3}{\times 3} = \frac{3}{21}$
$\frac{2}{3} = \frac{2}{3}\frac{\times 7}{\times 7} = \frac{14}{21}$

Finally, add the fractions by adding the numerators. Keep the common denominator. The sum is already in simplest form.

$\frac{1}{7} = \frac{3}{21}$, $+\frac{2}{3} = \frac{14}{21}$, $\frac{17}{21}$

Practice

Add. Write the answers in simplest form.

1. $\frac{1}{6} + \frac{1}{3} = \frac{1}{2}$
2. $\frac{1}{2} + \frac{3}{4} = 1\frac{1}{4}$
3. $\frac{2}{5} + \frac{7}{10} = 1\frac{1}{10}$
4. $\frac{1}{7} + \frac{1}{6} = \frac{13}{42}$

76 Operations with Fractions Simple Steps • Fifth Grade

Page 76

Adding Fractions with Unlike Denominators

Practice

Add. Write the answers in simplest form.

1. $\frac{3}{5} + \frac{1}{4} = \frac{17}{20}$
2. $\frac{2}{3} + \frac{2}{7} = \frac{20}{21}$
3. $\frac{1}{5} + \frac{1}{7} = \frac{12}{35}$
4. $\frac{3}{8} + \frac{1}{6} = \frac{13}{24}$
5. $\frac{1}{2} + \frac{1}{3} = \frac{5}{6}$
6. $\frac{2}{9} + \frac{5}{8} = \frac{61}{72}$
7. $\frac{6}{7} + \frac{1}{3} = 1\frac{4}{21}$
8. $\frac{2}{5} + \frac{5}{7} = 1\frac{4}{35}$
9. $\frac{7}{10} + \frac{1}{3} = 1\frac{1}{30}$
10. $\frac{3}{7} + \frac{1}{8} = \frac{31}{56}$
11. $\frac{2}{3} + \frac{1}{5} = \frac{13}{15}$
12. $\frac{4}{7} + \frac{5}{9} = 1\frac{8}{63}$
13. $\frac{3}{4} + \frac{3}{10} = 1\frac{1}{20}$
14. $\frac{7}{8} + \frac{2}{5} = 1\frac{11}{40}$
15. $\frac{8}{9} + \frac{6}{7} = 1\frac{47}{63}$
16. $\frac{3}{5} + \frac{17}{20} = 1\frac{9}{20}$

Simple Steps • Fifth Grade Operations with Fractions 77

Page 77

Subtracting Fractions with Unlike Denominators

When subtracting fractions with unlike denominators, rename the fractions to have a common denominator. Then, subtract the fractions and write the difference in simplest form.

Solve: Subtract $\frac{1}{3}$ from $\frac{8}{9}$.

First, list the multiples of the denominators, 3 and 9. The lowest number in both lists is 9. So, the lowest common denominator (LCD) is 9.

Multiples of 3: 3, 6, 9, 12, 15, 18, 21, 24, 27...
Multiples of 9: 9, 18, 27, 36, 45 ...
Note: 18 and 27 are also common multiples, but not the LCD.

Next, rewrite the fractions so that 9 is the denominator. To give 3 that denominator, multiply the numerator and denominator by 3. The fraction $\frac{8}{9}$ already has that denominator.

$\frac{1}{3} = \frac{1}{3}\frac{\times 3}{\times 3} = \frac{3}{9}$

Finally, subtract the fractions by subtracting the numerators. Keep the common denominator. The difference is already in simplest form.

$\frac{8}{9} = \frac{8}{9}$, $-\frac{1}{3} = \frac{3}{9}$, $\frac{5}{9}$

Practice

Subtract. Write the answers in simplest form.

1. $\frac{5}{6} - \frac{2}{9} = \frac{11}{18}$
2. $\frac{7}{10} - \frac{2}{3} = \frac{1}{30}$
3. $\frac{4}{5} - \frac{4}{7} = \frac{8}{35}$
4. $\frac{2}{5} - \frac{1}{4} = \frac{3}{20}$

78 Operations with Fractions Simple Steps • Fifth Grade

Page 78

Subtracting Fractions with Unlike Denominators

Practice

Subtract. Write the answers in simplest form.

1. $\frac{3}{4} - \frac{1}{2} = \frac{1}{4}$
2. $\frac{5}{6} - \frac{1}{3} = \frac{1}{2}$
3. $\frac{9}{10} - \frac{2}{5} = \frac{1}{2}$
4. $\frac{4}{7} - \frac{1}{8} = \frac{25}{56}$
5. $\frac{5}{9} - \frac{1}{3} = \frac{2}{9}$
6. $\frac{2}{5} - \frac{1}{9} = \frac{13}{45}$
7. $\frac{3}{5} - \frac{2}{7} = \frac{11}{35}$
8. $\frac{2}{3} - \frac{3}{8} = \frac{7}{24}$
9. $\frac{5}{6} - \frac{1}{3} = \frac{1}{2}$
10. $\frac{3}{4} - \frac{2}{9} = \frac{19}{36}$
11. $\frac{7}{10} - \frac{3}{6} = \frac{1}{5}$
12. $\frac{8}{9} - \frac{1}{4} = \frac{23}{26}$
13. $\frac{7}{8} - \frac{5}{12} = \frac{11}{24}$
14. $\frac{7}{10} - \frac{1}{4} = \frac{9}{20}$
15. $\frac{4}{5} - \frac{3}{7} = \frac{13}{35}$
16. $\frac{7}{9} - \frac{5}{12} = \frac{13}{36}$

Simple Steps • Fifth Grade Operations with Fractions 79

Page 79

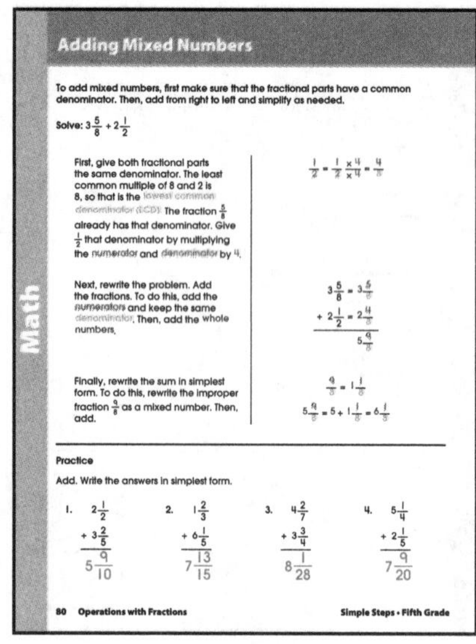

Adding Mixed Numbers

Math

To add mixed numbers, first make sure that the fractional parts have a common denominator. Then, add from right to left and simplify as needed.

Solve: $3\frac{5}{8} + 2\frac{1}{2}$

First, give both fractional parts the same denominator. The least common multiple of 8 and 2 is 8, so that is the lowest common denominator (LCD). The fraction $\frac{5}{8}$ already has that denominator. Give $\frac{1}{2}$ that denominator by multiplying the numerator and denominator by 4.

$\frac{1}{2} = \frac{1}{2}\frac{\times 4}{\times 4} = \frac{4}{8}$

Next, rewrite the problem. Add the fractions. To do this, add the numerators and keep the same denominator. Then, add the whole numbers.

$3\frac{5}{8} = 3\frac{5}{8}$; $+ 2\frac{1}{2} = 2\frac{4}{8}$; $5\frac{9}{8}$

Finally, rewrite the sum in simplest form. To do this, rewrite the improper fraction $\frac{9}{8}$ as a mixed number. Then, add.

$\frac{9}{8} = 1\frac{1}{8}$

$5\frac{9}{8} = 5 + 1\frac{1}{8} = 6\frac{1}{8}$

Practice

Add. Write the answers in simplest form.

1. $2\frac{1}{2} + 3\frac{2}{5} = 5\frac{9}{10}$
2. $1\frac{2}{3} + 6\frac{1}{5} = 7\frac{13}{15}$
3. $4\frac{2}{7} + 3\frac{3}{4} = 8\frac{1}{28}$
4. $5\frac{1}{4} + 2\frac{1}{5} = 7\frac{9}{20}$

80 Operations with Fractions — Simple Steps • Fifth Grade

Page 80

Adding Mixed Numbers

Math

Practice

Add mixed numbers to solve the problems. Write the answers in simplest form.

1. Caroline needs $3\frac{1}{7}$ cups of sugar for her first batch of brownies and $2\frac{8}{9}$ cups of sugar for a second batch. How much sugar does she need in all?
   1. $6\frac{2}{63}$ cups of sugar
2. Robert's gas tank has $5\frac{3}{5}$ gallons of gas in it. If he adds $7\frac{2}{3}$ gallons, how much gas will be in the tank?
   2. $13\frac{4}{15}$ gallons of gas
3. A hamburger weighs $\frac{1}{3}$ pound, and an order of french fries weighs $\frac{1}{4}$ pound. How many pounds total will a meal of hamburger and french fries weigh?
   3. $\frac{7}{12}$ pounds
4. John is $5\frac{6}{10}$ feet tall and Jamar is $\frac{5}{8}$ feet taller than John. How tall is Jamar?
   4. $6\frac{9}{40}$ feet tall
5. Mrs. Stevenson has used $4\frac{2}{3}$ inches of string. She needs $1\frac{6}{7}$ inches more. How much string will Mrs. Stevenson have used when she is done?
   5. $6\frac{11}{21}$ inches of string

Simple Steps • Fifth Grade — Operations with Fractions 81

Page 81

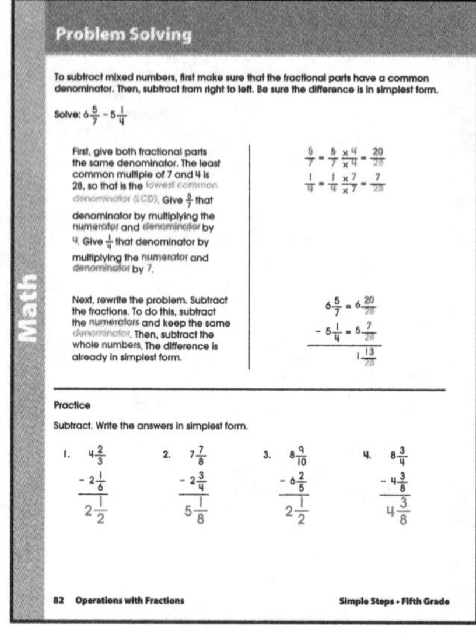

Problem Solving

Math

To subtract mixed numbers, first make sure that the fractional parts have a common denominator. Then, subtract from right to left. Be sure the difference is in simplest form.

Solve: $6\frac{5}{7} - 5\frac{1}{4}$

First, give both fractional parts the same denominator. The least common multiple of 7 and 4 is 28, so that is the lowest common denominator (LCD). Give $\frac{5}{7}$ that denominator by multiplying the numerator and denominator by 4. Give $\frac{1}{4}$ that denominator by multiplying the numerator and denominator by 7.

$\frac{5}{7} = \frac{5}{7}\frac{\times 4}{\times 4} = \frac{20}{28}$

$\frac{1}{4} = \frac{1}{4}\frac{\times 7}{\times 7} = \frac{7}{28}$

Next, rewrite the problem. Subtract the fractions. To do this, subtract the numerators and keep the same denominator. Then, subtract the whole numbers. The difference is already in simplest form.

$6\frac{5}{7} = 6\frac{20}{28}$; $- 5\frac{1}{4} = 5\frac{7}{28}$; $1\frac{13}{28}$

Practice

Subtract. Write the answers in simplest form.

1. $4\frac{2}{3} - 2\frac{1}{6} = 2\frac{1}{2}$
2. $7\frac{7}{8} - 2\frac{3}{4} = 5\frac{1}{8}$
3. $8\frac{9}{10} - 6\frac{2}{5} = 2\frac{1}{2}$
4. $8\frac{3}{4} - 4\frac{3}{8} = 4\frac{3}{8}$

82 Operations with Fractions — Simple Steps • Fifth Grade

Page 82

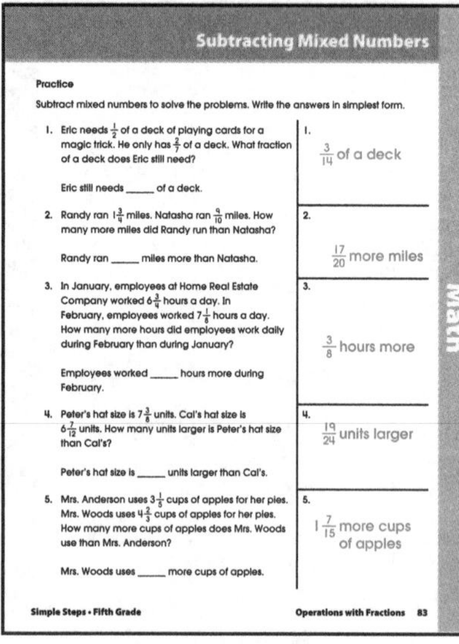

Subtracting Mixed Numbers

Math

Practice

Subtract mixed numbers to solve the problems. Write the answers in simplest form.

1. Eric needs $\frac{1}{2}$ of a deck of playing cards for a magic trick. He only has $\frac{2}{7}$ of a deck. What fraction of a deck does Eric still need?
   Eric still needs _____ of a deck.
   1. $\frac{3}{14}$ of a deck
2. Randy ran $1\frac{3}{4}$ miles. Natasha ran $\frac{9}{10}$ miles. How many more miles did Randy run than Natasha?
   Randy ran _____ miles more than Natasha.
   2. $\frac{17}{20}$ more miles
3. In January, employees at Home Real Estate Company worked $6\frac{3}{4}$ hours a day. In February, employees worked $7\frac{1}{8}$ hours a day. How many more hours did employees work daily during February than during January?
   Employees worked _____ hours more during February.
   3. $\frac{3}{8}$ hours more
4. Peter's hat size is $7\frac{3}{8}$ units. Cal's hat size is $6\frac{7}{12}$ units. How many units larger is Peter's hat size than Cal's?
   Peter's hat size is _____ units larger than Cal's.
   4. $\frac{19}{24}$ units larger
5. Mrs. Anderson uses $3\frac{1}{5}$ cups of apples for her pies. Mrs. Woods uses $4\frac{2}{3}$ cups of apples for her pies. How many more cups of apples does Mrs. Woods use than Mrs. Anderson?
   Mrs. Woods uses _____ more cups of apples.
   5. $1\frac{7}{15}$ more cups of apples

Simple Steps • Fifth Grade — Operations with Fractions 83

Page 83

Review

Math

Use everything you have learned so far about operations with fractions to solve the problems.

Add or subtract. Write the answers in simplest form.

1. $\frac{7}{12} + \frac{3}{5} = 1\frac{11}{60}$
2. $4 - \frac{5}{6} = 3\frac{1}{6}$
3. $\frac{2}{5} + \frac{9}{10} = 1\frac{3}{10}$
4. $6\frac{2}{3} - 4\frac{1}{3} = 2\frac{1}{3}$
5. $8\frac{3}{10} + 9\frac{2}{4} = 17\frac{4}{5}$
6. $\frac{5}{8} - \frac{1}{4} = \frac{3}{8}$
7. $\frac{5}{6} - \frac{7}{12} = \frac{1}{4}$
8. $5\frac{2}{7} - 4\frac{1}{4} = 1\frac{1}{28}$
9. $5\frac{2}{5} + 7\frac{2}{3} = 13\frac{1}{15}$
10. $2\frac{1}{2} - 1\frac{1}{12} = 1\frac{5}{12}$
11. $4\frac{3}{8} + 2\frac{11}{24} = 6\frac{5}{6}$
12. $9\frac{1}{8} - 8\frac{1}{16} = 1\frac{1}{16}$
13. $3\frac{3}{10} + 3\frac{2}{3} = 6\frac{29}{30}$
14. $6\frac{3}{5} - 2\frac{1}{4} = 4\frac{7}{20}$
15. $6\frac{1}{7} + 2\frac{3}{5} = 8\frac{26}{35}$
16. $3\frac{4}{5} - 1\frac{3}{10} = 2\frac{1}{2}$

84 Operations with Fractions — Simple Steps • Fifth Grade

Page 84

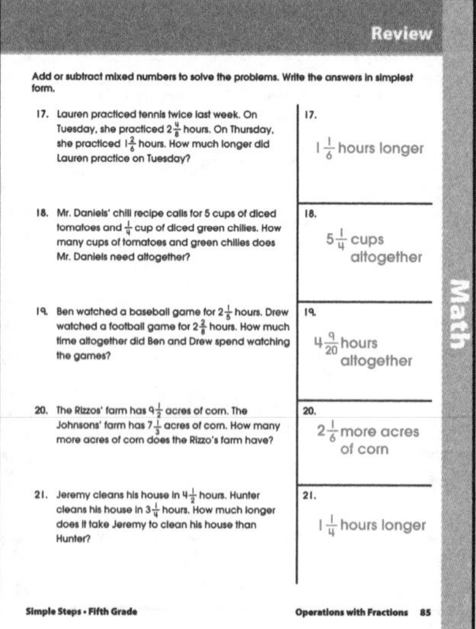

Review

Math

Add or subtract mixed numbers to solve the problems. Write the answers in simplest form.

17. Lauren practiced tennis twice last week. On Tuesday, she practiced $2\frac{4}{8}$ hours. On Thursday, she practiced $1\frac{2}{6}$ hours. How much longer did Lauren practice on Tuesday?
    17. $1\frac{1}{6}$ hours longer
18. Mr. Daniels' chili recipe calls for 5 cups of diced tomatoes and $\frac{1}{4}$ cup of diced green chilies. How many cups of tomatoes and green chilies does Mr. Daniels need altogether?
    18. $5\frac{1}{4}$ cups altogether
19. Ben watched a baseball game for $2\frac{1}{5}$ hours. Drew watched a football game for $2\frac{2}{8}$ hours. How much time altogether did Ben and Drew spend watching the games?
    19. $4\frac{9}{20}$ hours altogether
20. The Rizzos' farm has $9\frac{1}{2}$ acres of corn. The Johnsons' farm has $7\frac{1}{3}$ acres of corn. How many more acres of corn does the Rizzo's farm have?
    20. $2\frac{1}{6}$ more acres of corn
21. Jeremy cleans his house in $4\frac{1}{2}$ hours. Hunter cleans his house in $3\frac{1}{4}$ hours. How much longer does it take Jeremy to clean his house than Hunter?
    21. $1\frac{1}{4}$ hours longer

Simple Steps • Fifth Grade — Operations with Fractions 85

Page 85

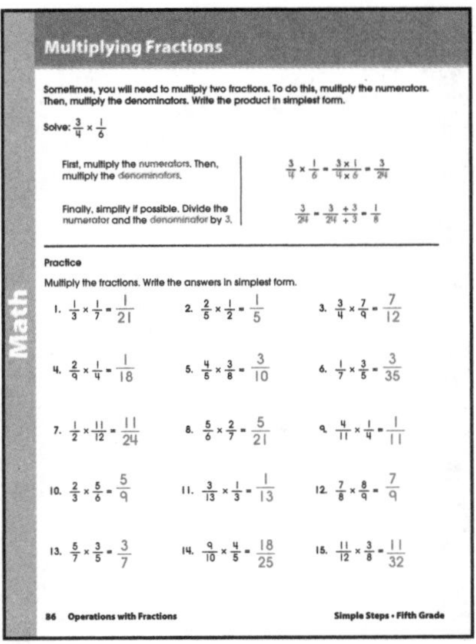

Multiplying Fractions

Sometimes, you will need to multiply two fractions. To do this, multiply the numerators. Then, multiply the denominators. Write the product in simplest form.

Solve: $\frac{3}{4} \times \frac{1}{6}$

First, multiply the numerators. Then, multiply the denominators. $\frac{3}{4} \times \frac{1}{6} = \frac{3 \times 1}{4 \times 6} = \frac{3}{24}$

Finally, simplify if possible. Divide the numerator and the denominator by 3. $\frac{3}{24} = \frac{3 \div 3}{24 \div 3} = \frac{1}{8}$

Practice

Multiply the fractions. Write the answers in simplest form.

1. $\frac{1}{3} \times \frac{1}{7} = \frac{1}{21}$ 2. $\frac{2}{5} \times \frac{1}{2} = \frac{1}{5}$ 3. $\frac{3}{4} \times \frac{7}{9} = \frac{7}{12}$

4. $\frac{2}{9} \times \frac{1}{4} = \frac{1}{18}$ 5. $\frac{4}{5} \times \frac{3}{8} = \frac{3}{10}$ 6. $\frac{1}{7} \times \frac{3}{5} = \frac{3}{35}$

7. $\frac{1}{2} \times \frac{11}{12} = \frac{11}{24}$ 8. $\frac{5}{6} \times \frac{2}{7} = \frac{5}{21}$ 9. $\frac{4}{11} \times \frac{1}{4} = \frac{1}{11}$

10. $\frac{2}{3} \times \frac{5}{6} = \frac{5}{9}$ 11. $\frac{3}{13} \times \frac{1}{3} = \frac{1}{13}$ 12. $\frac{7}{8} \times \frac{8}{9} = \frac{7}{9}$

13. $\frac{5}{7} \times \frac{3}{5} = \frac{3}{7}$ 14. $\frac{9}{10} \times \frac{4}{5} = \frac{18}{25}$ 15. $\frac{11}{12} \times \frac{3}{8} = \frac{11}{32}$

Math

86 Operations with Fractions Simple Steps • Fifth Grade

Page 86

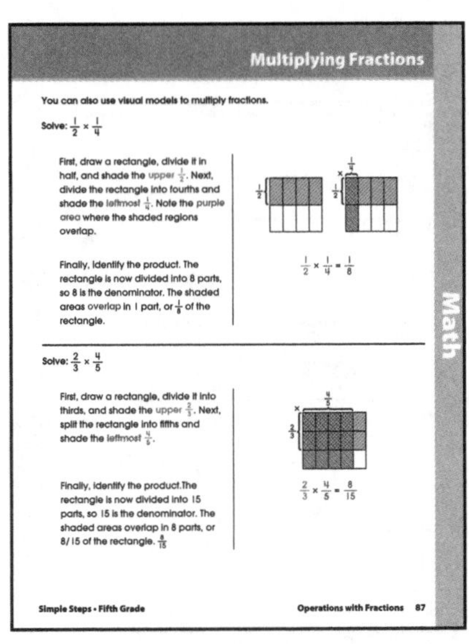

Multiplying Fractions

You can also use visual models to multiply fractions.

Solve: $\frac{1}{2} \times \frac{1}{4}$

First, draw a rectangle, divide it in half, and shade the upper $\frac{1}{2}$. Next, divide the rectangle into fourths and shade the leftmost $\frac{1}{4}$. Note the purple area where the shaded regions overlap.

Finally, identify the product. The rectangle is now divided into 8 parts, so 8 is the denominator. The shaded areas overlap in 1 part, or $\frac{1}{8}$ of the rectangle. $\frac{1}{2} \times \frac{1}{4} = \frac{1}{8}$

Solve: $\frac{2}{3} \times \frac{4}{5}$

First, draw a rectangle, divide it into thirds, and shade the upper $\frac{2}{3}$. Next, split the rectangle into fifths and shade the leftmost $\frac{4}{5}$.

Finally, identify the product. The rectangle is now divided into 15 parts, so 15 is the denominator. The shaded areas overlap in 8 parts, or 8/15 of the rectangle. $\frac{8}{15}$ $\frac{2}{3} \times \frac{4}{5} = \frac{8}{15}$

Math

Simple Steps • Fifth Grade Operations with Fractions 87

Page 87

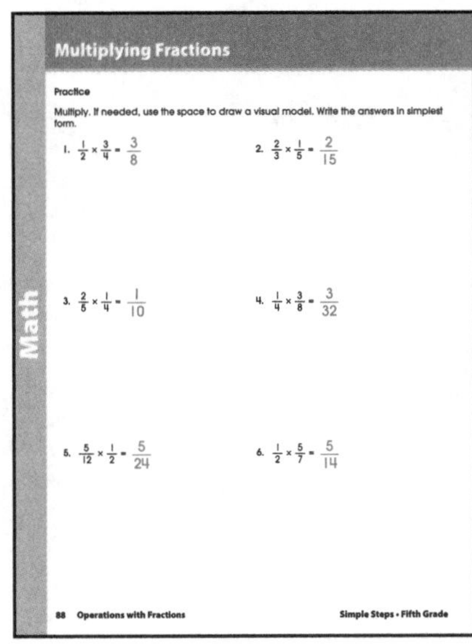

Multiplying Fractions

Practice

Multiply. If needed, use the space to draw a visual model. Write the answers in simplest form.

1. $\frac{1}{2} \times \frac{3}{4} = \frac{3}{8}$ 2. $\frac{2}{3} \times \frac{1}{5} = \frac{2}{15}$

3. $\frac{2}{5} \times \frac{1}{4} = \frac{1}{10}$ 4. $\frac{1}{4} \times \frac{3}{8} = \frac{3}{32}$

5. $\frac{5}{12} \times \frac{1}{2} = \frac{5}{24}$ 6. $\frac{1}{2} \times \frac{5}{7} = \frac{5}{14}$

Math

88 Operations with Fractions Simple Steps • Fifth Grade

Page 88

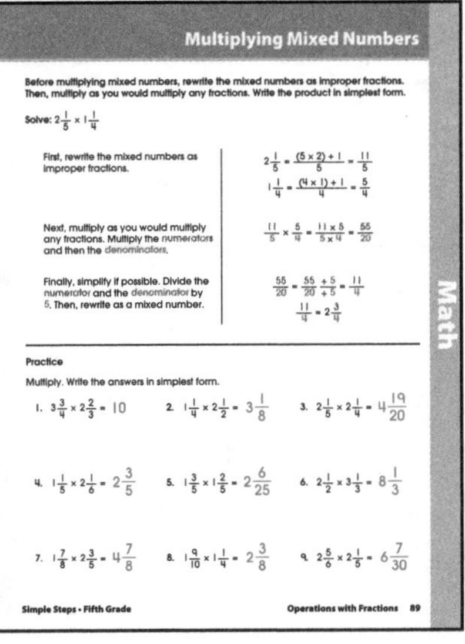

Multiplying Mixed Numbers

Before multiplying mixed numbers, rewrite the mixed numbers as improper fractions. Then, multiply as you would multiply any fractions. Write the product in simplest form.

Solve: $2\frac{1}{5} \times 1\frac{1}{4}$

First, rewrite the mixed numbers as improper fractions. $2\frac{1}{5} = \frac{(5 \times 2) + 1}{5} = \frac{11}{5}$ $1\frac{1}{4} = \frac{(4 \times 1) + 1}{4} = \frac{5}{4}$

Next, multiply as you would multiply any fractions. Multiply the numerators and then the denominators. $\frac{11}{5} \times \frac{5}{4} = \frac{11 \times 5}{5 \times 4} = \frac{55}{20}$

Finally, simplify if possible. Divide the numerator and the denominator by 5. Then, rewrite as a mixed number. $\frac{55}{20} = \frac{55 \div 5}{20 \div 5} = \frac{11}{4}$ $\frac{11}{4} = 2\frac{3}{4}$

Practice

Multiply. Write the answers in simplest form.

1. $3\frac{3}{4} \times 2\frac{2}{3} = 10$ 2. $1\frac{1}{4} \times 2\frac{1}{2} = 3\frac{1}{8}$ 3. $2\frac{1}{5} \times 2\frac{1}{4} = 4\frac{19}{20}$

4. $1\frac{1}{5} \times 2\frac{1}{6} = 2\frac{3}{5}$ 5. $1\frac{3}{5} \times 1\frac{2}{5} = 2\frac{6}{25}$ 6. $2\frac{1}{2} \times 3\frac{1}{3} = 8\frac{1}{3}$

7. $1\frac{7}{8} \times 2\frac{3}{5} = 4\frac{7}{8}$ 8. $1\frac{9}{10} \times 1\frac{1}{4} = 2\frac{3}{8}$ 9. $2\frac{5}{6} \times 2\frac{1}{5} = 6\frac{7}{30}$

Math

Simple Steps • Fifth Grade Operations with Fractions 89

Page 89

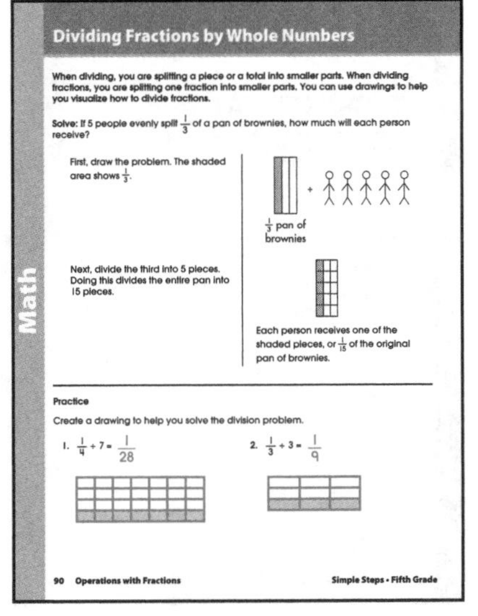

Dividing Fractions by Whole Numbers

When dividing, you are splitting a piece or a total into smaller parts. When dividing fractions, you are splitting one fraction into smaller parts. You can use drawings to help you visualize how to divide fractions.

Solve: If 5 people evenly split $\frac{1}{3}$ of a pan of brownies, how much will each person receive?

First, draw the problem. The shaded area shows $\frac{1}{3}$.

$\frac{1}{3}$ pan of brownies

Next, divide the third into 5 pieces. Doing this divides the entire pan into 15 pieces.

Each person receives one of the shaded pieces, or $\frac{1}{15}$ of the original pan of brownies.

Practice

Create a drawing to help you solve the division problem.

1. $\frac{1}{4} \div 7 = \frac{1}{28}$ 2. $\frac{1}{3} \div 3 = \frac{1}{9}$

Math

90 Operations with Fractions Simple Steps • Fifth Grade

Page 90

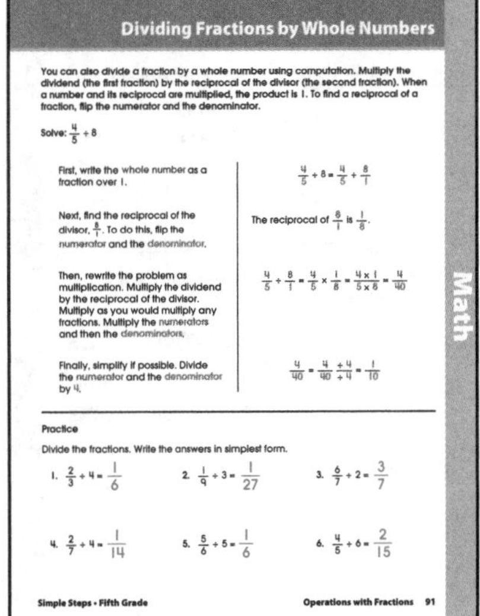

Dividing Fractions by Whole Numbers

You can also divide a fraction by a whole number using computation. Multiply the dividend (the first fraction) by the reciprocal of the divisor (the second fraction). When a number and its reciprocal are multiplied, the product is 1. To find a reciprocal of a fraction, flip the numerator and the denominator.

Solve: $\frac{4}{5} \div 8$

First, write the whole number as a fraction over 1. $\frac{4}{5} \div 8 = \frac{4}{5} \div \frac{8}{1}$

Next, find the reciprocal of the divisor, $\frac{8}{1}$. To do this, flip the numerator and the denominator. The reciprocal of $\frac{8}{1}$ is $\frac{1}{8}$.

Then, rewrite the problem as multiplication. Multiply the dividend by the reciprocal of the divisor. Multiply as you would multiply any fractions. Multiply the numerators and then the denominators. $\frac{4}{5} \div \frac{8}{1} = \frac{4}{5} \times \frac{1}{8} = \frac{4 \times 1}{5 \times 8} = \frac{4}{40}$

Finally, simplify if possible. Divide the numerator and the denominator by 4. $\frac{4}{40} = \frac{4 \div 4}{40 \div 4} = \frac{1}{10}$

Practice

Divide the fractions. Write the answers in simplest form.

1. $\frac{2}{3} \div 4 = \frac{1}{6}$ 2. $\frac{1}{9} \div 3 = \frac{1}{27}$ 3. $\frac{6}{7} \div 2 = \frac{3}{7}$

4. $\frac{2}{7} \div 4 = \frac{1}{14}$ 5. $\frac{5}{6} \div 5 = \frac{1}{6}$ 6. $\frac{4}{5} \div 6 = \frac{2}{15}$

Math

Simple Steps • Fifth Grade Operations with Fractions 91

Page 91

Dividing Fractions by Whole Numbers

Practice

Divide. Write the answers in simplest form.

1. $\frac{3}{5} \div 4 = \frac{3}{20}$
2. $\frac{5}{8} \div 5 = \frac{1}{8}$
3. $\frac{9}{4} \div 6 = \frac{3}{8}$
4. $\frac{5}{3} \div 4 = \frac{5}{12}$
5. $\frac{4}{3} \div 5 = \frac{4}{15}$
6. $\frac{8}{5} \div 5 = \frac{8}{25}$
7. $\frac{3}{8} \div 4 = \frac{3}{32}$
8. $\frac{9}{10} \div 3 = \frac{3}{10}$
9. $\frac{11}{12} \div 3 = \frac{11}{36}$
10. $\frac{7}{5} \div 2 = \frac{7}{10}$
11. $\frac{8}{5} \div 4 = \frac{2}{5}$
12. $\frac{7}{9} \div 7 = \frac{1}{9}$
13. $\frac{9}{5} \div 3 = \frac{3}{5}$
14. $\frac{8}{9} \div 2 = \frac{4}{9}$
15. $\frac{5}{4} \div 4 = \frac{5}{16}$
16. $\frac{9}{7} \div 3 = \frac{3}{7}$
17. $\frac{2}{15} \div 4 = \frac{1}{30}$
18. $\frac{9}{2} \div 12 = \frac{3}{8}$

92 Operations with Fractions — Simple Steps • Fifth Grade

Page 92

Dividing Whole Numbers by Fractions

You can also divide a whole number by a fraction using computation. Write the whole number dividend as a fraction over 1. Then, multiply by the reciprocal of the divisor. Simplify if possible.

Solve: $5 \div \frac{3}{4}$

First, write the whole number as a fraction over 1.	$5 \div \frac{3}{4} = \frac{5}{1} \div \frac{3}{4}$
Next, take the reciprocal of the divisor, $\frac{3}{4}$. To do this, flip the numerator and the denominator.	The reciprocal of $\frac{3}{4}$ is $\frac{4}{3}$.
Then, rewrite the problem as multiplication. Multiply the dividend by the reciprocal of the divisor. Multiply as you would multiply any fractions. Multiply the numerators and then the denominators.	$\frac{5}{1} \div \frac{3}{4} = \frac{5}{1} \times \frac{4}{3} = \frac{5 \times 4}{1 \times 3} = \frac{20}{3}$
Finally, simplify. Rewrite the improper fraction as a mixed number.	$\frac{20}{3} = 6\frac{2}{3}$

Practice

Divide. Write the answers in simplest form.

1. $2 \div \frac{1}{7} = 14$
2. $3 \div \frac{2}{5} = 7\frac{1}{2}$
3. $6 \div \frac{3}{8} = 16$
4. $4 \div \frac{6}{5} = 3\frac{1}{3}$
5. $2 \div \frac{5}{3} = 1\frac{1}{5}$
6. $4 \div \frac{1}{6} = 24$

Simple Steps • Fifth Grade — Operations with Fractions 93

Page 93

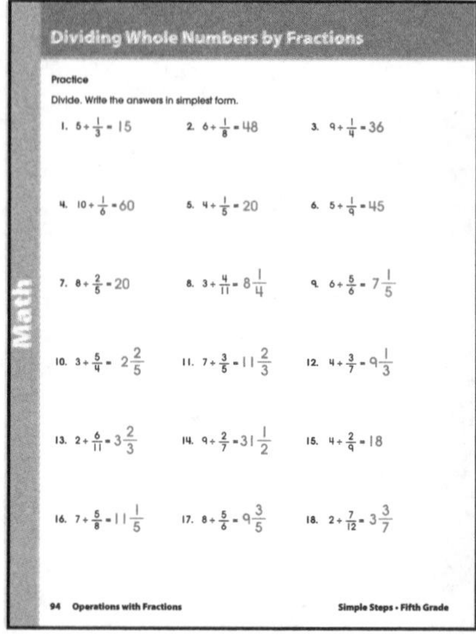

Dividing Whole Numbers by Fractions

Practice

Divide. Write the answers in simplest form.

1. $5 \div \frac{1}{3} = 15$
2. $6 \div \frac{1}{8} = 48$
3. $9 \div \frac{1}{4} = 36$
4. $10 \div \frac{1}{6} = 60$
5. $4 \div \frac{1}{5} = 20$
6. $5 \div \frac{1}{9} = 45$
7. $8 \div \frac{2}{5} = 20$
8. $3 \div \frac{4}{11} = 8\frac{1}{4}$
9. $6 \div \frac{5}{6} = 7\frac{1}{5}$
10. $3 \div \frac{5}{4} = 2\frac{2}{5}$
11. $7 \div \frac{3}{5} = 11\frac{2}{3}$
12. $4 \div \frac{3}{7} = 9\frac{1}{3}$
13. $2 \div \frac{6}{11} = 3\frac{2}{3}$
14. $9 \div \frac{2}{7} = 31\frac{1}{2}$
15. $4 \div \frac{2}{9} = 18$
16. $7 \div \frac{5}{8} = 11\frac{1}{5}$
17. $8 \div \frac{5}{6} = 9\frac{3}{5}$
18. $2 \div \frac{7}{12} = 3\frac{3}{7}$

94 Operations with Fractions — Simple Steps • Fifth Grade

Page 94

Problem Solving

You can use the multiplying and dividing with fractions strategies you have learned so far to solve more difficult problems.

First, underline the important information that you will need to solve the problem.	During Year 2, the size of a pond decreases to $\frac{1}{3}$ of what it was in Year 1. Assume that the same decrease occurs during Year 3. What fraction of the pond will remain after Year 3?
Next, determine which operation is best for solving the problem.	The size of the pond decreases by $\frac{1}{3}$ each year So, we can multiply by $\frac{1}{3}$ two times to find the answer.
Then, draw diagrams and write multiplication problems to represent the size of the pond in Year 1, Year 2, and Year 3.	Draw a rectangle to show the 1 whole pond in Year 1. Year 1 After Year 2, the pond is $\frac{1}{3}$ the size it was in Year 1. Divide the rectangle into thirds and shade $\frac{1}{3}$. Year 2 After Year 3, the pond is $\frac{1}{3}$ the size it was in Year 2. Divide each third into thirds and shade $\frac{1}{3}$ of the region showing Year 2. Year 3
Finally, solve the problem.	The diagram for Year 3 is $\frac{1}{9}$ shaded and $\frac{1}{3} \times \frac{1}{3} = \frac{1}{9}$. After Year 3, only $\frac{1}{9}$ of the pond remains.

Simple Steps • Fifth Grade — Operations with Fractions 95

Page 95

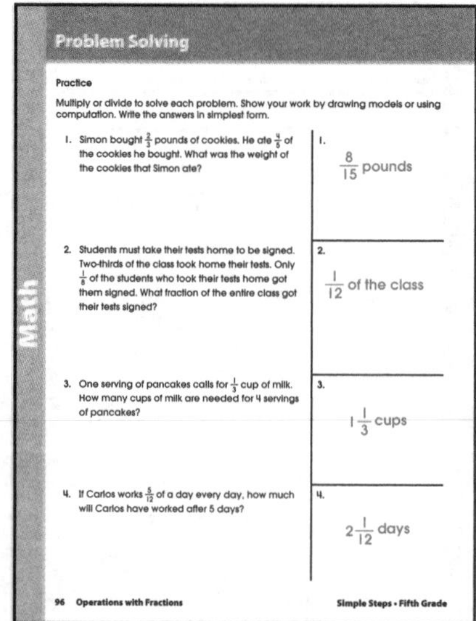

Problem Solving

Practice

Multiply or divide to solve each problem. Show your work by drawing models or using computation. Write the answers in simplest form.

1. Simon bought $\frac{2}{3}$ pounds of cookies. He ate $\frac{4}{5}$ of the cookies he bought. What was the weight of the cookies that Simon ate?
   1. $\frac{8}{15}$ pounds
2. Students must take their tests home to be signed. Two-thirds of the class took home their tests. Only $\frac{1}{8}$ of the students who took their tests home got them signed. What fraction of the entire class got their tests signed?
   2. $\frac{1}{12}$ of the class
3. One serving of pancakes calls for $\frac{1}{3}$ cup of milk. How many cups of milk are needed for 4 servings of pancakes?
   3. $1\frac{1}{3}$ cups
4. If Carlos works $\frac{5}{12}$ of a day every day, how much will Carlos have worked after 5 days?
   4. $2\frac{1}{12}$ days

96 Operations with Fractions — Simple Steps • Fifth Grade

Page 96

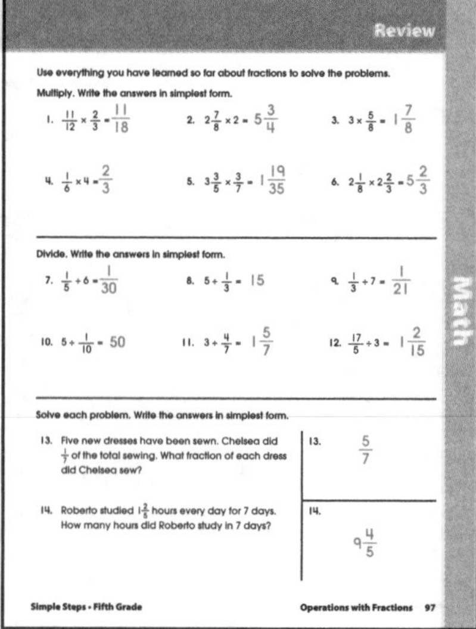

Review

Use everything you have learned so far about fractions to solve the problems.

Multiply. Write the answers in simplest form.

1. $\frac{11}{12} \times \frac{2}{3} = \frac{11}{18}$
2. $2\frac{7}{8} \times 2 = 5\frac{3}{4}$
3. $3 \times \frac{5}{8} = 1\frac{7}{8}$
4. $\frac{1}{6} \times 4 = \frac{2}{3}$
5. $3\frac{3}{5} \times \frac{3}{7} = 1\frac{19}{35}$
6. $2\frac{1}{8} \times 2\frac{2}{3} = 5\frac{2}{3}$

Divide. Write the answers in simplest form.

7. $\frac{1}{5} \div 6 = \frac{1}{30}$
8. $5 \div \frac{1}{3} = 15$
9. $\frac{1}{3} \div 7 = \frac{1}{21}$
10. $5 \div \frac{1}{10} = 50$
11. $3 \div \frac{4}{7} = 1\frac{5}{7}$
12. $\frac{17}{5} \div 3 = 1\frac{2}{15}$

Solve each problem. Write the answers in simplest form.

13. Five new dresses have been sewn. Chelsea did $\frac{1}{7}$ of the total sewing. What fraction of each dress did Chelsea sew?
    13. $\frac{5}{7}$
14. Roberto studied $1\frac{2}{5}$ hours every day for 7 days. How many hours did Roberto study in 7 days?
    14. $9\frac{4}{5}$

Simple Steps • Fifth Grade — Operations with Fractions 97

Page 97

Chapter Review

Add or subtract. Write the answers in simplest form.

1. $\frac{1}{2} + \frac{3}{4} = 1\frac{1}{4}$
2. $\frac{3}{3} + \frac{1}{10} = 1\frac{1}{10}$
3. $\frac{7}{10} - \frac{3}{6} = \frac{1}{5}$
4. $\frac{8}{9} - \frac{1}{4} = \frac{23}{36}$
5. $8\frac{1}{6} + 1\frac{4}{7} = 9\frac{31}{42}$
6. $2\frac{5}{6} + 6\frac{3}{5} = 9\frac{13}{30}$
7. $8\frac{8}{12} - 2\frac{3}{4} = 5\frac{11}{12}$
8. $9\frac{3}{10} - 6\frac{1}{8} = 3\frac{7}{40}$
9. $6\frac{4}{5} + 2\frac{1}{15} = 8\frac{13}{15}$
10. $7\frac{5}{9} - 3\frac{1}{3} = 4\frac{2}{9}$
11. $12\frac{7}{10} - 3\frac{1}{20} = 9\frac{13}{20}$
12. $\frac{9}{12} + \frac{2}{6} = 1\frac{1}{12}$
13. $2\frac{7}{8} - 1\frac{11}{16} = 1\frac{3}{16}$
14. $8\frac{8}{10} - 6\frac{2}{5} = 2\frac{2}{5}$
15. $\frac{7}{9} - \frac{1}{3} = \frac{4}{9}$
16. $\frac{9}{10} + \frac{11}{20} = 1\frac{9}{20}$

98 Operations with Fractions Simple Steps • Fifth Grade

Page 98

Chapter Review

Multiply or divide. Write the answers in simplest form.

17. $1\frac{5}{7} \times \frac{2}{3} = 1\frac{3}{5}$
18. $7 \div \frac{2}{5} = 17\frac{1}{2}$
19. $2\frac{8}{5} \times 1\frac{3}{8} = 4\frac{19}{20}$
20. $\frac{2}{7} \div 5 = \frac{2}{35}$
21. $\frac{9}{11} \times 1\frac{1}{4} = 1\frac{1}{44}$
22. $6 \div \frac{3}{8} = 16$
23. $1\frac{3}{6} \times 3\frac{4}{8} = 10\frac{1}{2}$
24. $\frac{4}{9} \div 6 = \frac{1}{13}$
25. $2\frac{8}{9} \times \frac{2}{7} = \frac{52}{63}$
26. $8 \div \frac{3}{5} = 13\frac{1}{3}$
27. $\frac{1}{2} \times \frac{1}{3} = \frac{1}{6}$
28. $6 \div \frac{1}{10} = 60$
29. $\frac{3}{4} \times \frac{2}{7} = \frac{3}{14}$
30. $3 \div \frac{1}{5} = 15$
31. $2\frac{3}{4} \times 2 = 5\frac{1}{2}$
32. $\frac{1}{8} \div 14 = \frac{1}{112}$
33. $1\frac{3}{8} \times 3 = 4\frac{1}{8}$
34. $\frac{1}{3} \div 8 = \frac{1}{24}$

Simple Steps • Fifth Grade Operations with Fractions 99

Page 99

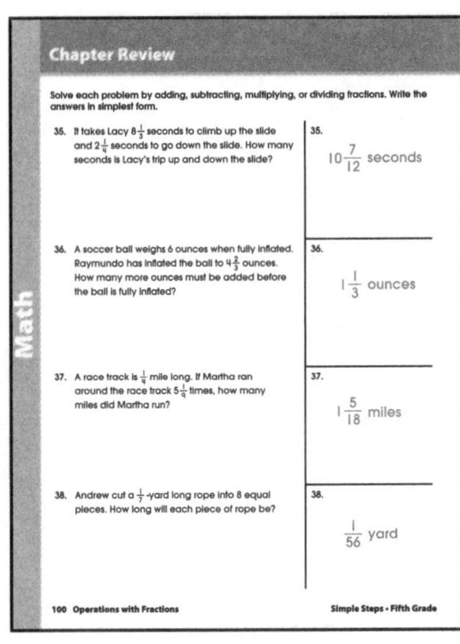

Chapter Review

Solve each problem by adding, subtracting, multiplying, or dividing fractions. Write the answers in simplest form.

35. It takes Lacy $8\frac{1}{3}$ seconds to climb up the slide and $2\frac{1}{4}$ seconds to go down the slide. How many seconds is Lacy's trip up and down the slide?

35. $10\frac{7}{12}$ seconds

36. A soccer ball weighs 6 ounces when fully inflated. Raymundo has inflated the ball to $4\frac{2}{3}$ ounces. How many more ounces must be added before the ball is fully inflated?

36. $1\frac{1}{3}$ ounces

37. A race track is $\frac{1}{4}$ mile long. If Martha ran around the race track $5\frac{1}{9}$ times, how many miles did Martha run?

37. $1\frac{5}{18}$ miles

38. Andrew cut a $\frac{1}{7}$-yard long rope into 8 equal pieces. How long will each piece of rope be?

38. $\frac{1}{56}$ yard

100 Operations with Fractions Simple Steps • Fifth Grade

Page 100

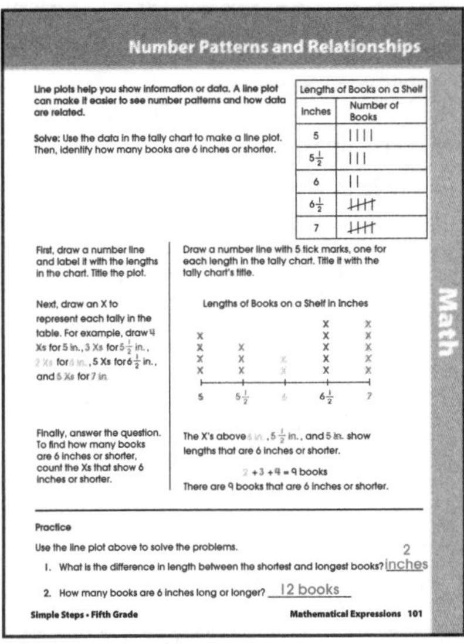

Number Patterns and Relationships

Line plots help you show information or data. A line plot can make it easier to see number patterns and how data are related.

Solve: Use the data in the tally chart to make a line plot. Then, identify how many books are 6 inches or shorter.

Lengths of Books on a Shelf	
Inches	Number of Books
5	||||
$5\frac{1}{2}$	|||
6	||
$6\frac{1}{2}$	~~||||~~
7	~~||||~~

First, draw a number line and label it with the lengths in the chart. Title the plot.

Draw a number line with 5 tick marks, one for each length in the tally chart. Title it with the tally chart's title.

Next, draw an X to represent each tally in the table. For example, draw 4 Xs for 5 in., 3 Xs for $5\frac{1}{2}$ in., 2 Xs for 6 in., 5 Xs for $6\frac{1}{2}$ in., and 5 Xs for 7 in.

Lengths of Books on a Shelf in Inches

Finally, answer the question. To find how many books are 6 inches or shorter, count the Xs that show 6 inches or shorter.

The X's above 6 in., $5\frac{1}{2}$ in., and 5 in. show lengths that are 6 inches or shorter.

2 + 3 + 4 = 9 books

There are 9 books that are 6 inches or shorter.

Practice

Use the line plot above to solve the problems.

1. What is the difference in length between the shortest and longest books? 2 inches
2. How many books are 6 inches long or longer? 12 books

Simple Steps • Fifth Grade Mathematical Expressions 101

Page 101

Number Patterns and Relationships

Practice

Use the information to complete each section of the table.

Long-distance swimmers generally need to take more breaths as they near the end of a race. Mark took 2 breaths on lap 2, he took 3 breaths on lap 4, and he took 4 breaths on lap 6. If the pattern continues, how many breaths will Mark take on lap 10?

1. Explain the pattern in words. laps increase by 2, breaths increase by 1
2. Use the pattern to fill in the table with ordered pairs. The first one has been done for you.

Lap Number	Breaths
2	2
4	3
6	4
8	5
10	6

3. Graph your points on the coordinate plane below. The first pair has been done for you.

0 1 2 3 4 5 6 7 8 9 10

4. How many breaths will Mark take on lap 10? 6 breaths

Simple Steps • Fifth Grade Mathematical Expressions 103

Page 103

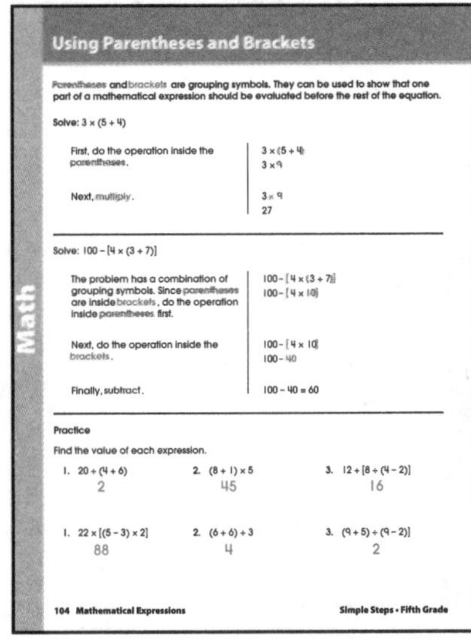

Using Parentheses and Brackets

Parentheses and brackets are grouping symbols. They can be used to show that one part of a mathematical expression should be evaluated before the rest of the equation.

Solve: 3 × (5 + 4)

First, do the operation inside the parentheses.	3 × (5 + 4) 3 × 9
Next, multiply.	3 × 9 27

Solve: 100 − [4 × (3 + 7)]

The problem has a combination of grouping symbols. Since parentheses are inside brackets, do the operation inside parentheses first.	100 − [4 × (3 + 7)] 100 − [4 × 10]
Next, do the operation inside the brackets.	100 − [4 × 10] 100 − 40
Finally, subtract.	100 − 40 = 60

Practice

Find the value of each expression.

1. 20 ÷ (4 + 6) — 2
2. (8 + 1) × 5 — 45
3. 12 + [8 ÷ (4 − 2)] — 16

1. 22 × [(5 − 3) × 2] — 88
2. (6 + 6) ÷ 3 — 4
3. (9 + 5) ÷ (9 − 2)] — 2

104 Mathematical Expressions Simple Steps • Fifth Grade

Page 104

Answer Key

Answer Key

Using Parentheses and Brackets

Practice

Find the value of each expression.

1. 2 × (4 − 2) 4	2. (3 + 13) − (2 + 8) 6	3. (452 − 448) × 6 24
4. 500 − [3 × (20 + 80)] 200	5. 25 ÷ (2 + 1 + 2) 5	6. [4 × (13 − 4)] × 3 108
7. (19 − 12) × (3 + 1) ÷ 4 7	8. (11 + 11 + 11) ÷ 11 3	9. 48 + [(19 + 3) ÷ 2] 59
10. 3 × [21 × (4 − 2)] 126	11. 56 ÷ (6 + 1) 8	12. (250 − 110) ÷ [7 × (2 + 3)] 4
13. (7 + 1) × (3 + 1) × (2 + 1) 96	14. 36 ÷ [(6 + 2) − (3 + 1)] 9	15. (9 + 3 + 6) ÷ (8 + 2 + 8) 1
16. 210 − [90 ÷ (7 + 3)] 201	17. (18 + 4 + 3) × (2 + 3) 105	18. (32 + 32) ÷ (4 + 4) 8

Simple Steps • Fifth Grade — Mathematical Expressions 105

Page 105

The Order of Operations

The order of operations is used to find the value of an expression with more than one operation.

Solve: 3 × (4 + 5) + 6 ÷ 3

First, do all operations within parentheses or other grouping symbols.	3 × (4 + 5) + 6 ÷ 3 3 × 9 + 6 ÷ 3
Second, multiply and divide in order, from left to right.	3 × 9 + 6 ÷ 3 27 + 6 ÷ 3 27 + 6 ÷ 3 27 + 2
Finally, add and subtract in order, from left to right.	27 + 2 = 29

Practice

Find the value of each expression.

1. 5 × (5 − 3) = 10
2. 5 + 4 × 3 ÷ 6 = 7
3. 20 − 4 × 3 = 8
4. 20 ÷ 5 × 2 = 8
5. (7 × 8) − (4 × 9) = 20
6. 6 × 5 − 5 × 4 = 10
7. 7 + 6 ÷ 2 − 2 = 8
8. 5 × 3 ÷ 5 + 12 = 15

106 Mathematical Expressions — Simple Steps • Fifth Grade

Page 106

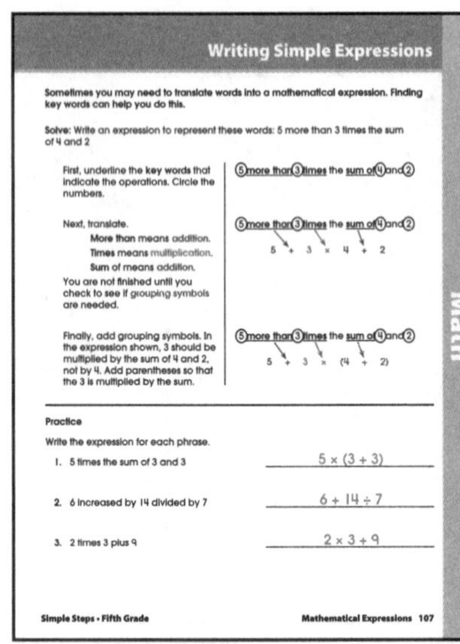

Writing Simple Expressions

Sometimes you may need to translate words into a mathematical expression. Finding key words can help you do this.

Solve: Write an expression to represent these words: 5 more than 3 times the sum of 4 and 2

First, underline the key words that indicate the operations. Circle the numbers.	(5) more than (3) times the sum of (4) and (2)
Next, translate. More than means addition. Times means multiplication. Sum of means addition. You are not finished until you check to see if grouping symbols are needed.	(5) more than (3) times the sum of (4) and (2) 5 + 3 × 4 + 2
Finally, add grouping symbols. In the expression shown, 3 should be multiplied by the sum of 4 and 2, not by 4. Add parentheses so that the 3 is multiplied by the sum.	(5) more than (3) times the sum of (4) and (2) 5 + 3 × (4 + 2)

Practice

Write the expression for each phrase.

1. 5 times the sum of 3 and 3 — 5 × (3 + 3)
2. 6 increased by 14 divided by 7 — 6 + 14 ÷ 7
3. 2 times 3 plus 9 — 2 × 3 + 9

Simple Steps • Fifth Grade — Mathematical Expressions 107

Page 107

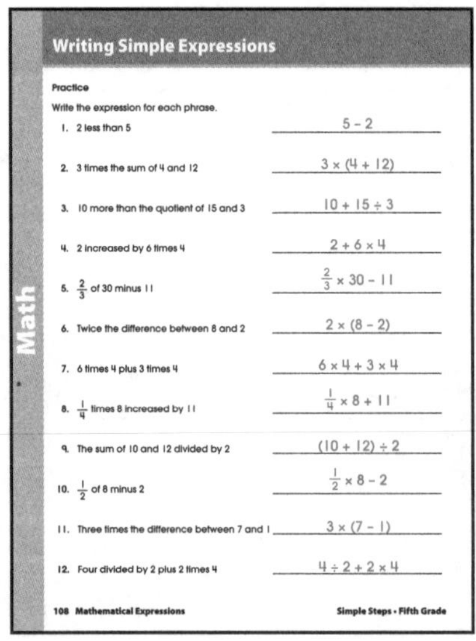

Writing Simple Expressions

Practice

Write the expression for each phrase.

1. 2 less than 5 — 5 − 2
2. 3 times the sum of 4 and 12 — 3 × (4 + 12)
3. 10 more than the quotient of 15 and 3 — 10 + 15 ÷ 3
4. 2 increased by 6 times 4 — 2 + 6 × 4
5. $\frac{2}{3}$ of 30 minus 11 — $\frac{2}{3}$ × 30 − 11
6. Twice the difference between 8 and 2 — 2 × (8 − 2)
7. 6 times 4 plus 3 times 4 — 6 × 4 + 3 × 4
8. $\frac{1}{4}$ times 8 increased by 11 — $\frac{1}{4}$ × 8 + 11
9. The sum of 10 and 12 divided by 2 — (10 + 12) ÷ 2
10. $\frac{1}{2}$ of 8 minus 2 — $\frac{1}{2}$ × 8 − 2
11. Three times the difference between 7 and 1 — 3 × (7 − 1)
12. Four divided by 2 plus 2 times 4 — 4 ÷ 2 + 2 × 4

108 Mathematical Expressions — Simple Steps • Fifth Grade

Page 108

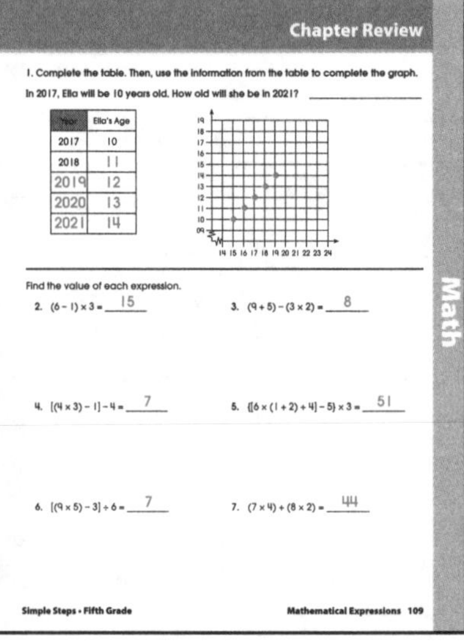

Chapter Review

1. Complete the table. Then, use the information from the table to complete the graph.

In 2017, Ella will be 10 years old. How old will she be in 2021? ______

Year	Ella's Age
2017	10
2018	11
2019	12
2020	13
2021	14

Find the value of each expression.

2. (6 − 1) × 3 = 15
3. (9 + 5) − (3 × 2) = 8
4. [(4 × 3) − 1] − 4 = 7
5. {[6 × (1 + 2) + 4] − 5} × 3 = 51
6. [(9 × 5) − 3] ÷ 6 = 7
7. (7 × 4) + (8 × 2) = 44

Simple Steps • Fifth Grade — Mathematical Expressions 109

Page 109

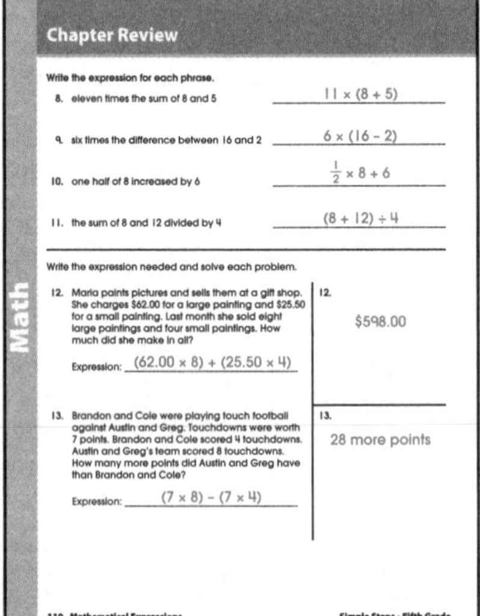

Chapter Review

Write the expression for each phrase.

8. eleven times the sum of 8 and 5 — 11 × (8 + 5)
9. six times the difference between 16 and 2 — 6 × (16 − 2)
10. one half of 8 increased by 6 — $\frac{1}{2}$ × 8 + 6
11. the sum of 8 and 12 divided by 4 — (8 + 12) ÷ 4

Write the expression needed and solve each problem.

12. Maria paints pictures and sells them at a gift shop. She charges $62.00 for a large painting and $25.50 for a small painting. Last month she sold eight large paintings and four small paintings. How much did she make in all?

Expression: (62.00 × 8) + (25.50 × 4)

12. $598.00

13. Brandon and Cole were playing touch football against Austin and Greg. Touchdowns were worth 7 points. Brandon and Cole scored 4 touchdowns. Austin and Greg's team scored 8 touchdowns. How many more points did Austin and Greg have than Brandon and Cole?

Expression: (7 × 8) − (7 × 4)

13. 28 more points

110 Mathematical Expressions — Simple Steps • Fifth Grade

Page 110

Metric Conversions

In many countries, and in the United States only for specific purposes, people use the metric system to measure length, mass, and volume. The metric system is based on units of 100. This table shows metric conversions for converting from one unit to another.

Length	Mass	Volume
1 kilometer (k) = 1,000 meters (m)	1 kilogram (kg) = 1,000 grams (g)	1 kiloliter (kL) = 1,000 liters (L)
1 meter (m) = 0.001 kilometers (km)	1 gram (g) = 0.001 kilograms (kg)	1 liter (L) = 0.001 kiloliters (kL)
1 meter (m) = 100 centimeters (cm)	1 gram (g) = 100 centigrams (cg)	1 liter = 100 centiliters (cL)
1 centimeter (cm) = 0.01 meters (m)	1 centigram (cg) = 0.01 grams (g)	1 centiliter (cL) = 0.01 liters (L)
1 meter (m) = 1,000 millimeters (mm)	1 gram (g) = 1,000 milligrams (mg)	1 liter (L) = 1,000 milliliters (mL)
1 millimeter (mm) = 0.001 meter (m)	1 milligram (mg) = 0.001 gram (g)	1 milliliter (mL) = 0.001 liters (L)

Solve: 6 grams = ________ milligrams

First, find the metric conversion you need. | Grams are units of mass. A useful metric conversion is: 1 g = 1,000 mg

Next, decide if you should multiply or divide. Since you are converting from a larger unit, grams, to a smaller unit, milligrams, multiply. | 6 g = (6 × 1,000) mg = 6,000 mg

Practice

Complete the following metric conversions.

1. 2 m = 200 cm
2. 500 mL = 0.5 L
3. 472 g = 472,000 mg
4. 1,200 mm = 1.2 m
5. 20 kg = 20,000 g
6. 5,100 m = 5.1 km
7. 15 cL = 0.15 L
8. 4,220 L = 4.22 kL

Simple Steps • Fifth Grade   Measurement, Geometry, and Graphing 111

Math

Page 111

Metric Conversions

Practice

Complete the following metric conversions.

1. 5 g = 5,000 mg
2. 117,000 g = 117 kg
3. 4,000 L = 4 kL
4. 51,000 mL = 51 L
5. 600 mm = 60 cm
6. 4 kL = 4,000 L
7. 42 m = 42,000 mm
8. 2 g 150 mg = 2,150 mg
9. 438 L = 438,000 mL
10. 500 cm = 50,000 mm
11. 2,500 g = 2.5 kg
12. 48 m = 48,000 mm
13. 1 kg, 520 mg = 1,520 mg
14. 482 cg = 4.82 g
15. 380 mm = 0.38 m
16. 59,600 mL = 59.6 L

112 Measurement, Geometry, and Graphing   Simple Steps • Fifth Grade

Math

Page 112

Standard Measurement Conversions

In the U.S. and some other countries, standard measurements are used. This table shows useful unit conversions in this measurement system.

Length	Volume	Weight
1 mile (mi.) = 1,760 yards (yd.)	1 gallon (gal.) = 4 quarts (qt.)	1 pound (lb.) = 16 ounces (oz.)
1 mile (mi.) = 5,280 feet (ft.)	1 gallon (gal.) = 8 pints (pt.)	
1 yard (yd.) = 36 inches (in.)	1 quart (qt.) = 2 pints (pt.)	
1 yard (yd.) = 3 feet (ft.)	1 quart (qt.) = 4 cups (c.)	2,000 pounds (lb.) = 1 ton (T.)
1 foot (ft.) = 12 inches (in.)	1 pint (pt.) = 2 cups (c.)	

Solve: 28,000 lb. = ________ T.

First, find the standard conversion you need. | Pounds are units of weight. A useful conversion is: 2,000 lb. = 1 T.

Next, decide if you multiply or divide. Since you are converting from a smaller unit, pounds, to a larger unit, tons, divide. | 28,000 lb = (28,000 ÷ 2,000) T. = 14 T.

Practice

Complete the following metric conversions.

1. 12 qt. = 24 pt.
2. 3 mi. = 5,280 yd.
3. 3 ft., 6 in. = 42 in.
4. 8 oz. = 0.5 lb.
5. 3 gal. = 24 pints
6. 2 qt., 1 c. = 9 c.
7. 48 in. = 4 ft.
8. 6.5 T. = 13,000 lb.

Simple Steps • Fifth Grade   Measurement, Geometry, and Graphing 113

Math

Page 113

Standard Measurement Conversions

Practice

Complete the following standard conversions.

1. 12 ft. = 4 yd.
2. 10 pt. = 5 qt.
3. 80 oz. = 5 lb.
4. 7 qt. = 28 c.
5. 14,000 lb. = 7 T.
6. 8 ft. 2 in. = 98 in.
7. 1 T. 5 oz. = 2,005 oz.
8. 8 gal. = 64 pt.
9. 7 yd. = 252 in.
10. 2 mi. 3,241 ft. = 13,801 ft.
11. 15 yd. = 540 in.
12. 30,000 lb. = 15 T.
13. 2 gal. 2 pt. = 9 qt.
14. 6 lb. 7 oz. = 103 oz.
15. 12 c. = 6 pt.
16. 1 mi. 372 yd. = 2,132 yd.

114 Measurement, Geometry, and Graphing   Simple Steps • Fifth Grade

Math

Page 114

Using Line Plots

Practice

Draw a line plot to organize the information. Then, write expressions to solve the problems.

1. Alexis is building a track for her toy train. She needs 3 more feet of track to reach the train station. She has 2 pieces of track that are each $\frac{1}{4}$ foot long, 1 piece of track that is $\frac{1}{2}$ foot long, and 1 piece of track that is $1\frac{1}{3}$ feet long. Are the pieces of track long enough to reach the station?

$$3 - \{(2 \times \frac{1}{4}) + \frac{1}{2} + 1\frac{1}{3}\} = \frac{2}{3} \text{ feet}$$

No, the track will be $\frac{2}{3}$ feet too short.

0 $\frac{1}{4}$ $\frac{1}{2}$ 1 $1\frac{1}{3}$

2. Getting ready for a science experiment, Mr. Yip poured water into 8 1-pint beakers. Two beakers hold $\frac{1}{4}$ pint, 3 beakers hold $\frac{3}{8}$ pint, 1 beaker holds $\frac{5}{8}$ pint, and 2 beakers hold $\frac{5}{6}$ pint. If Mr. Yip wants to split the water equally between the 8 beakers, how much water will be in each beaker?

$$\{(2 \times \frac{1}{4}) + (3 \times \frac{3}{8}) + (2 \times \frac{5}{6}) + \frac{5}{8}\} \div 8 = 3\frac{11}{12}$$

divided by 8 = $\frac{47}{96}$ pints each

0 $\frac{1}{4}$ $\frac{3}{8}$ $\frac{5}{8}$ $\frac{5}{6}$ 1

116 Measurement, Geometry, and Graphing   Simple Steps • Fifth Grade

Math

Page 116

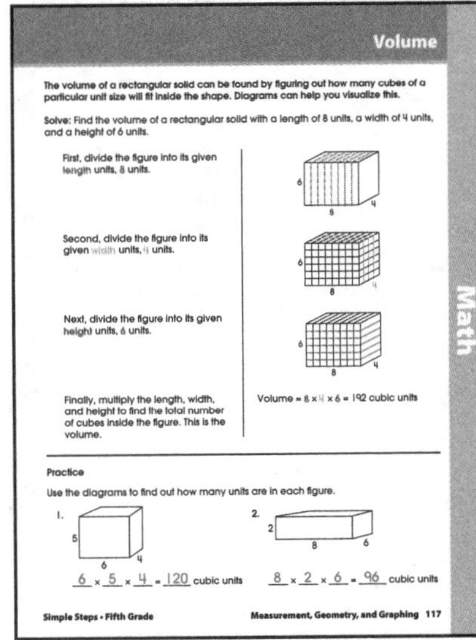

Volume

The volume of a rectangular solid can be found by figuring out how many cubes of a particular unit size will fit inside the shape. Diagrams can help you visualize this.

Solve: Find the volume of a rectangular solid with a length of 8 units, a width of 4 units, and a height of 6 units.

First, divide the figure into its given length units, 8 units.

Second, divide the figure into its given width units, 4 units.

Next, divide the figure into its given height units, 6 units.

Finally, multiply the length, width, and height to find the total number of cubes inside the figure. This is the volume. | Volume = 8 × 4 × 6 = 192 cubic units

Practice

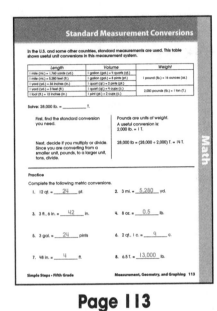

Use the diagrams to find out how many units are in each figure.

1. 6 × 5 × 4 = 120 cubic units
2. 8 × 2 × 6 = 96 cubic units

Simple Steps • Fifth Grade   Measurement, Geometry, and Graphing 117

Math

Page 117

Answer Key

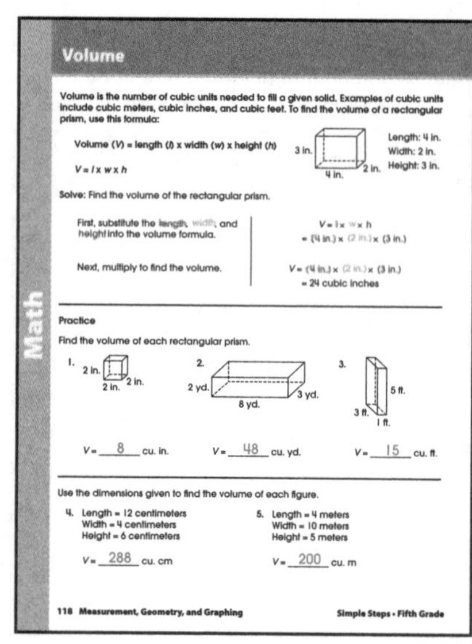

Volume

Volume is the number of cubic units needed to fill a given solid. Examples of cubic units include cubic meters, cubic inches, and cubic feet. To find the volume of a rectangular prism, use this formula:

Volume (V) = length (l) x width (w) x height (h)

V = l x w x h

Length: 4 in.
Width: 2 in.
Height: 3 in.

Solve: Find the volume of the rectangular prism.

First, substitute the length, width, and height into the volume formula. V = l x w x h = (4 in.) x (2 in.) x (3 in.)

Next, multiply to find the volume. V = (4 in.) x (2 in.) x (3 in.) = 24 cubic inches

Practice

Find the volume of each rectangular prism.

1. V = 8 cu. in.
2. V = 48 cu. yd.
3. V = 15 cu. ft.

Use the dimensions given to find the volume of each figure.

4. Length = 12 centimeters, Width = 4 centimeters, Height = 6 centimeters. V = 288 cu. cm
5. Length = 4 meters, Width = 10 meters, Height = 5 meters. V = 200 cu. m

118 Measurement, Geometry, and Graphing — Simple Steps • Fifth Grade

Page 118

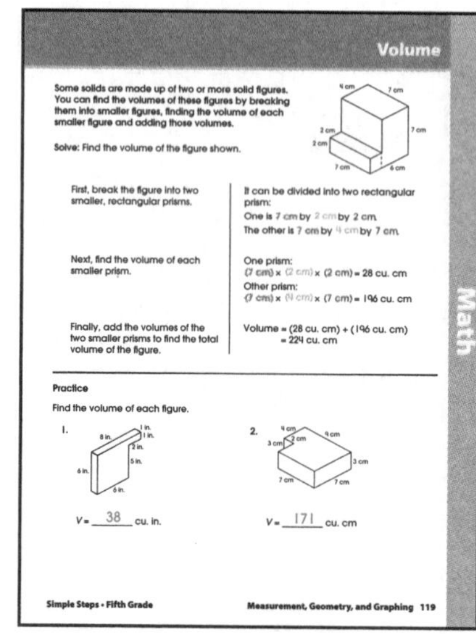

Volume

Some solids are made up of two or more solid figures. You can find the volumes of these figures by breaking them into smaller figures, finding the volume of each smaller figure and adding those volumes.

Solve: Find the volume of the figure shown.

First, break the figure into two smaller, rectangular prisms. It can be divided into two rectangular prism: One is 7 cm by 2 cm by 2 cm. The other is 7 cm by 4 cm by 7 cm.

Next, find the volume of each smaller prism. One prism: (7 cm) x (2 cm) x (2 cm) = 28 cu. cm. Other prism: (7 cm) x (4 cm) x (7 cm) = 196 cu. cm

Finally, add the volumes of the two smaller prisms to find the total volume of the figure. Volume = (28 cu. cm) + (196 cu. cm) = 224 cu. cm

Practice

Find the volume of each figure.

1. V = 38 cu. in.
2. V = 171 cu. cm

Simple Steps • Fifth Grade — Measurement, Geometry, and Graphing 119

Page 119

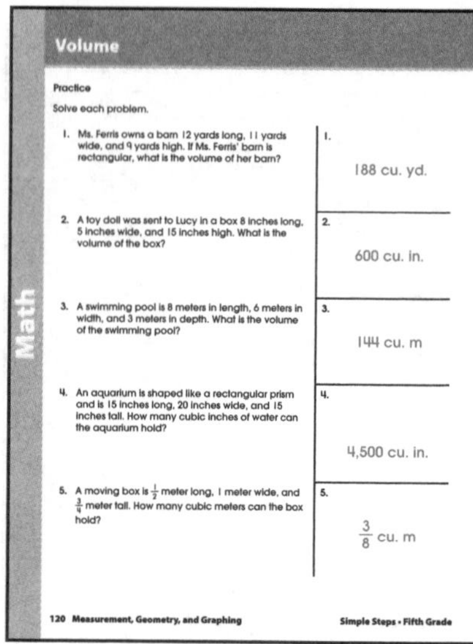

Volume

Practice

Solve each problem.

1. Ms. Ferris owns a barn 12 yards long, 11 yards wide, and 9 yards high. If Ms. Ferris' barn is rectangular, what is the volume of her barn? 188 cu. yd.
2. A toy doll was sent to Lucy in a box 8 inches long, 5 inches wide, and 15 inches high. What is the volume of the box? 600 cu. in.
3. A swimming pool is 8 meters in length, 6 meters in width, and 3 meters in depth. What is the volume of the swimming pool? 144 cu. m
4. An aquarium is shaped like a rectangular prism and is 15 inches long, 20 inches wide, and 15 inches tall. How many cubic inches of water can the aquarium hold? 4,500 cu. in.
5. A moving box is $\frac{1}{2}$ meter long, 1 meter wide, and $\frac{3}{4}$ meter tall. How many cubic meters can the box hold? $\frac{3}{8}$ cu. m

120 Measurement, Geometry, and Graphing — Simple Steps • Fifth Grade

Page 120

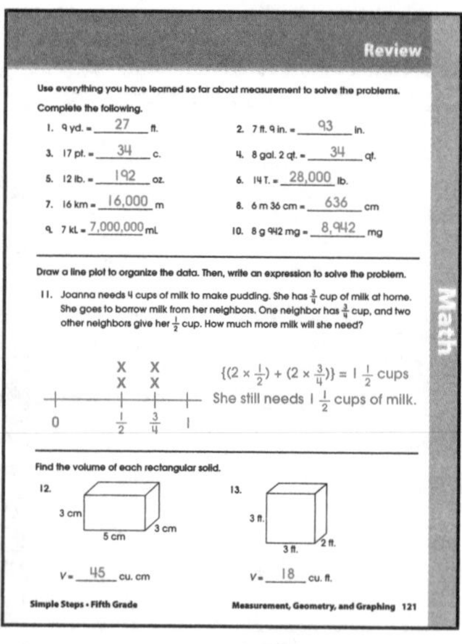

Review

Use everything you have learned so far about measurement to solve the problems.

Complete the following.

1. 9 yd. = 27 ft.
2. 7 ft. 9 in. = 93 in.
3. 17 pt. = 34 c.
4. 8 gal. 2 qt. = 34 qt.
5. 12 lb. = 192 oz.
6. 14 T. = 28,000 lb.
7. 16 km = 16,000 m
8. 6 m 36 cm = 636 cm
9. 7 kL = 7,000,000 mL
10. 8 g 942 mg = 8,942 mg

Draw a line plot to organize the data. Then, write an expression to solve the problem.

11. Joanna needs 4 cups of milk to make pudding. She has $\frac{3}{4}$ cup of milk at home. She goes to borrow milk from her neighbors. One neighbor has $\frac{3}{4}$ cup, and two other neighbors give her $\frac{1}{2}$ cup. How much more milk will she need?

$\{(2 \times \frac{1}{2}) + (2 \times \frac{3}{4})\} = 1\frac{1}{2}$ cups

She still needs $1\frac{1}{2}$ cups of milk.

Find the volume of each rectangular solid.

12. V = 45 cu. cm
13. V = 18 cu. ft.

Simple Steps • Fifth Grade — Measurement, Geometry, and Graphing 121

Page 121

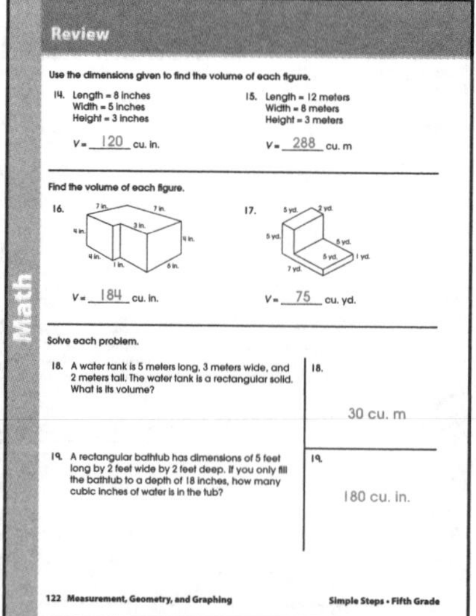

Review

Use the dimensions given to find the volume of each figure.

14. Length = 8 inches, Width = 5 inches, Height = 3 inches. V = 120 cu. in.
15. Length = 12 meters, Width = 8 meters, Height = 3 meters. V = 288 cu. m

Find the volume of each figure.

16. V = 184 cu. in.
17. V = 75 cu. yd.

Solve each problem.

18. A water tank is 5 meters long, 3 meters wide, and 2 meters tall. The water tank is a rectangular solid. What is its volume? 30 cu. m
19. A rectangular bathtub has dimensions of 5 feet long by 2 feet wide by 2 feet deep. If you only fill the bathtub to a depth of 18 inches, how many cubic inches of water is in the tub? 180 cu. in.

122 Measurement, Geometry, and Graphing — Simple Steps • Fifth Grade

Page 122

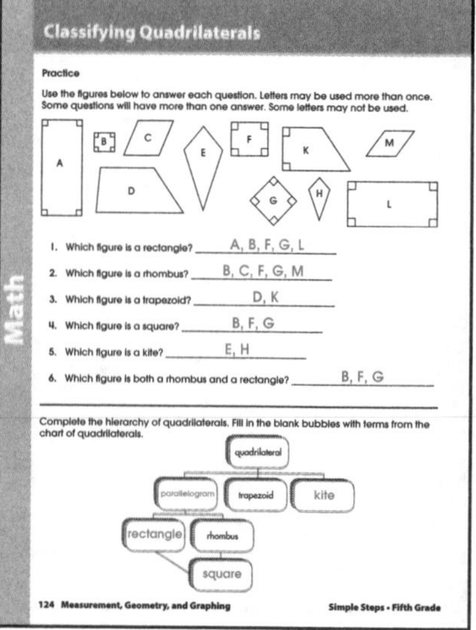

Classifying Quadrilaterals

Practice

Use the figures below to answer each question. Letters may be used more than once. Some questions will have more than one answer. Some letters may not be used.

1. Which figure is a rectangle? A, B, F, G, L
2. Which figure is a rhombus? B, C, F, G, M
3. Which figure is a trapezoid? D, K
4. Which figure is a square? B, F, G
5. Which figure is a kite? E, H
6. Which figure is both a rhombus and a rectangle? B, F, G

Complete the hierarchy of quadrilaterals. Fill in the blank bubbles with terms from the chart of quadrilaterals.

quadrilateral; parallelogram, trapezoid, kite; rectangle, rhombus; square

124 Measurement, Geometry, and Graphing — Simple Steps • Fifth Grade

Page 124

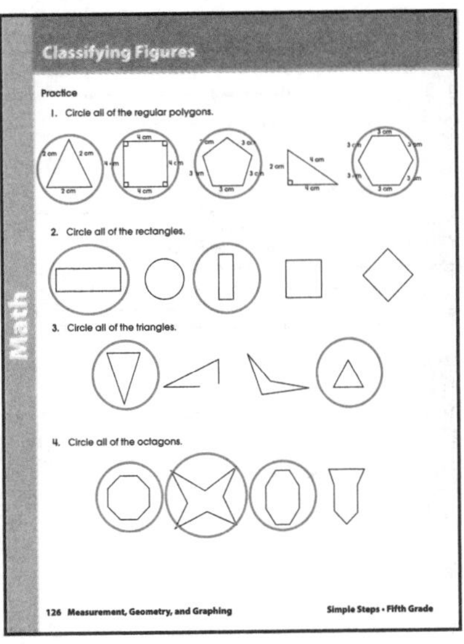
Classifying Figures

Practice

1. Circle all of the regular polygons.
2. Circle all of the rectangles.
3. Circle all of the triangles.
4. Circle all of the octagons.

126 Measurement, Geometry, and Graphing — Simple Steps • Fifth Grade

Page 126

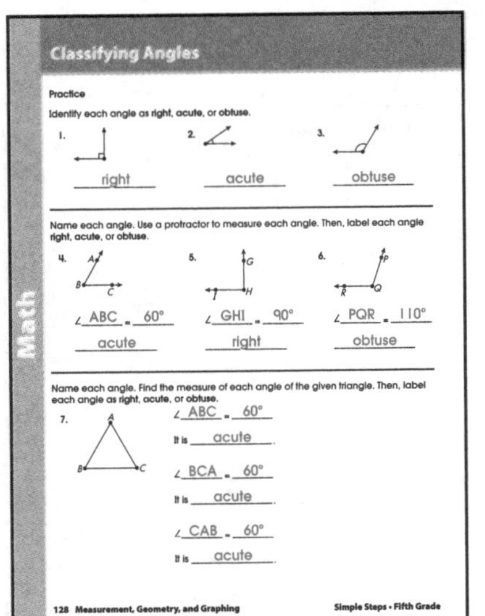
Classifying Angles

Practice

Identify each angle as right, acute, or obtuse.

1. right
2. acute
3. obtuse

Name each angle. Use a protractor to measure each angle. Then, label each angle right, acute, or obtuse.

4. ∠ ABC = 60° acute
5. ∠ GHI = 90° right
6. ∠ PQR = 110° obtuse

Name each angle. Find the measure of each angle of the given triangle. Then, label each angle as right, acute, or obtuse.

7. ∠ ABC = 60° It is acute.
∠ BCA = 60° It is acute.
∠ CAB = 60° It is acute.

128 Measurement, Geometry, and Graphing — Simple Steps • Fifth Grade

Page 128

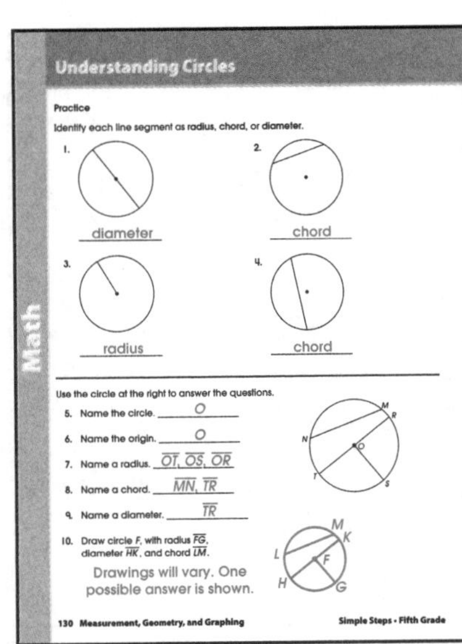
Understanding Circles

Practice

Identify each line segment as radius, chord, or diameter.

1. diameter
2. chord
3. radius
4. chord

Use the circle at the right to answer the questions.

5. Name the circle. O
6. Name the origin. O
7. Name a radius. OT, OS, OR
8. Name a chord. MN, TR
9. Name a diameter. TR
10. Draw circle F, with radius FG, diameter HK, and chord LM.
Drawings will vary. One possible answer is shown.

130 Measurement, Geometry, and Graphing — Simple Steps • Fifth Grade

Page 130

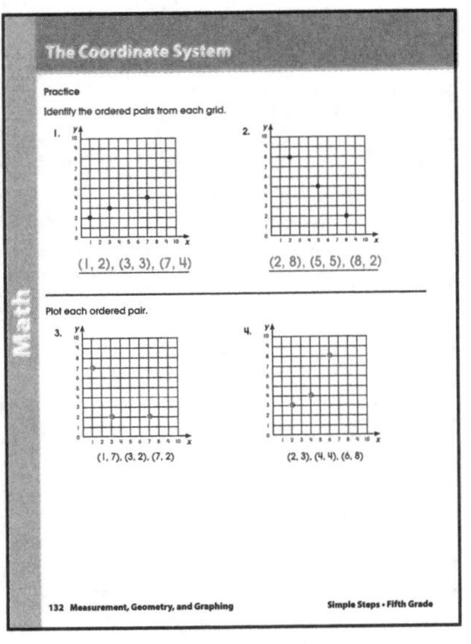
The Coordinate System

Practice

Identify the ordered pairs from each grid.

1. (1, 2), (3, 3), (7, 4)
2. (2, 8), (5, 5), (8, 2)

Plot each ordered pair.

3. (1, 7), (3, 2), (7, 2)
4. (2, 3), (4, 4), (6, 8)

132 Measurement, Geometry, and Graphing — Simple Steps • Fifth Grade

Page 132

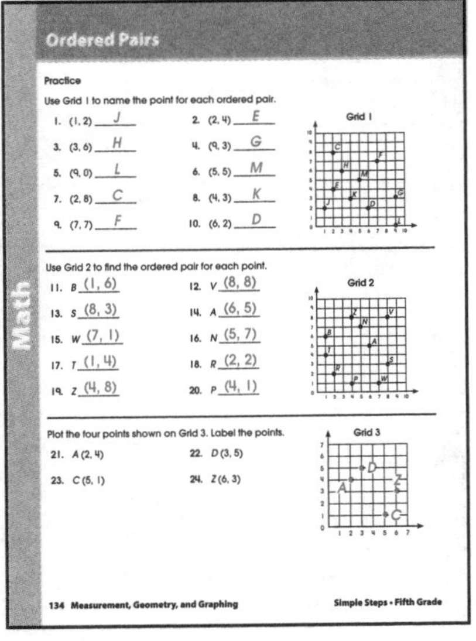
Ordered Pairs

Practice

Use Grid 1 to name the point for each ordered pair.

1. (1, 2) J
2. (2, 4) E
3. (3, 6) H
4. (9, 3) G
5. (9, 0) L
6. (5, 5) M
7. (2, 8) C
8. (4, 3) K
9. (7, 7) F
10. (6, 2) D

Use Grid 2 to find the ordered pair for each point.

11. B (1, 6)
12. V (8, 8)
13. S (8, 3)
14. A (6, 5)
15. W (7, 1)
16. N (5, 7)
17. T (1, 4)
18. R (2, 2)
19. Z (4, 8)
20. P (4, 1)

Plot the four points shown on Grid 3. Label the points.

21. A (2, 4)
22. D (3, 5)
23. C (5, 1)
24. Z (6, 3)

134 Measurement, Geometry, and Graphing — Simple Steps • Fifth Grade

Page 134

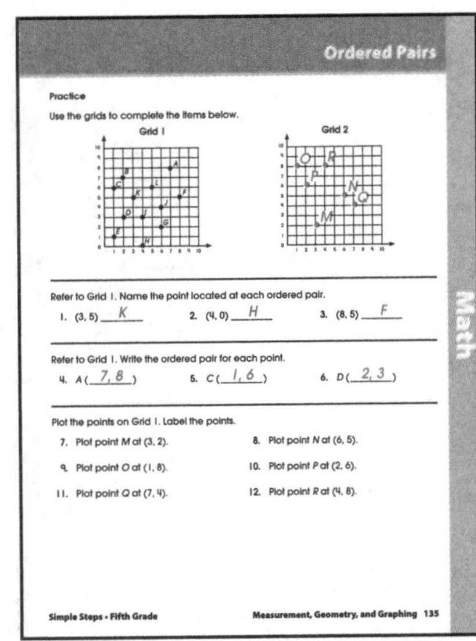
Ordered Pairs

Practice

Use the grids to complete the items below.

Refer to Grid 1. Name the point located at each ordered pair.

1. (3, 5) K
2. (4, 0) H
3. (8, 5) F

Refer to Grid 1. Write the ordered pair for each point.

4. A(7, 8)
5. C(1, 6)
6. D(2, 3)

Plot the points on Grid 1. Label the points.

7. Plot point M at (3, 2).
8. Plot point N at (6, 5).
9. Plot point O at (1, 8).
10. Plot point P at (2, 6).
11. Plot point Q at (7, 4).
12. Plot point R at (4, 8).

Simple Steps • Fifth Grade — Measurement, Geometry, and Graphing 135

Page 135

Answer Key

Ordered Pairs

You can use coordinate grids to solve problems.

Solve: A line segment runs from (3, 2) to (7, 2). How long is that line segment?

First, draw the line segment on a coordinate grid. Plot points at (3, 2) and (7, 2) and connect them.

Next, count the number of horizontal units between the end points of the segment. For a vertical line, you would count the number of vertical units between end points.

There are 4 units (spaces) between (3, 2) and (7, 2). The length of the line segment is 4 units.

Practice

Use the coordinate grid to solve the problems.

1. A line segment runs from (2, 8) to (4, 8). How long is the line segment? 2 units
2. A line segment runs from (3, 1) to (3, 7). How long is the line segment? 6 units
3. A rectangle has points at (4, 2), (6, 2), (6, 7), and (4, 7). What is the perimeter of the rectangle? 14 units

136 Measurement, Geometry, and Graphing — Simple Steps • Fifth Grade

Page 136

Problem Solving

You can use the coordinate grid strategies you have learned about so far to solve more difficult problems.

First, underline the important information that you will need to solve the problem.

Bob rides his bike from his home which is located at (6, 2) on the grid. He rides 4 blocks north, 3 blocks west, and then 4 blocks south. How many blocks will he have to ride to get home?

Next, determine which strategy is best for solving the problem.

Draw Bob's route on a coordinate grid. Then, determine the distance from his ending point to his home.

Then, represent Bob's route on a coordinate grid.

Finally, solve the problem. Count the distance between the ending point and Bob's home.

Bob's home is at (6, 2). He ends at (3, 2). There are 3 horizontal units between those points. Each unit shows 1 block, so Bob has to ride 3 blocks to get home.

Practice

Use the coordinate grid to solve the problems.

1. Carmen's mom drives from her home 8 blocks north to the store. Then, they go 4 blocks west for lunch and 6 blocks south for dessert. How far will they have to drive to get back home? 6 blocks—2 blocks south and 4 blocks east
2. On her way to school, Tisha walked 2 blocks east to her friend's house. Then, they walked together 5 blocks north to buy snacks. Finally, they walked 3 blocks east and 1 block south to get to school. How far will Tisha have to walk to get home from school if she makes no stops? 9 blocks—4 blocks south and 5 blocks west

Simple Steps • Fifth Grade — Measurement, Geometry, and Graphing 137

Page 137

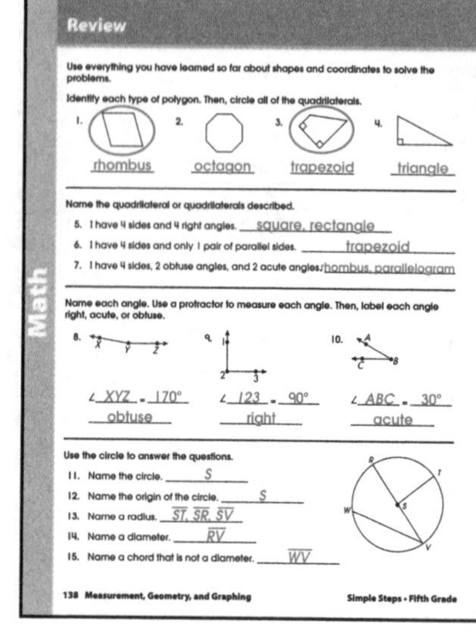

Review

Use everything you have learned so far about shapes and coordinates to solve the problems.

Identify each type of polygon. Then, circle all of the quadrilaterals.

1. rhombus 2. octagon 3. trapezoid 4. triangle

Name the quadrilateral or quadrilaterals described.

5. I have 4 sides and 4 right angles. square, rectangle
6. I have 4 sides and only 1 pair of parallel sides. trapezoid
7. I have 4 sides, 2 obtuse angles, and 2 acute angles. rhombus, parallelogram

Name each angle. Use a protractor to measure each angle. Then, label each angle right, acute, or obtuse.

8. ∠XYZ = 170° obtuse
9. ∠123 = 90° right
10. ∠ABC = 30° acute

Use the circle to answer the questions.

11. Name the circle. S
12. Name the origin of the circle. S
13. Name a radius. ST, SR, SV
14. Name a diameter. RV
15. Name a chord that is not a diameter. WV

138 Measurement, Geometry, and Graphing — Simple Steps • Fifth Grade

Page 138

Review

Identify the ordered pair from the grid.

16. (2, 4)

Plot the ordered pair.

17. (5, 5)

Use the grid to name the point for each ordered pair.

18. (3, 6) H
19. (9, 3) G

Use the coordinate grid to solve the problem.

20. Shane and Wesley want to meet and play baseball halfway between both of their houses. Shane lives at (4, 1) and Wesley lives at (10, 1). Plot both boys' houses on the grid. At which point should Shane and Wesley meet to play baseball? They should meet at point (7, 1).

Simple Steps • Fifth Grade — Measurement, Geometry, and Graphing 139

Page 139

Chapter Review

Complete the following.

1. 6 ft. = 2 yd.
2. 3 mi. = 15,840 ft.
3. 4 qt. = 8 pt.
4. 5 gal. = 20 qt.
5. 3 lb. = 48 oz.
6. 500 mm = 50 cm
7. 6 L = 6,000 mL
8. 8 kg = 8,000 g

Draw a line plot to organize the data. Then, solve the problem.

9. Joseph needs to run 3 miles during his workout for the soccer team. He begins practice by running $\frac{1}{2}$ mile. Then, he takes 3 breaks during practice to run $\frac{1}{4}$ mile each time. How much more will he need to run at the end of practice to finish his 3 miles? $1\frac{3}{4}$ miles

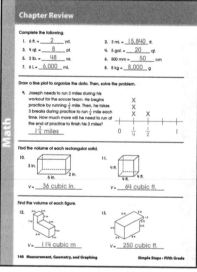

Find the volume of each rectangular solid.

10. V = 36 cubic in.
11. V = 64 cubic ft.

Find the volume of each figure.

12. V = 114 cubic m
13. V = 250 cubic ft.

140 Measurement, Geometry, and Graphing — Simple Steps • Fifth Grade

Page 140

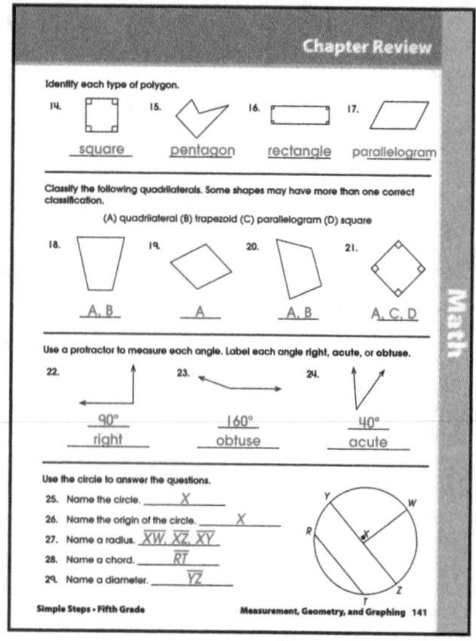

Chapter Review

Identify each type of polygon.

14. square 15. pentagon 16. rectangle 17. parallelogram

Classify the following quadrilaterals. Some shapes may have more than one correct classification.

(A) quadrilateral (B) trapezoid (C) parallelogram (D) square

18. A, B 19. A 20. A, B 21. A, C, D

Use a protractor to measure each angle. Label each angle right, acute, or obtuse.

22. 90° right 23. 160° obtuse 24. 40° acute

Use the circle to answer the questions.

25. Name the circle. X
26. Name the origin of the circle. X
27. Name a radius. XW, XZ, XY
28. Name a chord. RT
29. Name a diameter. YZ

Simple Steps • Fifth Grade — Measurement, Geometry, and Graphing 141

Page 141

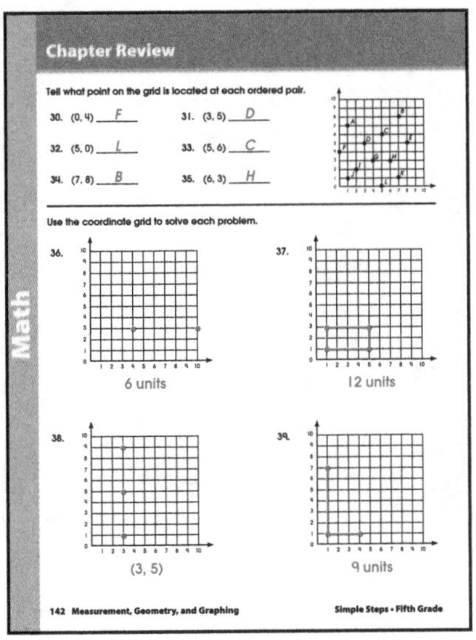

Chapter Review

Tell what point on the grid is located at each ordered pair.

30. (0, 4) F
31. (3, 5) D
32. (5, 0) L
33. (5, 6) C
34. (7, 8) B
35. (6, 3) H

Use the coordinate grid to solve each problem.

36. 6 units
37. 12 units
38. (3, 5)
39. 9 units

142 Measurement, Geometry, and Graphing — Simple Steps • Fifth Grade

Page 142

Math Review

Add, subtract, multiply, or divide.

1. 22.92 × 2.64 = 60.5088
2. \$67.52 + 20.18 = \$87.70
3. \$16.52 − 6.93 = \$9.59
4. 7.9)64.78 = 8.2

Multiply or divide by the power of ten to find the product.

5. 6.07 × 1,000 = 6,070
6. 3.457 ÷ 100 = 0.03457
7. 1×10^4 = 10,000

Write the number in expanded form.

8. 3,465 3,000 + 400 + 60 + 5

Write the numbers in order from least to greatest.

9. 1.5, 1.7, $\frac{1}{150}$, $\frac{8}{3}$ — $\frac{1}{150}$, 1.5, 1.7, $\frac{8}{3}$

Round each number to the place of the underlined digit.

10. 1,785,302 2,000,000
11. 7.3222 7.32
12. 4.397 4.4

Solve the problem.

13. Sami started with 5 pounds of flour. He used 2.25 pounds for bread and 1.5 pounds for cookies. How much did he use? He needs 1.15 lbs for pie. Does he have enough left? 3.75 pounds; Yes

Find the equivalent fraction.

14. $6 = \frac{18}{3}$
15. $\frac{7}{9} = \frac{14}{18}$
16. $8 = \frac{48}{6}$

Change each fraction to a decimal as indicated.

17. Change $2\frac{1}{5}$ to tenths. 2.2
18. Change $\frac{17}{50}$ to hundredths. 0.34

Simple Steps • Fifth Grade — Review 143

Page 143

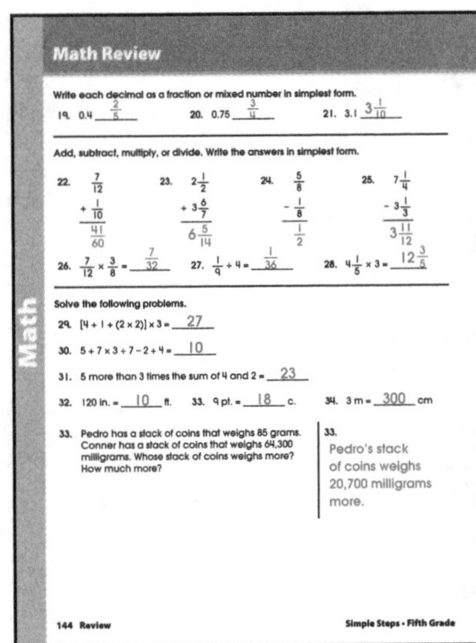

Math Review

Write each decimal as a fraction or mixed number in simplest form.

19. 0.4 $\frac{2}{5}$
20. 0.75 $\frac{3}{4}$
21. 3.1 $3\frac{1}{10}$

Add, subtract, multiply, or divide. Write the answers in simplest form.

22. $\frac{7}{12} + \frac{1}{10} = \frac{41}{60}$
23. $2\frac{1}{2} + 3\frac{6}{7} = 6\frac{5}{14}$
24. $\frac{5}{8} - \frac{1}{8} = \frac{1}{2}$
25. $7\frac{1}{4} - 3\frac{1}{3} = 3\frac{11}{12}$
26. $\frac{7}{12} \times \frac{3}{8} = \frac{7}{32}$
27. $\frac{1}{9} \div 4 = \frac{1}{36}$
28. $4\frac{1}{5} \times 3 = 12\frac{3}{5}$

Solve the following problems.

29. [4 + 1 + (2 × 2)] × 3 = 27
30. 5 + 7 × 3 ÷ 7 − 2 + 4 = 10
31. 5 more than 3 times the sum of 4 and 2 = 23
32. 120 in. = 10 ft.
33. 9 pt. = 18 c.
34. 3 m = 300 cm

33. Pedro has a stack of coins that weighs 85 grams. Conner has a stack of coins that weighs 64,300 milligrams. Whose stack of coins weighs more? How much more?

33. Pedro's stack of coins weighs 20,700 milligrams more.

144 Review — Simple Steps • Fifth Grade

Page 144

Math Review

Find the volume of each rectangular solid.

34. 8 in., 7 in., 2 in. V = 112 cu. in.

35. Length = 3 feet, Width = 2 feet, Height = 6 feet. V = 36 cu. ft.

Classify the following quadrilaterals. Some shapes may have more than one correct classification.

(A) parallelogram (B) quadrilateral (C) rectangle

36. A, B, C
37. A, B
38. B

Identify each angle as right, acute, or obtuse.

39. acute
40. right
41. obtuse

Use the grid to name the point for each ordered pair.

42. (6, 4) D
43. (1, 8) C
44. (1, 4) E
45. (3, 5) A
46. (8, 7) F
47. (4, 2) G

Simple Steps • Fifth Grade — Review 145

Page 145

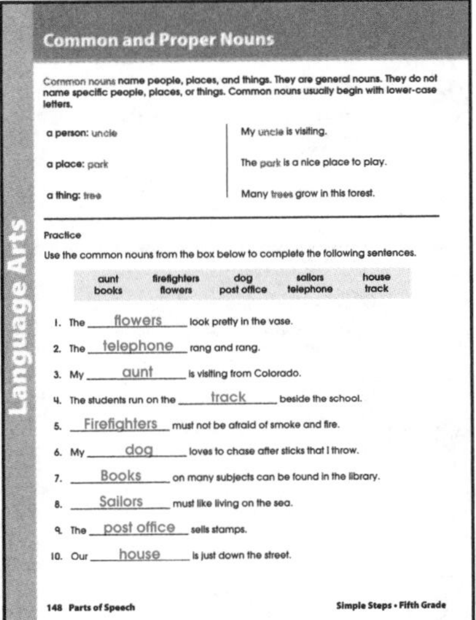

Common and Proper Nouns

Common nouns name people, places, and things. They are general nouns. They do not name specific people, places, or things. Common nouns usually begin with lower-case letters.

a person: uncle	My uncle is visiting.
a place: park	The park is a nice place to play.
a thing: tree	Many trees grow in this forest.

Practice

Use the common nouns from the box below to complete the following sentences.

aunt, books, firefighters, flowers, dog, post office, sailors, telephone, house, track

1. The flowers look pretty in the vase.
2. The telephone rang and rang.
3. My aunt is visiting from Colorado.
4. The students run on the track beside the school.
5. Firefighters must not be afraid of smoke and fire.
6. My dog loves to chase after sticks that I throw.
7. Books on many subjects can be found in the library.
8. Sailors must like living on the sea.
9. The post office sells stamps.
10. Our house is just down the street.

148 Parts of Speech — Simple Steps • Fifth Grade

Page 148

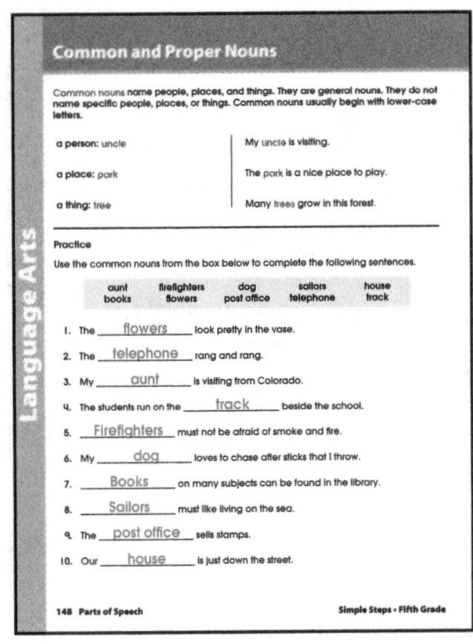

Common and Proper Nouns

Common nouns name people, places, and things. They are general nouns. They do not name specific people, places, or things. Common nouns usually begin with lower-case letters.

a person: uncle	My uncle is visiting.
a place: park	The park is a nice place to play.
a thing: tree	Many trees grow in this forest.

Practice

Use the common nouns from the box below to complete the following sentences.

aunt, books, firefighters, flowers, dog, post office, sailors, telephone, house, track

1. The flowers look pretty in the vase.
2. The telephone rang and rang.
3. My aunt is visiting from Colorado.
4. The students run on the track beside the school.
5. Firefighters must not be afraid of smoke and fire.
6. My dog loves to chase after sticks that I throw.
7. Books on many subjects can be found in the library.
8. Sailors must like living on the sea.
9. The post office sells stamps.
10. Our house is just down the street.

148 Parts of Speech — Simple Steps • Fifth Grade

Page 149

Answer Key

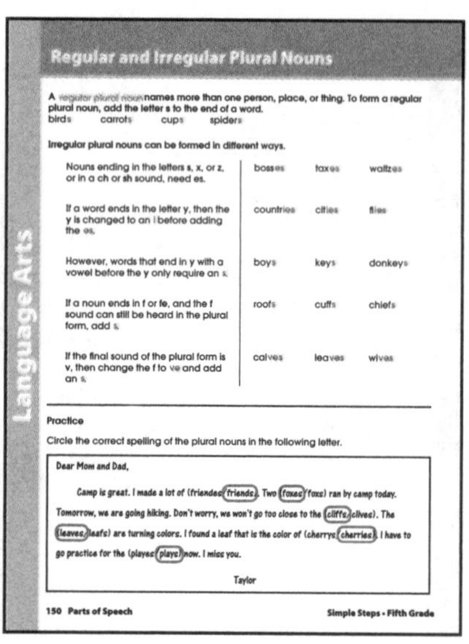

Regular and Irregular Plural Nouns

A regular plural noun names more than one person, place, or thing. To form a regular plural noun, add the letter s to the end of a word.
birds carrots cups spiders

Irregular plural nouns can be formed in different ways.

Nouns ending in the letters s, x, or z, or in a ch or sh sound, need es.	bosses	taxes	waltzes
If a word ends in the letter y, then the y is changed to an i before adding the es.	countries	cities	flies
However, words that end in y with a vowel before the y only require an s.	boys	keys	donkeys
If a noun ends in f or fe, and the f sound can still be heard in the plural form, add s.	roofs	cuffs	chiefs
If the final sound of the plural form is v, then change the f to ve and add an s.	calves	leaves	wives

Language Arts

Practice

Circle the correct spelling of the plural nouns in the following letter.

Dear Mom and Dad,

Camp is great. I made a lot of (friendes/friends). Two (foxes/foxs) ran by camp today. Tomorrow, we are going hiking. Don't worry, we won't go too close to the (cliffs/clives). The (leaves/leafs) are turning colors. I found a leaf that is the color of (cherrys/cherries). I have to go practice for the (playes/plays) now. I miss you.

Taylor

150 Parts of Speech Simple Steps • Fifth Grade

Page 150

Regular and Irregular Plural Nouns

Here are some other kinds of irregular plural nouns.

Irregular plural nouns do not have a pattern for changing from singular to plural. These nouns and their plural spellings have to be learned.	child (children) goose (geese) ox (oxen)	tooth (teeth) foot (feet)
Some irregular nouns do not change at all when they are in the plural form. These forms also have to be learned.	cod wheat deer	fish sheep series

Language Arts

Practice

Find the following irregular plurals in the word search puzzle. The words can be forward, backward, vertical, horizontal, or diagonal.

bass	mice
children	moose
cod	rye
deer	sheep
fish	trout
geese	wheat
men	women

c	h	i	l	d	r	e	n	a	z
o	s	b	y	c	y	w	d	v	e
d	i	u	t	t	e	g	s	h	r
i	f	q	j	p	m	l	o	n	a
b	z	y	c	d	x	l	w	d	e
f	v	e	g	h	t	s	c	e	i
w	o	m	e	n	e	s	e	e	g
h	j	e	q	r	k	p	i	r	p
e	o	n	i	m	n	e	m	a	x
a	m	s	u	c	n	e	o	c	c
t	o	h	t	f	k	h	r	i	l
e	i	t	u	n	e	s	o	o	m
g	d	o	r	e	e	b	s	a	b
i	r	e	d	r	o	w	j	a	m
t	t	n	t	c	a	h	s	l	b

Simple Steps • Fifth Grade Parts of Speech 151

Page 151

Subject and Object Pronouns

A pronoun is a word used in place of a noun. A subject pronoun replaces a noun that is the subject of a sentence. I, you, he, she, and it are subject pronouns.

Pancakes are great for breakfast. Pancakes taste good with syrup.
Pancakes are great for breakfast. They taste good with syrup.

Singular subject nouns	Singular subject pronouns
Dominique likes cats.	I like cats.
Lynn likes to run.	You like to run.
Ellis works for a newspaper.	He works for a newspaper.
Carol is a teacher.	She is a teacher.
Bicycling is their favorite sport.	It is their favorite sport.

Plural subject nouns	Plural subject pronouns
Gavin and Gabriel are brothers.	We are brothers.
Lisa and Chang are friends.	You are friends.
Jenna and Julia are tennis partners.	They are tennis partners.

Language Arts

Practice

Match the following pronouns with the nouns they could replace. Write the correct answer or answers to Column A in Column B. There may be more than one correct answer.

I	he	it	they
you	she	we	

Column A	Column B
Jack and Jennifer	you, we, they
Nicole	I, you, she
ball	it
Josh	I, you, he
cars	they

152 Parts of Speech Simple Steps • Fifth Grade

Page 152

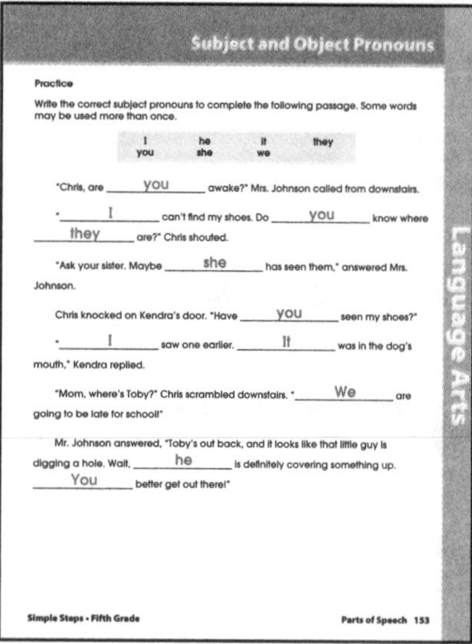

Subject and Object Pronouns

Practice

Write the correct subject pronouns to complete the following passage. Some words may be used more than once.

I	he	it	they
you	she	we	

"Chris, are you awake?" Mrs. Johnson called from downstairs.

"I can't find my shoes. Do you know where they are?" Chris shouted.

"Ask your sister. Maybe she has seen them," answered Mrs. Johnson.

Chris knocked on Kendra's door. "Have you seen my shoes?"

"I saw one earlier. It was in the dog's mouth," Kendra replied.

"Mom, where's Toby?" Chris scrambled downstairs. "We are going to be late for school!"

Mr. Johnson answered, "Toby's out back, and it looks like that little guy is digging a hole. Wait, he is definitely covering something up. You better get out there!"

Language Arts

Simple Steps • Fifth Grade Parts of Speech 153

Page 153

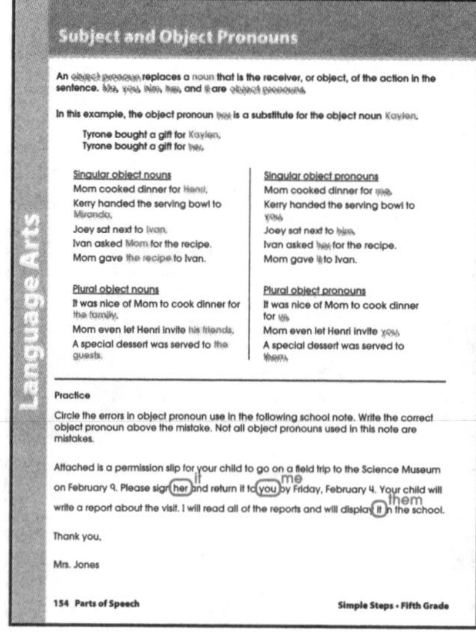

Subject and Object Pronouns

An object pronoun replaces a noun that is the receiver, or object, of the action in the sentence. Me, you, him, her, and it are object pronouns.

In this example, the object pronoun her is a substitute for the object noun Kaylen.

Tyrone bought a gift for Kaylen.
Tyrone bought a gift for her.

Singular object nouns	Singular object pronouns
Mom cooked dinner for Henri.	Mom cooked dinner for me.
Kerry handed the serving bowl to Miranda.	Kerry handed the serving bowl to you.
Joey sat next to Ivan.	Joey sat next to him.
Ivan asked Mom for the recipe.	Ivan asked her for the recipe.
Mom gave the recipe to Ivan.	Mom gave it to Ivan.

Plural object nouns	Plural object pronouns
It was nice of Mom to cook dinner for the family.	It was nice of Mom to cook dinner for us.
Mom even let Henri invite his friends.	Mom even let Henri invite you.
A special dessert was served to the guests.	A special dessert was served to them.

Language Arts

Practice

Circle the errors in object pronoun use in the following school note. Write the correct object pronoun above the mistake. Not all object pronouns used in this note are mistakes.

Attached is a permission slip for your child to go on a field trip to the Science Museum on February 9. Please sign (her) it and return it to (you) me by Friday, February 4. Your child will write a report about the visit. I will read all of the reports and will display (it) them in the school.

Thank you,

Mrs. Jones

154 Parts of Speech Simple Steps • Fifth Grade

Page 154

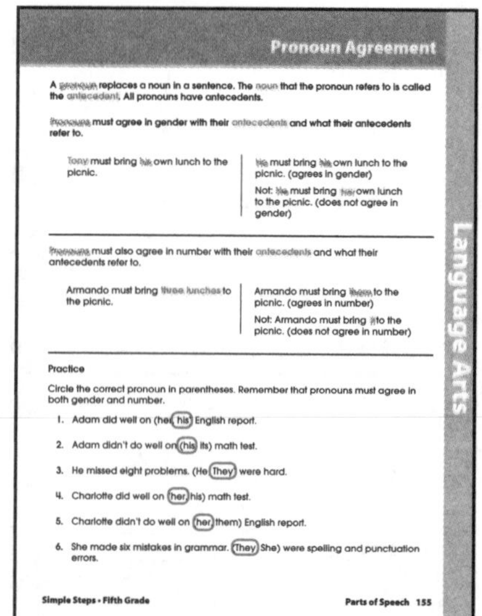

Pronoun Agreement

A pronoun replaces a noun in a sentence. The noun that the pronoun refers to is called the antecedent. All pronouns have antecedents.

Pronouns must agree in gender with their antecedents and what their antecedents refer to.

Tony must bring his own lunch to the picnic.	He must bring his own lunch to the picnic. (agrees in gender) Not: He must bring her own lunch to the picnic. (does not agree in gender)

Pronouns must also agree in number with their antecedents and what their antecedents refer to.

Armando must bring three lunches to the picnic.	Armando must bring them to the picnic. (agrees in number) Not: Armando must bring it to the picnic. (does not agree in number)

Language Arts

Practice

Circle the correct pronoun in parentheses. Remember that pronouns must agree in both gender and number.

1. Adam did well on (her/his) English report.
2. Adam didn't do well on (his/its) math test.
3. He missed eight problems. (He/They) were hard.
4. Charlotte did well on (her/his) math test.
5. Charlotte didn't do well on (her/them) English report.
6. She made six mistakes in grammar. (They/She) were spelling and punctuation errors.

Simple Steps • Fifth Grade Parts of Speech 155

Page 155

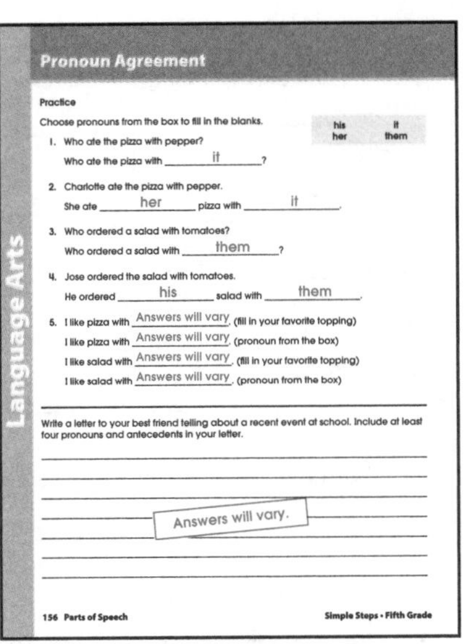

Pronoun Agreement

Practice

Choose pronouns from the box to fill in the blanks.

his	it
her	them

1. Who ate the pizza with pepper?
   Who ate the pizza with ___it___?
2. Charlotte ate the pizza with pepper.
   She ate ___her___ pizza with ___it___.
3. Who ordered a salad with tomatoes?
   Who ordered a salad with ___them___?
4. Jose ordered the salad with tomatoes.
   He ordered ___his___ salad with ___them___.
5. I like pizza with ___Answers will vary___. (fill in your favorite topping)
   I like pizza with ___Answers will vary___. (pronoun from the box)
   I like salad with ___Answers will vary___. (fill in your favorite topping)
   I like salad with ___Answers will vary___. (pronoun from the box)

Write a letter to your best friend telling about a recent event at school. Include at least four pronouns and antecedents in your letter.

Answers will vary.

156 Parts of Speech — Simple Steps • Fifth Grade

Page 156

Review

Use everything you have learned so far about nouns and pronouns to answer the questions.

Answer the following questions by circling the letter of the best answer.

1. Which sentence contains a common noun?
   a. I visited Yellowstone National Park.
   (b.) I liked seeing the animals.
   c. I heard that you went to Everglades National Park.
2. Which sentence contains a proper noun?
   (a.) The U.S. Capitol is in Washington, D.C.
   b. History is one of my favorite subjects.
   c. I like to study science.
3. Which sentence contains a regular plural noun?
   a. I liked seeing the moose at the park.
   b. The geese were in the pond and then they flew overhead.
   (c.) The cats liked playing together.
4. Which sentence contains an irregular plural noun?
   a. The dogs loved playing in the water.
   b. Rabbits make great pets.
   (c.) The mice scurried under the floorboards.
5. Which sentence contains a subject pronoun?
   a. Ava went on a science field trip.
   (b.) She went on a science field trip.
   c. Aaron went on a science field trip.
6. Which sentence contains an object pronoun?
   (a.) The team captain picked me.
   b. The team captain picked Sandy to play.
   c. He picked the best player to be on his side.
7. Which sentence has an incorrect use of pronoun agreement?
   (a.) The brothers left his jackets on the field.
   b. Diane picked up her books at the library.
   c. Jason forgot his books at the library.

Simple Steps • Fifth Grade — Parts of Speech 157

Page 157

Regular and Irregular Verbs

Practice

Answers will vary.
Possible answers include:

Use a present- or past-tense verb to complete each sentence below. There is more than one correct answer.

1. Quinten ___asked___ a good question in science class earlier.
2. As they look at the picture, the ladies ___gasp___ at its beauty.
3. I ___look___ at the stars as I walk through the planetarium.
4. Kelly and Taylor, please ___note___ that in your report.
5. Shelly and Dylan ___call___ when they are late.
6. The spectators ___yelled___ and cheered many times during the game last night.
7. Jim fell on the ice. But he ___joked___ about it later.
8. ___Load___ the luggage.
9. May I have some milk? I want to ___add___ it to my coffee.
10. Carl ___ordered___ waffles for breakfast.

Choose four present- and four past-tense irregular verbs from the list on page 158. Write a fictional paragraph using these verbs.

Answers will vary.

Simple Steps • Fifth Grade — Parts of Speech 159

Page 159

Helping Verbs

A helping verb is not a main verb. A helping verb helps form some of the tenses of a main verb.

The forms of the verb to be are helping verbs.	is, are, was, were, am, been
Helping verbs often help express express time and mood.	She could run for miles and miles. She will run for miles and miles.
Here are some examples of helping verbs.	shall, may, will, must, have, could, had, did, would, has, should, can, do

Practice

Circle the letter of the sentence that contains a helping verb. Remember, helping verbs help to set the time and mood of sentences.

1. (a.) We shall all go to the movies.
   b. We went to the movies.
   c. They ran to the movies.
2. a. Jake helped me with my homework.
   (b.) Jake will help me with my homework.
   c. Jake helps me with my homework every day.
3. (a.) I could study all night for the test.
   b. I studied for the test.
   c. I studied with Carol.

160 Parts of Speech — Simple Steps • Fifth Grade

Page 160

Helping Verbs

Helping verbs are often used with main verbs that end with ing.

An ing verb is a clue that there is a verb phrase or helping verb in the sentence.	She was running for miles and miles.
Sometimes, more than one helping verb is used in a sentence. This is called a verb phrase.	She had been running for miles and miles.

Practice

Choose a helping verb or verb phrase from the box to complete each sentence. Then, circle the main verb of the sentence. Sometimes there is a word between the helping and main verbs.

have	is	were
had	are	am
has	was	been

1. We ___have___ ___been___ (planning) our vacation for many months.
2. I ___am/was___ (looking) forward to it.
3. We ___are/were___ (traveling) by ship.
4. We ___had___ (to visit) a travel agent last week to get our tickets.
5. It ___was/is___ fun (choosing) the ship.

Simple Steps • Fifth Grade — Parts of Speech 161

Page 161

Linking Verbs

Linking verbs do not name an action. Linking verbs connect, or link, a subject to a noun or adjective. They do not express an action. A noun or adjective will follow a linking verb in a sentence.

The most common linking verbs are the forms of the verb to be.	It is time for bed. We are outside. That sound was loud! Many people were there. I have been sick. I am tired, Dad.
Some linking verbs express the five senses.	Do you smell that? You look beautiful. The milk tastes funny. I don't feel too well. That plan sounds good.
Other linking verbs reflect a state of being.	You appear ready. I seem better today. You have become tall. Tom and Tammy grow happier every day. He remains at home.

Practice

Circle the linking verb and underline the noun or adjective that is linked to the subject.

1. The book (is) good.
2. The flowers (smell) sweet.
3. The team (appears) disorganized.
4. The apples (are) bad.
5. Sharon (looks) fantastic tonight.
6. We (were) late.
7. The pear (was) tasty.
8. I (am) cold.

162 Parts of Speech — Simple Steps • Fifth Grade

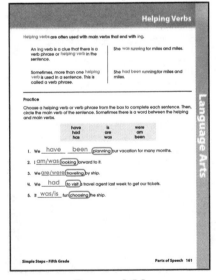

Page 162

Answer Key

Answer Key

Linking Verbs

Practice

Rewrite each of the sentences with a linking verb or more than one linking verb from the box. Notice how using other forms of linking verbs adds variety to your sentences.

grows	been	sounds
has	remained	tastes

1. The water from the faucet is bad.
   The water from the faucet tastes bad.
2. The older woman in the play is weary.
   The older woman in the play grows weary.
3. The trip is long.
   The trip has been long.
4. Walking, instead of riding, is great.
   Walking, instead of riding, sounds great.
5. The team is disorganized after half time.
   The team remained disorganized after half time.

Write a paragraph using at least five of the linking verbs on page 162. Remember, linking verbs link the subject of the sentence to either a noun or an adjective.

Answers will vary.

Simple Steps • Fifth Grade — Parts of Speech 163

Language Arts

Page 163

Verbs: Perfect Tense

Verb tenses tell when in time something happened.

The present perfect tense shows that something happened in the past and is still going on.	The Wilkinsons have been picking berries here for over a decade. I have not seen the person you're looking for. She has decided to try out for the soccer team.
The past perfect tense shows that an action was completed before another action in the past.	Yoko had thought about taking a photography class years before she registered. Juan enjoyed his lunch, but Joel had eaten too much at breakfast.
The future perfect tense shows that an action will be completed before a future time or a future action.	By the end of the summer, we will have visited the pool more than 50 times! Before Monday, I will have packed my suitcase for vacation. The rain will have stopped by the time we arrive at the picnic.

Practice

Read each sentence. If the underlined verb is in the past perfect tense, write PP on the line. If it is in the present perfect tense, write PR. If it is in the future perfect tense, write FP.

1. FP Soon, I <u>will have finished</u> reading this book.
2. PR I <u>have enjoyed</u> the first several chapters.
3. PP Until now, I <u>had not read</u> any other books by the author.
4. FP By next summer, I <u>will have read</u> all of her books.

164 Parts of Speech — Simple Steps • Fifth Grade

Language Arts

Page 164

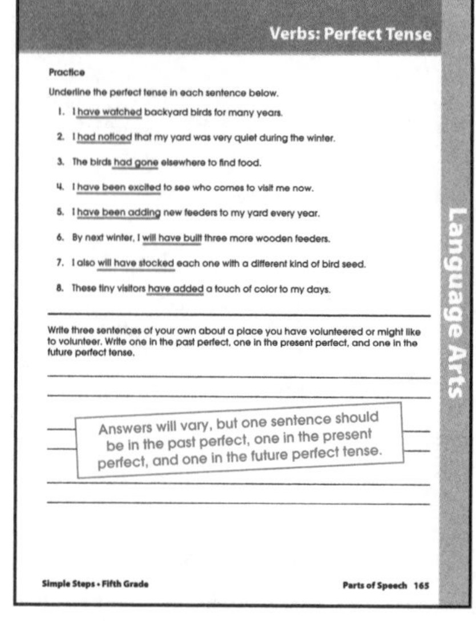

Verbs: Perfect Tense

Practice

Underline the perfect tense in each sentence below.

1. I have watched backyard birds for many years.
2. I had noticed that my yard was very quiet during the winter.
3. The birds had gone elsewhere to find food.
4. I have been excited to see who comes to visit me now.
5. I have been adding new feeders to my yard every year.
6. By next winter, I will have built three more wooden feeders.
7. I also will have stocked each one with a different kind of bird seed.
8. These tiny visitors have added a touch of color to my days.

Write three sentences of your own about a place you have volunteered or might like to volunteer. Write one in the past perfect, one in the present perfect, and one in the future perfect tense.

Answers will vary, but one sentence should be in the past perfect, one in the present perfect, and one in the future perfect tense.

Simple Steps • Fifth Grade — Parts of Speech 165

Language Arts

Page 165

Verbs: Perfect Tense

Practice

Read each sentence. On the line, write the boldface verb in the past, present, or future perfect tense. The words in parentheses will tell you which tense to use.

1. Audrey **volunteer** at Lakeside Waterfowl Rescue. (present perfect)
   has been volunteering
2. Aisha **work** with Audrey for the last six months. (present perfect)
   has been working
3. They **rescue** dozens of ducks, geese, herons, and other birds every month. (past perfect)
   had rescued
4. The rescue **provide** fresh food and water every day, rain or shine. (past perfect)
   had provided
5. They **raise** lots of money every year. (past perfect)
   had raised
6. The rescue **rely** on its volunteers to take care of the animals since its doors first opened. (present perfect)
   has been relying
7. At the end of the summer, Audrey **earn** an award for hours donated. (future perfect)
   will have earned
8. By next fall, Aisha **receive** the same award. (future perfect)
   will have received

166 Parts of Speech — Simple Steps • Fifth Grade

Language Arts

Page 166

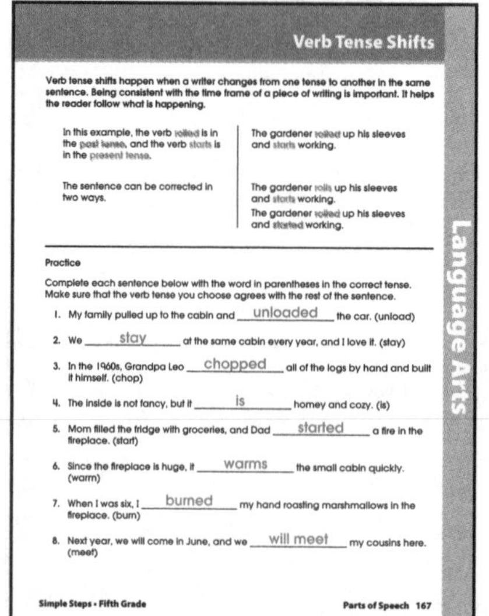

Verb Tense Shifts

Verb tense shifts happen when a writer changes from one tense to another in the same sentence. Being consistent with the time frame of a piece of writing is important. It helps the reader follow what is happening.

In this example, the verb rolled is in the past tense, and the verb starts is in the present tense.	The gardener rolled up his sleeves and starts working.
The sentence can be corrected in two ways.	The gardener rolls up his sleeves and starts working. The gardener rolled up his sleeves and started working.

Practice

Complete each sentence below with the word in parentheses in the correct tense. Make sure that the verb tense you choose agrees with the rest of the sentence.

1. My family pulled up to the cabin and unloaded the car. (unload)
2. We stay at the same cabin every year, and I love it. (stay)
3. In the 1960s, Grandpa Leo chopped all of the logs by hand and built it himself. (chop)
4. The inside is not fancy, but it is homey and cozy. (is)
5. Mom filled the fridge with groceries, and Dad started a fire in the fireplace. (start)
6. Since the fireplace is huge, it warms the small cabin quickly. (warm)
7. When I was six, I burned my hand roasting marshmallows in the fireplace. (burn)
8. Next year, we will come in June, and we will meet my cousins here. (meet)

Simple Steps • Fifth Grade — Parts of Speech 167

Language Arts

Page 167

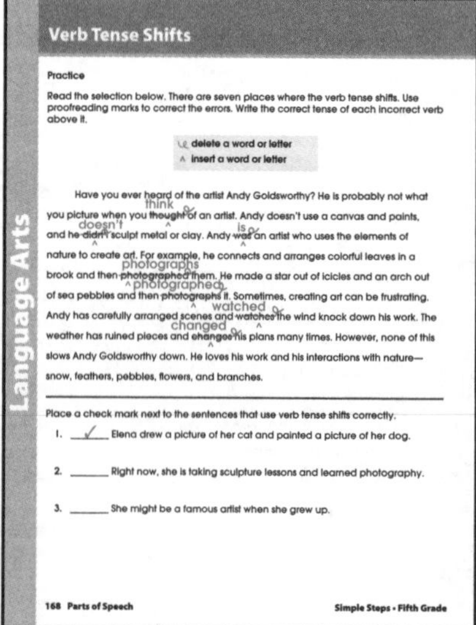

Verb Tense Shifts

Practice

Read the selection below. There are seven places where the verb tense shifts. Use proofreading marks to correct the errors. Write the correct tense of each incorrect verb above it.

delete a word or letter
^ insert a word or letter

Have you ever heard of the artist Andy Goldsworthy? He is probably not what you picture when you ~~thought~~ think of an artist. Andy doesn't use a canvas and paints, and he ~~didn't~~ doesn't sculpt metal or clay. Andy ~~was~~ is an artist who uses the elements of nature to create art. For example, he connects and arranges colorful leaves in a brook and then ~~photographed~~ photographs them. He made a star out of icicles and an arch out of sea pebbles and then ~~photographs~~ photographed it. Sometimes, creating art can be frustrating. Andy has carefully arranged scenes and ~~watches~~ watched the wind knock down his work. The weather has ruined pieces and ~~changes~~ changed his plans many times. However, none of this slows Andy Goldsworthy down. He loves his work and his interactions with nature—snow, feathers, pebbles, flowers, and branches.

Place a check mark next to the sentences that use verb tense shifts correctly.

1. ✓ Elena drew a picture of her cat and painted a picture of her dog.
2. ____ Right now, she is taking sculpture lessons and learned photography.
3. ____ She might be a famous artist when she grew up.

168 Parts of Speech — Simple Steps • Fifth Grade

Language Arts

Page 168

Answer Key

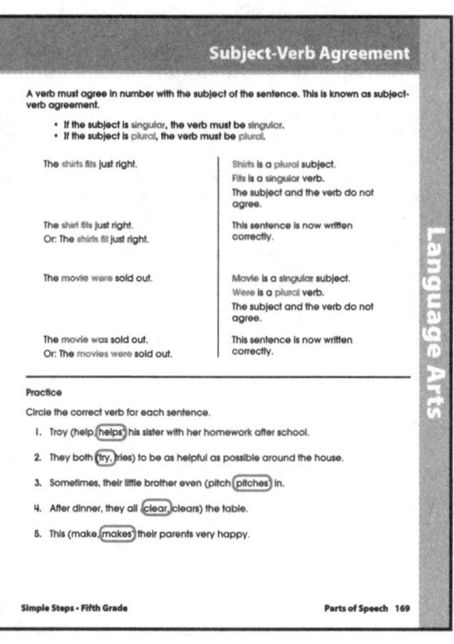

Subject-Verb Agreement

A verb must agree in number with the subject of the sentence. This is known as subject-verb agreement.

- If the subject is singular, the verb must be singular.
- If the subject is plural, the verb must be plural.

The shirts fits just right.	Shirts is a plural subject. Fits is a singular verb. The subject and the verb do not agree.
The shirt fits just right. Or: The shirts fit just right.	This sentence is now written correctly.
The movie were sold out.	Movie is a singular subject. Were is a plural verb. The subject and the verb do not agree.
The movie was sold out. Or: The movies were sold out.	This sentence is now written correctly.

Practice

Circle the correct verb for each sentence.

1. Troy (help, **helps**) his sister with her homework after school.
2. They both (**try**, tries) to be as helpful as possible around the house.
3. Sometimes, their little brother even (pitch, **pitches**) in.
4. After dinner, they all (**clear**, clears) the table.
5. This (make, **makes**) their parents very happy.

Simple Steps • Fifth Grade Parts of Speech 169

Language Arts

Page 169

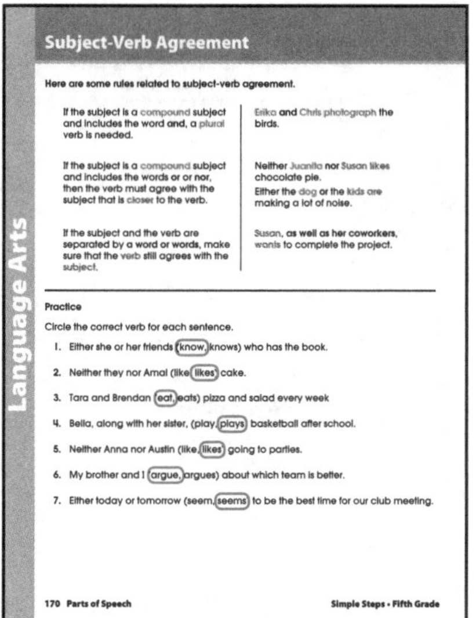

Subject-Verb Agreement

Here are some rules related to subject-verb agreement.

If the subject is a compound subject and includes the word and, a plural verb is needed.	Erika and Chris photograph the birds.
If the subject is a compound subject and includes the words or or nor, then the verb must agree with the subject that is closer to the verb.	Neither Juanita nor Susan likes chocolate pie. Either the dog or the kids are making a lot of noise.
If the subject and the verb are separated by a word or words, make sure that the verb still agrees with the subject.	Susan, as well as her coworkers, wants to complete the project.

Practice

Circle the correct verb for each sentence.

1. Either she or her friends (**know**, knows) who has the book.
2. Neither they nor Amal (like, **likes**) cake.
3. Tara and Brendan (**eat**, eats) pizza and salad every week.
4. Bella, along with her sister, (play, **plays**) basketball after school.
5. Neither Anna nor Austin (like, **likes**) going to parties.
6. My brother and I (**argue**, argues) about which team is better.
7. Either today or tomorrow (seem, **seems**) to be the best time for our club meeting.

170 Parts of Speech Simple Steps • Fifth Grade

Language Arts

Page 170

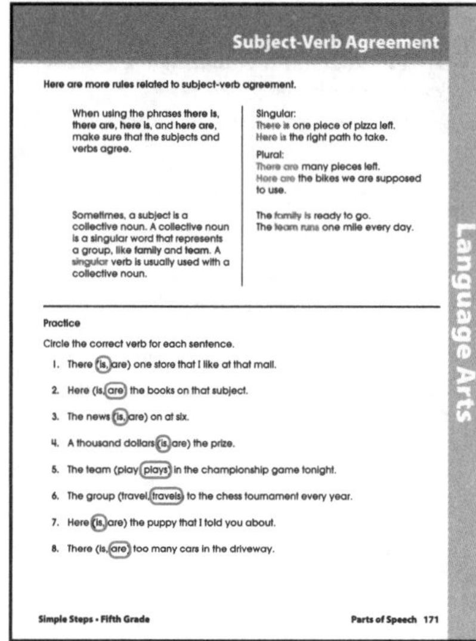

Subject-Verb Agreement

Here are more rules related to subject-verb agreement.

When using the phrases there is, there are, here is, and here are, make sure that the subjects and verbs agree.	Singular: There is one piece of pizza left. Here is the right path to take. Plural: There are many pieces left. Here are the bikes we are supposed to use.
Sometimes, a subject is a collective noun. A collective noun is a singular word that represents a group, like family and team. A singular verb is usually used with a collective noun.	The family is ready to go. The team runs one mile every day.

Practice

Circle the correct verb for each sentence.

1. There (**is**, are) one store that I like at that mall.
2. Here (is, **are**) the books on that subject.
3. The news (**is**, are) on at six.
4. A thousand dollars (**is**, are) the prize.
5. The team (play, **plays**) in the championship game tonight.
6. The group (travel, **travels**) to the chess tournament every year.
7. Here (**is**, are) the puppy that I told you about.
8. There (is, **are**) too many cars in the driveway.

Simple Steps • Fifth Grade Parts of Speech 171

Language Arts

Page 171

Review

Use everything you have learned so far about nouns and verbs to answer the questions.

Draw a line from the word or phrase in Column A to the word or phrase that it describes in Column B.

Column A	Column B
1. sound	Regular Verb
2. whispered.	Irregular Verb
3. should	Helping Verb
4. taught	Linking Verb

Read each sentence. If the underlined verb is in the past perfect tense, write PP on the line. If it is in the present perfect, write PR, and if it is in the future perfect, write FP.

6. PP Lola had dreamed the same dream three nights last week.
7. FP By the end of our trip, we will have visited more than ten state parks.
8. PR Emilio has been getting his hair cut here for his entire life.
9. FP Aaron will have made twelve new paintings at the end of this semester.
10. PP Dr. Mohammed had thought that Mom had shingles before the examination.

Write two sentences about your favorite activities to do with friends or family. Make sure the subjects and the verbs agree.

11.
12.

Answers will vary.

172 Parts of Speech Simple Steps • Fifth Grade

Language Arts

Page 172

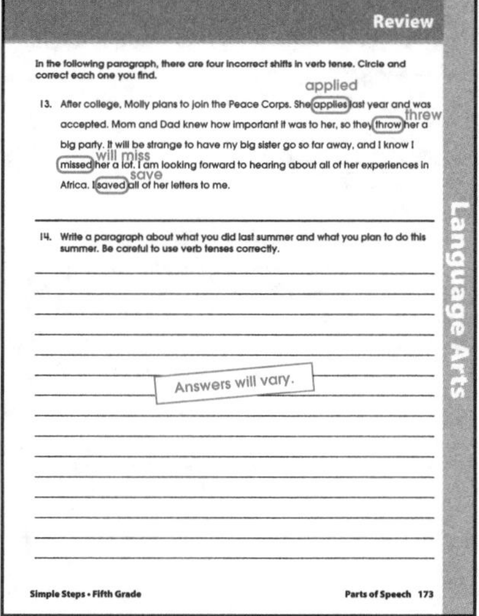

Review

In the following paragraph, there are four incorrect shifts in verb tense. Circle and correct each one you find.

13. After college, Molly plans to join the Peace Corps. She **applies** (applied) last year and was accepted. Mom and Dad knew how important it was to her, so they **throw** (threw) her a big party. It will be strange to have my big sister go so far away, and I know I **missed** (will miss) her a lot. I am looking forward to hearing about all of her experiences in Africa. I **saved** (save) all of her letters to me.

14. Write a paragraph about what you did last summer and what you plan to do this summer. Be careful to use verb tenses correctly.

Answers will vary.

Simple Steps • Fifth Grade Parts of Speech 173

Language Arts

Page 173

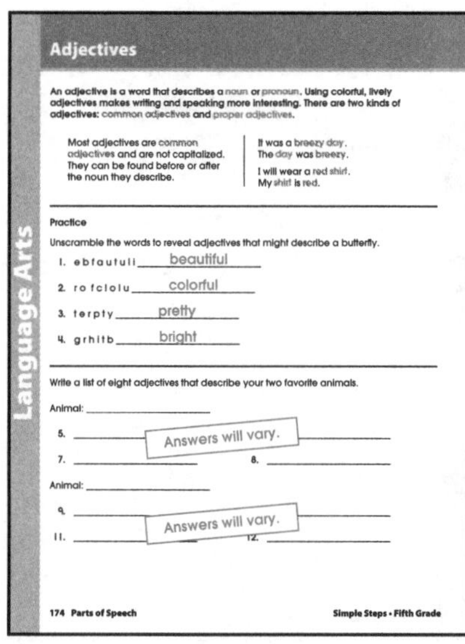

Adjectives

An adjective is a word that describes a noun or pronoun. Using colorful, lively adjectives makes writing and speaking more interesting. There are two kinds of adjectives: common adjectives and proper adjectives.

Most adjectives are common adjectives and are not capitalized. They can be found before or after the noun they describe.	It was a breezy day. The day was breezy. I will wear a red shirt. My shirt is red.

Practice

Unscramble the words to reveal adjectives that might describe a butterfly.

1. ebfautuil beautiful
2. rofclolu colorful
3. terpty pretty
4. grhitb bright

Write a list of eight adjectives that describe your two favorite animals.

Animal:

5. 6.
7. 8.

Animal:

9. 10.
11. 12.

Answers will vary.

174 Parts of Speech Simple Steps • Fifth Grade

Language Arts

Page 174

Answer Key

Adjectives

Nouns and pronouns can also be described by proper adjectives.

Proper adjectives are formed from proper nouns. They are always capitalized.	The chef likes baking his pizzas in the Italian oven. My civics class was invited to attend a Congressional hearing in Washington, D.C.

Practice

Circle only the proper adjectives in each sentence.

1. (Pacific) waves are often perfect for surfing.
2. It was a beautiful (February) day for downhill skiing.
3. A diet of double cheeseburgers and (French) fries is bad for your health.
4. The little children waved as the enormous plane flew over the (Alaskan) village.
5. She liked many types of (Asian) food, including (Thai) curry, (Japanese) sushi, and (Chinese) dumplings.

Write a paragraph about places you would like to visit. Use at least three proper adjectives.

6. Answers will vary.

Simple Steps • Fifth Grade   Parts of Speech 175

Language Arts

Page 175

Adverbs

An adverb is a word used to describe a verb, an adjective, or another adverb. An adverb can tell how, why, when, where, how often, and how much. How much?

How?	John drove carefully on the slick road.
Where?	It was a good day to stay inside.
How often?	The rain seemed like it would never stop.
How much?	The puddle completely covered the sidewalk.
When?	The weather might be better tomorrow.

Practice

Circle the letter of the sentence that contains an adverb. Remember, adverbs modify verbs, adjectives, and other adverbs.

1. (a.) Lisa quickly finished work so she could go to dinner.
   b. Lisa finished work so she could go to dinner.
   c. Lisa did not finish her work.
2. a. Fruit makes a delicious dessert.
   (b.) Fruit often makes a delicious dessert.
   c. Fruit is dessert.
3. a. You take the biggest slice of pizza.
   (b.) You always take the biggest slice of pizza.
   c. May I take the biggest slice of pizza?

176 Parts of Speech   Simple Steps • Fifth Grade

Language Arts

Page 176

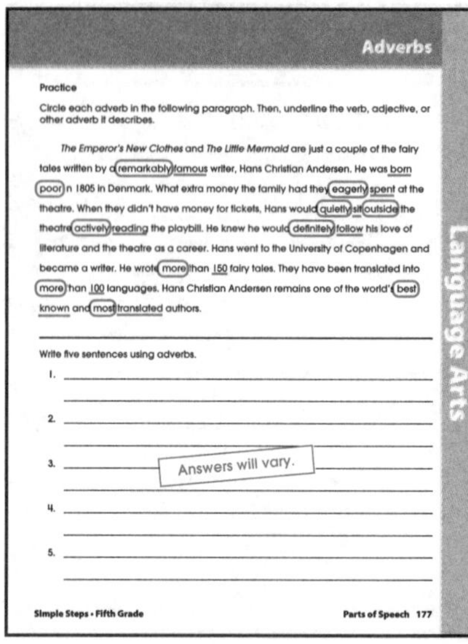

Adverbs

Practice

Circle each adverb in the following paragraph. Then, underline the verb, adjective, or other adverb it describes.

The Emperor's New Clothes and *The Little Mermaid* are just a couple of the fairy tales written by a (remarkably) famous writer, Hans Christian Andersen. He was born (poor) in 1805 in Denmark. What extra money the family had they (eagerly) spent at the theatre. When they didn't have money for tickets, Hans would (quietly) sit (outside) the theatre (actively) reading the playbill. He knew he would (definitely) follow his love of literature and the theatre as a career. Hans went to the University of Copenhagen and became a writer. He wrote (more) than 150 fairy tales. They have been translated into (more) than 100 languages. Hans Christian Andersen remains one of the world's (best) known and (most) translated authors.

Write five sentences using adverbs.

1.–5. Answers will vary.

Simple Steps • Fifth Grade   Parts of Speech 177

Language Arts

Page 177

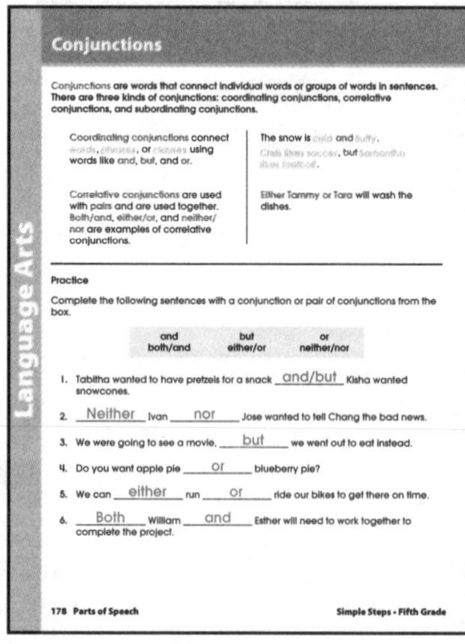

Conjunctions

Conjunctions are words that connect individual words or groups of words in sentences. There are three kinds of conjunctions: coordinating conjunctions, correlative conjunctions, and subordinating conjunctions.

Coordinating conjunctions connect words, phrases, or clauses using words like and, but, and or.	The snow is cold and fluffy. Chris likes soccer, but Samantha likes football.
Correlative conjunctions are used with pairs and are used together. Both/and, either/or, and neither/nor are examples of correlative conjunctions.	Either Tammy or Tara will wash the dishes.

Practice

Complete the following sentences with a conjunction or pair of conjunctions from the box.

and	but	or
both/and	either/or	neither/nor

1. Tabitha wanted to have pretzels for a snack and/but Kisha wanted snowcones.
2. Neither Ivan nor Jose wanted to tell Chang the bad news.
3. We were going to see a movie, but we went out to eat instead.
4. Do you want apple pie or blueberry pie?
5. We can either run or ride our bikes to get there on time.
6. Both William and Esther will need to work together to complete the project.

178 Parts of Speech   Simple Steps • Fifth Grade

Language Arts

Page 178

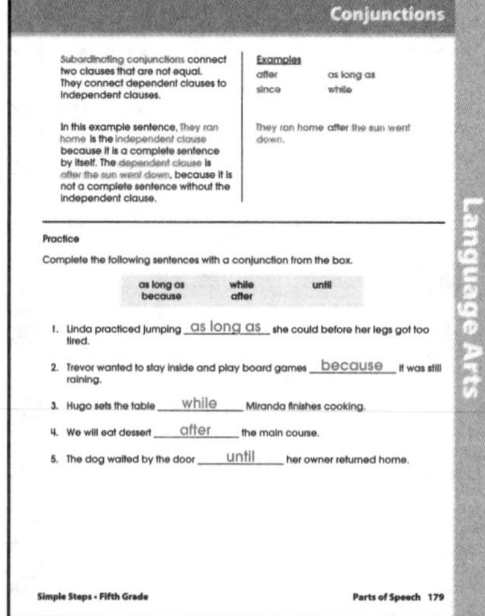

Conjunctions

Subordinating conjunctions connect two clauses that are not equal. They connect dependent clauses to independent clauses.	<u>Examples</u> after as long as since while
In this example sentence, They ran home is the independent clause because it is a complete sentence by itself. The dependent clause is after the sun went down, because it is not a complete sentence without the independent clause.	They ran home after the sun went down.

Practice

Complete the following sentences with a conjunction from the box.

as long as	while	until
because	after	

1. Linda practiced jumping as long as she could before her legs got too tired.
2. Trevor wanted to stay inside and play board games because it was still raining.
3. Hugo sets the table while Miranda finishes cooking.
4. We will eat dessert after the main course.
5. The dog waited by the door until her owner returned home.

Simple Steps • Fifth Grade   Parts of Speech 179

Language Arts

Page 179

Conjunctions

Practice

Identify the conjunctions in the following sentences as coordinate, correlative, or subordinate. Write CD for coordinating, CR for correlative, or S for subordinate before each sentence.

1. CD Are we going to go biking or hiking on Saturday?
2. CR Neither pasta nor pizza was offered on the menu.
3. S As long as it's raining, we may as well get our homework done.
4. CR Either Rachel or Carrie will be voted president of the class.
5. S Let's walk to school since it is a sunny, warm day.
6. CD Todd wants to play baseball this weekend, but he has a class in the morning.
7. S While we are waiting in line, let's get some popcorn.
8. CR Both the girls' and the boys' teams are going to the championship.

Write four sentences of your own using conjunctions. Use two conjunctions from each category.

9.–12. Answers will vary.

180 Parts of Speech   Simple Steps • Fifth Grade

Language Arts

Page 180

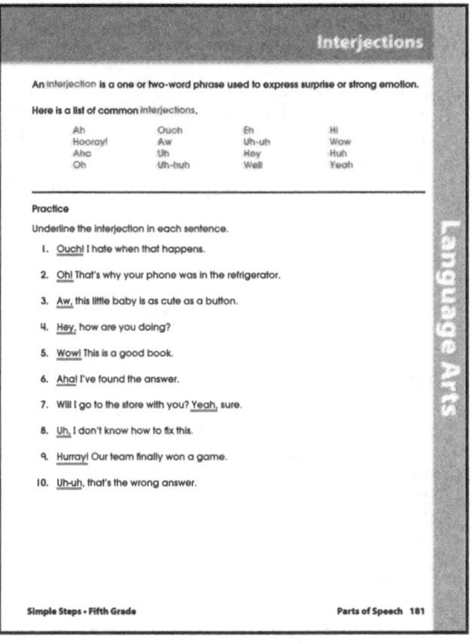

Interjections

An interjection is a one or two-word phrase used to express surprise or strong emotion.

Here is a list of common interjections.

Ah	Ouch	Eh	Hi
Hooray!	Aw	Uh-uh	Wow
Aha	Uh	Hey	Huh
Oh	Uh-huh	Well	Yeah

Practice

Underline the interjection in each sentence.

1. Ouch! I hate when that happens.
2. Oh! That's why your phone was in the refrigerator.
3. Aw, this little baby is as cute as a button.
4. Hey, how are you doing?
5. Wow! This is a good book.
6. Aha! I've found the answer.
7. Will I go to the store with you? Yeah, sure.
8. Uh, I don't know how to fix this.
9. Hurray! Our team finally won a game.
10. Uh-uh, that's the wrong answer.

Language Arts

Simple Steps • Fifth Grade   Parts of Speech 181

Page 181

Interjections

Interjections can be used with exclamation marks, commas, or question marks.

An exclamation mark is usually used after an interjection to separate it from the rest of the sentence.	Oh! I'm so happy that you can make the trip.
If the feeling isn't quite as strong, a comma is used in place of the exclamation mark.	Oh, it's too bad he won't be joining us.
Sometimes question marks are used as an interjection's punctuation.	Eh? Is that really true?

Practice

Use each interjection in a sentence.

1. aha
2. hey
3. oh
4. huh
5. ah

Answers will vary.

Language Arts

182 Parts of Speech   Simple Steps • Fifth Grade

Page 182

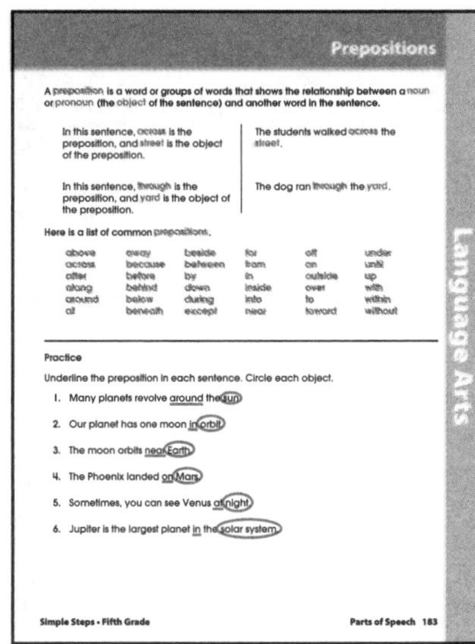

Prepositions

A preposition is a word or groups of words that shows the relationship between a noun or pronoun (the object of the sentence) and another word in the sentence.

In this sentence, across is the preposition, and street is the object of the preposition.	The students walked across the street.
In this sentence, through is the preposition, and yard is the object of the preposition.	The dog ran through the yard.

Here is a list of common prepositions.

above	away	beside	for	off	under
across	because	between	from	on	until
after	before	by	in	outside	up
along	behind	down	inside	over	with
around	below	during	into	to	within
at	beneath	except	near	toward	without

Practice

Underline the preposition in each sentence. Circle each object.

1. Many planets revolve around the sun.
2. Our planet has one moon in orbit.
3. The moon orbits near Earth.
4. The Phoenix landed on Mars.
5. Sometimes, you can see Venus at night.
6. Jupiter is the largest planet in the solar system.

Language Arts

Simple Steps • Fifth Grade   Parts of Speech 183

Page 183

Prepositions

A prepositional phrase includes a preposition and the object that follows. It can also include objectives or adverbs that modify the object. Prepositional phrases often tell when or where something is happening.

The prepositional phrase in this sentence includes the preposition beneath, the object the waves, and the modifier frothing.	The ship sank beneath the frothing waves.
The prepositional phrase in this sentence includes the preposition around, the object the room, and the modifiers crowded and noisy.	The dancers whirled around the crowded, noisy room.

Practice

Write a journal entry about what you did yesterday. Use at least five prepositional phrases. After you have written your entry, underline all of the prepositional phrases you used.

Answers will vary.

Language Arts

184 Parts of Speech   Simple Steps • Fifth Grade

Page 184

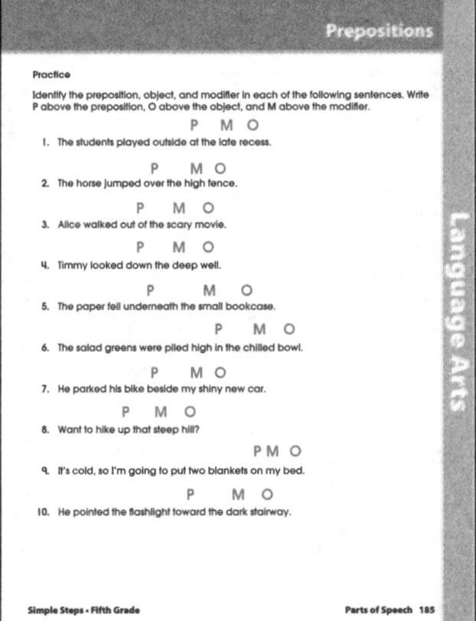

Prepositions

Practice

Identify the preposition, object, and modifier in each of the following sentences. Write P above the preposition, O above the object, and M above the modifier.

1. The students played outside of the late recess. (P M O)
2. The horse jumped over the high fence. (P M O)
3. Alice walked out of the scary movie. (P M O)
4. Timmy looked down the deep well. (P M O)
5. The paper fell underneath the small bookcase. (P M O)
6. The salad greens were piled high in the chilled bowl. (P M O)
7. He parked his bike beside my shiny new car. (P M O)
8. Want to hike up that steep hill? (P M O)
9. It's cold, so I'm going to put two blankets on my bed. (P M O)
10. He pointed the flashlight toward the dark stairway. (P M O)

Language Arts

Simple Steps • Fifth Grade   Parts of Speech 185

Page 185

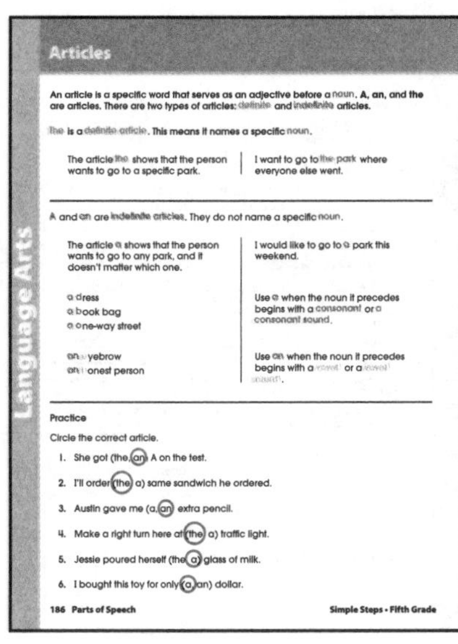

Articles

An article is a specific word that serves as an adjective before a noun. A, an, and the are articles. There are two types of articles: definite and indefinite articles.

The is a definite article. This means it names a specific noun.

The article the shows that the person wants to go to a specific park.	I want to go to the park where everyone else went.

A and an are indefinite articles. They do not name a specific noun.

The article a shows that the person wants to go to any park, and it doesn't matter which one.	I would like to go to a park this weekend.
a dress a book bag a one-way street	Use a when the noun it precedes begins with a consonant or a consonant sound.
an eyebrow an honest person	Use an when the noun it precedes begins with a vowel or a vowel sound.

Practice

Circle the correct article.

1. She got (the, an) A on the test.
2. I'll order (the, a) same sandwich he ordered.
3. Austin gave me (a, an) extra pencil.
4. Make a right turn here at (the, a) traffic light.
5. Jessie poured herself (the, a) glass of milk.
6. I bought this toy for only (a, an) dollar.

Language Arts

186 Parts of Speech   Simple Steps • Fifth Grade

Page 186

Answer Key

Answer Key

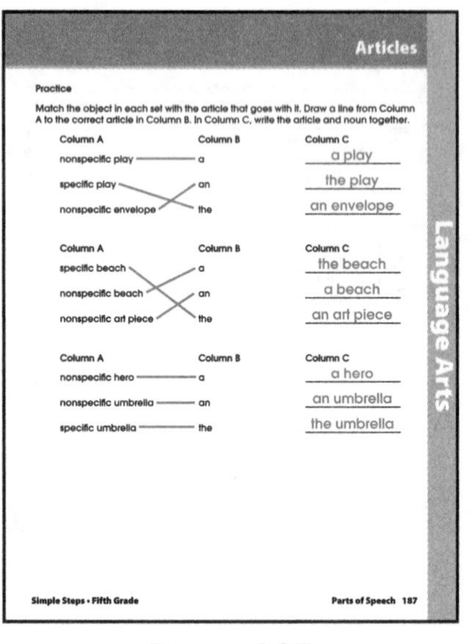

Articles

Practice

Match the object in each set with the article that goes with it. Draw a line from Column A to the correct article in Column B. In Column C, write the article and noun together.

Column A	Column B	Column C
nonspecific play	a	a play
specific play	an	the play
nonspecific envelope	the	an envelope

Column A	Column B	Column C
specific beach	a	the beach
nonspecific beach	an	a beach
nonspecific art piece	the	an art piece

Column A	Column B	Column C
nonspecific hero	a	a hero
nonspecific umbrella	an	an umbrella
specific umbrella	the	the umbrella

Language Arts

Simple Steps • Fifth Grade   Parts of Speech 187

Page 187

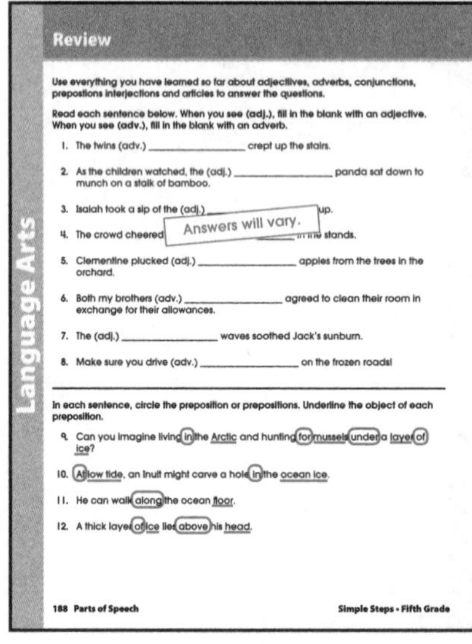

Review

Use everything you have learned so far about adjectives, adverbs, conjunctions, prepostions interjections and articles to answer the questions.

Read each sentence below. When you see (adj.), fill in the blank with an adjective. When you see (adv.), fill in the blank with an adverb.

1. The twins (adv.) ________ crept up the stairs.
2. As the children watched, the (adj.) ________ panda sat down to munch on a stalk of bamboo.
3. Isaiah took a sip of the (adj.) ________ up.
4. The crowd cheered ________ in the stands.
5. Clementine plucked (adj.) ________ apples from the trees in the orchard.
6. Both my brothers (adv.) ________ agreed to clean their room in exchange for their allowances.
7. The (adj.) ________ waves soothed Jack's sunburn.
8. Make sure you drive (adv.) ________ on the frozen roads!

Answers will vary.

In each sentence, circle the preposition or prepositions. Underline the object of each preposition.

9. Can you imagine living in the Arctic and hunting for mussels under a layer of ice?
10. At low tide, an Inuit might carve a hole in the ocean ice.
11. He can walk along the ocean floor.
12. A thick layer of ice lies above his head.

Language Arts

188 Parts of Speech   Simple Steps • Fifth Grade

Page 188

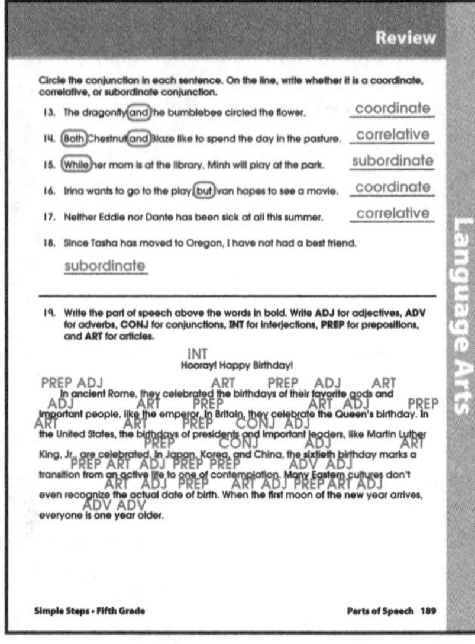

Review

Circle the conjunction in each sentence. On the line, write whether it is a coordinate, correlative, or subordinate conjunction.

13. The dragonfly and the bumblebee circled the flower. coordinate
14. Both Chestnut and Blaze like to spend the day in the pasture. correlative
15. While her mom is at the library, Minh will play at the park. subordinate
16. Irina wants to go to the play, but Ivan hopes to see a movie. coordinate
17. Neither Eddie nor Dante has been sick at all this summer. correlative
18. Since Tasha has moved to Oregon, I have not had a best friend. subordinate

19. Write the part of speech above the words in bold. Write **ADJ** for adjectives, **ADV** for adverbs, **CONJ** for conjunctions, **INT** for interjections, **PREP** for prepositions, and **ART** for articles.

INT
Hooray! Happy Birthday!

PREP ADJ ART PREP ADJ ART
In ancient Rome, they celebrated the birthdays of their favorite gods and
ADJ ART PREP ART ADJ PREP
important people, like the emperor. In Britain, they celebrate the Queen's birthday. In
ART ART PREP CONJ ADJ
the United States, the birthdays of presidents and important leaders, like Martin Luther
PREP CONJ ADJ ART
King, Jr., are celebrated. In Japan, Korea, and China, the sixtieth birthday marks a
PREP ART ADJ PREP PREP ADV ADJ
transition from an active life to one of contemplation. Many Eastern cultures don't
ART ADJ PREP ART ADJ PREP ART ADJ
even recognize the actual date of birth. When the first moon of the new year arrives,
ADV ADV
everyone is one year older.

Language Arts

Simple Steps • Fifth Grade   Parts of Speech 189

Page 189

Chapter Review

Write the correct words from the box to complete this excerpt from Elena's journal. Use only proper nouns.

national park school	Mount Rushmore South Dakota	Pierce School states

My family is planning a trip to (1.) Mount Rushmore. We will drive through the state of (2.) South Dakota to get there. On Monday the 17th, it's back to (3.) Pierce School.

Give an example for each of the rules below about regular and irregular plural nouns.

4. Rule: Nouns ending in the letters s, x, or z, or in a ch or sh sound, add es.
   Example: Answers will vary. Possible answers include: foxes, dresses, brushes
5. Rule: If a word ends in the letter y, then the y is changed to an i before adding the es.
   Example: Answers will vary. Possible answers include: parties, countries, duties

Rewrite the following sentences. Replace the underlined subject and object nouns with the correct subject and object pronouns.

6. My cousin and I wanted to go the movies. Dad drove my cousin and me.
   We wanted to go the movies. Dad drove us.
7. Cathy and Marie won the game. The trophy goes to Cathy and Marie.
   They won the game. The trophy goes to them.

Circle the correct pronoun for each sentence.

8. Janice tutored Renata in (its her) grammar skills.
9. Renata tutored the twins in (his their) math skills.

Language Arts

190 Parts of Speech   Simple Steps • Fifth Grade

Page 190

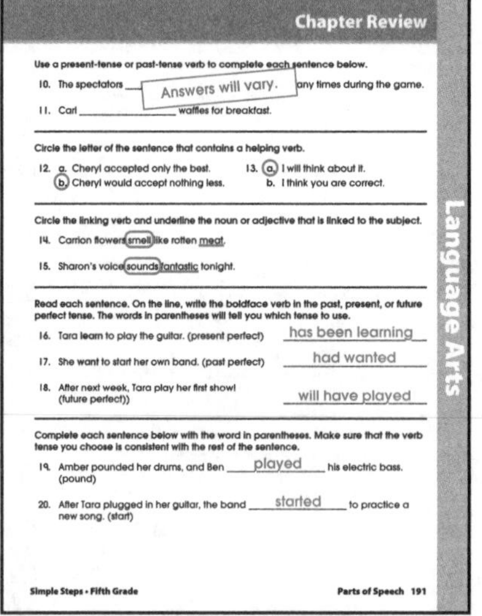

Chapter Review

Use a present-tense or past-tense verb to complete each sentence below.

10. The spectators ________ many times during the game.
11. Carl ________ waffles for breakfast.

Answers will vary.

Circle the letter of the sentence that contains a helping verb.

12. a. Cheryl accepted only the best.
    b. Cheryl would accept nothing less.
13. a. I will think about it.
    b. I think you are correct.

Circle the linking verb and underline the noun or adjective that is linked to the subject.

14. Carrion flowers smell like rotten meat.
15. Sharon's voice sounds fantastic tonight.

Read each sentence. On the line, write the boldface verb in the past, present, or future perfect tense. The words in parentheses will tell you which tense to use.

16. Tara **learn** to play the guitar. (present perfect) has been learning
17. She **want** to start her own band. (past perfect) had wanted
18. After next week, Tara **play** her first show! (future perfect)) will have played

Complete each sentence below with the word in parentheses. Make sure that the verb tense you choose is consistent with the rest of the sentence.

19. Amber pounded her drums, and Ben played his electric bass. (pound)
20. After Tara plugged in her guitar, the band started to practice a new song. (start)

Language Arts

Simple Steps • Fifth Grade   Parts of Speech 191

Page 191

Chapter Review

Add an adjective that describes each noun in bold.

21. Candice and Danny were twins and wanted a Answers will vary **pet** for their birthday.
22. Their mother said, "Pets are a Answers will vary **responsibility**. Are you ready for this?"

Circle the adverb in each sentence.

23. My dog happily gobbled its dinner.
24. Let's go inside and play a board game.

Circle the conjunctions in the following sentences. On the line, write whether the conjunction is coordinate, correlative, or subordinate.

25. Do you want tomatoes or pickles on your sandwich? coordinate
26. We carried umbrellas because it was a soggy, cloudy day. subordinate
27. Neither dogs nor cats are allowed in the building. correlative

Underline the interjection in each sentence.

28. Well, we are learning about Egyptian pyramids.
29. Wow! The first pyramid was built in 2780 BC.

Identify the preposition, object, and modifier in each of the following sentences. Write P above the preposition, O above the object, and M above the modifier.

30. P M O
We ducked under the low-hanging branches.
31. P M M O
The hikers made their way up the steep mountain trail.

Language Arts

192 Parts of Speech   Simple Steps • Fifth Grade

Page 192

Answer Key

Declarative Sentences

A declarative sentence is a sentence that makes a statement.

Declarative sentences say something about a place, person, thing, or idea. When punctuating a declarative sentence, use a period at the end of the sentence.

Richard Pough was the founder of The Nature Conservancy.
Salad is my favorite food.

Practice

Write a dialogue between two people. Write 10 declarative sentences they say about a place they are visiting. Be sure to use periods when you are making writing declarative sentences.

Answers will vary.

Language Arts

Simple Steps • Fifth Grade Sentences 193

Page 193

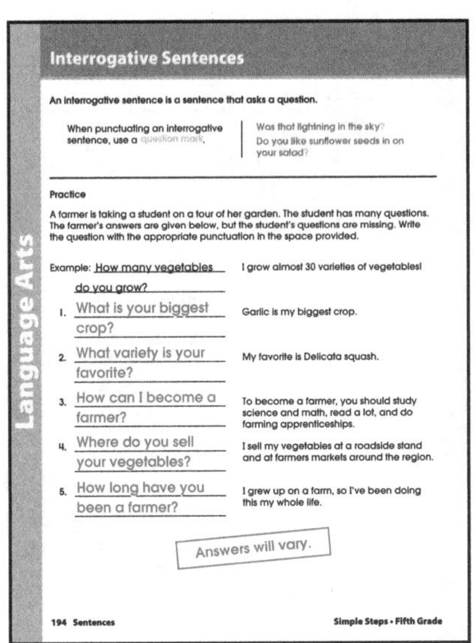

Interrogative Sentences

An interrogative sentence is a sentence that asks a question.

When punctuating an interrogative sentence, use a question mark.

Was that lightning in the sky?
Do you like sunflower seeds in on your salad?

Practice

A farmer is taking a student on a tour of her garden. The student has many questions. The farmer's answers are given below, but the student's questions are missing. Write the question with the appropriate punctuation in the space provided.

Example: How many vegetables do you grow? I grow almost 30 varieties of vegetables!

1. What is your biggest crop? Garlic is my biggest crop.
2. What variety is your favorite? My favorite is Delicata squash.
3. How can I become a farmer? To become a farmer, you should study science and math, read a lot, and do farming apprenticeships.
4. Where do you sell your vegetables? I sell my vegetables at a roadside stand and at farmers markets around the region.
5. How long have you been a farmer? I grew up on a farm, so I've been doing this my whole life.

Answers will vary.

Language Arts

194 Sentences Simple Steps • Fifth Grade

Page 194

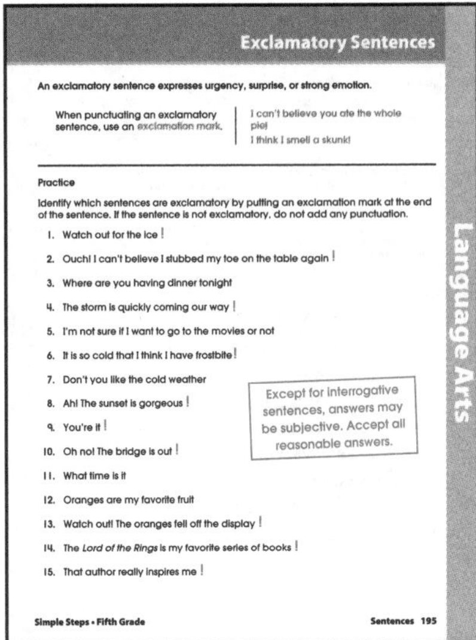

Exclamatory Sentences

An exclamatory sentence expresses urgency, surprise, or strong emotion.

When punctuating an exclamatory sentence, use an exclamation mark.

I can't believe you ate the whole pie!
I think I smell a skunk!

Practice

Identify which sentences are exclamatory by putting an exclamation mark at the end of the sentence. If the sentence is not exclamatory, do not add any punctuation.

1. Watch out for the ice !
2. Ouch! I can't believe I stubbed my toe on the table again !
3. Where are you having dinner tonight
4. The storm is quickly coming our way !
5. I'm not sure if I want to go to the movies or not
6. It is so cold that I think I have frostbite !
7. Don't you like the cold weather
8. Ah! The sunset is gorgeous !
9. You're it !
10. Oh no! The bridge is out !
11. What time is it
12. Oranges are my favorite fruit
13. Watch out! The oranges fell off the display !
14. The *Lord of the Rings* is my favorite series of books !
15. That author really inspires me !

Except for interrogative sentences, answers may be subjective. Accept all reasonable answers.

Language Arts

Simple Steps • Fifth Grade Sentences 195

Page 195

Imperative Sentences

An imperative sentence makes an order or a demand. It is often written in the present tense. The subjects of imperative sentences are usually not expressed, because it is usually understood that the subject is you.

Look at the rabbit behind the trees.
Write the note here.
Throw me the ball!

(You look at the rabbit behind the trees.)
(You write the note here.)
(You throw me the ball!)

Practice

Choose a verb from the box to complete each imperative sentence. Remember, the subject you is implied in the sentences.

carry	drive	pick	swing	vote
drink	pass	shoot	throw	yell

1. Vote for Simon for president!
2. Pass the potatoes, please.
3. Pick up the paper from the floor.
4. Carry that bag for your aunt.
5. Throw the ball to second base!
6. Drive slowly when on ice.
7. Swing the racket higher.
8. Yell the cheers louder!
9. Drink all of your tomato juice.
10. Shoot the basketball through the hoop!

Language Arts

196 Sentences Simple Steps • Fifth Grade

Page 196

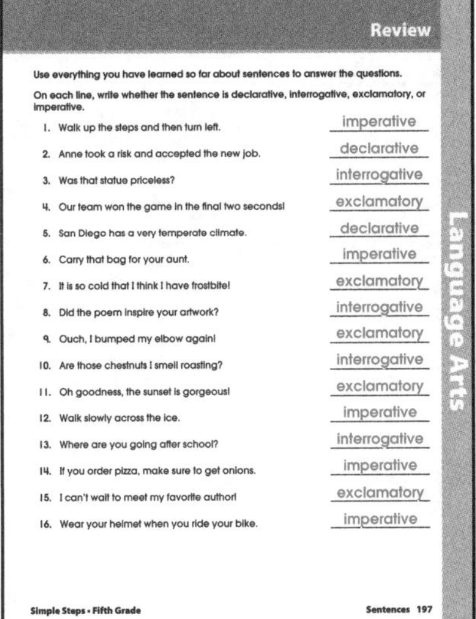

Review

Use everything you have learned so far about sentences to answer the questions.

On each line, write whether the sentence is declarative, interrogative, exclamatory, or imperative.

1. Walk up the steps and then turn left. imperative
2. Anne took a risk and accepted the new job. declarative
3. Was that statue priceless? interrogative
4. Our team won the game in the final two seconds! exclamatory
5. San Diego has a very temperate climate. declarative
6. Carry that bag for your aunt. imperative
7. It is so cold that I think I have frostbite! exclamatory
8. Did the poem inspire your artwork? interrogative
9. Ouch, I bumped my elbow again! exclamatory
10. Are those chestnuts I smell roasting? interrogative
11. Oh goodness, the sunset is gorgeous! exclamatory
12. Walk slowly across the ice. imperative
13. Where are you going after school? interrogative
14. If you order pizza, make sure to get onions. imperative
15. I can't wait to meet my favorite author! exclamatory
16. Wear your helmet when you ride your bike. imperative

Language Arts

Simple Steps • Fifth Grade Sentences 197

Page 197

Simple Sentences

A simple sentence is a sentence with one independent clause. A simple sentence does not have any dependent clauses.

An independent clause is a complete thought that can stand alone as a sentence. Chantal brushed her teeth.

A dependent clause is not a complete thought and cannot stand alone as a sentence. after washing her face

Practice

The following sentences contain both independent and dependent clauses. Rewrite each of the following sentences as two simple sentences.

Example:
Sarah wanted to go swimming, but it rained.
Sarah wanted to go swimming. It rained.

1. The car broke down, so I took a taxi.
The car broke down. I took a taxi.
2. The boy started a new painting while his first painting was drying.
The boy started a new painting. His first painting was drying.
3. The baby cried because she was hungry.
The baby cried. She was hungry.
4. I watered the plant after it wilted.
I watered the plant. It wilted.

Language Arts

198 Sentences Simple Steps • Fifth Grade

Page 198

Answer Key

Simple Sentences

Simple subjects can take different forms.

Simple sentences can have one or more subjects.	The costumes glittered. The costumes and the jewelry glittered.
Simple sentences can have one or more verbs or verb phrases.	The costumes glittered. The costumes glittered and sparkled.
Simple sentences can have more than one subject and more than one verb or verb phrase.	The costumes and the jewelry glittered and sparkled.

Practice

Underline the subjects and circle the verbs or verb phrases in the following simple sentences.

1. Elsa liked baking cookies and liked cooking spaghetti.
2. Elsa and her grandmother liked baking and liked cooking together.
3. Tanya liked eating her grandmother's cookies.
4. Grandma liked eating Tanya's spaghetti.
5. Aaron washed and dried the dishes.
6. My brother and I walked and fed the dog.
7. Fire trucks and ambulances surrounded the burning building.
8. The firefighters saved our lives.

Simple Steps • Fifth Grade Sentences 199

Page 199

Compound Sentences

A compound sentence is a sentence with two or more independent clauses joined by a coordinate conjunction, punctuation, or both. Compound sentences express more than one complete thought.

A compound sentence can be two simple sentences joined by a comma and a coordinate conjunction.	The costumes glittered, but the jewelry was dull.
A compound sentence can also be two simple sentences joined by a semicolon.	The costumes glittered; the jewelry was dull.

Practice

Match simple sentences in Column A with simple sentences in Column B to create compound sentences. Add either a comma with a coordinate conjunction or a semicolon.

Column A	Column B
1. The seats were bad. ________	The snack bar line was long.
2. The actors were funny. ________	We can stay late.
3. The intermission was short. ________	The show was good.
4. The ushers were nic[e]. ________	The ticket takers were rude.
5. We can leave early. ________	The orchestra played well.
6. The theater lights were low. ________	The actors were serious.
7. The audience laughed. ________	The audience applauded.
8. The actors' voices were loud. ________	The seats were sold out.
9. The play had good reviews. ________	The music was soft.
10. The actors bowed. ________	The stage lights were bright.

Answers will vary.

200 Sentences Simple Steps • Fifth Grade

Page 200

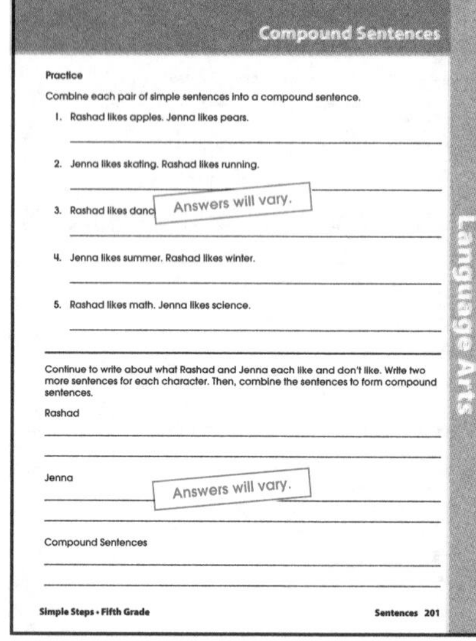

Compound Sentences

Practice

Combine each pair of simple sentences into a compound sentence.

1. Rashad likes apples. Jenna likes pears.
2. Jenna likes skating. Rashad likes running.
3. Rashad likes danc[ing]...
4. Jenna likes summer. Rashad likes winter.
5. Rashad likes math. Jenna likes science.

Answers will vary.

Continue to write about what Rashad and Jenna each like and don't like. Write two more sentences for each character. Then, combine the sentences to form compound sentences.

Rashad

Jenna

Answers will vary.

Compound Sentences

Simple Steps • Fifth Grade Sentences 201

Page 201

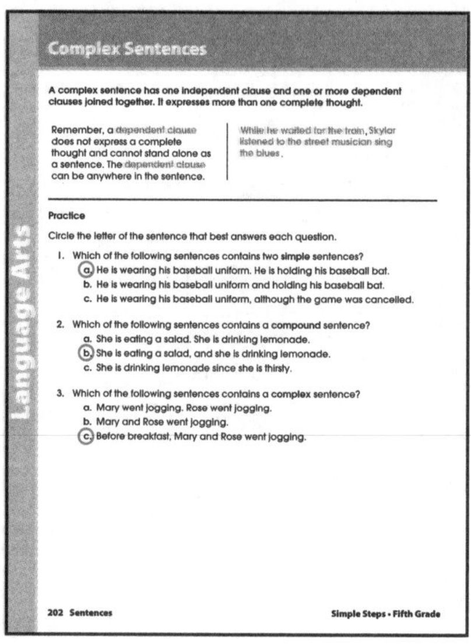

Complex Sentences

A complex sentence has one independent clause and one or more dependent clauses joined together. It expresses more than one complete thought.

Remember, a dependent clause does not express a complete thought and cannot stand alone as a sentence. The dependent clause can be anywhere in the sentence.	While he waited for the train, Skylar listened to the street musician sing the blues.

Practice

Circle the letter of the sentence that best answers each question.

1. Which of the following sentences contains two simple sentences?
   a. He is wearing his baseball uniform. He is holding his baseball bat.
   b. He is wearing his baseball uniform and holding his baseball bat.
   c. He is wearing his baseball uniform, although the game was cancelled.
2. Which of the following sentences contains a compound sentence?
   a. She is eating a salad. She is drinking lemonade.
   b. She is eating a salad, and she is drinking lemonade.
   c. She is drinking lemonade since she is thirsty.
3. Which of the following sentences contains a complex sentence?
   a. Mary went jogging. Rose went jogging.
   b. Mary and Rose went jogging.
   c. Before breakfast, Mary and Rose went jogging.

202 Sentences Simple Steps • Fifth Grade

Page 202

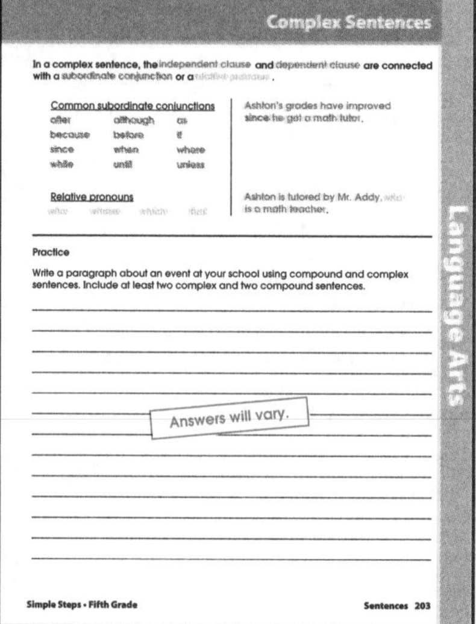

Complex Sentences

In a complex sentence, the independent clause and dependent clause are connected with a subordinate conjunction or a relative pronoun.

Common subordinate conjunctions: after, although, as, because, before, if, since, when, where, while, until, unless	Ashton's grades have improved since he got a math tutor.
Relative pronouns: who, whom, which, that	Ashton is tutored by Mr. Addy, who is a math teacher.

Practice

Write a paragraph about an event at your school using compound and complex sentences. Include at least two complex and two compound sentences.

Answers will vary.

Simple Steps • Fifth Grade Sentences 203

Page 203

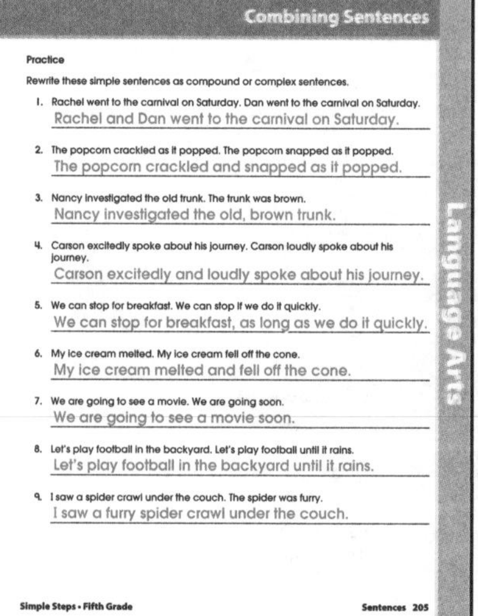

Combining Sentences

Practice

Rewrite these simple sentences as compound or complex sentences.

1. Rachel went to the carnival on Saturday. Dan went to the carnival on Saturday.
   Rachel and Dan went to the carnival on Saturday.
2. The popcorn crackled as it popped. The popcorn snapped as it popped.
   The popcorn crackled and snapped as it popped.
3. Nancy investigated the old trunk. The trunk was brown.
   Nancy investigated the old, brown trunk.
4. Carson excitedly spoke about his journey. Carson loudly spoke about his journey.
   Carson excitedly and loudly spoke about his journey.
5. We can stop for breakfast. We can stop if we do it quickly.
   We can stop for breakfast, as long as we do it quickly.
6. My ice cream melted. My ice cream fell off the cone.
   My ice cream melted and fell off the cone.
7. We are going to see a movie. We are going soon.
   We are going to see a movie soon.
8. Let's play football in the backyard. Let's play football until it rains.
   Let's play football in the backyard until it rains.
9. I saw a spider crawl under the couch. The spider was furry.
   I saw a furry spider crawl under the couch.

Simple Steps • Fifth Grade Sentences 205

Page 205

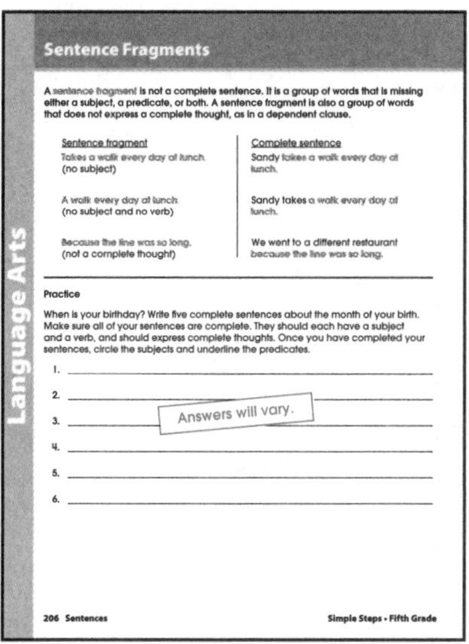

Sentence Fragments

A sentence fragment is not a complete sentence. It is a group of words that is missing either a subject, a predicate, or both. A sentence fragment is also a group of words that does not express a complete thought, as in a dependent clause.

Sentence fragment	Complete sentence
Takes a walk every day at lunch. (no subject)	Sandy takes a walk every day at lunch.
A walk every day at lunch. (no subject and no verb)	Sandy takes a walk every day at lunch.
Because the line was so long. (not a complete thought)	We went to a different restaurant because the line was so long.

Practice

When is your birthday? Write five complete sentences about the month of your birth. Make sure all of your sentences are complete. They should each have a subject and a verb, and should express complete thoughts. Once you have completed your sentences, circle the subjects and underline the predicates.

1.
2.
3. Answers will vary.
4.
5.
6.

206 Sentences · Simple Steps • Fifth Grade

Page 206

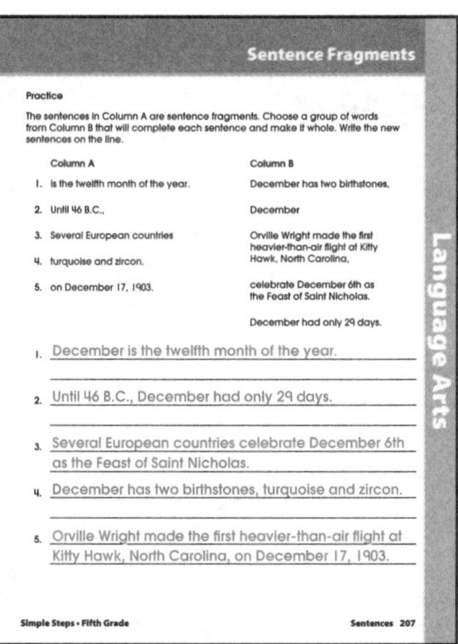

Sentence Fragments

Practice

The sentences in Column A are sentence fragments. Choose a group of words from Column B that will complete each sentence and make it whole. Write the new sentences on the line.

Column A	Column B
1. is the twelfth month of the year.	December has two birthstones,
2. Until 46 B.C.,	December
3. Several European countries	Orville Wright made the first heavier-than-air flight at Kitty Hawk, North Carolina,
4. turquoise and zircon.	celebrate December 6th as the Feast of Saint Nicholas.
5. on December 17, 1903.	December had only 29 days.

1. December is the twelfth month of the year.
2. Until 46 B.C., December had only 29 days.
3. Several European countries celebrate December 6th as the Feast of Saint Nicholas.
4. December has two birthstones, turquoise and zircon.
5. Orville Wright made the first heavier-than-air flight at Kitty Hawk, North Carolina, on December 17, 1903.

Simple Steps • Fifth Grade · Sentences 207

Page 207

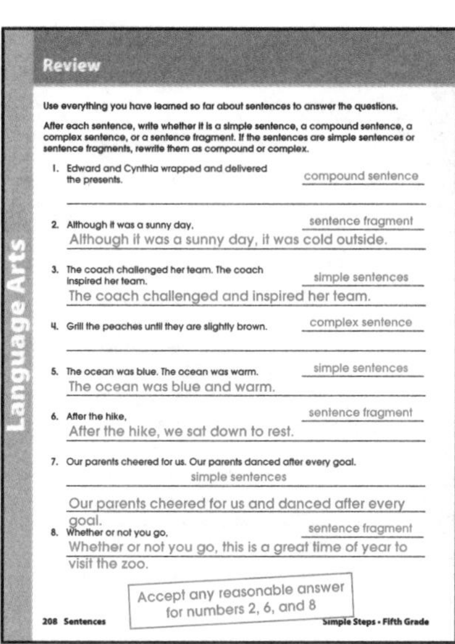

Review

Use everything you have learned so far about sentences to answer the questions.

After each sentence, write whether it is a simple sentence, a compound sentence, a complex sentence, or a sentence fragment. If the sentences are simple sentences or sentence fragments, rewrite them as compound or complex.

1. Edward and Cynthia wrapped and delivered the presents. compound sentence
2. Although it was a sunny day, sentence fragment
   Although it was a sunny day, it was cold outside.
3. The coach challenged her team. The coach inspired her team. simple sentences
   The coach challenged and inspired her team.
4. Grill the peaches until they are slightly brown. complex sentence
5. The ocean was blue. The ocean was warm. simple sentences
   The ocean was blue and warm.
6. After the hike, sentence fragment
   After the hike, we sat down to rest.
7. Our parents cheered for us. Our parents danced after every goal. simple sentences
   Our parents cheered for us and danced after every goal.
8. Whether or not you go, sentence fragment
   Whether or not you go, this is a great time of year to visit the zoo.

Accept any reasonable answer for numbers 2, 6, and 8

208 Sentences · Simple Steps • Fifth Grade

Page 208

Chapter Review

On each line, write whether the sentence is declarative, interrogative, exclamatory, or imperative.

1. Walk up the steps and then turn left. imperative
2. The weather is fantastic! exclamatory
3. Three bridges cross the Grand Canal. declarative
4. Did your dad make chicken and rice for dinner last night? interrogative
5. What a beautiful bridge that is! exclamatory
6. How warm does it get in Venice in the summer? interrogative

On each line, write whether the sentence is simple, compound, or complex.

7. She jogged through the mist. simple
8. The chefs cooked and baked in the competition. compound
9. After dinner, I'm going for a walk. complex
10. Farm Sanctuary rescues and protects farm animals. compound
11. Mr. Baum, who is also the baseball coach, is my favorite teacher. complex
12. He didn't think he was a fan of Shakespeare, yet he enjoyed the play. complex
13. You can go to the movies if you finish your homework. complex
14. Before the party, she will pick up Maria. complex
15. Mike, who loved animals, was learning about moose and caribou at school. complex

Simple Steps • Fifth Grade · Sentences 209

Page 209

Chapter Review

16. Rewrite the paragraph by combining simple sentences and correcting sentence fragments.

Recycling is important to our environment. It is important for many reasons. Recycling saves trees. If we recycle the paper products we use. Fewer trees will have to be cut down. It also protects our natural habitats. When we cut down trees, birds and squirrels lose their homes. Rabbits and many other forest animals lose their homes. Recycling greatly reduces our need for landfills. If we recycle what would be trash. There will be less garbage to put into the landfills. It also reduces curbside pollution. Less garbage means less trash on our streets. Less garbage means less pollution on our streets. These are excellent reasons why we should encourage our friends to recycle. These are excellent reasons why we should encourage our families to recycle. We should all be committed to a recycling program.

Recycling is important to our environment for many reasons. Recycling saves trees. If we recycle the paper products we use, fewer trees will have to be cut down. It also protects our natural habitats. When we cut down trees, birds, squirrels, rabbits, and many other forest animals lose their homes. Recycling greatly reduces our need for landfills. If we recycle what would be trash, there will be less garbage to put into the landfills. It also reduces curbside pollution. Less garbage means less trash and pollution on our streets. These are excellent reasons why we should encourage our friends and families to recycle. We should all be committed to a recycling program.

210 Sentences · Simple Steps • Fifth Grade

Page 210

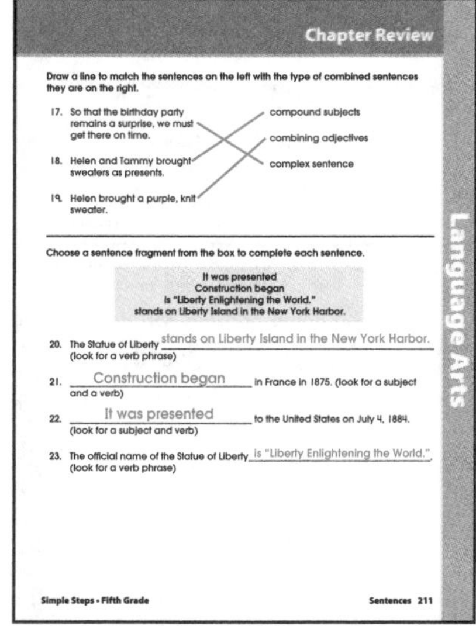

Chapter Review

Draw a line to match the sentences on the left with the type of combined sentences they are on the right.

17. So that the birthday party remains a surprise, we must get there on time. — complex sentence
18. Helen and Tammy brought sweaters as presents. — compound subjects
19. Helen brought a purple, knit sweater. — combining adjectives

Choose a sentence fragment from the box to complete each sentence.

It was presented
Construction began
is "Liberty Enlightening the World."
stands on Liberty Island in the New York Harbor.

20. The Statue of Liberty stands on Liberty Island in the New York Harbor. (look for a verb phrase)
21. Construction began in France in 1875. (look for a subject and a verb)
22. It was presented to the United States on July 4, 1884. (look for a subject and verb)
23. The official name of the Statue of Liberty is "Liberty Enlightening the World.". (look for a verb phrase)

Simple Steps • Fifth Grade · Sentences 211

Page 211

Answer Key

Answer Key

Capitalizing Proper Nouns

Proper nouns are specific people, places, and things. They always begin with a capital letter.

Capitalize names of cities.	Anchorage, Los Angeles, Detroit, Kona, Columbus, New York
Capitalize names of states.	Maine, Florida, Ohio, Alaska, Hawaii, Michigan
Capitalize names of countries.	United States, Brazil, Senegal, Japan, Israel, Denmark

Practice

Circle the correct answer that completes each of the following sentences.

1. California is the most populated (State, state) in the United States.
2. The least populated state in the United States is (Wyoming, wyoming).
3. China is the most populated (Country, country).
4. Australia is the only continent that is its own (Country, country).
5. The capital of California is (Sacramento, sacramento).
6. This (City, city) has a population of approximately 485,000.
7. (Los Angeles, los Angeles), has the largest population in California.
8. The city in the United States with the largest population is (New York, new york).
9. The (City, city) of New York has a population of approximately 22 million.
10. The capital city of the state of (New York, new york) is Albany.
11. Albany, (New York, new york) has a population of approximately 98,500.

Language Arts

212 Capitalization and Punctuation — Simple Steps • Fifth Grade

Page 212

Capitalizing Proper Nouns

Proper nouns include the days of the week and the months of the year. They always begin with a capital letter.

Capitalize days of the week.	Sunday, Monday, Tuesday, Wednesday, Thursday, Friday, Saturday
Capitalize days of the year.	January, February, March, April, May, June, July, August, September, October, November, December

Practice

Complete the following sentences by writing the correct month of the year on the line. Remember to capitalize the month when you write it in. Use an encyclopedia or the Internet if you need help.

1. The chrysanthemum is the flower for November, the eleventh month of the year.
2. The United States celebrates Independence Day on July 4th.
3. February is the shortest month of the year.
4. In the Northern Hemisphere, summer begins in the month of June.
5. August was named for the Roman emperor, Augustus.
6. Fools come out to play on this April day.
7. The month of January was named for the Roman god, Janus.
8. Cinco de Mayo is a holiday celebrated in Mexico on the fifth day of May.
9. The sapphire is the birthstone for September.
10. Farmers start to bring in their crops, including pumpkins, in the month of October.

Language Arts

Simple Steps • Fifth Grade — Capitalization and Punctuation 213

Page 213

Capitalizing Proper Nouns

The names of specific streets, places, and people are proper nouns and are capitalized.

Capitalize the names of specific streets.	Blue Street, Ohio Avenue, Wind Boulevard
Nonspecific words like street and road are not capitalized.	I live one street over from you.
Capitalize the names of specific places.	Rocky Mountain National Park
Capitalize first and last names of people, including special titles, initials, and abbreviations that go with the names.	President Barack Obama
Do not capitalize nonspecific street names, places, or titles.	My best friend is our class president.

Practice

Circle the proper nouns.

1. Our neighbors stayed at Water's Edge Hotel near the beach.
2. Cross the highway and then turn right on Riverbend Drive.
3. The veterinarian, Dr. Green, vaccinated all of the dogs in town.
4. Her soccer practices are at Barry Field.
5. Hawaii Volcanoes National Park is located on the island Hawaii.
6. Kari lives on Lane Road.

Language Arts

214 Capitalization and Punctuation — Simple Steps • Fifth Grade

Page 214

Capitalizing Proper Nouns

Correct the mistakes in the use of capitalization with proper nouns. Use the proofreading marks explained in the box to the right.

≡ capitalize a letter
/ lowercase a letter

Do you believe in haunted houses? How about haunted hotels? Granville, Ohio, is home to the buxton inn. The buxton inn, located on broadway street, has a haunting reputation. The Hotel was built in 1812 by orrin granger, founder of the City of Granville. The Hotel was named after major buxton, who ran the inn from 1865 to 1905. So whose ghosts have supposedly appeared in this Inn? orrin granger was first seen in the 1920s eating a piece of pie in the kitchen. major buxton has been seen by Guests, mostly in the Dining Room. The ghosts of other Owners have also been spotted. Even a kitty of days gone by has been seen roaming throughout the buxton inn. Of course the ghost cat now has a name—Major Buxton.

Write a short autobiography. Write about the city where you were born, the name of the first street where you lived, your parents' and siblings' names, and the name of your first school and your first teacher. Write about a few of your favorite memories growing up. Make sure that all of the proper nouns in your autobiography are capitalized.

Answers will vary.

Language Arts

Simple Steps • Fifth Grade — Capitalization and Punctuation 215

Page 215

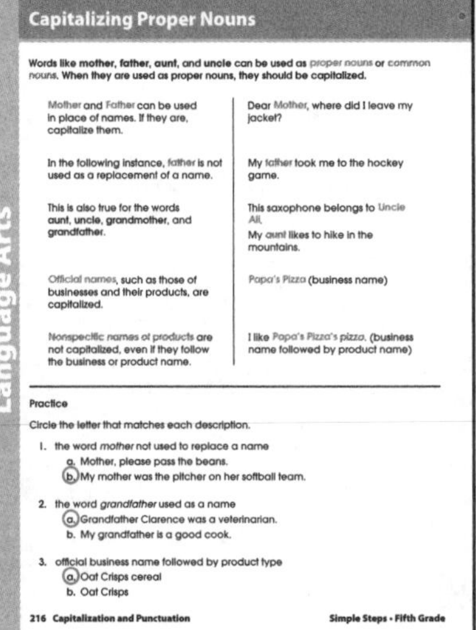

Capitalizing Proper Nouns

Words like mother, father, aunt, and uncle can be used as proper nouns or common nouns. When they are used as proper nouns, they should be capitalized.

Mother and Father can be used in place of names. If they are, capitalize them.	Dear Mother, where did I leave my jacket?
In the following instance, father is not used as a replacement of a name.	My father took me to the hockey game.
This is also true for the words aunt, uncle, grandmother, and grandfather.	This saxophone belongs to Uncle Al. My aunt likes to hike in the mountains.
Official names, such as those of businesses and their products, are capitalized.	Papa's Pizza (business name)
Nonspecific names of products are not capitalized, even if they follow the business or product name.	I like Papa's Pizza's pizza. (business name followed by product name)

Practice

Circle the letter that matches each description.

1. the word *mother* not used to replace a name
   a. Mother, please pass the beans.
   (b.) My mother was the pitcher on her softball team.
2. the word *grandfather* used as a name
   (a.) Grandfather Clarence was a veterinarian.
   b. My grandfather is a good cook.
3. official business name followed by product type
   (a.) Oat Crisps cereal
   b. Oat Crisps

Language Arts

216 Capitalization and Punctuation — Simple Steps • Fifth Grade

Page 216

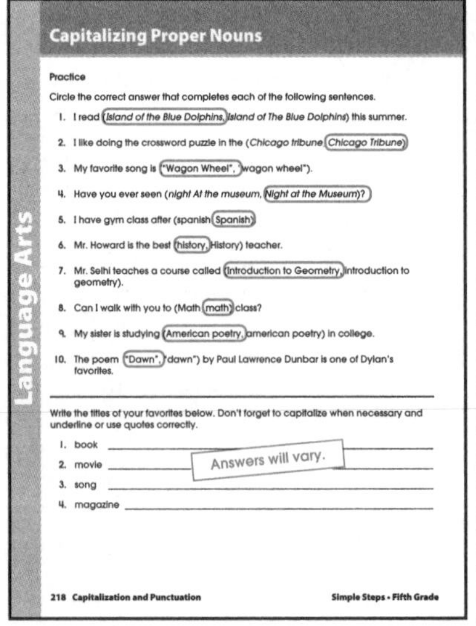

Capitalizing Proper Nouns

Practice

Circle the correct answer that completes each of the following sentences.

1. I read (*Island of the Blue Dolphins*, *Island of The Blue Dolphins*) this summer.
2. I like doing the crossword puzzle in the (*Chicago tribune*, *Chicago Tribune*).
3. My favorite song is ("Wagon Wheel", "wagon wheel").
4. Have you ever seen (*night At the museum*, *Night at the Museum*)?
5. I have gym class after (spanish, Spanish).
6. Mr. Howard is the best (history, History) teacher.
7. Mr. Selhi teaches a course called (Introduction to Geometry, introduction to geometry).
8. Can I walk with you to (Math, math) class?
9. My sister is studying (American poetry, american poetry) in college.
10. The poem ("Dawn", "dawn") by Paul Lawrence Dunbar is one of Dylan's favorites.

Write the titles of your favorites below. Don't forget to capitalize when necessary and underline or use quotes correctly.

1. book
2. movie
3. song
4. magazine

Answers will vary.

Language Arts

218 Capitalization and Punctuation — Simple Steps • Fifth Grade

Page 218

Answer Key

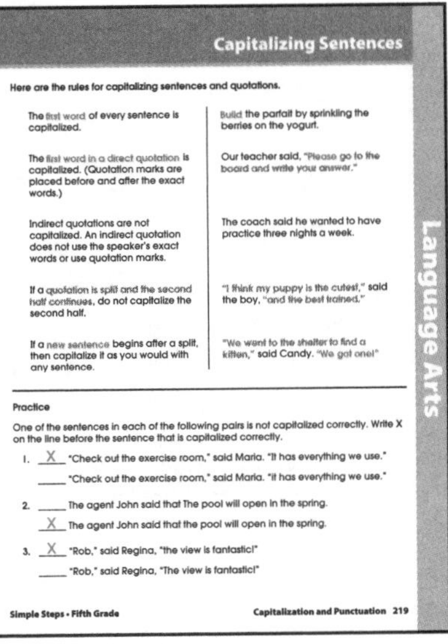

Capitalizing Sentences

Here are the rules for capitalizing sentences and quotations.

The first word of every sentence is capitalized.	Build the parfait by sprinkling the berries on the yogurt.
The first word in a direct quotation is capitalized. (Quotation marks are placed before and after the exact words.)	Our teacher said, "Please go to the board and write your answer."
Indirect quotations are not capitalized. An indirect quotation does not use the speaker's exact words or use quotation marks.	The coach said he wanted to have practice three nights a week.
If a quotation is split and the second half continues, do not capitalize the second half.	"I think my puppy is the cutest," said the boy, "and the best trained."
If a new sentence begins after a split, then capitalize it as you would with any sentence.	"We went to the shelter to find a kitten," said Candy. "We got one!"

Practice

One of the sentences in each of the following pairs is not capitalized correctly. Write X on the line before the sentence that is capitalized correctly.

1. __X__ "Check out the exercise room," said Maria. "It has everything we use."
   _____ "Check out the exercise room," said Maria. "it has everything we use."
2. _____ The agent John said that The pool will open in the spring.
   __X__ The agent John said that the pool will open in the spring.
3. __X__ "Rob," said Regina, "the view is fantastic!"
   _____ "Rob," said Regina, "The view is fantastic!"

Simple Steps • Fifth Grade Capitalization and Punctuation 219

Language Arts

Page 219

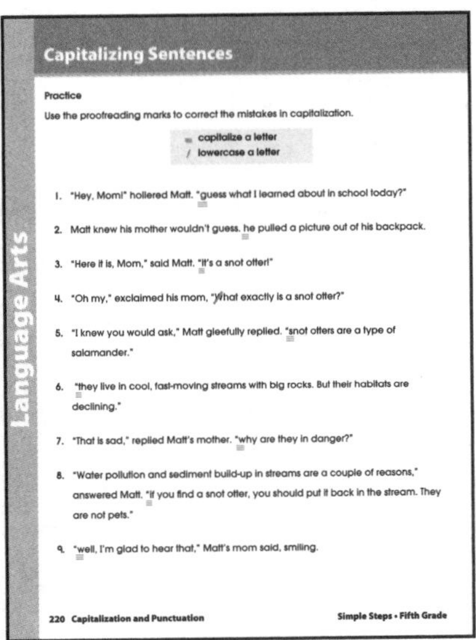

Capitalizing Sentences

Practice

Use the proofreading marks to correct the mistakes in capitalization.

≡ capitalize a letter
/ lowercase a letter

1. "Hey, Mom!" hollered Matt. "guess what I learned about in school today?"
2. Matt knew his mother wouldn't guess. he pulled a picture out of his backpack.
3. "Here it is, Mom," said Matt. "it's a snot otter!"
4. "Oh my," exclaimed his mom, "What exactly is a snot otter?"
5. "I knew you would ask," Matt gleefully replied. "snot otters are a type of salamander."
6. "they live in cool, fast-moving streams with big rocks. But their habitats are declining."
7. "That is sad," replied Matt's mother. "why are they in danger?"
8. "Water pollution and sediment build-up in streams are a couple of reasons," answered Matt. "if you find a snot otter, you should put it back in the stream. They are not pets."
9. "well, I'm glad to hear that," Matt's mom said, smiling.

220 Capitalization and Punctuation Simple Steps • Fifth Grade

Language Arts

Page 220

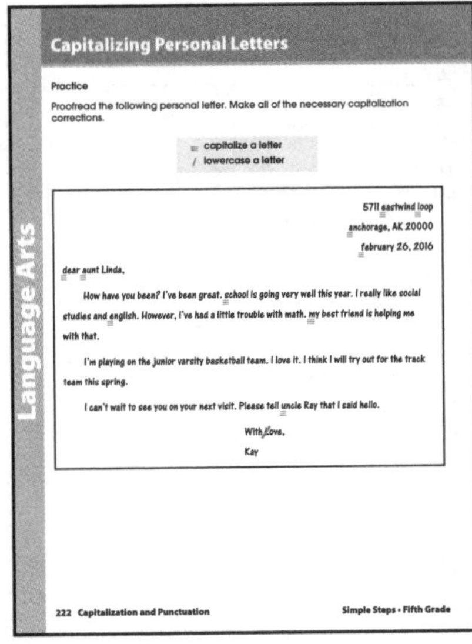

Capitalizing Personal Letters

Practice

Proofread the following personal letter. Make all of the necessary capitalization corrections.

≡ capitalize a letter
/ lowercase a letter

5711 eastwind loop
anchorage, AK 20000
february 26, 2016

dear aunt Linda,

How have you been? I've been great. school is going very well this year. I really like social studies and english. However, I've had a little trouble with math. my best friend is helping me with that.

I'm playing on the junior varsity basketball team. I love it. I think I will try out for the track team this spring.

I can't wait to see you on your next visit. Please tell uncle Ray that I said hello.

With Love,
Kay

222 Capitalization and Punctuation Simple Steps • Fifth Grade

Language Arts

Page 222

Review

Use everything you have learned so far about capitalization to proofread the following personal letter. Make all of the necessary capitalization corrections.

≡ capitalize a letter
/ lowercase a letter

4064 palm tree lane
oakdale, FL 20000
March 19, 2016

dear Perry,

How do you like anaheim, California, and your new school? things are about the same here. I'm getting ready for baseball season. Our first game is next thursday. coach Washington says That I can start as pitcher.

The basketball team won the division, but we didn't get very far in state. I think the baseball team will do well. we already have a sponsor for the team. Fast Feet Sporting Goods has already signed on. I like Fast Feet Shoes, but I'm still going to buy my gloves from your Uncle's store.

My family is going on vacation this summer. We're going to chicago, illinois. My Grandpa and Grandma are going too. We are going to visit aunt Christina. We're also going to navy pier and the sears tower. Did you know that the Sears Tower used to be the tallest Building in the world?

Are you trying out for the track team this year? Aren't tryouts in march? I hope you get to come back to visit soon. maybe we can meet somewhere in the middle next winter break? Write when you can.

your Friend,
Denny

Simple Steps • Fifth Grade Capitalization and Punctuation 223

Language Arts

Page 223

Periods

A period is placed at the end of different kinds of sentences.

Place a period at the end of a declarative sentence.	They left for their trip on Friday.
Place a period at the end of an imperative sentence when the statement is not urgent.	Take this coffee to your father, please.

Practice

Add the correct punctuation mark in each sentence.

1. Diedre lives in the house on the right __.__
2. I'm so excited to visit her this weekend __!__
3. Look at the bright plants her mom planted __.__
4. Lilac bushes were growing under the window __.__
5. Have you ever been here before __?__

Write two declarative sentences and two imperative sentences. Make sure to use periods at the end of each sentence.

6. ______
7. ______
8. ______
9. ______

Answers will vary.

224 Capitalization and Punctuation Simple Steps • Fifth Grade

Language Arts

Page 224

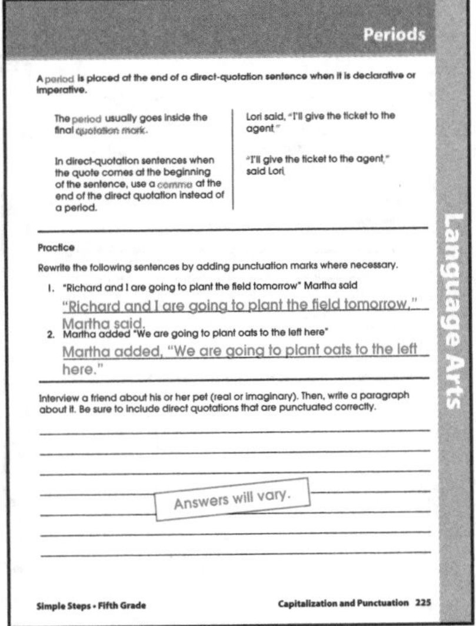

Periods

A period is placed at the end of a direct-quotation sentence when it is declarative or imperative.

The period usually goes inside the final quotation mark.	Lori said, "I'll give the ticket to the agent."
In direct-quotation sentences when the quote comes at the beginning of the sentence, use a comma at the end of the direct quotation instead of a period.	"I'll give the ticket to the agent," said Lori.

Practice

Rewrite the following sentences by adding punctuation marks where necessary.

1. "Richard and I are going to plant the field tomorrow" Martha said
   "Richard and I are going to plant the field tomorrow," Martha said.
2. Martha added "We are going to plant oats to the left here"
   Martha added, "We are going to plant oats to the left here."

Interview a friend about his or her pet (real or imaginary). Then, write a paragraph about it. Be sure to include direct quotations that are punctuated correctly.

Answers will vary.

Simple Steps • Fifth Grade Capitalization and Punctuation 225

Language Arts

Page 225

Answer Key

Periods

Periods are also used in abbreviations, initials, and titles before names.

Use a period after each part of an abbreviation. Do not leave a space between the period and the following letter.	B.C. A.D. P.M.
Use a period after each letter of an initial.	J.R.R. Tolkien
Use a period with abbreviated titles before names.	Dr. Ms.
Do not use periods if the abbreviation is an acronym. Acronyms are words formed from the first letters of words in a phrase.	ASAP (as soon as possible)

Practice

The following people were either misidentified or are not pleased with how their names appeared in a recent magazine article. Rewrite them as they request.

1. Donna Kay Dell — "I prefer my middle name to be an initial."
   Donna K. Dell
2. Melissa Sarah Oliver — "I prefer first and middle initials."
   M. S. Oliver
3. M. L. Roberts — "I am a doctor."
   Dr. M. L. Roberts

226 Capitalization and Punctuation — Simple Steps • Fifth Grade

Page 226

Periods

Practice

Draw a line to match the following abbreviations, titles, and acronyms in Column A with their meanings in Column B.

Column A	Column B
1. P.O.	Public Broadcasting System
2. PBS	Also Known As
3. Mr.	Post Office
4. LOL	Avenue
5. M.D.	Medical Doctor
6. Ave.	United Sates of America
7. J. K. Rowling	Joanne Kathleen Rowling
8. AKA	Laugh Out Loud
9. U.S.A.	Mister

You are having a formal party. Make a formal list of 10 people you would like to invite. Include their titles and abbreviations, like Mr., Dr., and Mrs.

Answers will vary.

Simple Steps • Fifth Grade — Capitalization and Punctuation 227

Page 227

Question Marks

Question marks are used in interrogative sentences (sentences that ask a question).

Ending a sentence with a question mark shows that a question is being asked.	How many students are in the class? Can I play too?

When used in quotations, questions marks can be placed either inside or outside of the closing quotation mark depending on the meaning of the sentence.

When the question mark is punctuating the quotation itself, it is placed inside the quotation mark.	The customer asked, "How much does the car cost?"
When the question mark is punctuating the entire sentence, it is placed outside the quotation mark.	Did the sales person say, "It's the most expensive car on the lot"?
For indirect quotations, a period is used instead of a question mark.	I asked my sister if she would help us with our math homework.

Practice

Place a question mark in the appropriate place in the sentences that need one. Add quotation marks where needed. In the sentences that do not need a question mark, place a period at the end of the sentence.

1. Did you hear back from the admissions office ?
2. Jason said he saw the movie 12 times .
3. My mom asked, "How much homework do you have tonight ?"
4. Did your teacher say, "Finish the entire chapter tonight "?
5. I asked Jill if she had a good day .
6. There must have been 200 people in the theatre .

228 Capitalization and Punctuation — Simple Steps • Fifth Grade

Page 228

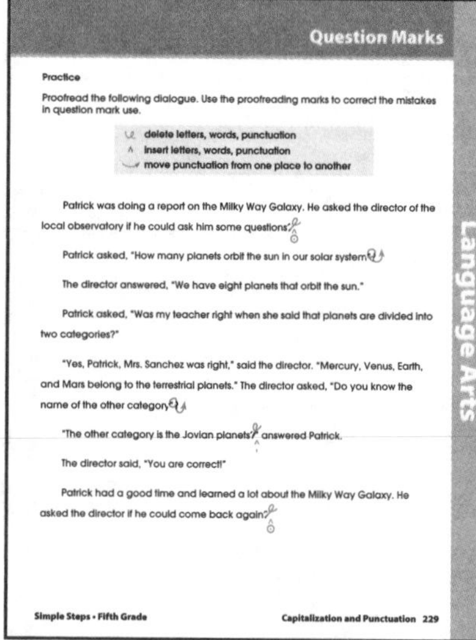

Question Marks

Practice

Proofread the following dialogue. Use the proofreading marks to correct the mistakes in question mark use.

- delete letters, words, punctuation
- insert letters, words, punctuation
- move punctuation from one place to another

Patrick was doing a report on the Milky Way Galaxy. He asked the director of the local observatory if he could ask him some questions?

Patrick asked, "How many planets orbit the sun in our solar system"?

The director answered, "We have eight planets that orbit the sun."

Patrick asked, "Was my teacher right when she said that planets are divided into two categories?"

"Yes, Patrick, Mrs. Sanchez was right," said the director. "Mercury, Venus, Earth, and Mars belong to the terrestrial planets." The director asked, "Do you know the name of the other category"?

"The other category is the Jovian planets?" answered Patrick.

The director said, "You are correct!"

Patrick had a good time and learned a lot about the Milky Way Galaxy. He asked the director if he could come back again?

Simple Steps • Fifth Grade — Capitalization and Punctuation 229

Page 229

Exclamation Marks

Exclamation marks are used with exclamatory sentences and interjections.

Exclamation marks help exclamatory sentences express surprise or a strong emotion.	I'm so excited that you made it into the first college on your list!
Exclamation marks also help interjections express surprise or a strong emotion.	Oh, no! I left my homework at home.

Practice

Place an ! at the end of each sentence that needs an exclamation mark.

1. Watch out The stove is hot !
2. The soup should be on medium high _____
3. Thank you for my beautiful flowers !
4. Tulips are my favorite flower _____
5. Ouch My fingers were still in the door !
6. After all of my hard work, I finally got an A on the test !
7. I have a lot of homework to do tonight _____
8. I won the race !
9. Oh, no The rain is coming down really hard now !
10. I like the sound of rain on the rooftop _____
11. The cars are coming fast !
12. My favorite color is green _____

230 Capitalization and Punctuation — Simple Steps • Fifth Grade

Page 230

Commas

Commas have a variety of uses. Three uses for commas are to set off items in a series, in direct address, and with multiple adjectives.

A series is at least three items listed together in a sentence. The items can be words, phrases, or clauses. Commas are used to separate them.	I must clean the kitchen, the bathroom, and the family room this weekend.
When multiple adjectives are used to describe a noun, they are separated by commas.	The sweet, cool apple tasted good on the hot day.
Make sure each adjective describes the noun.	The piping hot pizza was ready to come out of the oven. There is no comma because the pizza is not piping. The adverb piping describes the adjective hot.
When the name of a person being spoken to is used in a sentence, it is called direct address. A comma is used to separate the name from the rest of the sentence.	Ming, after our chores are done, we can go to the park. Pass the ball here, Ming!

Practice

Write three sentences describing your favorite foods. In each sentence, use commas in a series or with multiple adjectives.

1.
2.
3.

Answers will vary.

Simple Steps • Fifth Grade — Capitalization and Punctuation 231

Page 231

Answer Key

Commas

Practice

Draw a line to match the following sentences in Column A to the type of commas they require in Column B.

Column A	Column B
1. The soft, sweet, loving kitten purred.	commas in a series
2. They stayed out of the biting cold water.	commas in direct address
3. Daphne, please answer the door.	commas separating adjectives
4. I worked out on the treadmill, bike, and	no comma necessary between adverb and adjective elliptical cycle.

Column A	Column B
5. The sizzling hot sauce was too hot to eat.	commas in a series
6. Stephanie, please pass the strawberries.	commas in direct address
7. The sweet, juicy, ripe peaches were perfect.	commas separating adjectives
8. The tennis players grabbed their towels, bags, and balls on their way off the court.	no comma necessary between adverb and adjective

Rewrite the following sentences by adding commas where necessary.

9. John wanted pasta vegetables and rolls for dinner.
John wanted pasta, vegetables, and rolls for dinner.

10. Tiffany make the reservation for 7:30.
Tiffany, make the reservation for 7:30.

11. The new black car was just what he wanted.
The new, black car was just what he wanted.

12. I checked in on the slowly boiling water.
I checked in on the slowly boiling water.

232 Capitalization and Punctuation — Simple Steps • Fifth Grade

Language Arts

Page 232

Commas

Practice

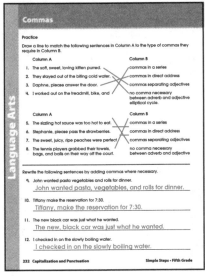

Make a list of five of your favorite things. Then, make a list of words that describe these things. Write five sentences about your favorite things using the words that describe them. Be sure to include commas in the appropriate places.

1.

2. Answers will vary.

3.

4.

5.

Simple Steps • Fifth Grade — Capitalization and Punctuation 233

Language Arts

Page 233

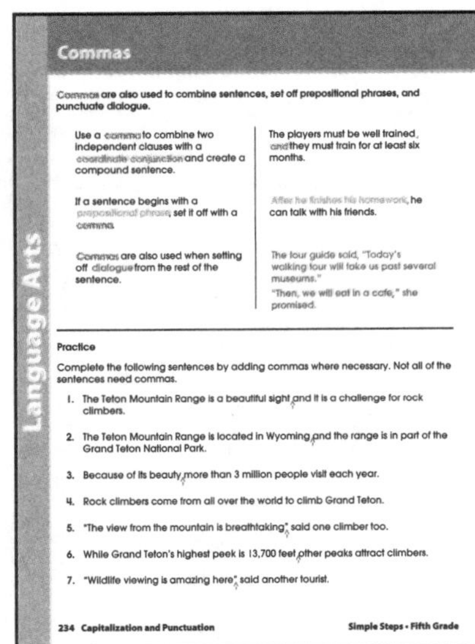

Commas

Commas are also used to combine sentences, set off prepositional phrases, and punctuate dialogue.

Use a comma to combine two independent clauses with a coordinate conjunction and create a compound sentence.	The players must be well trained, and they must train for at least six months.
If a sentence begins with a prepositional phrase, set it off with a comma.	After he finishes his homework, he can talk with his friends.
Commas are also used when setting off dialogue from the rest of the sentence.	The tour guide said, "Today's walking tour will take us past several museums." "Then, we will eat in a cafe," she promised.

Practice

Complete the following sentences by adding commas where necessary. Not all of the sentences need commas.

1. The Teton Mountain Range is a beautiful sight, and it is a challenge for rock climbers.
2. The Teton Mountain Range is located in Wyoming, and the range is in part of the Grand Teton National Park.
3. Because of its beauty, more than 3 million people visit each year.
4. Rock climbers come from all over the world to climb Grand Teton.
5. "The view from the mountain is breathtaking," said one climber too.
6. While Grand Teton's highest peek is 13,700 feet, other peaks attract climbers.
7. "Wildlife viewing is amazing here," said another tourist.

234 Capitalization and Punctuation — Simple Steps • Fifth Grade

Language Arts

Page 234

Commas

Practice

Proofread the following paragraph. Use a proofreading mark to add commas where necessary.

^ inserts letter, words, punctuation

What is a marathon? Most runners know that a marathon is a foot race of 26.2 miles, but not everyone knows how the marathon began. Now popular worldwide, the marathon has its roots in Greece. We are familiar with bicycle couriers, but ancient Greeks used foot couriers. Many of them had to run city to city to make deliveries. In 490 B.C., Persia was at war with Greece. A Persian army landed 25 miles from Athens at the city of Marathon. After a mighty battle, the Greeks were victorious. A runner was sent from Marathon to Athens to spread the news of the victory. Pheidippides ran the 25 miles from Marathon to Athens. When he reached the city, legend says he said, "Rejoice, we conquer." Then, Pheidippides fell dead. Although the facts are not known for sure, the legend prevails. The modern race got a name, and the marathon was born.

Write a paragraph explaining your favorite sport or hobby, how it got its beginning, and why you like it. Use a variety of sentences. Add a quotation of your own.

Answers will vary.

Simple Steps • Fifth Grade — Capitalization and Punctuation 235

Language Arts

Page 235

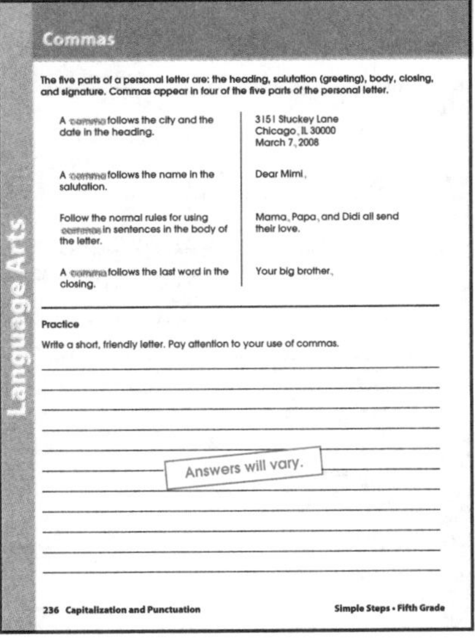

Commas

The five parts of a personal letter are: the heading, salutation (greeting), body, closing, and signature. Commas appear in four of the five parts of the personal letter.

A comma follows the city and the date in the heading.	3151 Stuckey Lane Chicago, IL 30000 March 7, 2008
A comma follows the name in the salutation.	Dear Mimi,
Follow the normal rules for using commas in sentences in the body of the letter.	Mama, Papa, and Didi all send their love.
A comma follows the last word in the closing.	Your big brother,

Practice

Write a short, friendly letter. Pay attention to your use of commas.

Answers will vary.

236 Capitalization and Punctuation — Simple Steps • Fifth Grade

Language Arts

Page 236

Commas

Practice

Proofread the following friendly letter. Use proofreading marks to insert commas where necessary.

deletes letter, words, punctuation
^ inserts letter, words, punctuation

5512 Alpine Lane
Ridgeview, CO 55214
April 26, 2015

Dear Marina,

How are you? Are you getting excited for summer? I am going to volunteer at the local animal shelter, and I am going to learn all about the different kinds of animals there. I am sure that it will be a hard job, but it will be rewarding too.

What are your plans for summer? Will you be going camping with your parents like you did last year? That sounds like so much fun! After you get back, I want to hear all about it.

I need to get back to reading about animal care, but I hope to hear from you soon!

Your friend,
Sharon

Simple Steps • Fifth Grade — Capitalization and Punctuation 237

Language Arts

Page 237

Quotation Marks

Practice

Draw a line to match the following sentences or titles from Column A to the type of quotation in Column B.

Column A	Column B
1. Susan said, "Let's go to lunch at 12:30."	direct quotation
2. "Right," Connie answered. "My boss said, 'Our lunch meeting is scheduled for 12:00 sharp.'"	quote within a quote
3. "Mary Had a Little Lamb"	title

Column A	Column B
4. "Cinderella"	direct quotation
5. My sister said, "The coach said 'Eat a good dinner the night before the game.'"	quote within a quote
6. "I'm heading for the beach," Sheryl said.	title

Practice writing sentences with quotation marks. Write two sentences that are direct quotations, two that are quotes within quotes, and two that include titles.

7. ______
8. ______ Answers will vary.
9. ______
10. ______
11. ______
12. ______

Simple Steps • Fifth Grade — Capitalization and Punctuation 239

Page 239

Apostrophes

Practice

Choose a contraction from the box to replace each phrase in parentheses and complete each sentence.

We're	It's	He'd
I'm	We've	let's

1. (I am) I'm hungry and thirsty.
2. (We are) We're on our way to the café.
3. (It is) It's not too far away, and it has the best muffins.
4. Do you think we should take something back for Pablo? (He would) He'd appreciate it.
5. (We have) We've been eating for almost an hour.
6. Come on, (let us) let's hurry.

Rewrite the following sentences, adding apostrophes where necessary.

1. Myras grades really improved after she started studying with her two older sisters.
   Myra's grades really improved after she started studying with her two older sisters.
2. With her sisters help and her parents encouragement, she is now a much better student.
   With her sister's help and her parents' encouragement, she is now a much better student.
3. Math isnt her best subject, but she was determined to work hard.
   Math isn't her best subject, but she was determined to work hard.
4. Much to her teachers surprise, Myra got an A on the years final test.
   Much to her teacher's surprise, Myra got an A on the year's final test.

Simple Steps • Fifth Grade — Capitalization and Punctuation 241

Page 241

Colons

A colon is used to introduce a series, to set off a clause, for emphasis, and in time.

Colons are used to introduce a series in a sentence. Usually, but not always, the list is proceeded by the words following, these, or things.	The chef does the following: washes the vegetables, chops the vegetables, and steams the vegetables.
Colons are sometimes used instead of a comma in more formal cases to set off a clause.	The weather reporter said: "We can expect six more inches of snow overnight."
Colons are used to set off a word or phrase for emphasis.	We hoped to see some activity in the night sky. And then we saw it: a shooting star.
Colons are used when writing the time.	Are we meeting at 9:00 or 10:00?

Practice

Identify why the colon is used in each sentence. Write S for series, C for clause, E for emphasis, or T for time.

1. E One of the most violent types of storms occurs primarily in the United States: tornados.
2. C A tornado is defined as the following: "a violent rotating column of air extending from a thunderstorm to the ground."
3. S Thunderstorms that develop in warm, moist air in advance of a cold front can produce these things: hail, strong wind, and tornados.
4. S Staying aware is very important for safety. During storms, look for the following: dark, greenish skies; large hail; loud roars; and flash floods.
5. S You can prepare for tornados by doing the following: developing a safety plan, practicing house drills, and listening to weather reports.

242 Capitalization and Punctuation — Simple Steps • Fifth Grade

Page 242

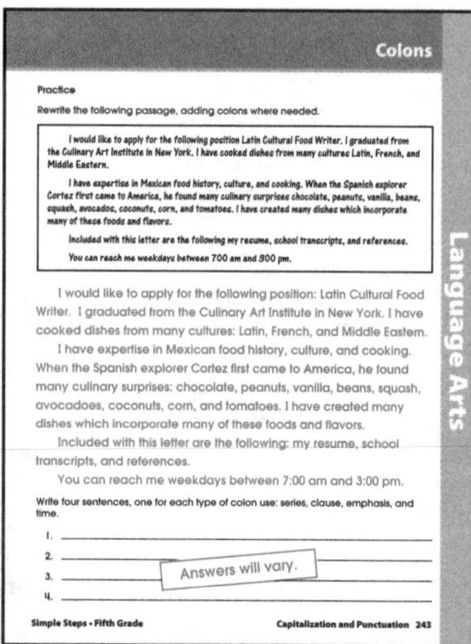

Colons

Practice

Rewrite the following passage, adding colons where needed.

I would like to apply for the following position Latin Cultural Food Writer. I graduated from the Culinary Art Institute in New York. I have cooked dishes from many cultures Latin, French, and Middle Eastern.

I have expertise in Mexican food history, culture, and cooking. When the Spanish explorer Cortez first came to America, he found many culinary surprises chocolate, peanuts, vanilla, beans, squash, avocadoes, coconuts, corn, and tomatoes. I have created many dishes which incorporate many of these foods and flavors.

Included with this letter are the following my resume, school transcripts, and references.

You can reach me weekdays between 700 am and 300 pm.

I would like to apply for the following position: Latin Cultural Food Writer. I graduated from the Culinary Art Institute in New York. I have cooked dishes from many cultures: Latin, French, and Middle Eastern.

I have expertise in Mexican food history, culture, and cooking. When the Spanish explorer Cortez first came to America, he found many culinary surprises: chocolate, peanuts, vanilla, beans, squash, avocadoes, coconuts, corn, and tomatoes. I have created many dishes which incorporate many of these foods and flavors.

Included with this letter are the following: my resume, school transcripts, and references.

You can reach me weekdays between 7:00 am and 3:00 pm.

Write four sentences, one for each type of colon use: series, clause, emphasis, and time.

1. ______
2. ______ Answers will vary.
3. ______
4. ______

Simple Steps • Fifth Grade — Capitalization and Punctuation 243

Page 243

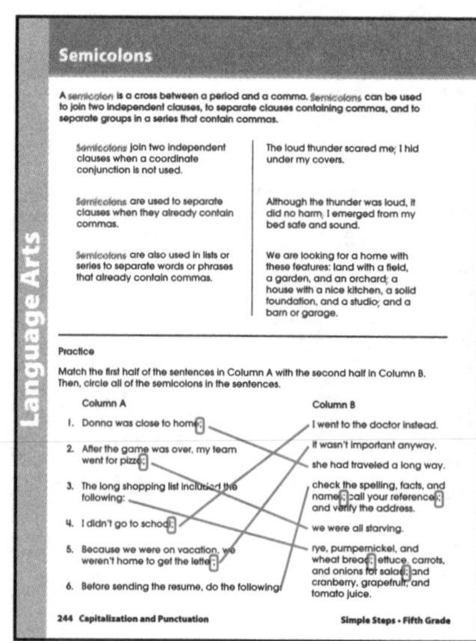

Semicolons

A semicolon is a cross between a period and a comma. Semicolons can be used to join two independent clauses, to separate clauses containing commas, and to separate groups in a series that contain commas.

Semicolons join two independent clauses when a coordinate conjunction is not used.	The loud thunder scared me; I hid under my covers.
Semicolons are used to separate clauses when they already contain commas.	Although the thunder was loud, it did no harm; I emerged from my bed safe and sound.
Semicolons are also used in lists or series to separate words or phrases that already contain commas.	We are looking for a home with these features: land with a field, a garden, and an orchard; a house with a nice kitchen, a solid foundation, and a studio; and a barn or garage.

Practice

Match the first half of the sentences in Column A with the second half in Column B. Then, circle all of the semicolons in the sentences.

Column A	Column B
1. Donna was close to home;	I went to the doctor instead.
2. After the game was over, my team went for pizza;	it wasn't important anyway.
3. The long shopping list included the following:	she had traveled a long way.
4. I didn't go to school;	check the spelling, facts, and names; call your references; and verify the address.
5. Because we were on vacation, we weren't home to get the letter;	we were all starving.
6. Before sending the resume, do the following:	rye, pumpernickel, and wheat bread; lettuce, carrots, and onions for salad; and cranberry, grapefruit, and tomato juice.

244 Capitalization and Punctuation — Simple Steps • Fifth Grade

Page 244

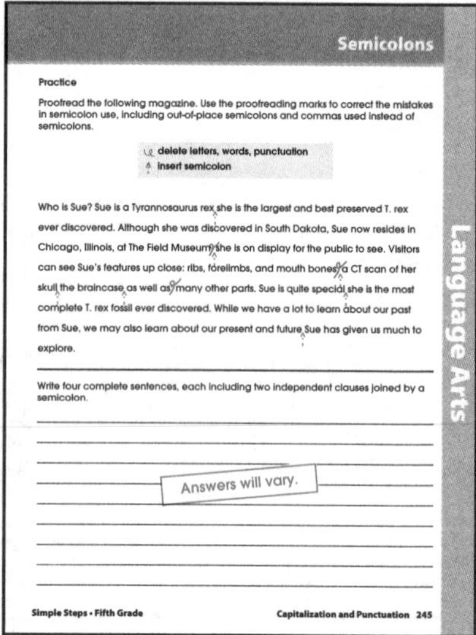

Semicolons

Practice

Proofread the following magazine. Use the proofreading marks to correct the mistakes in semicolon use, including out-of-place semicolons and commas used instead of semicolons.

delete letters, words, punctuation
insert semicolon

Who is Sue? Sue is a Tyrannosaurus rex, she is the largest and best preserved T. rex ever discovered. Although she was discovered in South Dakota, Sue now resides in Chicago, Illinois, at The Field Museum, she is on display for the public to see. Visitors can see Sue's features up close: ribs, forelimbs, and mouth bones; a CT scan of her skull, the braincase, as well as; many other parts. Sue is quite special; she is the most complete T. rex fossil ever discovered. While we have a lot to learn about our past from Sue, we may also learn about our present and future, Sue has given us much to explore.

Write four complete sentences, each including two independent clauses joined by a semicolon.

______ Answers will vary.

Simple Steps • Fifth Grade — Capitalization and Punctuation 245

Page 245

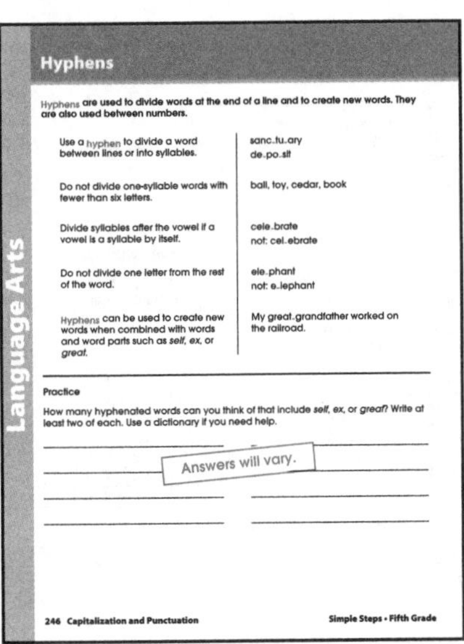

Hyphens

Hyphens are used to divide words at the end of a line and to create new words. They are also used between numbers.

Use a hyphen to divide a word between lines or into syllables.	sanc.tu.ary de.po.sit
Do not divide one-syllable words with fewer than six letters.	ball, toy, cedar, book
Divide syllables after the vowel if a vowel is a syllable by itself.	cele.brate not: cel.ebrate
Do not divide one letter from the rest of the word.	ele.phant not: e.lephant
Hyphens can be used to create new words when combined with words and word parts such as *self*, *ex*, or *great*.	My great.grandfather worked on the railroad.

Practice

How many hyphenated words can you think of that include *self*, *ex*, or *great*? Write at least two of each. Use a dictionary if you need help.

Answers will vary.

246 Capitalization and Punctuation — Simple Steps • Fifth Grade

Page 246

Hyphens

Practice

Solve the following puzzle. Write the words from the box in the appropriate spaces. The words must be divided correctly in order to fit into the spaces.

basket	compose	dinosaur	graduate	puppy
bicycle	crocodile	embankment	personal	television

1. t e l e - v i s i o n
2. b a s - k e t
3. p e r - s o n a l
4. c r o c o - d i l e
5. g r a d u - a t e
6. c o m - p o s e
7. e m b a n k - m e n t
8. b i c y - c l e
9. p u p p y
10. d i n o - s a u r

Simple Steps • Fifth Grade — Capitalization and Punctuation 247

Page 247

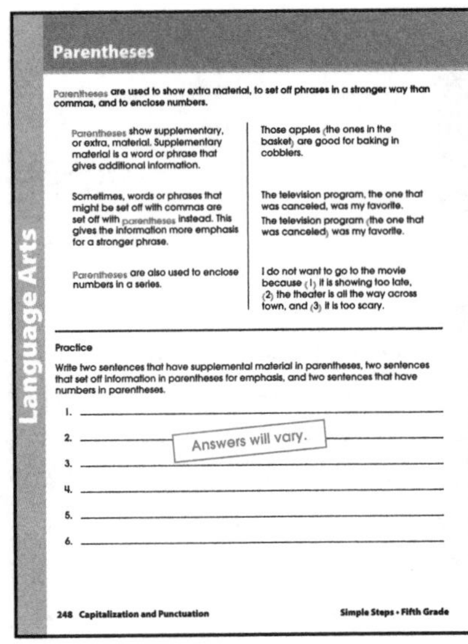

Parentheses

Parentheses are used to show extra material, to set off phrases in a stronger way than commas, and to enclose numbers.

Parentheses show supplementary, or extra, material. Supplementary material is a word or phrase that gives additional information.	Those apples (the ones in the basket) are good for baking in cobblers.
Sometimes, words or phrases that might be set off with commas are set off with parentheses instead. This gives the information more emphasis for a stronger phrase.	The television program, the one that was canceled, was my favorite. The television program (the one that was canceled) was my favorite.
Parentheses are also used to enclose numbers in a series.	I do not want to go to the movie because (1) it is showing too late, (2) the theater is all the way across town, and (3) it is too scary.

Practice

Write two sentences that have supplemental material in parentheses, two sentences that set off information in parentheses for emphasis, and two sentences that have numbers in parentheses.

1.
2.
3.
4.
5.
6.

Answers will vary.

248 Capitalization and Punctuation — Simple Steps • Fifth Grade

Page 248

Parentheses

Practice

Complete the following sentences by adding parenthetical phrases from the box. Add the parentheses where they belong. The first one is done for you.

(1) (2) (3) with four doors	(1) (2) (3) my best friend	my great-great-grandmother's see key

1. The road on this map looks like a two-lane road.
   The road on this map (see key) looks like a two-lane road.
2. The recipe is the best!
   The recipe (my great-great-grandmother's) is the best!
3. Andy is moving to another state.
   Andy (my best friend) is moving to another state.
4. I love to exercise because it is good for my heart, it gives me energy, and I feel good afterward.
   I love to exercise because (1) it is good for my heart, (2) it gives me energy, and (3) I feel good afterward.
5. The new, blue car is the one I want.
   The new, blue car (with four doors) is the one I want.
6. Pigs are my favorite animal because they are intelligent, they are cute, and they make "oinking" sounds.
   Pigs are my favorite animal because (1) they are intelligent, (2) they are cute, and (3) they make "oinking" sounds.

Simple Steps • Fifth Grade — Capitalization and Punctuation 249

Page 249

Review

Use everything you have learned so far about sentences to answer the questions.

1. Proofread the following letter. Use a proofreading mark to insert the missing periods and commas.

^ inserts letter, words, punctuation

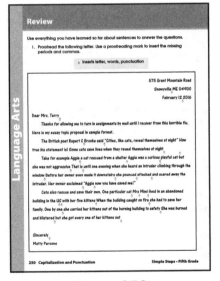

575 Grant Mountain Road
Snowyville ME 04900
February 12 2016

Dear Mrs. Terry

Thanks for allowing me to turn in assignments by mail until I recover from this horrible flu. Here is my essay topic proposal in sample format.

The British poet Rupert C Brooke said "Cities, like cats, reveal themselves at night" How true his statement is! Some cats save lives when they reveal themselves at night

Take for example Aggie a cat rescued from a shelter Aggie was a curious playful cat but she was not aggressive That is until one evening when she heard an intruder climbing through the window Before her owner even made it downstairs she pounced attacked and scared away the intruder. Her owner exclaimed "Aggie now you have saved me!"

Cats also rescue and save their own. One particular cat Mrs Mimi lived in an abandoned building in the US with her five kittens When the building caught on fire she had to save her family. One by one she carried her kittens out of the burning building to safety She was burned and blistered but she got every one of her kittens out

Sincerely
Matty Parsons

250 Capitalization and Punctuation — Simple Steps • Fifth Grade

Page 250

Review

Add question marks and exclamation marks where they are needed.

2. May I go with you to the baseball game?
3. Wait for me!
4. We won! We won!
5. The hiker asked, "Is this as far as the trail goes?"
6. Did the coach say, "Run three more laps"?

Use proofreading marks to insert single and double quotation marks, apostrophes and semicolons.

7. "Claude Monet lived in France from 1840 to 1926 and was the founder of Impressionism. Many of Monet's paintings were landscapes," said Mrs. Konikow.
8. "Did Mrs. Konikow say, 'Many of Monet's paintings were landscapes?'" Patricia asked Doug.
9. "Someday, I would like to go to France," said Patricia, "but for now I think I'll just take a trip to the library."
10. This summer, I learned how to swim; played baseball, soccer, and tennis; and ate lots of fresh corn, tomatoes, and cucumbers.
11. Before I go back to school, I have one thing left on my summer to-do list: a cookout at my best friend's house.

Simple Steps • Fifth Grade — Capitalization and Punctuation 251

Page 251

Answer Key

Answer Key

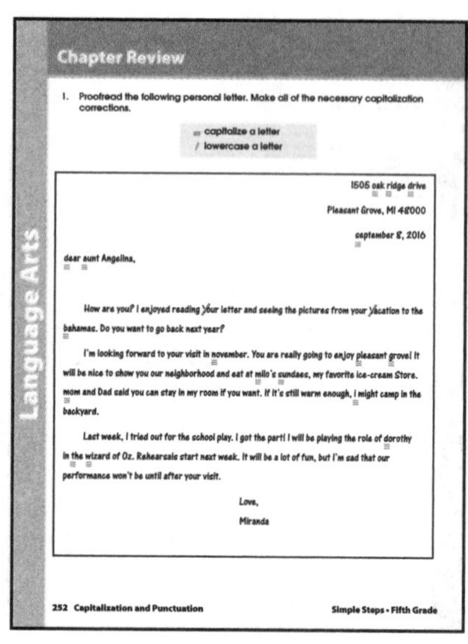

Chapter Review

Language Arts

1. Proofread the following personal letter. Make all of the necessary capitalization corrections.

≡ capitalize a letter
/ lowercase a letter

1505 oak ridge drive
Pleasant Grove, MI 48000
september 8, 2016

dear aunt Angelina,

How are you? I enjoyed reading Your letter and seeing the pictures from your Vacation to the bahamas. Do you want to go back next year?

I'm looking forward to your visit in november. You are really going to enjoy pleasant grove! It will be nice to show you our neighborhood and eat at milo's sundaes, my favorite ice-cream Store. mom and Dad said you can stay in my room if you want. If it's still warm enough, I might camp in the backyard.

Last week, I tried out for the school play. I got the part! I will be playing the role of dorothy in the wizard of Oz. Rehearsals start next week. It will be a lot of fun, but I'm sad that our performance won't be until after your visit.

Love,
Miranda

252 Capitalization and Punctuation — Simple Steps • Fifth Grade

Page 252

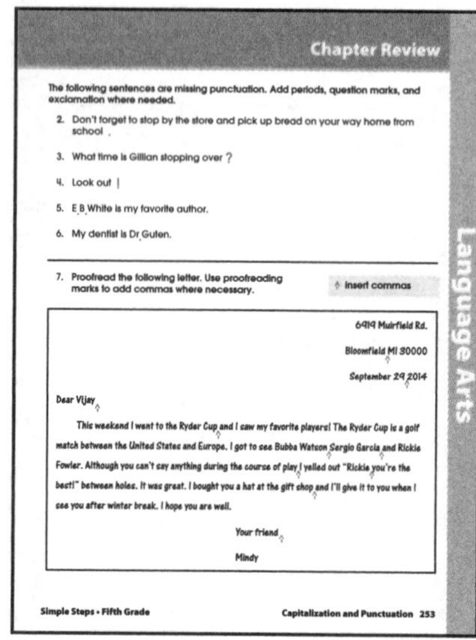

Chapter Review

Language Arts

The following sentences are missing punctuation. Add periods, question marks, and exclamation marks where needed.

2. Don't forget to stop by the store and pick up bread on your way home from school .
3. What time is Gillian stopping over ?
4. Look out !
5. E.B. White is my favorite author.
6. My dentist is Dr. Guten.

7. Proofread the following letter. Use proofreading marks to add commas where necessary.

^ insert commas

6414 Muirfield Rd.
Bloomfield, MI 30000
September 29, 2014

Dear Vijay,

This weekend I went to the Ryder Cup, and I saw my favorite players! The Ryder Cup is a golf match between the United States and Europe. I got to see Bubba Watson, Sergio Garcia, and Rickie Fowler. Although you can't say anything during the course of play, I yelled out "Rickie, you're the best!" between holes. It was great. I bought you a hat at the gift shop, and I'll give it to you when I see you after winter break. I hope you are well.

Your friend,
Mindy

Simple Steps • Fifth Grade — Capitalization and Punctuation 253

Page 253

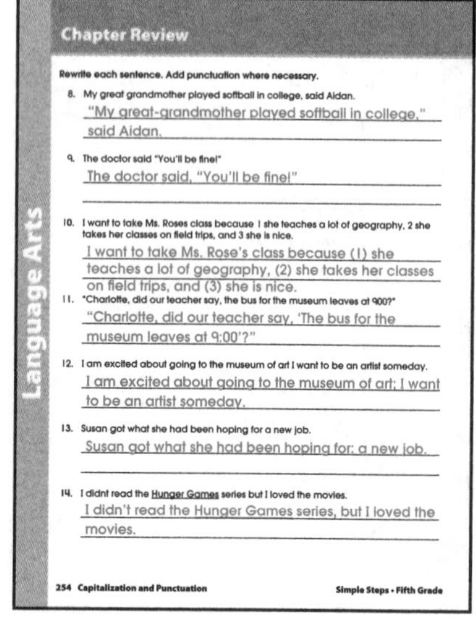

Chapter Review

Language Arts

Rewrite each sentence. Add punctuation where necessary.

8. My great grandmother played softball in college, said Aidan.
"My great-grandmother played softball in college," said Aidan.

9. The doctor said "You'll be fine!"
The doctor said, "You'll be fine!"

10. I want to take Ms. Roses class because 1 she teaches a lot of geography, 2 she takes her classes on field trips, and 3 she is nice.
I want to take Ms. Rose's class because (1) she teaches a lot of geography, (2) she takes her classes on field trips, and (3) she is nice.

11. "Charlotte, did our teacher say, the bus for the museum leaves at 900?"
"Charlotte, did our teacher say, 'The bus for the museum leaves at 9:00'?"

12. I am excited about going to the museum of art I want to be an artist someday.
I am excited about going to the museum of art; I want to be an artist someday.

13. Susan got what she had been hoping for a new job.
Susan got what she had been hoping for: a new job.

14. I didnt read the Hunger Games series but I loved the movies.
I didn't read the Hunger Games series, but I loved the movies.

254 Capitalization and Punctuation — Simple Steps • Fifth Grade

Page 254

Using Tenses with Irregular Verbs

Language Arts

When they change tenses, irregular verbs do not follow the same rules as regular verbs.

The present tense of a verb tells that the action is taking place now or continuously. — I do the crossword puzzles on Sunday.

The past tense of a verb tells that the action took place in the past. — Renee and Kristen went on an archaeological dig last semester.

The past participle of a verb tells that the action began in the past and was completed in the past. In order to form the past participle, the verb must be preceded by one of the following verbs: was, were, has, had, or have. — Yuki, Lori, and Blair had come with us on our vacation three years in a row, but last year they didn't.

Practice

Complete the following sentences by circling the correct verb in parentheses.

1. Timmy (come, **has come**) over for dinner every night this week.
2. I can (did, **do**) my homework now.
3. The class (go, **had gone**) to the same exhibit last year.
4. Bianca and Nicole (gone, **went**) to see the butterflies at the butterfly house.
5. Please (came, **come**) and pick up your order.
6. Andrea (do, **has done**) that assignment many times before.

Simple Steps • Fifth Grade — Usage, Vocabulary, and Spelling 255

Page 255

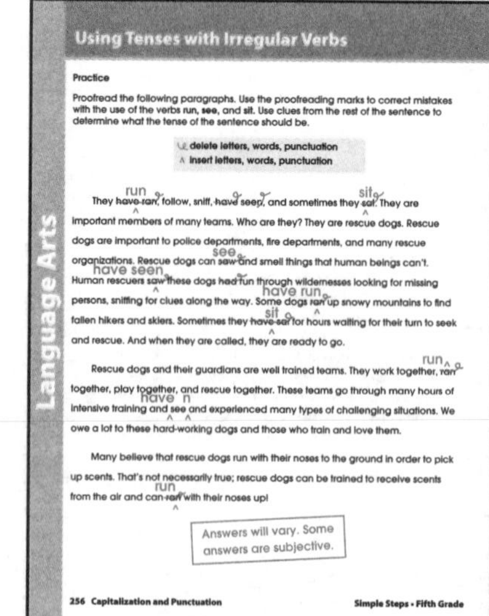

Using Tenses with Irregular Verbs

Language Arts

Practice

Proofread the following paragraphs. Use the proofreading marks to correct mistakes with the use of the verbs run, see, and sit. Use clues from the rest of the sentence to determine what the tense of the sentence should be.

⌒ delete letters, words, punctuation
^ insert letters, words, punctuation

They ~~have ran~~ run, follow, sniff, ~~have~~ seen, and sometimes they ~~sat~~ sit. They are important members of many teams. Who are they? They are rescue dogs. Rescue dogs are important to police departments, fire departments, and many rescue organizations. Rescue dogs can ~~saw~~ see and smell things that human beings can't. Human rescuers ~~saw~~ have seen these dogs ~~had~~ ~~run~~ through wildernesses looking for missing persons, sniffing for clues along the way. Some dogs ~~ran~~ have run up snowy mountains to find fallen hikers and skiers. Sometimes they ~~have sat~~ sit for hours waiting for their turn to seek and rescue. And when they are called, they are ready to go.

Rescue dogs and their guardians are well trained teams. They work together, ~~ran~~ run together, play together, and rescue together. These teams go through many hours of intensive training and ~~see~~ have seen and experienced many types of challenging situations. We owe a lot to these hard-working dogs and those who train and love them.

Many believe that rescue dogs run with their noses to the ground in order to pick up scents. That's not necessarily true; rescue dogs can be trained to receive scents from the air and can ~~ran~~ run with their noses up!

Answers will vary. Some answers are subjective.

256 Capitalization and Punctuation — Simple Steps • Fifth Grade

Page 256

Comparative and Superlative Adjectives

Language Arts

All types of adjectives describe nouns.

Regular adjectives describe one noun. — cute/cuter/cutest: Phoebe has a cute puppy.

Comparative adjectives compare two nouns. — big/bigger/biggest: Joe's sandwich is bigger than Barney's.

Superlative adjectives compare three or more nouns. — light/lighter/lightest: This windbreaker is the lightest jacket in my closet.

The word more before an adjective means it is comparative, comparing two nouns. — Students in the morning class are more energetic than students in the afternoon class.

The word most before an adjective means it is superlative, comparing three or more nouns. — Please sign the three yellow forms first; they are the most important.

The words more and most are normally used instead of er and est with adjectives that have more than two syllables.

Practice

Complete the following sentences by circling the correct word or words in parentheses.

1. Of the three bats, Henry's is the (light, **lightest**).
2. Christina has a very (**cute**, cuter) kitten.
3. My notebook is (**bigger**, biggest) than yours.
4. (**Light**, Lightest) rain fell on the roof.
5. Every mother thinks her child is the (cute, **cutest**) in the class.

Simple Steps • Fifth Grade — Usage, Vocabulary, and Spelling 257

Page 257

Answer Key

Comparative and Superlative Adjectives

Language Arts

Practice

Identify each of the following sentences as either a comparative sentence or a superlative sentence. Write C for comparative and S for superlative. Then, underline the adjectives (including the words more or most) in the sentences.

1. S The most challenging sports competition in the world is the Tour de France.
2. S The Tour de France can be ridden in some of the worst weather conditions.
3. S One of the best shirts to earn in the Tour de France is the polka-dot jersey.
4. S The world's most famous bicyclers come to France to compete.
5. C Athletes now have more specialized training than they did years ago.
6. C The more training an athlete has, the more prepared they will be.

Write a paragraph describing a performance or sporting event you have seen. Use at least six comparative or superlative adjectives.

Answers will vary.

258 Usage, Vocabulary, and Spelling — Simple Steps • Fifth Grade

Page 258

Adjective or Adverb?

Language Arts

Practice

Complete the following sentences by circling the correct adjective or adverb in parentheses. Underline the verb, adjective, or adverb that it modifies. Then, identify what type of word the adjective or adverb modifies: write V for verb, ADJ for adjective, ADV for adverb, and N for noun.

1. V Jim was sick and ran (bad, badly) during the race.
2. V Amy had a great day and ran (good, well) in her race.
3. N The day I lost the race was a (bad, badly) day for me.
4. ADJ I was a (bad, badly) beaten runner.
5. N But it was a (good, well) day for my friend.
6. V She accepted her praises (good, well).
7. V I will train harder so I do (good, well) in my next race.
8. N That will be a (good, well) day for the whole team.

Write a paragraph describing a school event in which some things went well, and some things didn't go so well. Use each of the words bad, badly, good, well, really, and very at least once.

Answers will vary.

260 Usage, Vocabulary, and Spelling — Simple Steps • Fifth Grade

Page 260

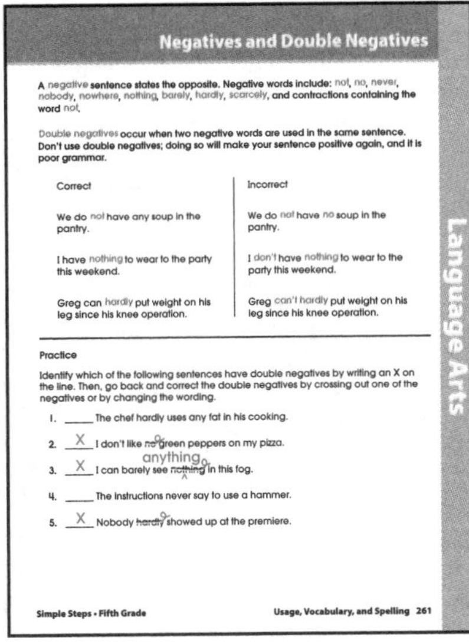

Negatives and Double Negatives

Language Arts

A negative sentence states the opposite. Negative words include: not, no, never, nobody, nowhere, nothing, barely, hardly, scarcely, and contractions containing the word not.

Double negatives occur when two negative words are used in the same sentence. Don't use double negatives; doing so will make your sentence positive again, and it is poor grammar.

Correct	Incorrect
We do not have any soup in the pantry.	We do not have no soup in the pantry.
I have nothing to wear to the party this weekend.	I don't have nothing to wear to the party this weekend.
Greg can hardly put weight on his leg since his knee operation.	Greg can't hardly put weight on his leg since his knee operation.

Practice

Identify which of the following sentences have double negatives by writing an X on the line. Then, go back and correct the double negatives by crossing out one of the negatives or by changing the wording.

1. ____ The chef hardly uses any fat in his cooking.
2. X I don't like ~~no~~ green peppers on my pizza.
3. X I can barely see ~~nothing~~ anything in this fog.
4. ____ The instructions never say to use a hammer.
5. X Nobody ~~hardly~~ showed up at the premiere.

Simple Steps • Fifth Grade — Usage, Vocabulary, and Spelling 261

Page 261

Negatives and Double Negatives

Language Arts

Practice

Rewrite this paragraph to correct the double negatives.

Firefighting is a brave and courageous job. If you can't imagine yourself not working hard, then this job isn't for you. Firefighters go through special training. They don't never take training lightly. Firefighters must wear special gear and use special equipment. It isn't easy to use the equipment. They spend many class hours learning about it and training with it. Firefighters must train in actual fires. Some trainees don't make it through this training. They may find they don't like climbing no ladders that are so high. Some may find they aren't scarcely strong enough. The firefighters who graduate are ready for the job. They don't never know what dangers each day will bring, but they are trained and ready. Firefighters keep us, our pets, and our homes safe. Firefighting is a brave and courageous career to explore.

Firefighting is a brave and courageous job. If you can't imagine yourself working hard, then this job isn't for you. Firefighters go through special training. They don't take training lightly. Firefighters must wear special gear and use special equipment. It isn't easy to use the equipment. They spend many class hours learning about it and training with it. Firefighters must train in actual fires. Some trainees don't make it through this training. They may find they don't like climbing ladders that are so high. Some may find they aren't strong enough. The firefighters who graduate are ready for the job. They never know what dangers each day will bring, but they are trained and ready. Firefighters keep us, our pets, and our homes safe. Firefighting is a brave and courageous career to explore.

262 Usage, Vocabulary, and Spelling — Simple Steps • Fifth Grade

Page 262

Synonyms and Antonyms

Language Arts

Synonyms and antonyms are two types of word relationships. Synonyms describe things that are similar, and antonyms describe things that are different.

Synonyms are words that have the same, or almost the same, meaning. Using synonyms can help you avoid repeating words and can make your writing more interesting.	Here are some examples of synonyms: clever/smart, reply/answer, wreck/destroy, applaud/clap
Antonyms are words that have opposite meanings. Using antonyms can help you show how people, places, situations, and things are different.	Here are some examples of antonyms: wide/narrow, accept/decline, break/repair, borrow/lend

Practice

Read each sentence below. If the underlined words are synonyms, write S on the line. If they are antonyms, write A on the line.

1. A Do you know if the house at the end of the street is vacant or occupied?
2. S Although Tamika is shy now, I don't expect that she'll be timid her whole life.
3. S The hero of the story was courageous, and he was rewarded for being so brave.
4. A The plane departs at 11:00 and arrives at its destination at 2:30.
5. S The commander was well respected by his men, and they were happy to follow their leader.

Simple Steps • Fifth Grade — Usage, Vocabulary, and Spelling 263

Page 263

Homophones

Language Arts

Homophones are words that sound the same but have different spellings and different meanings. There are hundreds of homophones in the English language.

allowed: to have permission	Are you allowed to go to the midnight movie?
aloud: in a speaking voice	Practice saying your multiplication tables aloud.
threw: propelled through the air with the hand and arm	Tomas threw the football to me.
through: movement into one point and out another	The tunnel goes through the mountain.

Practice

Read the following sentences. Circle the letter of the definition of the underlined homophone that fits the sentence. If you are unsure about which homophone to use, look up the meanings in a dictionary.

1. Taylor will have many books to buy when he starts college.
   - (a.) to purchase
   - b. to be near
2. The horse's mane glistened in the morning sunshine.
   - a. the most important
   - (b.) hair
3. Ellen lives by the pond with the ducks and geese.
   - a. to purchase
   - (b.) to be near
4. Please underline the sentence with the main idea in this paragraph.
   - (a.) the most important
   - b. hair

264 Usage, Vocabulary, and Spelling — Simple Steps • Fifth Grade

Page 264

Answer Key

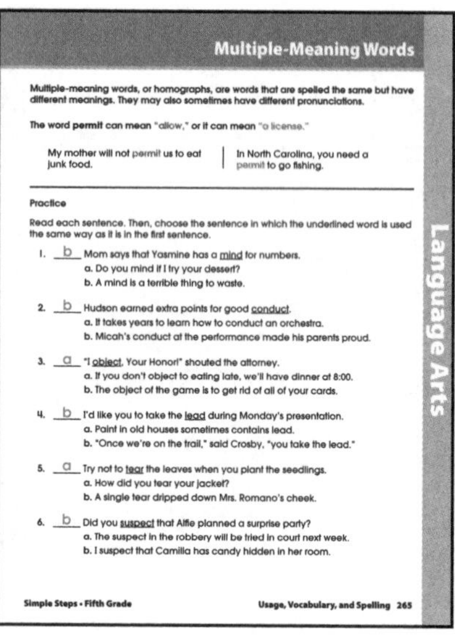

Multiple-Meaning Words

Multiple-meaning words, or homographs, are words that are spelled the same but have different meanings. They may also sometimes have different pronunciations.

The word **permit** can mean "allow," or it can mean "a license."

My mother will not permit us to eat junk food. | In North Carolina, you need a permit to go fishing.

Practice

Read each sentence. Then, choose the sentence in which the underlined word is used the same way as it is in the first sentence.

1. b Mom says that Yasmine has a mind for numbers.
   a. Do you mind if I try your dessert?
   b. A mind is a terrible thing to waste.
2. b Hudson earned extra points for good conduct.
   a. It takes years to learn how to conduct an orchestra.
   b. Micah's conduct at the performance made his parents proud.
3. a "I object, Your Honor!" shouted the attorney.
   a. If you don't object to eating late, we'll have dinner at 8:00.
   b. The object of the game is to get rid of all of your cards.
4. b I'd like you to take the lead during Monday's presentation.
   a. Paint in old houses sometimes contains lead.
   b. "Once we're on the trail," said Crosby, "you take the lead."
5. a Try not to tear the leaves when you plant the seedlings.
   a. How did you tear your jacket?
   b. A single tear dripped down Mrs. Romano's cheek.
6. b Did you suspect that Alfie planned a surprise party?
   a. The suspect in the robbery will be tried in court next week.
   b. I suspect that Camilla has candy hidden in her room.

Language Arts

Simple Steps • Fifth Grade   Usage, Vocabulary, and Spelling 265

Page 265

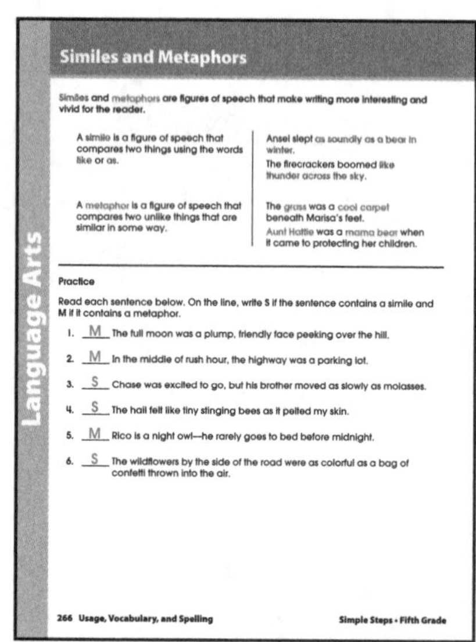

Similes and Metaphors

Similes and metaphors are figures of speech that make writing more interesting and vivid for the reader.

A simile is a figure of speech that compares two things using the words like or as. | Ansel slept as soundly as a bear in winter. The firecrackers boomed like thunder across the sky.

A metaphor is a figure of speech that compares two unlike things that are similar in some way. | The grass was a cool carpet beneath Marisa's feet. Aunt Hattie was a mama bear when it came to protecting her children.

Practice

Read each sentence below. On the line, write S if the sentence contains a simile and M if it contains a metaphor.

1. M The full moon was a plump, friendly face peeking over the hill.
2. M In the middle of rush hour, the highway was a parking lot.
3. S Chase was excited to go, but his brother moved as slowly as molasses.
4. S The hail felt like tiny stinging bees as it pelted my skin.
5. M Rico is a night owl—he rarely goes to bed before midnight.
6. S The wildflowers by the side of the road were as colorful as a bag of confetti thrown into the air.

Language Arts

266 Usage, Vocabulary, and Spelling   Simple Steps • Fifth Grade

Page 266

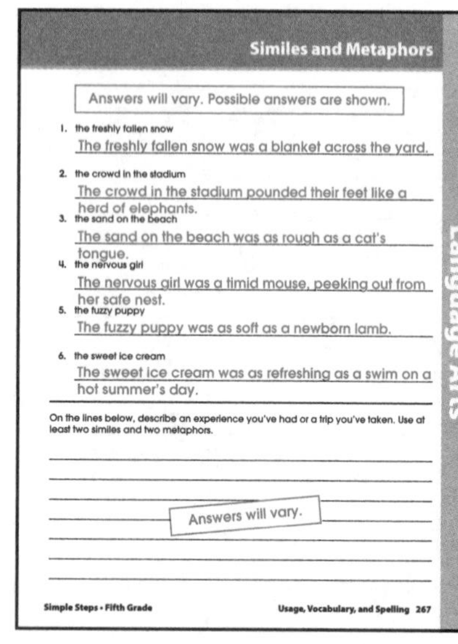

Similes and Metaphors

Answers will vary. Possible answers are shown.

1. the freshly fallen snow
   The freshly fallen snow was a blanket across the yard.
2. the crowd in the stadium
   The crowd in the stadium pounded their feet like a herd of elephants.
3. the sand on the beach
   The sand on the beach was as rough as a cat's tongue.
4. the nervous girl
   The nervous girl was a timid mouse, peeking out from her safe nest.
5. the fuzzy puppy
   The fuzzy puppy was as soft as a newborn lamb.
6. the sweet ice cream
   The sweet ice cream was as refreshing as a swim on a hot summer's day.

On the lines below, describe an experience you've had or a trip you've taken. Use at least two similes and two metaphors.

Answers will vary.

Language Arts

Simple Steps • Fifth Grade   Usage, Vocabulary, and Spelling 267

Page 267

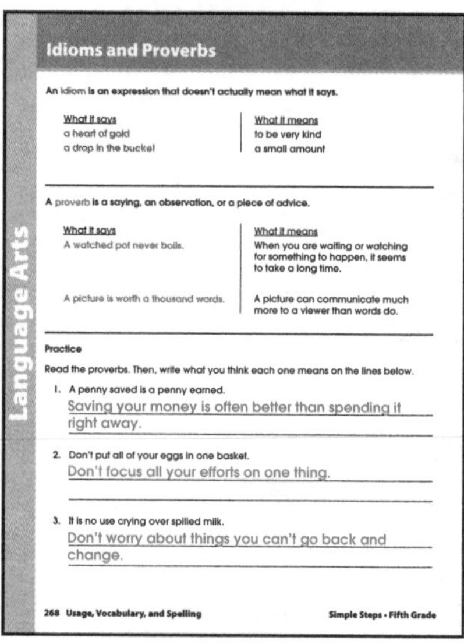

Idioms and Proverbs

An idiom is an expression that doesn't actually mean what it says.

What it says	What it means
a heart of gold	to be very kind
a drop in the bucket	a small amount

A proverb is a saying, an observation, or a piece of advice.

What it says	What it means
A watched pot never boils.	When you are waiting or watching for something to happen, it seems to take a long time.
A picture is worth a thousand words.	A picture can communicate much more to a viewer than words do.

Practice

Read the proverbs. Then, write what you think each one means on the lines below.

1. A penny saved is a penny earned.
   Saving your money is often better than spending it right away.
2. Don't put all of your eggs in one basket.
   Don't focus all your efforts on one thing.
3. It is no use crying over spilled milk.
   Don't worry about things you can't go back and change.

Language Arts

268 Usage, Vocabulary, and Spelling   Simple Steps • Fifth Grade

Page 268

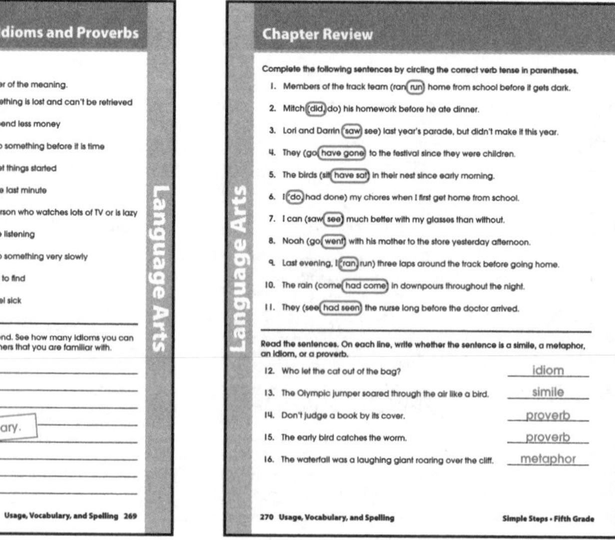

Idioms and Proverbs

Practice

Read each idiom below. On the line, write the letter of the meaning.

1. h at a snail's pace
2. c to jump the gun
3. a down the drain
4. f couch potato
5. j under the weather
6. d get the ball rolling
7. i a needle in a haystack
8. e at the 11th hour
9. b to tighten your belt
10. g all ears

a. something is lost and can't be retrieved
b. to spend less money
c. to do something before it is time
d. to get things started
e. at the last minute
f. a person who watches lots of TV or is lazy
g. to be listening
h. to do something very slowly
i. hard to find
j. to feel sick

Imagine that you are writing a short e-mail to a friend. See how many idioms you can include. You may use idioms from the lesson or others that you are familiar with.

Answers will vary.

Language Arts

Simple Steps • Fifth Grade   Usage, Vocabulary, and Spelling 269

Page 269

Chapter Review

Complete the following sentences by circling the correct verb tense in parentheses.

1. Members of the track team (ran, **run**) home from school before it gets dark.
2. Mitch (**did**, do) his homework before he ate dinner.
3. Lori and Darrin (**saw**, see) last year's parade, but didn't make it this year.
4. They (go, **have gone**) to the festival since they were children.
5. The birds (sit, **have sat**) in their nest since early morning.
6. I (**do**, had done) my chores when I first get home from school.
7. I can (saw, **see**) much better with my glasses than without.
8. Noah (go, **went**) with his mother to the store yesterday afternoon.
9. Last evening, I (**ran**, run) three laps around the track before going home.
10. The rain (come, **had come**) in downpours throughout the night.
11. They (see, **had seen**) the nurse long before the doctor arrived.

Read the sentences. On each line, write whether the sentence is a simile, a metaphor, an idiom, or a proverb.

12. Who let the cat out of the bag? idiom
13. The Olympic jumper soared through the air like a bird. simile
14. Don't judge a book by its cover. proverb
15. The early bird catches the worm. proverb
16. The waterfall was a laughing giant roaring over the cliff. metaphor

Language Arts

270 Usage, Vocabulary, and Spelling   Simple Steps • Fifth Grade

Page 270

Chapter Review

Proofread the following sentences. Use the proofreading marks to correct mistakes with homophones and double negatives.

delete letters, words, punctuation
insert letters, words, punctuation

17. Diane was ~~aloud~~ allowed to visit her friends after she finished her homework.
18. Lynn wants to ~~by~~ buy earrings with the money she earns from shoveling snow.
19. Elise brushes her horse's ~~main~~ mane every morning and every night.
20. Mr. and Mrs. Jones ~~past~~ passed the turn they were supposed to make into the school.
21. Andrew ~~through~~ threw the football the farthest.
22. Amy wanted to go to the game to**o**.

Make up your own metaphor, simile, and proverb. Write one of each on the lines below.

23. ______________________
24. ______________________ Answers will vary.
25. ______________________

Simple Steps • Fifth Grade — Usage, Vocabulary, and Spelling 271

Language Arts

Page 271

Chapter Review

Complete the following sentences by circling the correct use of adjective or adverb in parentheses.

26. Stephanie thought *The Wizard of Oz* was the (cute, **(cutest)**) play she had seen all year.
27. We have to climb over one (**(big,)** biggest) rock in order to pass the test.
28. That is the (bigger, **(biggest)**) mountain I've ever seen.
29. Clint makes (**(more,)** most) money mowing lawns than Perry does selling lemonade.
30. The ice storm we had last night was (**(worse,)** worst) than the one we had last year.
31. The blizzard brought the (more, **(most)**) snow I had ever seen.
32. I think swimming in the lake in the winter is a (**(bad,)** badly) idea.

In each sentence below, a pair of words is underlined. On the line, write **S** if the words are synonyms, **A** if they are antonyms, or **M** if they are multiple-meaning words.

33. __A__ Do you store your summer clothes in the attic or the basement?
34. __M__ Be careful that when you bow, your bow doesn't slip out of your hair.
35. __S__ The presents are on the table, and the guests can't wait for you to open your gifts.
36. __S__ Did Rascal eat the entire bone, or did he consume only part of it?
37. __A__ That bread is stale, but I did make some fresh bread today.
38. __M__ Mom put Clare's down comforter down the laundry chute.

272 Usage, Vocabulary, and Spelling — Simple Steps • Fifth Grade

Language Arts

Page 272

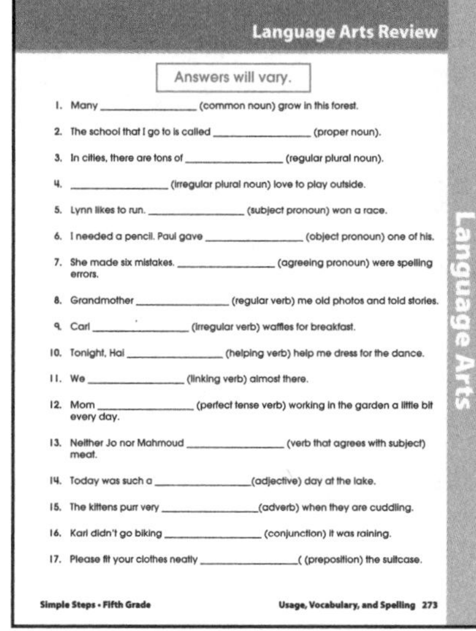

Language Arts Review

Answers will vary.

1. Many ________ (common noun) grow in this forest.
2. The school that I go to is called ________ (proper noun).
3. In cities, there are tons of ________ (regular plural noun).
4. ________ (irregular plural noun) love to play outside.
5. Lynn likes to run. ________ (subject pronoun) won a race.
6. I needed a pencil. Paul gave ________ (object pronoun) one of his.
7. She made six mistakes. ________ (agreeing pronoun) were spelling errors.
8. Grandmother ________ (regular verb) me old photos and told stories.
9. Carl ________ (irregular verb) waffles for breakfast.
10. Tonight, Hal ________ (helping verb) help me dress for the dance.
11. We ________ (linking verb) almost there.
12. Mom ________ (perfect tense verb) working in the garden a little bit every day.
13. Neither Jo nor Mahmoud ________ (verb that agrees with subject) meat.
14. Today was such a ________(adjective) day at the lake.
15. The kittens purr very ________(adverb) when they are cuddling.
16. Karl didn't go biking ________ (conjunction) it was raining.
17. Please fit your clothes neatly ________((preposition) the suitcase.

Simple Steps • Fifth Grade — Usage, Vocabulary, and Spelling 273

Language Arts

Page 273

Language Arts Review

On each line, write whether the sentence declarative, interrogative, exclamatory, or imperative.

18. Oh no! The bridge is closed! — exclamatory
19. I want to read my book all day tomorrow. — declarative
20. Be nice to your sister. — imperative
21. Did you hear the thunder? — interrogative

On each line, write whether the sentence is simple, compound, or complex.

22. Henry liked baking bread and making soup. — simple
23. We played a lot; we slept a lot. — compound
24. Frida, my best friend, wants to be a neuroscientist. — complex

Rewrite each pair of simple sentences and sentence fragments as one combined, complete sentence.

25. Mikaela jogged through the buggy forest. Mikaela jogged quickly.
    Mikaela jogged quickly through the buggy forest.
26. Strawberries and blueberries. The earliest fruit to ripen.
    Strawberries and blueberries are the earliest fruit to ripen.

Add periods, question marks, and exclamation points where needed.

27. When will you get home ?
28. Jamie said, "Mr. Hammond said to do Lesson Eight for homework."
29. Careful, the path is very muddy ! OR .
30. At the M.L.K. School, everybody reads Isabelle Allende in sixth grade.

274 Usage, Vocabulary, and Spelling — Simple Steps • Fifth Grade

Language Arts

Page 274

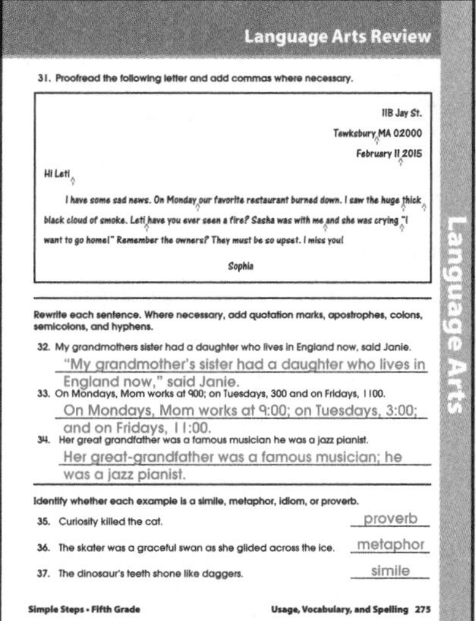

Language Arts Review

31. Proofread the following letter and add commas where necessary.

IIB Jay St.
Tewksbury, MA 02000
February 11, 2015

Hi Leti,

I have some sad news. On Monday, our favorite restaurant burned down. I saw the huge, thick, black cloud of smoke. Leti, have you ever seen a fire? Sasha was with me, and she was crying, "I want to go home!" Remember the owners? They must be so upset. I miss you!

Sophia

Rewrite each sentence. Where necessary, add quotation marks, apostrophes, colons, semicolons, and hyphens.

32. My grandmothers sister had a daughter who lives in England now, said Janie.
    "My grandmother's sister had a daughter who lives in England now," said Janie.
33. On Mondays, Mom works at 900; on Tuesdays, 300 and on Fridays, 1100.
    On Mondays, Mom works at 9:00; on Tuesdays, 3:00; and on Fridays, 11:00.
34. Her great grandfather was a famous musician he was a jazz pianist.
    Her great-grandfather was a famous musician; he was a jazz pianist.

Identify whether each example is a simile, metaphor, idiom, or proverb.

35. Curiosity killed the cat. — proverb
36. The skater was a graceful swan as she glided across the ice. — metaphor
37. The dinosaur's teeth shone like daggers. — simile

Simple Steps • Fifth Grade — Usage, Vocabulary, and Spelling 275

Language Arts

Page 275

Answer Key

Notes

Notes

Notes